THE
PASIEGOS

THE
PÆSIEGOS
Spaniards in No Man's Land

SUSAN TAX FREEMAN

THE UNIVERSITY OF CHICAGO PRESS / CHICAGO AND LONDON

SUSAN TAX FREEMAN is professor of anthropology at the
University of Illinois, Chicago Circle, and the author
of *Neighbors: The Social Contract in a Castilian Hamlet*,
also published by the University of Chicago Press.

THE UNIVERSITY OF CHICAGO PRESS, CHICAGO 60637
THE UNIVERSITY OF CHICAGO PRESS, LTD., LONDON
© 1979 by The University of Chicago
All rights reserved. Published 1979
Printed in the United States of America
83 82 81 80 79   54321

Library of Congress Cataloging in Publication Data

Freeman, Susan Tax.
    The Pasiegos: Spaniards in no man's land.

    Includes bibliographical references and index.
    1. Pas Valley, Spain—Rural conditions.
2. Marginality, Social—Spain—Pas Valley. 3. Herders—
Spain—Pas Valley. I. Title.
HN590.P35F73   309.1'46'351082   78-13928
ISBN 0-226-26173-5

for Les and Sarah

CONTENTS

ILLUSTRATIONS

MAPS
follow p. 245

TABLES

ACKNOWLEDGMENTS

My reconnaissance in Santander in 1966 was conducted under a grant-in-aid from the Wenner-Gren Foundation for Anthropological Research. The field research and a subsequent period of data analysis were funded by the National Institute of Mental Health under research grants MH 15379-01 and 15379-02. The University of Illinois at Chicago Circle funded additional research assistance in 1973, through its Research Board, and manuscript typing through the Office of Social Science Research and the Department of Anthropology.

The active support and involvement of my colleagues in Santander, who are my close friends of more than a decade, aided my research beyond measure. They are María del Cármen González Echegaray, Joaquín González Echegaray, Celia Valbuena, Benito Madariaga, and José María García Cáraves, and they would insist that there is no need for members of our community to say "thank you" to one another. This is true in that there is a need for more than the writing down of insufficient phrases.

I was given every assistance in my work in the Centro de Estudios Montañeses, under its late director Tomás Maza Solano; the Diputación Provincial; the Biblioteca Municipal; the Archivo Histórico Provincial; and the cadastral section of the Ministerio de Hacienda. My perspectives on archival materials of the province were deepened as I worked alongside María del Cármen González Echegaray, whose sensitivity as a local historian is unmatched, and one of the archivists, Agustín Rodríguez Fernández.

The sustained cooperation of a number of people in Vega de Pas was crucial in different aspects of my research: Frutos

Gómez Ruíz; Santiago Carral Gómez; Eladio Diego Sainz; and the municipal secretary, Jesús Saiz López. I also received guidance from the late, retired priest, Manuel Ruíz Cagigas; the two parish priests then stationed in La Vega; the secretary of the Hermandad Sindical, Jesús Gómez Ruíz; and two of the barrio teachers, Emilia González and Dora Rivas. I have let the families who housed me, in Casco and barrio, remain anonymous, but to them, and to the tolerant cooperation of all their neighbors, this book owes its existence. All names used in the book are fictitious so that individual identities may be protected, but the identity of their town cannot be concealed.

I am grateful to the officials of San Pedro del Romeral and San Roque de Ríomiera for their cooperation and cordiality on my visits to their towns.

In Madrid, I owe thanks to Nieves de Hoyos Sancho not only for sending me to Pas but for her continuing guidance and hospitality. I am grateful to my colleagues Carmelo Lisón Tolosana and María Cátedra Tomás, also researchers of Spain's far North, for their lively personal and professional friendship. Julio Caro Baroja and Julio González y González both gave me the same critical guidance in my second Castilian research they had given me in my first.

Two formal conferences with Spanish colleagues gave me a chance to present data on the Pasiegos for critical discussion. In addition to Lisón and Cátedra, I am indebted in this context to the other regular participants—Enrique Luque Baena, Teresa San Román, Joan F. Mira, and Ramón Valdés.

María Dolores Echaide and Blanca Izquierdo, of San Sebastián, have been important critics and editors of my work in preparing parts of it for translation. My father and mother have read and criticized all my work on Pas, beginning with field notes. Drafts of various papers have been shared with William Christian, my companion in Santander research, and with James Fernández, next door in Asturias: I am the beneficiary of both their commentaries and their published work.

Marion Sirefman helped me organize cadastral data in Santander. In Chicago, James Turner assisted in the codification of land tenure data. Laura R. Walters worked with me during most of a year in analysis of data from genealogies on marriage, occupation, and emigration. I could not have asked for more intelligent help.

From the beginning of this lengthy research, my husband has been a steady source of encouragement, critique, and professional companionship. Our daughter has always known me amidst the clutter of the book in progress. It has been completed on time stolen from her.

A NOTE ON USAGES IN THE TEXT

I have followed Pasiego usage in various matters. Grass, both fresh and dried, is referred to as grass (*hierba*) rather than hay (*heno*). Milk production is generally measured by daily yield under different feeding regimens rather than averaged over the length of the lactation period. Similarly, La Montaña refers only to the coastal plain of Santander province and not to the entire province. However, Pasiegos refer to their meadows indiscriminately as *prados* (meadows) or *fincas* (fields). I use the English "meadow" exclusively in reference to meadows (enclosed for cows) and reserve "fields" for reference to areas of cereal cultivation—that is, the former maize fields.

Terms from the dialect are identified by "dial." Terms in standard Spanish are contrasted, where necessary, by "Sp." If no notation is given, terms are in standard Spanish. The line between standard Spanish and dialect is hard to draw, however: it is partly an artifact of the Spanish Academy's decision to recognize or not to recognize forms. Many "dialect" terms can be found in the dictionary as archaic forms, but would not be recognized as legitimate Spanish by many speakers of the language. Conversely, some terms in local use are not necessarily considered dialectic yet are not recognized by the Academy.

Foreign terms which recur in the text are listed in the Glossary.

All translations from non-English sources are my own.

INTRODUCTION

The Montes de Pas, homeland of the Pasiegos, lies on the northern slopes of the Cantabrian mountains facing the Atlantic Ocean and the port city of Santander. The mountain crests which form the divide between coastal and inland Spain and some of the major access routes onto the Spanish meseta from the coastal plain lie within the Montes. To come here from Madrid and Burgos is to leave Spain's high, dry, windswept uplands—a landscape of grainlands and sheep pasture—and to enter, through the Escudo Pass, a green world of meadows, cabbage patches, and forested slopes, whitened here and there by the stone fences which enclose properties, by snow-capped peaks, and often also by blankets of mist. Abundant streams water the alpine slopes and join to form several large rivers to water the coastal plain. Here the landscape is dotted with cows, so scarce on the meseta, and Spaniards have long come from other, hotter places to pass cool summers at bathing spots near inland springs or on the seacoast itself. Settlement is more dispersed than it is on most of the meseta, though there is the same high esteem for living in cities and the centers, rather than the peripheries, of rural districts. The capital city, Santander, is Castile's only seaport and thus, in past times, housed her only shipyards and fisheries and accommodated much of her sea traffic to Europe, although competition came early from the Basque port of Bilbao, which today monopolizes most heavy shipping.

Santander's history is primarily a northern one, long before it becomes Castilian. A few elements of it are reviewed in chapter 1, especially as they illuminate the character of the lower nobility, but a more general outline will be helpful in giving background both to the history of the Montes de Pas and to the questions of interethnic contacts raised in chapter 10. The coastal region is, of course, the far northern frontier of Iberia and of difficult access. The major land routes from mainland Europe, for example, have crossed the Pyrenees into Navarra and the meseta, while the coast from Galicia to Basque country and France has not been a major avenue of land travel. This is still true today, as major communications radiate from points on the meseta to northern centers, while those centers are less well connected to one another.

The tribal area of the Cantabrians, along with the neighboring zones of Basques and Asturians on either side, were the last on the peninsula to submit to the Romans: their defense endured for two centuries. The Visigothic movement into Spain of the beginning of the fifth century did not reach Cantabria until the end of the sixth (A.D. 574). The leading historian of early Cantabria, Joaquín González Echegaray (1966a, 1969, 1977), attributes the ultimate Romanization of Cantabria not to the Romans but to the influence of the Visigoths as they moved into the coastal region. Until then, Romance culture was a veneer on a small segment of Cantabrian society and old customs and pagan cults dominated the countryside. The area was missionized under the Visigoths. However, the evidence for thoroughgoing Romanization and Christianization both come from the eighth century, when the North became a refuge area for Christian Spaniards and Visigoths fleeing the Muslim armies, which began their eight-century Spanish campaigns in the year 711. Until then, the inroads of Christian beliefs, the establishment of Christian sacred centers, were fragmentary and gradual.

The coastal zone was not a place of heavy settlement in all these centuries. Major towns of what is modern Santander province were Julióbriga, near Reinosa, and later Santa Juliana, the modern Santillana. The tiny port of Santander itself was Julióbriga's port—Portus Victoriae Iuliobrigensium—and took its modern name from the martyr San Emeterio, whose remains were probably not moved into the region (from Calahorra, in modern Logroño) until they were endangered by the advance of Islam in the eighth century. The influences of that time were Christian, carried by Hispano-Visigothic people from farther south. Cantabria was never an area of heavy Jewish settlement: the Jewish population remained affixed to the larger towns of the meseta and the South. Muslim contact was extremely brief and largely of a military nature. Yet despite the increasing dominance of Christianity there, coastal Cantabria remained something of a frontier of ecclesiastical establishment: Amaya, in

Burgos, was the northernmost shrine of importance in the early period, and Cantabria did not house the seat of a bishopric until the eighteenth century.

Muslim penetration was greater in what is now the province of Oviedo, or modern Asturias, than farther east in Cantabria or Basque country. In Asturias, before they had been on Iberian soil for a decade, the armies of Islam met with resistance from Visigothic nobles, under Pelayo, and countrymen—the legendary beginning of the Reconquest. The kingdom of Asturias was born, and grew, and the Reconquest with it, emanating from various points in the mountains of the North. Modern Santander, with modern Oviedo, was part of Las Asturias: there were Asturias of Oviedo, Santillana, and Trasmiera, and all were Visigothic strongholds, proud in the maintenance of their traditions and in their Christianity. The Visigoths, the only conquerors of Spain truly to penetrate the far North, came ultimately to lodge there. The survival of the Visigothic kingdoms became one with the Reconquest itself and the early beginnings of the Christian Spanish nation (see Menéndez y Pidal 1963, 1964 for the detailed summary of these processes). By the time Spain was born, and in the northernmost regions where this happened first, her very identity was Romance, Visigothic, and Christian. History gives evidence that Basques, too, identified themselves with Spain and her historic mission (Greenwood 1977). These were all the lands where large segments of the population could claim purity of blood to become the untitled nobility—*hijosdalgo*—which peopled the armies of the Reconquest to seize Spain for Christianity. Moors and Jews were foreign to the far North, but their presence at its frontiers served to raise the regional consciousness and to charge the concern for purity which was to define the course of the nation's history.

I worked between 1962 and 1966 on the meseta, in an upland border region between Old and New Castile, the Sierra Ministra —a land of small, tightly clustered villages of people who produce bread from their own wheat and pasture their sheep locally for meat and wool. With their negative appraisal of herding activities, and of people who spend their time exclusively in them (including their own family herdsmen), these people were my eloquent first instructors in attitudes which I have come to see as Spanish in the widest sense. Much of their tightly woven community life depends upon their nearly constant presence in the cluster of houses which is the village. Cooperation is a crucial element of their social and economic life, and people's visibility by their neighbors keeps them subject to the social controls—especially public opinion—which ensure the continuing success of the cooperative venture. Spanish historical ethnography teaches us that this has been the most widespread form of traditional community life in Spain, even though the inventory of collective concerns has typically been much smaller in some regions, particularly the South. My book on the Sierra Ministra was called _Neighbors_ and it documented, more than anything, a successful venture in social control and close community living.

In 1966, I made plans to begin work in the province of Santander. My initial interests were in comparing the two parts of Old Castile—the meseta and the coastal zone—with particular attention to differences in settlement pattern and the expectable concomitant differences in the dynamics of community life and informal social controls. My friend Nieves de Hoyos Sancho, the conservator of the Museo del Pueblo Español, in Madrid, urged me to consider working among the Pasiegos, who are known to have what is probably the most systematically dispersed settlement pattern in Iberia. Following a visit to the Montes de Pas, preliminary survey of the literature, and consultation with colleagues in Santander in 1966, I began eighteen months of fieldwork in July of 1968, beginning in archives and then residing in Vega de Pas from early October, 1968, until December of 1969. There, my plan of comparative study lost all semblance of simplicity and my original focus became enmeshed in a far broader and more complex analysis than I had been able to predict.

Of the extant literature on Pas, only the article by the geographer Terán (1947) gave any hint of the true nature of Pasiego transhumance and the striking periodicity of movement from meadow to meadow. Even Terán, however, gave slightly greater emphasis to the fact that cows are stabled for long periods than to the periodicity of movement. I found myself not only among herders in a landscape of scattered dwellings, then, but in a herding community so uniquely itinerant and so dedicated to the rearing of animals at the expense of all cultivation that the expectable differences between them and settled Spanish farmers must be of tremendous import. The writings of other Spaniards about the Pasiegos assured that Spaniards themselves felt the differences to be extraordinary. My study came thus to deal with Pasiego ethnography in the context of the rest of Spain and of Europe; with Spanish views of Pasiego ethnography as it is represented in literature and popular belief; and with the obstacles which the real differences and supposed differences of the Pasiegos have posed for them in their relations with non-Pasiegos in their home province and in the nation at large. Further, my study of Vega de Pas itself became more nearly two community studies than one, for the differences between herders and settled people which are writ large in the nation become evident first at home: the Casco, or town center, is largely a sedentary and commercial community of Pasiegos who are themselves quick to show how different and superior they are to Pasiego herders, their kinsmen.

This book grows out of concern with all of these features. To the extent that the Casco and the herding barrios are describably different from one another, they are dealt with in separate chapters. The dynamics of their interaction and of the movement of herders into the settled center are the subject of a separate chapter. In all of these, and particularly in chapter 6, I have tried to bring the ethnography of the Pasiegos into the spectrum of Spanish and European ethnography in order to suggest the extent to which Pasiego distinctiveness is partly a fabrication of a few Spanish writers and partly a confusion by them of what is supposedly unique or non-Spanish with what is simply archaic but widely European. Most of the comparative suggestions are contained in footnotes to prevent the text from becoming unwieldy.

The element of Pasiego ethnography which is truly distinctive is the one that has received the least explicit attention from Spanish writers (except for Terán), and this is Pasiego transhumance. However, the accentuated and truly unique transhumance practiced today is only a century old; in the past it was more comparable to that of the Alps or of Pyrenean zones like Andorra. Ironically it was in a period when Pasiegos were somewhat less distinctive that the literature on their distinctiveness began to grow. The growth of Pasiego lore is presented in chapter 1, along with the documentary history of the Montes de Pas. A broader historical and cultural line of questioning is taken up in chapter 10, where the way in which Spaniards have dealt with the Pasiegos is compared with the ways in which a number of other marginal Spaniards have been viewed within their nation. This leads necessarily to a consideration of the tenets of Spanish culture which govern the definition of the society's margins and the placement there of certain peoples. The exploration of such large questions as the ones dealt with in chapter 10 is necessarily partial and tentative, but it is essential to a full understanding of the Pasiegos' situation.

Indeed, most aspects of Pasiego life are best comprehended only with reference to the Spanish whole. Without this, it is difficult to see what it is about the herders that brings them to be so harshly viewed by settled Pasiegos; it is difficult to identify the points of reference of the settled Pasiegos when they import material and behavioral styles to confound the herders in moving up the social ladder; and it is difficult to see what in either the Pasiego reality or stereotype has led other Spaniards to view Pasiegos as too different to be Spanish. Pasiego ethnology is central to this book, then, but the book is also about Spain and Spanish notions of esteem. To me, the greatest personal benefit of this research has been its profound lessons about Spain, the mosaic of her history and the historical depth of her cultural judgments.

I arrived in Vega de Pas with many blank notebooks, my earlier experience in Spain, and a compass. I rented a room in a family home above a busy tavern in the center of town, owned and run by the family, and I arranged to share meals with them in the kitchen. This was the best available space for rent, placed me as centrally as possible for work in the different barrios (which in Pas are separate valleys), permitted me to use the tavern as a natural place for meeting people, and involved me in family living.

I did not use my compass, for the complications of the landscape are not of a kind to be undone by an orientation to the cardinal points. The problems of moving through the landscape bear brief mention, as they are among the first cited by outsiders, and I was warned of them by friends in Santander. The characteristics of the Pasiego landscape have made the use of the wheel in Pas minimal, with obvious implications for both communication and mechanization, and contribute to making trespassing a perennial problem between neighbors—a problem taken up in chapter 5. To outsiders who really do not know the landscape, the difficulties are all reduced to an alleged refusal on the part of Pasiegos to give directions to outsiders. Anyone who has learned his way around a bit and poses himself the problem of verbalizing what he has learned will realize how one-sided this allegation is. There is simply no way of giving directions to someone who doesn't know his way except by going along with him. Meadows look alike and are not oriented along paths; the *cabañas* (house-stable structures) on them look alike; the only way to direct someone to a given place is to name people and known landmarks by which he may orient himself.

To orient an outsider who has no knowledge of these is impossible, and even the most helpful Pasiego is reduced to the position of the proverbial Vermonter who concluded, "You can't get there from here."

The landscape posed serious difficulties in making acquaintances with herders in the barrios and in sustaining contacts over wide spaces, but I remained committed to working in more than a single barrio and managed slowly to increase my inventory of known people. I used children (from my host family) in helping to initiate contacts in roadways and meadows, for many people refused to become involved in conversation under ordinary circumstances but could be pressed in the presence of a third person who was both known and socially more or less neutral—the child. I often planted myself in public places to force myself on people's notice. Sometimes I exploited links with a third party in order to visit someone at a distance from the center: these attempts were not always successful. Mostly, I persevered and tried to let acquaintances develop naturally.

A happy encounter in the Casco helped me to work in one barrio of difficult access from the center. A man of barrio origins who was retired and lived near the center of town became fascinated with genealogies after I recorded his own and was interested that I should have a full record of the town. He and one of his cousins accompanied me to visit a mutual relation and found it great sport. Afterward, he declared that I could never make contacts in his father's barrio without introduction, and he enlisted to join me in a number of visits up that valley with his own family's friends, selected by him to represent complementary webs of kinship. The total number of visits we made together was not large, but his presence gave me the introduction I needed for further work. His acknowledgement of the difficulty of my task was evident in his conduct of our visits. Sometimes we would chat idly about barrio and family affairs for as long as three hours. When he felt that the way was laid for formal inquiry, he would say to our hosts, "Do you think you can win the prize for the longest family in La Vega?" and to me, "Get out your notebook!" This man's companionship and sustained pleasure in my work were unique. I worked intensively with many people in different aspects of my study, and with mutual pleasure, but no single person was as instrumental in my entry into the barrios in the difficult first months.

Conversance in Spanish language and culture, which, in retrospect, seems more crucial for work in Pas than in most other regions, had its drawbacks. I learned gradually, from encounters with a few incredulous people, that I was not being granted the status of foreigner by barrio people but, rather, was assumed to be Spanish. Therefore, I was suspected both of unpleasant motives, such as property assessment for tax collection, and of holding the prejudices against Pasiegos which Spaniards could be expected to hold. When, to counteract this, I advertised my foreignness, I was disbelieved. I did not notice much general success in my campaign until after about five months. By this time, I had outstayed any property assessor or other official in memory (and taxes had not been raised); in addition, the concession had been made in some quarters that I could be Mexican. I had also developed enough friendships among herders to acquire spokesmen, and fewer people had to react to me in a vacuum. The community of herders is dispersed, however, and I was never uniformly known in all barrios nor did word of my foreignness reach everyone.

My difficulties were not in extracting sensitive information; they were in making acquaintances on the most casual level with people who were often loathe even to exchange greetings. By the time I had close visiting relationships and had lived in the high pastures with a barrio family, had photographed people's cows for them and given them the prints, and had participated in those few public social events which exist in barrio life, I felt that I was quite well accepted. There were some people, however, who refused ever to enter into even minimal exchange with me. Sometimes, I would see them seated in their house doors or meadows, staring into space (a fourteen-hour-a-day pastime for some), and when I passed they would say quickly, "I'm busy." I respected this refusal to interact, of course, but always found it distressing. This, and a widespread lack of curiosity, which can destroy anthropological work, when it did not depress me completely often cast me in much more aggressive roles than I am comfortable in or have ever been forced to play in Spain, and my fieldwork in Pas was as unpleasant in some ways as it was rewarding in others.

The difficulties I cite were largely in the barrios, or with barrio people in the center, and were governed by the quality of *recelo* —suspicious reserve—often attributed to Pasiegos by outsiders and also to the herders by the residents of the Casco. Recelo is discussed in chapter 9. Here it is important to say that there are good reasons for Pasiego herders to behave with recelo, for outsiders' interactions with them give Pasiegos ample cause for mistrust and dislike. While I could not be happy with the superficiality of many relationships, I became more and more sympathetic with their cause as I learned, gradually, about outsiders' approaches to Pasiegos. I myself, as a researcher living in Pas, had to deal with members of the provincial press, academic establishments, and some aficionados of local ethnography who tried to have me confirm publicly their own theories about Pasiego origins and behavior or to use me as an entrée into this forbidding community. In more sensitive situations of the same kind, of course, anthropologists are simply not permitted to work—by circumstances or by decision of their potential subjects. This danger was not evident in Pas, though I suppose one irresponsible researcher could have made it so. The problem was, rather, to combat suspicion with a steady demonstration of sympathy and loyalty. Time is the most important factor in such an effort. After one and one-half years in Pas, I felt that I was finally ready to begin my fieldwork in the barrios.

My awareness of people's reactions to outsiders, as well as my own ability to respond to these, grew with time. I had begun in ignorance. A woman from the barrio of Guzparras made me aware for the first time of the problem my presence gave people. I had never met her, and was sent by her sister-in-law in another barrio to seek her out. I found her washing bed sheets near her cabaña, the herder's combined home and stable. She invited me to talk as she laundered, but expressed worry whether my questions might bring her trouble. I spoke casually and was reassuring, and she continued to converse. I discovered only late in the visit that her daughter had just given birth to a child and that the linens of the childbed were being washed. I realized that I was being treated very cordially for the circumstances. I apologized for having come at such a time and expressed thanks for her reception. She seemed to regret her first hesitation and tried to explain it: "Here they only teach us enough so we can write a letter and sign our name; when somebody like you comes along, we don't even know if we're speaking with the right words." I had been in Pas for seven months, but this comment made me fully conscious of Pasiego reactions for the first time.

The woman's comment points up, by the way, the Pasiegos' own view of their dialect as nothing but incorrect Spanish and the fact that Pasiegos measure themselves by Spanish standards. Most Spaniards consider themselves successful in being Spanish. Foreigners who live and work in Spain are used to having their presence met by a prideful assertion of local and national identity. The absence of this kind of pride in Pasiego herders is as noteworthy as it is depressing.

A sustained demonstration of sympathy and loyalty in the barrios required a personal style which was foreign—sometimes almost unacceptable—in the Casco. There, my foreignness, level of education, and professional status were considered major attractions, but people—particularly women—found it impossible to understand that I would not display enough jewelry, clothing, or other signs of my supposed status and purchasing power. Reactions to me in the town center gave me a very early awareness of the importance of conspicuous display there and led me to pay close attention to people's manipulation of material symbols of status as they move from barrios to the town center and out into other parts of Spain. Two papers, dated 1973 and 1976b, contain preliminary explorations of the matter of styles. I have attempted to show in the photographs something of the evolution of styles through space in Vega de Pas. I was never really misunderstood in the Casco, nor was my work, and I have good friendships there, but I was necessarily seen as something of an eccentric. The simultaneous demands of both communities on me created pressures which I had continually to deal with. Fortunately, I was usually able to explain my procedures, and my stylistic failures, in the Casco and be understood.

One measure of the distance between the two Pasiego communities is that very few Casco residents have a good notion of what the herding economy is like, and almost none of them knows what Pasiego transhumance really entails: most believe, for example, that the possession of three meadows involves only three moves per year. This ignorance, which is in many respects reciprocated by barrio people, and the contrasting styles of Casco and barrios, became important foci of my study.

I left Vega de Pas late in 1969, although I continue to visit there and to maintain contacts. The research in archival and secondary sources continues, for I was unable fully to explore all dimensions of Pasiego history and ethnography on the spot and the sources for it are rich. I used the municipal and church archives in Vega de Pas while I was living there and studied a variety of sources in Santander—at the Archivo Histórico Provincial, the Biblioteca Municipal, and the Centro de Estudios Montañeses—during 1968 and 1969. I returned to the Archivo for further work in 1974. Much of the comparative work on which chapter 10 is based has been done over the years since then and still continues.

Of the writers on Pas, I was the first to live there for more than a few days at a time. Many of the early writings are described in chapter 1; they represent time spent in archives and armchairs and in only the briefest excursions to the Montes de Pas. Of the major recent works, Terán's article on the geography of the

Montes (1947) gives a concise summary of the prior literature, describes the stereotype, and is dedicated to an analysis of the herding economy and its extension into adjacent zones. Although his focus is limited, Terán's personal familiarity with the zone is evident.

In his book, *Los Pasiegos* (1960), the late Adriano García-Lomas expands on all of the topics expounded in earlier literature and on a few additional ones, such as surnames and dialect. It is discursive and its language convoluted but its message—in the light of the earliest works—is refreshing. Part of the book is dedicated to exploring the world distribution of traits which have been assumed peculiar to Pas, and the lesson that these are montane adaptations rests between the lines. Such a focus contributes little to the study of the Pasiegos in their own setting, however, and the book is otherwise a compendium of Pasiego lore and history, often without satisfactory citation of sources. I have worked at verifying some of García-Lomas's statements and have found sources in popular literature rather than in Pasiego memory. His data are not necessarily false, but are often partial, as is the case, for example, with his description of the nature and location of the Madrid marketplace for wet-nurses, discussed in chapter 9.

García-Lomas was seventy-nine years old when he published *Los Pasiegos* and, I understand, he made only a few trips into the Montes de Pas during the book's preparation. His chief informant on the dialect, I was told in Pas, was a Casco tavern keeper in Vega de Pas who enjoyed performing in dialect but was not from a barrio. There are errors of ethnographic detail, and all of this has led me to avoid specific dependence on the book unless I was able to verify facts elsewhere as well. The extent to which the book itself has affected my consciousness of Pasiego history and lore is thus not adequately reflected in these pages: it and Terán's article were the informing sources of my own interest in Pas.

A British dialectologist, Ralph Penny, spent one and one-half years in Santander province preparing a study, *El habla pasiega*, which appeared in 1969. His research probably ended shortly before my own began. He spent, by his own description, two or three days a week in Pas and adjacent zones, administering a linguistic questionnaire and conducting directed interviews. He worked in two barrios of Selaya as well as the three towns of Pas, and with ten chief informants, three each in Vega de Pas and Selaya and two each in San Pedro and San Roque. With these key relationships established, Penny and his wife apparently did not enter into the larger social life of the towns they studied—at least in Vega de Pas I found no evidence of this— nor was that their purpose. Penny's work in syntax contains a good deal of ethnographic information, but as indicated, its sources were very limited in number. Again, wherever our interests overlapped, I have relied on data of my own collection. This is not at all to diminish Penny's contribution to the subject of the Pasiego dialect. In addition to its descriptive contribution, his work is important in affiliating the Pasiegos, in their language, with other peoples of the northwest quadrant of Spain who have retained variants of the once widespread Leonese dialect.

Since the time of my fieldwork, several short studies have been conducted in Pas and published. Celia Valbuena's report (1970) on children's toys (cows whittled from twigs) includes those from the Montes de Pas. More specifically focused on Pas are the results of a research project conducted from the University of Toulouse, largely in dialectology (see, for example, Leal 1972, 1974), and based on questionnaires and sporadic travel into Vega de Pas. José Ortega Valcárcel, a geographer, published in 1978 a study (dated 1975) dealing with the evolution of Pasiego transhumance. His focus is heavily on the Burgos side of the mountains. This work does not evidence control of all of the literature on the Pasiegos nor are many of the author's deductions supportable by available documents, but he brings to light a few relatively late sources available in Burgos and Simancas not cited by other authors. Finally, Diez Manrique (1975) published a "psychological" study based on questionnaires administered in schools in Pas and on records housed in one of the province's main clinics. This work contains a great many factual and inferential errors, perpetuates the Pasiego stereotype by a reiteration of its elements as if they were facts, and is not responsibly conceived. Two reports of my own research which I published locally (1970b, 1975) have inspired heated correspondence, my colleagues tell me, from within the province and from as far away as South America. The responses are largely concerned with arguing that the Pasiegos must indeed be non-Spanish in origin. Such arguments, and some of the recent literature, indicate that the era of unbridled speculation about the Pasiegos has not ended.

Tista's Year

Those people should be rewarded, not despised.

a Casco man

Tista Pelayo Maza, his wife, and their three children, move twenty times each year (see table 1), between seven cabañas, stabling their cows on the ground floor under the cabaña's combined loft and living quarters, pasturing them on the adjacent meadow or stall-feeding them inside when the weather is bad or the grass crop being prepared for harvest.

The year begins in May with the ripening on the lowest lying meadows of the grass crop called the *retoño*.[1] The cows are put out to graze for the first time since February. By the end of May, when the crop has been consumed and perhaps supplemented with the last of last year's grass stored in the cabaña, the family moves its herd to its highest meadow, the summer meadow or *braniza*. The cattle are stall-fed there on last year's grass while as many family members as can be spared return below to harvest the five intermediate fields of their retoño grass, moving slowly back up the mountainsides during June and July, storing the newly dried grass from each meadow in the attached cabaña. As the harvesters return to the lowest field to harvest and store the second growth, the *brena*, so that cabaña too will be filled with grass, whoever is above in the braniza, usually Elisa and two of the children, harvest and store the retoño there. Then they descend, not to the lowest meadow whose brena has just

1. Details of transhumance patterns are discussed in chapter 4. A concise review of the concomitants of the transhumance system is given in Freeman 1973.

1

been cut, but to the next lowest one, where the brena is grazed.
And so on back up the mountainsides, with the harvest in and
the family together, the cows are put to pasture through August
and September on the second growth on each meadow. This
journey terminates again at the highest meadow, where the cows
now graze outside.

TABLE 1
TISTA'S YEAR (THE TRANSHUMANCE CYCLE)
Meadows are listed by altitude in ascending order from bottom of table.
Movements of harvesters are shown in italics.

7 Braniza	end May-end July *harvest* retoño	end September graze brena			
6 Ladera	*June-July 8 days harvest* retoño	ca. mid-September graze brena	until end November graze brena	end April stall feeding (leaving some animals in cabaña 4)	
5 Ladera	*June 8 days harvest* retoño	September 18–20 days graze brena	graze brena	April 15–20 days stall feeding	
4 Ladera	*June 8 days harvest* retoño	August-September 8–15 days graze brena	graze brena	end March-early April 15–20 days stall feeding	
3 Ladera	*June 8 days harvest* retoño	August-September 8–15 days graze brena	graze brena	March stall feeding	
2 Ladera	*early June 8 days harvest* retoño	August 8–15 days graze brena	graze brena	February stall feeding	
1 Ribera	May graze retoño some stall-feeding	*early July 8 days harvest brena*	early October graze brena	December-January graze brena	May graze retoño some stall feeding

In early October, the third crop is ripe in the valley, and a new
ascent begins. The third crop is grazed on all meadows in ascending order, but this time there is no visit to the braniza: it does
not produce a third crop. And so, when six meadows have been

grazed, sometime in December, Tista's family moves back down to their lowest field and the cows are put to pasture on its fourth and last crop of grass, which may last through January. In February, the year's last ascent begins through the five intermediate meadows, whose third and last crop was grazed on the previous ascent: from February through April, in each cabaña on the ascent, the cows are fed on the stored retoño crop. When this is consumed, by the end of April, and the new retoño can be grazed in the valley meadow, the family descends once more, and another year begins.

There have been twenty moves in the year, excluding those of the harvesters. Twice, at most, once in the highest meadow and perhaps again in the lowest, the family has remained in one place for as long as two months. Most of their sojourns are of one to two weeks' duration. In the seven meadow-clusters or *praderas* in which he lives, Tista has a total of fifty-four neighbors. Forty-five of these neighbor families are ones with which Tista's family coincides at only one point in space, and the precise dates of their visits to that pradera do not always exactly coincide. Five neighbors exploit meadows in two of the same praderas Tista does, and four co-reside in three praderas. In one pradera, Tista's meadow is the only one: he has no neighbors there.

The barrio school is located centrally to the valley-bottom meadows, but the summer meadows and many of the intermediate ones are distant. Classes are held from mid-September until early June, disbanding in time for the harvest. Nonetheless, the continual ascents out of the lower meadows make the children's school attendance at best sporadic unless they are able, as they are at times, to stay with their grandparents, who are retired on a meadow in the valley bottom.

Tista regards the cabaña in his lowest meadows as his "dwelling cabaña" because it is the lowest place, nearest to the town's commercial center, and stands on a large enough field to support fairly long visits. As a dwelling cabaña, or *vividora*, this cabaña contains more furniture and equipment than the others, and the loft is neatly separated from the living quarters by partitions; even the sleeping quarters are partitioned from the kitchen as they are not in the other cabañas. Cooking here, as elsewhere, is still done on an open wood fire, built on a wide, low stone hearth, but not all of Tista's cabañas have chimneys as this one does: in the braniza house, the smoke simply rises through a hole in the slate roof. Here below, there are a cupboard, a couple of chests, a standard-sized table and chairs, as well as bedsteads for all the family. In the other houses there are only the low, three-legged milking stools and crude, squat tables which Tista has made himself in each place. In most of the cabañas, over time, Tista and Elisa have tried to maintain at least one crude bed-frame so that they can sleep apart from the children. But in the braniza, the bed has long since broken and, given the difficulty of getting another one up to the house and the short periods for which it is needed, the couple has forgotten it and, like so many parents in so many of their cabañas, they as well as their children make their beds in the dried grass.

ONE
Pasiegos and Pasieguería: *History and Fable*

. . . that the people who live there . . . may go with all security with their stock, cows, mares, goats and pigs, wherever they wish to graze in the said territory . . .

donation to the Monastery of San Salvador,
in Oña, by Don Sancho,
Count of Castile, A.D. 1011 (Appendix A)

I say that the Pasiegos do not descend from the Cantabrians but are of Semitic family, descended from Ismael, preserved without admixture in their mountains by the tendency not to intermarry with the inhabitants of the valleys . . .

Lasaga Larreta 1889

Some five and a-half thousand of the people known as Pasiegos today inhabit the Montes de Pas, a mountain district within the Cantabrian range comprising one portion of the provincial boundary between Santander and Burgos (maps 1, 2, and 4).[1] The bulk of the population inhabits the Santander municipalities of San Pedro del Romeral, San Roque de Ríomiera, and Vega de Pas, which are known officially as Las Tres Villas Pasiegas (The Three Pasiego Villas). Here they live in dispersion, for the most part, along the montane valleys of the River Miera and the River Pas and its tributaries, all on the northwestern slope of the mountains, facing the Atlantic coast. Also on the Santander side, outside the municipal limits of the Pasiego villas but contiguous

1. For census purposes, I include as Pasiegos not only the inhabitants of the three "official" Pasiego towns, but also those of three immediately contiguous settlements whose mode of livelihood marks them as Pasiegos to their fellow townsmen as well as to "official" Pasiegos. The following figures are, with the one noted exception, from the 1960 census (Instituto Nacional de Estadística 1960), which was the point of reference during

with them, people who are for all practical purposes Pasiegos inhabit the Pisueña district of Selaya municipality, on the headwaters of the River Pisueña below the Braguía Pass (map 4), and the portion of Soba municipality on the River Miera, adjacent to San Roque.[2] On the Burgos side of the mountains, facing southeast, Pasiegos inhabit the municipality of Espinosa de los Monteros in the montane localities collectively called Los Cuatro Ríos Pasiegos (The Four Pasiego Rivers), the four rivers being the upper tributaries of the Trueba (map 4) in the zone between the Estacas de Trueba Pass (Vega de Pas) and Portilla la Lunada (San Roque). The major permanently settled center of Los Cuatro Ríos Pasiegos is Las Machorras.[3]

---

fieldwork. There is some basis for assuming all census figures to be on the low side in these towns: some families have eluded enrollment. The official census figures for 1970 show net losses primarily for Vega de Pas and the Espinosa zone.

The Pasiego Villas (Santander)	
San Pedro del Romeral	1165
San Roque de Ríomiera	977
Vega de Pas	1858
*Soba (Santander) (contiguous with San Roque)	200
Pisueña (municipality of Selaya, Santander)	
(contiguous with Vega de Pas and San Roque)	304
Los Cuatro Ríos Pasiegos (municipality of Espinosa de los	
Monteros, Burgos) (continguous with Vega de Pas	
and San Roque)	955
Total	5459

*Approximate figure suggested by the *alcalde* of San Roque.

2. There is some incidence of Pasiego life-style in the municipality of Luena, adjacent to San Pedro. From my vantage point in Vega de Pas, I never heard herders refer to Luena transhumant herders as fellow Pasiegos, as they did to the other adjacent groups mentioned above. The number of Luena people practicing Pasiego transhumance there is difficult to assess, though greater familiarity with San Pedro might have helped me to do so. Unquestionably, though, there are a few people living like Pasiegos (and recognized as such at least in San Pedro and Luena) in the sectors of Luena bordering San Pedro, north from the Magdalena Pass (map 4). Luena is excluded from the census figures in note 1 above.

3. The Pasiego sector of Espinosa is included in a geographic study by Ortega Valcárcel (1974) of the region known as Las Montañas de Burgos. The area of his concern ends at the modern provincial boundary and hence he considers only a small part of the Pasiego zone. The Pasiegos of Espinosa are as marginal to the rest of the Montañas de Burgos as the Santander Pasiegos are to the rest of their province. Historically, the designation (in singular) Montaña de Burgos was applied to a much wider zone and apparently evolved into the name by which the entire province of Santander is called today—La Montaña.

The outstanding characteristic of the localities of Pasiego residence, all on or at the foot of major slopes, is the pronounced altitudinal variation along the montane rivers; rivers descend from their mountain sources as much as 1000 meters in a matter of 10 to 15 kilometers. Beyond the limits of this zone, in gentler terrain with no such descents, there is not sufficient altitudinal variation within short distances to allow the rapidly repetitive, sequential exploitation of meadows which marks the Pasiego way of life.[4]

Within the Montes de Pas, it is not major differences in lifestyle which distinguish herders of the three villas from the other, adjacent Pasiegos. The distinction of the three villas is that their populations are Pasiego in their entirety, while in Soba, Pisueña, Espinosa, and perhaps Luena (see note 2 above), Pasiegos live and move in local structural settings dominated by non-Pasiegos. Beyond the limits of the three villas, Pasiegos live as outsiders, for to be a Pasiego is not only to practice (or have forbears who practiced) a certain kind of transhumance; it is also to share a legal and ethnic history.

In 1011 A.D., Don Sancho, Count of Castile, donated extensive rights in what are now primarily the provinces of Burgos and Santander to the Monastery of San Salvador, in Oña (Burgos).[5] This was the same year in which Don Sancho had founded the Monastery itself, for his daughter Tigridia, placing in its jurisdiction 167 population centers of varied size and legal status, with their lands, and nearly one hundred churches (Pérez de Urbel 1969–70, 3:122–25).[6] The magnitude of the original donation, plus numerous subsequent ones, made Oña a major center of ecclesiastical power in the emerging Castile, parts of which in the eleventh century were experiencing repopulation in the wake of local reconquest by Christian forces.[7]

The Montes de Pas were included in the 1011 grant of pasturage rights to Oña. This is the first documented mention of the

4. Cattle transhumance is practiced elsewhere in Santander, for example (see de los Ríos y Ríos 1878), but is not "rapidly repetitive" as it is in Pas, and is of a truly different nature, with different implications for community life.

5. The donation is published in various sources, such as R. Amador de los Ríos 1891:884–86 and Escagedo Salmón 1921. It is reproduced here in appendix A.

6. Oña, today a minor town, lies about forty kilometers south-southeast of Espinosa.

7. Many of these donations are published by González y González (1960, vols. 2, 3).

zone, though, as Terán (1947) points out, this does not mean that the Montes were uninhabited before 1011 (or that they were necessarily inhabited from that moment), but simply that they did not contain independent centers of population at that time. Indeed, there is no evidence even for permanent settlements there, not to mention administratively independent ones, until much later.[8] As late as 1467, in the confirmation of grazing privileges issued by Enrique IV, the Montes were still described as "wild and deserted mountains" (*montañas bravas y desiertas*) (Escagedo Salmón 1921:50; Terán 1947:16) and as "uncultivated, uninhabited wasteland" (*montañas yermas*) (Vega de Pas Archive [VPA] 1790).

As early as in the donation of 1011, the Montes de Pas were primarily considered a natural extension of the territory of Espinosa de los Monteros, lying beyond the mountain called El Castro Valnera, which towers at the modern provincial divide above the Estacas de Trueba Pass (maps 4 and 5). Pasiego history is most intimately linked with that of Espinosa, and some understanding both of the nature of the linkage and the events of the history are important for understanding aspects of the Pasiegos' contemporary situation.

From 1011 until the early part of the nineteenth century, virtually all sources on Pasiego history are documentary in nature. Some of the more important documents were studied, and many published, from the nineteenth century onward. I have studied some of these locally, but I am certain that the totality of relevant sources has never been studied by scholars with particular interest in Pas: relevant local sources are of only marginal interest to the general historian, and local historians have made only partial approaches at best to the wider issues of regional history. The following resumé of Pasiego history, based on published pri-

8. A document of 1170 records a donation to Oña of the monasteries of "Sancti Petri del Romeral" and "Sancte Marie de Laebega." In publishing the donation, González y González identifies "Romeral" with Ramales (1960, 2:242), but he agrees (pers. comm.) that this might be incorrect. The juxtaposition of San Pedro del Romeral and Santa María de "Laebega" might support the argument that the reference is to the Montes de Pas, but the existence there of monasteries in 1170 is doubtful at best. González y González points out that the document contains erasures and rewriting (particularly in the monastery names, and especially "Laebega") and he gives the document little weight. We know also that a document (authentic?) of 817 makes reference to monasteries of San Pedro (or Santos Pedro y Pablo) and Santa María at a place called Eçe, near the River Pas (cited in García-Lomas 1960:20n) and that in this eçe and in later documents the references might reasonably be interpreted as pertaining to the Valley of Toranzo, adjacent to the Montes de Pas and on the main stream of the River Pas (M. C. González Echegaray 1974:153ff.).

mary and some secondary sources, and on some local archives, is not meant to inventory the welter of recorded events: of these I am sure my knowledge is incomplete, and some of the sources are themselves contradictory on questions of detail. Rather, I have attempted to generalize from the tortuous legal history of Pas its general course.

The first requisite to an understanding of Pasiego history is an understanding of the categories of rights and privileges which were separable from one another and individually transferrable from one party to another. Thus, community of pasture (the chief resource at issue in this area) did not necessarily imply common enrollment (*vecindad* or *vecino* status) in a single co-residential locality. Further, vecinos of dependencies, or localities outside the designated capital town of a municipality, did not always enjoy precisely the same status as vecinos of the capital itself. Parish membership was not always fully coincident with place of secular enrollment, either. Legal jurisdiction, civil and criminal, was not necessarily exercised by the same local entity in which individuals were enrolled as vecinos. And, finally, rights to the collection of various fees, tribute, and taxes from a particular locality often lay with numerous individuals or establishments of various other localities. In the case of the Montes de Pas, many of the legally separable categories of rights and obligations were in fact separated at one time or another, and the implications of rights in certain areas for rights in others became the subject of much litigation, and decisions were reversed again and again in favor of alternative arguments. In the Montes de Pas, litigation focused almost entirely on questions of pasturage rights, but many other aspects of the complex relationship between different localities were brought as evidence in support of one or another party.[9] Thus, the court cases themselves bring together the largest body of data on the various arrangements prevailing in the period following 1011 until the litigations ceased, apparently around 1790.[10]

9. A short series of litigations dating from the mid-fifteenth to the mid-sixteenth centuries relates to problems of clearing and enclosure in Pas. This is fully reviewed in chapter 3; it is the only body of litigation—and it is a small one—whose review is deferred until later.

10. Appendix B lists the cases filed in the town archive of Vega de Pas (VPA). The San Pedro Archive, when I studied it, yielded nothing of this nature. I did not study archives in San Roque. However, the cases filed in Vega de Pas, and particularly that of 1790, make wide reference, often in great detail, to earlier, related cases, and thus together they present a fair summary of the legal proceedings and principal concerns of the preceding centuries.

There is little question that the dispersion of rights in Pas among a variety of outside entities, and the ambiguities of Pasiegos' status with regard to the surrounding localities, were such complicated issues precisely because the Montes de Pas began as a no-man's-land, an inhospitable and unpeopled zone at the northern, Cantabrian margin of the emerging County of Castile at a time when much of Cantabria and Castile were yet to be populated by both the *presura*—the informal movement into uninhabited regions—and by the formal charters of the Repopulation (Pérez de Urbel 1951 and 1969–70). It is not likely that zones constituting less of a no-man's-land, or those more systematically populated, were plagued to the same extent by legal ambiguities of the type which troubled the history of Pas.

In the social landscape of the period, religious centers like the monastery at Oña were important in receiving tribute and redistributing it, or rights to collect it, to other, subsidiary centers or individuals. Subsidiary centers thus acquired the financial base for the further amassing of power, secular or ecclesiastical. Espinosa de los Monteros in all probability received some of its early revenue by the grace of Oña. We know that in 1576 (VPA 1790:467ff.), the inhabitants of the Montes de Pas still paid tithes and first fruits (*diezmos* and *primicias*) to Oña, but that by 1666 (VPA 1789:589–91) or even earlier (Arroyo del Prado 1958:406) these were being paid either wholly or in part to Espinosa (Escalera 1735:241). But Espinosa had independent privileges as well. In 1006, the Count Don Sancho had created the corps of monteros.[11] These were originally masters of the royal hunt. Though documentation of its first two centuries seems scanty, the corps of monteros had an early close association with a few localities, Espinosa de los Monteros among them. Espinosa's monteros eventually became *monteros de cámara*, guards of the king's private chambers, as distinct from *monteros mayores*, royal huntsmen. In 1206, Alfonso VIII, King of Castile, named twelve monteros, all natives of Espinosa, and decreed that their family lines be thereafter exempt from the payment of all tribute. A second decree, in 1208, named an additional twenty-five Espinosa families from which men might be called, and be obliged, to serve as monteros (González y González 1960, 3:364, 445).[12]

11. Arroyo del Prado (1958) summarizes numerous archives concerning the monteros, Espinosa, and Pas, but his citations are often imprecise. See Uría Ríu (1976) on the monteros as huntsmen.

12. These privileges are also detailed in Escalera (1735 edition of a 1632 work). Escalera insisted that the 1206 privilege must really have proceeded from 1208 instead.

As the home of the monteros, Espinosa was in 1369 granted extensive grazing privileges by Enrique III, and these were confirmed at various later times (Escagedo Salmón 1921).[13] The most often cited confirmation and statement of privileges was that of 1467, by Enrique IV (for example, Escalera 1735 and Escagedo Salmón 1921). The grant covered the area of the Montes de Pas and all of the contiguous zones, and more (Escalera 1735:250–51), though it was not as extensive as the grant to Oña in 1011. At least in the case of Pas, this grant was probably a confirmation of established practice, but the 1369–1467 privilege became the important referent for the subsequent litigation, none of which makes mention of the prior grant to Oña.[14] By 1666, Espinosa and not Oña was the focus not only of grazing rights in Pas: inhabitants of the Montes de Pas were now also paying their tithes and first fruits in part to Espinosa (Escalera 1735:241), and Escalera listed in 1735 (p. 239) only one Espinosa shrine that was at that time a dependency of the Oña monastery.

For five centuries following the 1011 donation, the Montes de Pas contained no parishes, and their inhabitants received sacraments and brought their dead to be buried in Espinosa. Some of the earliest litigation to be initiated from Pas sought the establishment of parish churches in Pas (cited VPA 1790:712ff, 784 ff.).[15] The suit was filed, either in 1535 or in 1538, by the *Bachiller* (at that period a clerical title) Pedro Ruiz Carriazo. He was identified in the suit (as cited in 1790) as the priest of the church of Nuestra Señora del Porrato, which was identified as a private chapel (*oratorio*) on the land of Martín de Vivanco, a porter of the King.[16] The name of El Porrato is still borne by one of the riverside meadows in the barrio of Viaña, in Vega de Pas, and modern informants identify it as the site of the former

13. Espinosa was also, by other decrees, privileged to select two *alcaldes* rather than one and to hold a weekly free market (Escalera 1735). See also Arroyo del Prado 1958.

14. The dates of the privilege are given by Arroyo del Prado (1958) as 1392 and 1458, and he refers to the 1392 grant as being, in actuality, a confirmation of yet a prior grant.

15. There was a slightly earlier (1534) sentence regarding pasturage in Ríolangos, to be described presently. The only significantly earlier date given for litigation is cited by Escagedo Salmón (1921:54) and Arroyo del Prado (1958:405) in reference to a 1384 suit between Espinosa and Valdeporres over pasturage in Pas. None of the cases filed in Vega de Pas makes reference to this or any other case of the fourteenth century, but Escagedo Salmón implies that the 1384 suit underlay the ensuing confirmation of the 1369 privilege.

16. This reference also gives early evidence of social stratification in the Montes de Pas, a problem discussed further in chapter 7.

chapel. (Escagedo's transcription of the documents gives the church the name of Santa María del Patronato.) There is also local knowledge in Vega de Pas of Bachiller Carriazo, who in his first acquaintance with the Viaña people was supposed to have been given lodging there as he journeyed from Villacarriedo, his place of study, to his home in Valdeporres. A heavy snowfall kept him in Viaña for a week, during which time he met a Viaña family who were unable to bury a deceased member because the deep snow made it impossible to get to Espinosa. Carriazo apparently took the Pasiegos' plight to heart and filed suit on their behalf. Escagedo Salmón (1921) reports that Carriazo was accused of giving the sacraments and establishing chapels in Pas when the people were still parishioners of Espinosa.

Carriazo won his case in part. A sentence of 1538 (cited in VPA 1790) distinguishes between parishioners of Espinosa who pastured their stock temporarily in Pas and permanent inhabitants of Pas. The former were ordered to pay their tithes to Espinosa and the latter to El Porrato. The sentence was apparently carried out without subsequent long-term reversals, though there is evidence that it was appealed more than once (Archive of the Centro de Estudios Montañeses [CEMA] 1767). However, Carriazo's legal victory apparently did not win for Pasiegos the right to bury their dead at home. There is a reference, probably to the year 1666 (VPA 1789:589–91), indicating that Pasiegos were still buried in Espinosa at that time, and they certainly still were in 1576, when the Archbishop of Burgos ordered two clerics to take up residence in Pas (Escagedo Salmón 1921:65; Arroyo del Prado 1958:406). Further, informants in Vega de Pas have told me that Bárcenas—a dependency of Espinosa lying between the villa of Espinosa and Las Machorras—served for a period as an intermediate burial ground for Pasiegos, before the establishment of cemeteries in Pas. Here is another case of separation of the elements proper to full parish status: the presence of an altar and a baptismal font do not imply the presence of a cemetery as well. (According to Escalera, the Pas settlements had baptismal fonts by 1632; Arroyo del Prado [1957] cites this statement from the first edition of Escalera's book.) The ambiguity of Pasiego parish status persisted into later years and seemed primarily due to the continued dependence on the Espinosa (or Bárcenas) cemetery.[17]

17. The right of possession of a baptismal font without rights to an independent cemetery as well is extremely rare if not unique in Spanish history (González y González, pers. comm.) and serves to underline the peculiarities attending Pas' marginal situation. However, there was per-

The three Pas parishes were classified as *feligresías* (rural parishes), dependencies of Espinosa. Between the time of the establishment of the feligresías and 1689, when the Pas towns became independent municipal centers, the territories in the Montes de Pas were known almost exclusively as the feligresías of San Pedro, San Roque, and Nuestra Señora de la Vega (or sometimes Santa María de la Vega, the modern Vega de Pas): they were named for their major churches. Their most detailed description, with an enumeration of chapels and shrines, is by Escalera (1735:240–41) and it is interesting that by 1735 there was no mention of any place of worship called El Porrato. The three clergymen then attached to the Pas feligresías were said by Escalera to receive their support from the Archbishop of Burgos, the Abbot of Oña, and the *cabildo* of Espinosa (doubtless the collegiate church there). And to these three parties the Pasiegos at that time paid their tithes.

Despite their partial independence, the three feligresías continued as political-administrative dependents of Espinosa, and they shared the pasturage privileges enjoyed by Espinosa. A lengthy series of litigations between Espinosa and the territories of Valdeporres and Sotoscueva over grazing rights in the Río de la Engaña won a confirmation of privileges which were shared by San Pedro and Vega de Pas as Espinosa's dependents (VPA 1699, 1789). (San Roque was not a party in the case, evidently because it shares no common boundaries with Valdeporres and Sotoscueva and probably did not pasture there.) San Pedro also shared in Espinosa's victory in a suit with the Valley of Toranzo over pasturage in Ríolangos, on what is today the border between San Pedro and Luena. (VPA 1790 cites a 1534 decision, as do Escagedo Salmón 1921 and Arroyo del Prado 1958.) Further, in 1666 (cited in VPA 1789), certain named inhabitants of Pas were serving as monteros. These facts, and the apparent fact of continued burial in Espinosa territory, stood in favor of the Pasiegos' claim to share Espinosa's privileges, while the existence of separate feligresías, even though dependent, was repeatedly taken as a counterargument. So was the fact, cited for 1657 (VPA 1790), that inhabitants of San Pedro had to pay

haps an economic motive behind Espinosa's retention of Pas' burial rights: one-fifth (*el quinto*) of a person's earned property (*gananciales*) (as opposed to the *legítima*, his inherited property) could, in instances, go to the parish, and Espinosa would have stood to benefit in such cases (González y González, pers. comm.). However, Escagedo Salmón notes (1921:65) that the Pas priests were themselves entitled to collect the burial fees attending burial in the Espinosa cemetery.

alcabalas (excise fees or duties on market exchange) to sell in the market at Espinosa, fees which vecinos of the villa of Espinosa did not have to pay. Here, evidently, enters the distinction between categories of citizenship within and outside the *chef lieu* of a territory.

In 1646 and 1648 (cited in VPA 1790), there was litigation between Espinosa and the Carriedo Valley north of Pas concerning rights to civil and criminal jurisdiction in the Montes de Pas. The judge ordered that jurisdiction over half of the Montes, for reasons of geographic proximity, be ceded by Espinosa to Carriedo, and each contestant was ordered to pay one half of the price of 11,000 ducats fixed by the judge.[18] Espinosa's failure to pay gave jurisdictional rights to Carriedo alone, and these were held for approximately forty years, until the towns of Pas purchased rights to their own jurisdiction. The events of the acquisition by Carriedo of jurisdiction in Pas are explained in the record of a later court proceeding (VPA 1790:230ff.). Another reference (VPA 1689:3a ff.) emphasizes that the judicial order to divide jurisdiction in Pas between Carriedo and Espinosa specified that "the community of pastures remain as it was before."

The purchase by the Pas feligresías of their own jurisdiction (which followed some continued litigation on the part of Pas) shortly preceded the date—1689—when the three Pasiego towns were, by royal decree, named independent villas. But for the forty years preceding the royal decree, separation of jurisdiction (Carriedo) from other aspects of civil membership (Espinosa), and the continued ambiguity of parish status, fueled arguments in the litigations over pasturage being pressed at the time. Only in 1689 did the ambiguities of status disappear, for the creation of the new villas evidently made the associated parishes independent: as soon as the royal decree was effected, the Pas settlements were no longer referred to as feligresías. (Thus, on March 17, 1689, Nuestra Señora de la Vega was called a villa, but San Pedro remained a feligresía until March 20, and San Roque remained one until May, for reasons of inaccessibility due to heavy snow.) Villa status brought both civil and religious membership to focus fully in the Pas settlements; the jailhouse at Santibañez (Carriedo) was no longer to be used for Pasiegos, and new ones were ordered established in the Pas villas; the administrative officials of independent municipalities were named, apparently all residents of their respective villas; and

18. The separation of jurisdiction from locality of vecindad or civil enrollment is also perhaps unique (González y González, pers. comm.).

the limits of the municipal territories, as previously established, were carefully recorded. The three new villas were to retain whatever community of pasture they had previously enjoyed.

The *Real Privilegio*, or royal grant of villa status, of 1689, is the only document which I studied which was apparently not seen, or at least not studied in substance, by those authors who have recorded Pasiego documentary history in greatest detail—Escagedo Salmón (1921), Terán (1947), and García-Lomas (1960).[19] Knowledge of its substance would undoubtedly have given them better perspective on the legal history of Pas (though Escagedo Salmón demonstrates fair perspective in any case). The locally preserved litigation all post-dates 1689, with the exception of the royal grant itself, and it was apparently the act of 1689 which caused all prior litigation and sentences to be reviewed in a new context. The establishment of the villas reopened the questions of the community of pasture which had before been fought by Espinosa and Pas together. Now a new era of litigation began: the three new villas of Pas went to court against Espinosa in order to preserve, despite their new independence, the ancient community of pasture which they had enjoyed.

Even though Espinosa and the Pas settlements had, until 1689, been successful in retaining the pasturage privileges as granted in the fourteenth and fifteenth centuries,[20] the judicial sentences were, throughout the seventeenth century, continually being appealed and reversed, sometimes on an almost annual basis. As early as the period when Espinosa had lost the right of jurisdiction in Pas, the Pas-Espinosa community of pasture was apparently called into question: one of the court records (VPA 1789)

19. Maza Solano (1956) cites the 1689 date for purchase of jurisdiction but does not associate it with the establishment of the villas. Arroyo del Prado apparently saw the document in Vega de Pas, where its binding bears a misleading date of 1843, though no 1843 document is included. He lists the royal grant as an 1843 document (Arroyo del Prado 1958:408) and gives no evidence of having read the binder's actual contents. Escagedo Salmón (1921:66) correctly identifies 1689 as the date of villa establishment but, strangely, he cites none of the document's substance. Both he (1921:56) and Arroyo del Prado (1958:407) list a document giving 1692 as the date at which Pas purchased its own jurisdiction from Carriedo. This is so contradictory to the events recorded in VPA 1689 that I have omitted reference to it in my narrative; I assume the 1692 document to be a simple confirmation or official closing of the purchase made earlier. Neither author gives detail of the 1692 document or its archival source.

20. As I have already noted, the documents reviewing pasturage privileges (that is, the court records themselves) never cite the 1011 rights of Oña but rather the 1369 grant to Espinosa and/or its 1467 confirmation.

cites a document found in San Roque recording a legal victory for Pas over Espinosa, but no date is given. The former co-litigants had become adversaries. Espinosa evidently reopened the question when the territorial limits of the three new villas were officially recorded in 1689, and so litigation between the new adversaries continued into the eighteenth century. Finally, in 1790, the Pas villas won their case, and we have no record of appeals or subsequent reversals of the decision. The community of pasture survived intact and was confirmed even in the face of Pasiego municipal independence. This appears to have put to rest the question of grazing rights, at least as regards Pas and her immediate neighbors: Pasiegos evidently continued to enjoy the wide privileges they had won with Espinosa in the centuries of prior litigation, and there is no further record of full-scale conflict. The community of pasture would change, as municipalities ultimately obtained the general right to charge outsiders on their communal lands if they wished, and as the use of the pastures themselves would change, but not as results of litigation.

The three villas of Pas were, from the time of their establishment, *realengas*—that is, they were directly subject to (and taxable by) the Crown with no intermediate lords. While some local historians advised me that the Duchy of Frías, near Oña, might have possessed rights in Pas, I have found none mentioned. The royal decree of villa status states that, in 1689, the Duke of Infantado possessed some rights to the *montazgos* collected in Pas (fees for passage of stock across the communal lands—a fee from which all enjoying community of pasture were, according to the Oña grant and later ones, exempt). Whether the House of Infantado acquired rights to some form of payment from the inhabitants themselves (a possible implication of the term *montazgo*), or whether its rights were only to fees paid in Pas by outsiders, is unclear. This reference is the only one I have seen detailing any relationship at all of the Pasiegos with a secular power other than the Crown. The Duchy of Infantado was not founded until 1475, in any case, though the first Duke also held the older title, dating from 1445, of Marqués of Santillana.

Freedom from rule by feudal lords is hardly unusual in northern Old Castile and adjacent areas. Many whole population centers were at one time classed as *behetrías* (see Valdeavellano 1968 or, for detail, Ferrari Nuñes 1958). Briefly, the behetría territory or individual enjoyed the right of shifting allegiance at will from one overlord to another, in some instances to the legal limit of seven times in one day, and in some instances (*behetría de mar a mar*) to any lord whatever in the entire Castilian-Leonese realm—thus "from sea to sea," from the Cantabrian (Bay of Biscay) to the open Atlantic (Valdeavellano 1968:342). Espinosa de los Monteros, however, was not listed in the mid-fourteenth century *Libro* or *Becerro de las Behetrías* (see Ferrari Nuñez 1958), and, indeed, it is hardly surprising that Espinosa, with its special relation to the Crown, apparently was not subject to secular intermediacy, for there is no hint of any in the records I have seen. Thus, as dependencies of Espinosa, the Pas settlements were subject primarily to ecclesiastical authorities only, and as villas they were, like Espinosa, subject directly to the Crown.[21]

Espinosans who were designated as monteros had to demonstrate purity of blood, and the population of Espinosa in general appears to have enjoyed noble status at some level (see Escalera 1735:252ff.). There were conscious attempts to preserve the purity and noble status of the general population, as in such acts as the severe restriction of contact with Jews, or people of Jewish family, and New Christians ordered by Juana la Loca in 1511 (reprinted in full by Escalera 1735:254–58 and Escagedo Salmón 1921:89–91). There is good evidence that virtually all inhabitants of Pas as well enjoyed status in the lower nobility as *hijosdalgo (hidalgos), hombres buenos, hijos de algo notorio,* and so on, before as well as following their independence from Espinosa.[22] Citation in court records (VPA 1790:324ff.) of a *padrón* or census roll of the Pas settlements drawn up in 1613 lists virtually all individuals as *hijos dalgo*. Again, more than a century later, in the Cadaster of the Marqués de la Ensenada, drawn up for Pas about 1753, virtually the entire population was listed as having noble status (as *nobles*).[23]

21. Ecclesiastical establishments such as monasteries, cathedrals, or collegiate churches were, in the Spanish feudal system, generally far more important as collectors and redistributors of revenue than were secular powers, which often depended heavily on revenues directed to them by religious establishments. The manor associated with "classic" feudalism, the attendant many-stranded relationship between lords and their dependents, and even geographic proximity of subject to lord were virtually absent in the Castilian system we are dealing with here.
22. These terms, as that of *noble de sangre,* or simply *noble,* were wholly interchangeable, in this region at least, and often it was apparently the scribe or recorder who was responsible for applying one or the other term.
23. The town rolls of the Ensenada cadaster were studied and published by Maza Solano (1956), but the crucial volume containing the *padrón*, or rolls, for Vega de Pas was missing. Maza Solano thus deals

Status in the lower nobility was based largely on genealogical, or presumed genealogical, credentials, and this is indicated by the frequent designation of this category by the term *nobleza de sangre*, or blood nobility. Blood nobles were not necessarily also titled nobles, and it was to the higher nobility—the titled nobles —that property and rights to revenue collection pertained. The blood nobility, on the contrary, did not possess significant social and economic power, though its members were freed of various taxes, and its numbers included destitute poor along with simple farmers and herders and their wealthier landlords. In parts of northern Spain, the proportion of nobles (not necessarily titled) in the general population is very high. This is owing to the special statuses enjoyed by many localities in those regions which were Christian strongholds during the centuries of Muslim dominion, and to the fact that individuals and whole populations of northern areas played special roles in the early years of the Christian Reconquest of Spain. Northerners moved southward in the armies of the Reconquest, earning honors and gaining dominions as they went, and the oldest Spanish titles are, of course, tied to northern localities.

Much of what is today the province of Santander was formerly part of the Asturias. These were, from west to east, the Asturias of Oviedo (in the modern province of Oviedo) and, in modern Santander, the Asturias of Santillana (from the basin of the Deva to the basin of the Miera) and the Asturias of Trasmiera (from the Miera basin to the Asón basin). When historians name "Asturias" as the seat of the Reconquest, and its legendary center the cave of Covadonga, they refer to what was in fact the Asturias de Oviedo and, more specifically, to the mountainous borderlands between the modern provinces of Santander and Oviedo dominated by the Picos de Europa Range (see, for example, González Camino y Aguirre 1930). But all of the Asturias, in the older and broader application of the name, together enjoyed a history which was virtually unbroken by the Moorish invasion and, as I have mentioned, many localities there assumed special status for their roles in the formative events of Spanish nationhood. This was not seignieurial terrain but rather the land of the behetría *par excellence*; not so much the land of

---

only with the other two villas. Arroyo del Prado (1958:409ff.) took from the general volumes on landholdings in San Pedro and San Roque all references to people from Vega de Pas who, as landholders outside their own town, identified themselves fully, and these again were virtually all *hijos de algo notorio*.

the titled nobility and *rico hombre* (though it was that, too) as the land of the noble common man, who could demonstrate purity of blood and, in instances, claim with pride to be *más noble que el rey*—nobler than the king—in this respect.

In towns like those of Pas, with everyone a noble, the status probably meant little; in W. S. Gilbert's words, "When everyone is somebody, then no one's anybody." But the noble status of the Pasiego population requires introduction here, and mention at later points in the text, first for the respects in which Pasiegos' own consciousness of it differs from one sector to another of the Pas community and, second, for the respects in which it has concerned outsiders.

In the preceding pages, I have taken as the chief source for the study of Pasiego history the documents themselves. Until the middle of the nineteenth century, documents of a largely legal nature were the only sources for such an endeavor. In the nineteenth century, however, the array of both sources and issues became more complex.

Pasiegos had long been leaving Pas, at least temporarily, to ply trades outside. Their presence outside Pas is clearly documented in archives of the seventeenth century (M. C. González Echegaray, pers. comm.). Most of their trades were in the category of petty commerce and peddling, often seasonal. The migrations were of several general types. Peddling focused by and large on rural communities along the north coast and in regions neighboring Pas. Market vending of local products (butter and cheese) focused, of course, on market centers, mostly in the province of Santander, as far as the capital city, and in the adjacent zones of Burgos, especially Espinosa and Soncillo. But Pasiegos also, possibly as early as 1586, were purveyors of butter and cheese to the royal palace and "Burgos, Nájera, Logroño, Santo Domingo, Victoria, Bilbao and other villas and localities."[24]

Finally, a certain amount of peddling of specific products was tied to the demand for these products in centers of tourism or major population centers: Pasiegos sold hydromel in Madrid cafés in the summers, or ice cream and butter-wafers at resorts in Santander and, more generally, along coastal districts into France as far as Bayonne. They also ran contraband from southwestern France across the Basque provinces and into Castile via the eastern districts of the Montes de Pas, and from Vega de Pas

24. Document cited in Escagedo Salmón (1921:80).

out of Castile again and westward into Asturias (Oviedo province). All of these activities, to be described later in other contexts, were in full swing during the nineteenth century, and one further occurrence acted as a catalyst in bringing the Pasiego presence outside of Pas to full public attention.

In 1830, a Pasiego woman was selected as wet-nurse for the royal infant who was to become Isabel II. Medical doctors in the service of the Crown had long recruited wet-nurses from the countryside of León and northern Castile. The province of Burgos had been in favor, and the search for likely candidates extended from there into Santander, bringing a Pasiega to the Court for the first time (Cortés Echánove 1958).[25] And thus was initiated the era of *pasieguería*, Pasiego lore, in the published literature and the public mind.

There were apparently no appreciable secondary sources on the Pasiegos (other than the 1632 and 1735 editions of Escalera's work) until around 1830, when the Pasiega's presence in Court nudged the public curiosity and brought writers, mostly local to Santander province, to focus their attention on Pas.[26] Perhaps the first excursion into Pas which became the subject of a published description was a brief one—to Vega de Pas—by a poet, Enrique Gil, published in 1839. A close survey of provincial newspapers and periodicals of the time would probably reveal further references to the picturesque qualities of Pas and its people, and the Pasiego "type" and "character" and "homeland" gradually became the subjects of a romantic literature by travelers, local artists, and local historians. García-Lomas (1960) reproduces commemorative plates, lithographs, even cheese wrappers and labels from other products which depicted Pasiegos and/or bore their name. The early post-1830 literature has been reviewed by Terán (1947) and García-Lomas (1960), and a glance

25. The wet-nurse of Isabel II was Francisca Ramón, a Pasiega, but actually from Peñacastillo on the coastal plain near the city of Santander. She was not the first Santanderina chosen to join the corps of potential wet-nurses (*nodrizas, amas de leche*) in the palace, but the first chosen as the ranking nodriza for a royal infant (see Cortés Echánove 1958). The next Pasiega to assume such an important rank as wet-nurse was María Gómez, of Vega de Pas, one of the two chief nodrizas of the infant Alfonso XII.

26. This was the era of Spain's division into its modern provinces (in 1833), and I should remark that, possibly in an atmosphere of heightened consciousness of the new political identity, the Pasiego lore originated from and was associated almost exclusively with the province of Santander, where most Pasiegos and the three villas are located, and not with the province of Burgos. This remains the case today.

at the bibliographies of these authors reveals nothing prior to 1830 of the type that appeared after that date.[27]

In the first decades following 1830, works on Pas and its people were mostly concerned with the landscape (the precipitous mountains, the slate-roofed cabañas set in emerald-green meadows, the ultra-rural quality lent by the dispersion of the dwellings), on the local costume and equipment (the herder's staff, the carrying baskets which took the place of all wheeled vehicles, the combined stable and home which was the cabaña), on the diet (milk and cornbread), and on the local products (butter and cheese) which were brought into regional markets on the backs of these "curious" people. Madoz, writing in 1849 and evidently using such sources, gave the following description, which, significantly, is contained in his article on Villacarriedo, where Pasiegos came to market, rather than in those on the three villas themselves. (His description of administrative seats like Villacarriedo are more comprehensive, so the inclusion of the Pasiegos here is in part by design.) ". . . Among all the residents of this zone there are to be distinguished the inhabitants of the pueblos of Pas, known throughout Spain by the name Pasiegos; their industry, their fondness for and disposition toward commerce, their agility, their robustness, their costume, and their deserved fame as smugglers . . ." (Madoz 1849, 16: 101–3). In 1865, the literature on the Pasiegos left the realm of the purely picturesque and entered that of conjectural history. Gregorio Lasaga Larreta, in a work entitled *Compilación histórica, biográfica y marítima de la provincia de Santander*, doubted that any people as unusual as the Pasiegos could possibly be of Cantabrian stock.[28] A possible precursor for this idea is Esperón's 1851 statement that "the Pasiegos, like the Jews, are a separate nation" (cited in Terán 1947 from Esperón 1851). Lasaga argued that the Pasiego population must instead be of Moorish origin, descended specifically from captives of the group which entered Spain with Tariq. All that was offered in support

27. García-Lomas, however, reproduces two eighteenth-century paintings depicting Pasiego costumes, one from a general collection on Spanish dress (1960: 142–43).

28. The Cantabrian tribes, at the time of the Romanization of the Iberian peninsula, occupied a territory covering the eastern portion of the modern Asturias (from the River Sella) and most of modern Santander, with a probable eastern boundary in eastern Santander at the frontier of the territory of the Autrigones and Basques, and stretching southward from the sea over the Cantabrian range into Burgos, well south of the location of modern Espinosa (see J. González Echegaray 1966a).

of this argument was a description of the elements of Pasiego dress and aspects of Pasiegos' physiognomy and bearing. And the accompanying citation of Pasiego customs regarding diet (including the method of cooking pork!), transhumance, use of the carrying basket, bedding in the cabañas, and funeral observances were no doubt intended as further support for how "different" Pasiegos were.[29] Lasaga restated his convictions in an 1889 publication.

Lasaga's groundless speculations were dignified in 1921 by a more painstakingly documented but no better founded theory set forth by Mateo Escagedo Salmón. Escagedo began by presenting a resumé of archival materials which apparently served as the single most important source or guide for later authors writing on the same subject (especially Terán 1947, Arroyo del Prado 1958, García-Lomas 1960). Escagedo then goes on to cite Lasaga Larreta and to offer a different interpretation of Pasiego origins. Instead of assuming all Pasiegos to be of Semitic stock, as did Lasaga, Escagedo admitted that some of the population must indeed be Christian and of Cantabrian stock, or how else could there be such an incidence of clean-blooded nobles among them? However, how could a predominantly Christian and Cantabrian population be so very different in its ways? Escagedo resolved this conundrum by postulating that the ancient nucleus of the population of Pas dating from 1011 must have been Semitic and that people who moved there subsequently simply assumed the same distinguishing (Semitic) characteristics which have come to characterize the Pasiego people as a whole.

The speculative literature involves the assumption of facts which are so obviously foreign to the body of documented history of prior centuries that the theories of Lasaga and Escagedo scarcely seem to need refutation. But Escagedo's arguments, in particular, have proven very convincing in provincial circles, so much so that there is today an extensive mythology in the province of Santander regarding the Semitic origin of the Pasiegos, widespread in rural areas as well as in intellectual circles in the capital city. Once expounded in these circles, points of view dif-

29. Many items in this list are simple adaptations to local circumstances and are not unknown in similar settings elsewhere. The questions of funeral customs and costume, however, are of a different order, and, in fact, I can find in neither one grounds for distinguishing Pasiegos from their neighbors any more than their neighbors are distinguishable from each other. Also, it is unlikely that any of the authors of this period had sufficient exposure to Pasiego life to have any but superficial and unrepresentative views of the various modes of dress in use or of the full context of funeral customs.

fuse quickly and widely; publications on topics of local interest or lectures presented in such forums as the Ateneo (Atheneum) receive wide coverage in the press, and their diffusion and repetition are based more on their authors' personal and family renown than on the logic or scholarship of their arguments. In this setting, by the third or fourth decade of this century, the Pasiegos were widely believed to be a race apart, and this is still the case today. In this context, it is fitting to lay bare the details of Escagedo's argument rather than simply to mark it as removed from documented facts, a product of the post-1830 period.

Escagedo began by assuming the existence of a farflung social structure in which the first inhabitants of Pas were serfs (or *familias de criación*) of the Abbot or Abbess of Oña. Thus, in his discussion of the 1011 donation to Oña, he fails to cite the text in its original language—"*. . . hominibus de Abate de Onia . . .*" (see appendix A)—and freely translates the above phrase as *"vasallos* [vassals] *del abad de Oña"* (1921:47). The liberty is inexcusable, and the tendency of Escagedo's translation should be contrasted with that published in 1891 by R. Amador de los Ríos (see appendix A) which leaves *homin[es]* as *hombres*. Further, as I have suggested earlier, there is no documentary evidence to support the assumption that vecinos or any other inhabitants of Oña itself were at any time consistently present in Pas. None of the earliest documents, in presenting information on the population of the Montes de Pas, mentions anyone who did not have the status of vecino in one of the immediately adjacent localities—Espinosa, Sotoscueva, Valdeporres, Toranzo, Carriedo, and so on. The original donation (appendix A), after detailing the region in question as territory adjacent to Espinosa, states that the grazing privileges are to be enjoyed by *"illi homines qui sub domine Abate, vel domine Abatissa Sancti Salvatoris Oniae populaberint . . ."* (Sp. *hombres que allí poblaren y habitaren bajo el dominio de . . . San Salvador de Oña . . .*); that is, by the population of Espinosa and not specifically that of Oña. The whole of Escagedo's interpretation, which is in part accepted by Terán (1947:17), suggests that "dependents" of Oña were more people than places and that they wandered far afield; the whole of documented history indicates that the "dependents" referred to were usually localities—and only sometimes the populations of those localities, who entered only lands adjacent to theirs and even then did so slowly. There are not sufficient data to permit resolution of this question, and this fact itself puts Escagedo's theory out of place. However, the absence of any real basis for his further assumptions should also be exposed. Escagedo cites a donation of fifty Moorish slaves by Garci-Fernández, Count of Castile, to his daughter. Next, he cites the foundation in 780 of the Monastery of Obona, which involved *familias de criación* (serf families) and appointed these to various functions, designating some of them as cowherds. Finally, Escagedo repeats that Juana la Loca did, in 1511, place restrictions upon the sojourn in Espinosa of Jews and/or New Christians, and this is taken (quite properly—see J. Amador de los Ríos 1960:922, 996) as evidence for the historical presence of Jews in the region. Thus are brought together diverse data, from diverse times and places, on the presence of both Moors and Jews, the fact that serf families were in one instance part of a donation, and that serfs in another instance had been cowherds. Thus, without further ado, Escagedo concludes that the 1011 donation to Oña, as well, involved the sending of subject peoples of Semitic stock into the Montes de Pas as cowherds. And he assumes that the New Christians and people of Jewish origin who were the subject of the Queen's decree in 1511 must have been the descendants of the first herders to enter Pas.

Finally, to close his argument, Escagedo reverts from the semblance of scholarship to the impressionism of Lasaga: "The transhumant Pasiego, going from cabaña to cabaña in search of pasture for his animals, reminds me of the nomadic Arab shepherd, nor are the Pasiego's commercial habits very different; he does not remain behind the counter but, like the son of Hagar, carries his wares to the towns where they are consumed, and fatigue and danger do not turn him back" (Escagedo Salmón 1921:88).

While Lasaga and Escagedo were hardly responsible for creating the Pasiegos' distinctiveness, which is closely associated with their transhumant way of life rather than anything else, they were indeed responsible for elevating to a new level the local consciousness of Pasiego distinctiveness, and this had inevitable effects on the self-consciousness of the Pasiegos themselves. The discussion of Pasiego origins has led scholars to classify the Pasiegos among the *pueblos malditos* (damned or despised peoples) of the North, in company with the Vaqueiros de Alzada (Asturias), the Maragatos (León), and the Agotes (Navarra).[30]

---

30. Cf. Caro Baroja 1943:142–3; 1946:306–7. Both citations make primary reference to the work of Lasaga and repeat his statement, for which I have found no support elsewhere, that Pasiegos were locally suspected even of having tails. Caro himself (1943:143) views the Pasiegos

While the social dynamics of the relations of all these groups with outsiders are in many ways comparable, it is historically important to note that the Pasiegos are a recent addition to the roster of the damned: the classic, early sources on the pueblos malditos do not concern themselves with the Pasiegos.[31] The earliest source cited as basis for connecting the Pasiegos with the other despised groups is Lasaga's work of 1865.

Ironically, another phenomenon began to occur in the same period which saw the heightening of popular notions of Pasiego distinctiveness. The stereotype of the Pasiego, the most "picturesque" of the province, became increasingly identified with the province as a whole. Literati immortalized versions of rural life and dialect which, romanticized in themselves, were then assumed by a general public to derive from Pas (which was sometimes untrue) *and* to typify rural Santander. The word *pasiega*, for example, entered the Spanish dictionary (where it still stands) as an accepted synonym for *nodriza*, or wet-nurse.[32] This is true despite the fact that non-Pasiegas of Santander province served as wet-nurses in greater proportion than Pasiegas themselves, be they from Pas or be they Pasiego emigrants to other localities in the province. Artists had been depicting Pasiegos since even before 1830, and some of the paintings and drawings are reproduced by García-Lomas (1960); the physical image of the Pasiego apparently became sufficiently engraved in the public consciousness that it dominated the images from other regions of the province. Given the growing speculation in Santander concerning Pasiego origins and the general disdain for their way of life, it is not surprising that equating Pasiegos with Santander called forth some angry comment from local writers. Less angered than bewildered, José María de Pereda, the Santander novelist, is reported by García-Lomas (1960: 41–42) to have written to Menéndez Pelayo, in 1886, while writing his *Peñas Arriba*, the following disclaimer:

(and other similar groups) as primarily occupational enclaves with a history of relative social isolation but no verifiable foreign origins. J. González Echegaray (1966b) reaches similar conclusions regarding the Pasiegos and comparable groups.

31. Principal early sources are Lardizábal y Uribe 1786, Michel 1847, and de Rochas 1876. They make no reference to the Pasiegos.

32. One sector of the Cathedral square in the city of Granada is named Plaza de las Pasiegas, presumably for the wet-nurses. I have been unable to discover anything further about the history of the plaza's name, but the earliest dated map in Granada's municipal museum bearing the name is from 1894.

I don't know if you've noticed that these newspapers, like almost all Spanish papers, keep stating with certainty that I'm writing a novel, with a prologue by you, entitled *Los de Pas*. That was announced by a paper in this city [probably Santander] on the Día de Inocentes. The singular thing about the case is not that the rumor spreads as it does, but that it ought to be true, because in that part of the Montaña [Santander province] and among those people there *is* a novel which I ought to write; but I'll never write it, because I know no more about that country-side and those people than I do about the Chinese Empire.[33]

Peñas Arriba (1894) was modeled on the town of Tudanca, in the Nansa Valley of western Santander.[34] Nonetheless, when the book appeared, so did a caricature of Pereda atop a mountain, wearing wooden clogs stuffed with straw and carrying a *cuévano* —the Pasiego carrying basket.[35]

Today, in addition to elements of material culture, village traditions, and fragments of Pas' real history, the stereotype of the Pasiego is sharpened by historical conjecture and by caricatures of Pasiego behavior derived largely from contact in the marketplace and elsewhere outside Pas. In the surrounding parts of the province, Pasiego jokes play on the stereotype of the Pasiego as the driver of a hard bargain in the market or at the stock fair, tight-fisted, shrewd in all dealings; an inveterate wanderer, a person who lives among cows and is out of place in the urban world and who, when questioned, is devious, close-mouthed, and suspicious—unblinking, he swallows information and divulges none.

Images of the Pasiego are more diverse, however, and have sprung up, even if in attenuated form, in whatever contexts Pasiegos have left Pas. Outside Santander, in Basque towns, for example, a "Pasiego" is a vendor of cloth; in certain circles, and in the dictionary, a "Pasiega" is a wet-nurse; and in urban areas —and largely since the end of the nineteenth century—a Pasiego is the neighborhood retailer of milk.

Among Pasiegos, also, there are varying self-images, different for the Pasiego herder, the sedentary Pasiego living in Pas, the

33. Pereda apparently saw some sincere misunderstanding here and not the simple humor appropriate to the Día de Inocentes, which is equivalent to April Fool's Day. For a character evidently styled as Pasiego, if only in name, and identified as *montañés* (from Santander), see Clarín's Fermín de Pas in *La Regenta*, published in 1884.

34. For the contrast between the Nansa towns and Pas, compare Christian 1972.

35. From the review *Blanco y Negro* 16:3 (1895), reproduced by García-Lomas 1960:47.

Pasiego herder who raises cattle outside Pas, and the child of Pasiego emigrants who was reared in the city. For each group, the elements of Pasiego tradition are differently weighted and differently colored. To understand this, we must first understand the basis for differentiation of the various segments of the Pasiego community.

TWO

Vega de Pas

*Don't think we're not afraid, up there in the branizas all alone.
It's down here, by the Plaza, that we like to be.*

a barrio girl

The municipality of Vega de Pas, called simply La Vega by most
of its residents, is officially subdivided into seven parts: the villa
proper—commonly called the Casco (for *casco urbano*, urban
nucleus), sometimes called the Plaza, after the Casco's social
center—and six barrios, Pandillo, Yera, Viaña, Candolías, La
Gurueba, and Guzparras (see map 5). In general, these divisions
are true social ones, corresponding also with geographically separate entities. The barrios of Pandillo, Yera, and Viaña are the
basins of the rivers of those names, with their boundaries along
the mountain crests which divide the separate drainages. The
Casco is located at the confluence of the Pandillo and the Yera,
where they assume the name of Pas; the Viaña flows into the
Pas about two kilometers downstream of the Casco.[1] The barrio
of Candolías extends from the boundary of the Casco to the
point of confluence with the Viaña and from the low meadows
on both sides of the main stream of the Pas to the crests dividing Vega de Pas from the neighboring municipalities of Selaya
and Villacarriedo, in the Valley of Carriedo. La Gurueba, immediately adjacent to Candolías and Viaña, occupies both sides of
the Pas, on the north to the crest overlooking Carriedo and on
the south to the relatively artificial boundary with the munici-

1. The distances of barrios from the Plaza listed in the official census
(Instituto Nacional de Estadística 1960 or 1970) are measured from selected points within the barrios, and in these terms "Viaña" is 3 km. distant from the Plaza. Likewise, the official distances for Pandillo and Yera
from the Plaza, listed in note 2 below, are strangely arbitrary.

28

pality of San Pedro. The barrio of Guzparras, the smallest both in territory and in number of inhabitants, is bounded by La Gurueba and by its non-Pasiego neighbors in Carriedo and Luena. It is watered by a small tributary of the Pas but is not located on the Pas itself or on any major stream. The lack here is not of water, which is plentiful, but of fertile, valley-bottom land.

The barrios display different patterns in marriage, occupation, and emigration; these are described in chapter 9 and appendix C. These differences accompany the differences in geography, economy, and communications to which I turn now.

The three alpine barrios of Pandillo, Yera, and Viaña are social entities which are also naturally bounded—they are separate montane river basins. The inhabitants of these three barrios are dedicated almost exclusively to cattle-herding and to the transhumant regime described in Tista's Year. As shown in maps 3 and 4, the three alpine barrios embrace territories varying in altitude from about 360 m. (represented by the Plaza at 358 m.), or lower, at the mouths of the tributaries, to well over 1000 m. in the highest utilized meadows, whose altitudes are fairly well represented by the figures given for the major passes at the mountain crests—1116 m. at the Estacas de Trueba (Yera and Pandillo) and rising along the Pandillo crests toward the municipality of San Roque and the Lunada Pass there, which stands at 1350 m. These passes are actually within the high meadow areas; they are overshadowed by peaks, such as that of Castro Valnera at more than 1700 m., which stand high above the utilized lands and are occasionally covered with snow even in summer.

The barrios of Candolías, La Gurueba, and Guzparras are smaller than Pandillo, Yera, and Viaña, and while the former do not necessarily have a smaller proportion of bottom land (see table 2), they range over territories with less altitudinal variation.[2] The highest pastures in these barrios lie at altitudes rep-

2. The official altitudes recorded by the Census and cadastral survey are taken at specified distances from the town center and are as follows:

Place	Distance from center	Altitude
Pandillo	3.5 km	534 m
Yera	2.5	569
Viaña	3.0	548
Candolías	1.3	410
La Gurueba	5.0	241
Guzparras	7.0	514
Casco	—	358

These figures are not indicative of much, however, in the cases of the barrios, since an arbitrary selection of points of reference can give a very

TABLE 2

APPROXIMATE AMOUNTS OF MEADOW IN EACH OF THE THREE
ALTITUDE ZONES, BY BARRIO[a]

Barrio	Ribera Total			Ladera Total			Braniza Total			Total Meadow			Percent Ribera	Percent Ladera	Percent Braniza
	Ha[b]	a[b]	ca[b]	Ha	a	ca	Ha	a	ca	Ha	a	ca			
Pandillo	111	16	20	192	76	60	305	46	00	609	38	80	18.24	31.63	50.13
Yera	152	56	40	123	25	00	184	33	60	460	15	00	33.16	26.78	40.06
Viaña	69	57	40	141	11	00	104	75	00	315	43	40	22.06	44.74	33.21
Candolías	197	30	40	72	58	40	39	28	40	309	17	20	63.82	23.48	12.71
La Gurueba	51	01	20	81	91	60	107	74	50	240	67	30	21.20	34.04	44.77
Guzparras[c]	—	—	—	—	—	—	103	44	40	103	44	40	—	—	100.00
Casco	48	88	00	—	—	—	—	—	—	48	88	00	100.00	—	—

[a]These figures are adapted from the modern cadaster but categorized by informants according to traditional classification of meadow by relative altitude. Thus, the total amount of meadow in town is larger than shown in the official figures on table 6 below, because these combine some of the types distinguished in the cadaster. These figures are only approximate, as the data reviewed by informants did not include later corrections registered in the cadaster, but these do not affect the general patterns summarized in the last columns.

[b]Ha = hectares; a = areas = 1/10 hectare; ca = centiareas = 1/100 hectare.

[c]Informants named a group of three meadows in a zone classified as ribero in Guzparras, which is shown here as having no ribero land. The three meadows in question were either omitted from the cadaster or mistakenly designated as braniza under another name, and no measurements are available for them. The status of all the rest of Guzparras as low braniza is discussed in chap. 2, n. 15.

resented by that of the Braguía Pass, at 720 m. The economies of Candolías, La Gurueba, and Guzparras are more mixed than those of the three larger barrios, and the social and geographic boundaries between them are not always as clear as those of Pandillo, Yera, and Viaña. Proportionally more land is under cultivation, particularly in La Gurueba and Guzparras, and transhumance is more attenuated in nature. Guzparras was the only barrio of Vega de Pas included in the agronomic survey of the Pas Valley (Ministerio de Agricultura 1949). The variance between the two groups of barrios is evident in many of the respects in which I shall be comparing them. The reasons for the variance are not necessarily more environmental than they are cultural, but some weight must be given to true differences in altitude and microclimate. In questions of cultural style, however, and in the contrast of barrio style to that of the Plaza, all of the barrios are as one. The question of barrio style and identity will be of concern through most of this study. In inquiring into the differences in barrio economies, however, it is important to remember that all of Pasiego herding, transhumance, and economic relations with the outside world have changed greatly since the end of the nineteenth century, and when we come later to review these changes it is crucial to wonder if the three larger barrios did not simply select differently for change than did the others, for the three smaller barrios are, by contrast, closer or better connected to regions outside Pas and have evidently turned more frequently away from herding as the exclusive means of earning a living. A hundred years ago, the differences visible today appear to have been considerably smaller.

Of the three alpine barrios, Yera stands slightly apart, for it shares, particularly with Candolías and La Gurueba, access to the Entrambasmestas-Espinosa highway, which has brought greater outside contact to these barrios since the beginning of the twentieth century. The approximate beginning date for the improvement of this early eighteenth-century highway—at least of its sector through La Vega—was 1895. Improvement of the local segment of the highway from Selaya over the Braguía Pass into Vega de Pas (and ultimately to Entrambasmestas and Reinosa) was begun around 1907. Prior to this period, those roads were dirt roads open to traffic by cart or by foot and only

---

false picture of relative altitudes, and this appears to be true especially for Candolías relative to the Plaza. The figure for Guzparras, however, even though it is far downstream from the center, seems accurately to reflect its location in the flanks of the hills above the Pas.

as conditions permitted. Palacio Atard (1959:55) describes the condition of all the "highways" from Burgos to the Santander coast in the late eighteenth century as "irregular and, in general, detestable." There is no evidence that they were improved until a century later. Mail service to La Vega was by pedestrian carrier working out of Entrambasmestas (Blanchard 1892).

The barrios touched by the roads have made use of them in the development of enterprises not related to herding. There has been a greater concentration in these areas of carting and other kinds of ambulatory commerce; recently there is trucking as well; with roads available for transport, there has been more lumbering and quarrying; there has been greater incidence of home production of items which might attract tourists and travelers, or trade items for market; and more people in these zones have—at least in a supplementary way—found work on the road crews or in the telegraph and postal services.

The population of the Casco itself is heavily dedicated to commercial callings and, for the most part, only indirectly to exploitation of land and livestock, though the juxtaposition of herders and non-herders there is substantial and has special interest (see chap. 7).

Table 3 gives the numbers of Pasiego households for the various sectors of town (though the official rolls lend rigidity to the relatively fluid household composition to be described later). This count includes all barrio households—even those which somehow escaped enrollment in 1965—for all of these are Pasiegos, as well as including the vast majority of Casco households, excluding only the resident outsiders who are both from outside Pas and have non-Pasiego spouses. Outsiders with affinal or blood ties in Pas are included in the household count.

The resident outsiders enrolled in La Vega during my period of fieldwork were the Pandillo and Casco schoolteachers (though they, like the other teachers, maintained residences outside Pas and never lived in La Vega for the entire year); various members of the Civil Guard, the military police, who resided in a headquarters at the edge of the Casco and who, by dint of the Guard's regulations, do not remain more than four years in a single town; one of the two active priests, and a retired priest with his niece; the pharmacist and his family; the game warden and his family; and the doctor and his family. Other professionals who resided in the Casco but were enrolled outside of Pas were a barrio teacher, a Casco teacher, and an active priest. Finally, the secretary of the *ayuntamiento* (municipal government) is married to a Pasiega from the Plaza and his household is included in the count on table 3. The veterinarian, a native of the Plaza, completes the roster of resident professionals, and his household is also included on the table. Vega de Pas is also served by a notary, but he visits the town from outside Pas only once a month.

TABLE 3
PASIEGO HOUSEHOLDS[a]

| | Genealogical Data[b] | | | Special Cases Not | | Total |
	None	Incomplete	Complete	Enrolled[b]	Total	Individuals[c]
Pandillo	2	1	93	1	97	481
Yera	4	1	60	1	66	296
Viaña	3	1	32	1	37	172
Candolías	5	3	46	3	57	283
La Gurueba	33	0	9	0	42	189
Guzparras	12	0	3	1	16	66
Casco (excluding resident outsiders)	0	0	75	2	77	371
Total	59	6	318	9	392	1,858

[a]Figures are based on town rolls for 1965 and adjusted by my field census.
[b]See appendix C.
[c]Figures are from 1960 census (Instituto Nacional de Estadística 1960). The number of individuals cannot be divided by the number of households to yield a true description of family size, for families do not always co-reside and their size is best studied from genealogical data (see appendix C).

Certain special facilities are manned by natives of the Casco who (like the game warden) are not strictly career men. These are the branch savings bank and the local office of the farmers' and herders' trade guild (Hermandad Sindical de Labradores y Ganaderos). The man who runs the *despacho sindical* is also the town's chief postal official.

Professionals and non-Pasiego service people are, by and large, located in the Casco. Only the Viaña teacher, during part of my residence in La Vega, took weekday pension with a Candolías family located on the highway close to the entrance to Viaña. The teacher for La Gurueba lived, I believe, in one of the adjacent settlements of San Pedro del Romeral.[3]

3. The Casco school was the only one with two teachers, with boys and girls taught separately. Pandillo, Yera, Viaña, and La Gurueba had separate schools, located at points marked on map 5. Candolías children attended the Casco school, an arrangement of long standing. Guzparras had a school but, in the term of my residence, no teacher, and there were only three children of school age in that barrio; their families had to arrange for their attendance at other schools. The need for such adjustments is not infrequent in Pas.

Certain of the tradesmen and professionals of the Casco travel into the barrios regularly in the normal execution of their work. These are the veterinarian, who also serves San Pedro in its entirety; the butchers, who inspect stock—mostly male calves—to purchase, slaughter, and sell (or in the case of the few mature animals, to export for slaughter outside Pas, since beef is neither eaten nor sold in Pas); the doctor, where house calls are necessary; the bakers, who truck bread to specified points in the barrios for sale on certain days of each week. (Milk collectors from dairying enterprises outside Pas travel likewise to specified localities for twice-daily milk pick-ups, and in a few cases, local people are employed as collectors.) Truckers (who transport animals and occasionally fodder) or anyone who functions as a stock dealer (*tratante*) also travel regularly through the barrios as well as through other towns in and beyond the Montes de Pas. Finally, the priests living in the Casco serve the chapel in La Gurueba, when necessary, and the church in Guzparras.

Guzparras, for its distance from the Plaza, has both a church and a cemetery of its own (though I know no date for their establishment), but it does not form a separate parish. The Gurueba chapel, dedicated to the Virgin of the Cármen, is the site only of occasional functions. There were formerly more active chapels and shrines in locations outside the Plaza, and these will be mentioned later, but their demise is apparently part of the general trend toward concentration in the Casco of almost all services and public meeting places, as well as of their personnel.[4]

Let us turn, then, to an overview of the nature of this concentration—and to the general absence of services and public places in the barrios. Table 4 gives a rough breakdown of the kinds of occupations followed in the various territorial entities. The categories under "herding" will be described later (pp. 75–87); for the present, it suffices to note that, although only two trans-

---

4. Two of the public facilities merit special mention, and they are markets of contrasting type. The occasional Sunday market, held in the Plaza of the Casco, is a minuscule remnant of what it once was (see chap. 3). Today the only vendors are outsiders, who peddle items of clothing almost exclusively; most of the same items are available in one or two of the general stores, and the chief clients of the market are inhabitants of the barrios. The Sunday market is not an outlet for any local products. By contrast, the stock fair, or *feria*, to be discussed at length, is the major single selling place for Pasiego cattle to outsiders (or emigrants), and it is not only the single most crucial locus in the transactional field of Vega de Pas; it is also one of the crucial marketplaces for dairy stock in all of Spain. Here, Pasiegos and not outsiders are the chief vendors.

TABLE 4
OCCUPATIONAL BREAKDOWN OF PASIEGO HOUSEHOLDS

	Total Units[a]	Transhumant		Sedentary[b]		Retired (= Sedentary)		Total Herding		Commercial or Employed		Other (Rents, etc.)	
		Number	Per-cent	Number	Per-cent	Number	Per-cent	Number	Per-cent	Number	Per-cent	Number	Per-cent
Pandillo	94	77	81.9	4	4.3	13	13.8	94	100.0	0	—	0	—
Yera	64	33	51.6	11	17.2	10	15.6	54	84.4	8	12.5	2	3.1
Viaña	36	29	80.5	2	5.5	5	13.9	36	100.0	0	—	0	—
Candolias	52	26	50.0	7	13.5	5	9.6	38	73.1	5	9.6	9	17.3
La Gurueba	42	8	19.1	17	40.5	9	21.4	34	81.0	5	11.9	3	7.1
Guzparras	14	4	28.6	5	35.7	5	35.7	14	100.0	0	—	0	—
Casco (excluding resident outsiders)	73	2	2.7	10	13.7	9	12.3	21	28.8	30	41.1	22	30.1
Total	375	179	47.7	56	14.9	56	14.9	291	77.6	48	12.8	36	9.6

[a]These figures do not correspond with household totals given in table 2 for two reasons: (1) the nine unregistered households on table 2 are not included here, and (2) in a few cases, for certain purposes, households which are otherwise separately enrolled combine to form joint units (see p. 00).

[b]The fact that not all members of all of these "sedentary" households are necessarily totally sedentary is considered in chap. 4.

humant herding households were officially enrolled in the Casco, sixteen other families, from various barrios, owned or rented meadows within the Casco limits, and thus moved in and out of the Casco on their yearly rounds. In addition, two permanent Casco residents (listed in table 4 as sedentary herders) were primarily herders by profession, with over ten cows apiece. The other sedentary herders in the Casco were, on the contrary, primarily commercial families who normally keep three or four cows, or a half dozen at most. The point here is that the overall incidence of herding activity within the Casco is appreciable, and its extent is not properly reflected by the official Casco rolls. It is also true in the Casco that if a person has any calling other than *ganadero* (herder), he enrolls himself in the other occupation, even if he also keeps cattle. The opposite is true of the barrios; most herders with other callings nonetheless enroll as ganaderos. Though there are bureaucratic reasons for enrolling in certain ways, it is also true that people begin to project their images differently when they move into the Casco.

The difference between barrio and Casco is not simply one of enrollment style, however. This is evident when, from the field census, we review the types of specialization (other than herding) present in the various sectors of town. Table 5 lists, by sector, all of the non-herding occupations practiced in Vega de Pas by heads of families who are self-employed. The list thus excludes such people as postal employees or construction workers; these employments are, further, usually subsidiary for herders or small landowners, and they do not provide services exchangeable for cash or goods within the population. Similarly excluded are the numerous women who, subsidiary to other household activities, produce the local baked specialties, *sobaos* and *quesadas*, and carry them to market or to establishments outside Pas for sale. Other forms of peddling, to be discussed later, are also excluded. Livestock trading, too, will be considered separately. With these exclusions, table 5 offers the most complete commercial census which I could compile, with informants' help.

With little exception, the Casco obviously holds a monopoly on business—that is, it is the location of most people who make their primary living at the businesses listed. Its closest rival, Candolías, is also its closest neighbor; the Candolías businesses are all located along the Entrambasmestas-Espinosa highway fairly close to the Casco and, with the exception of the smithy and the store-tavern, serve much the same market. The Candolías store-tavern, like the one in La Gurueba, primarily at-

TABLE 5
BUSINESSES, SPECIALTIES, AND PUBLIC FACILITIES

Casco
  Businesses
    3 butcher shops
    2 bread bakeries
    5 general stores (3 large-scale)
    7 bars
    1 pharmacy
    1 mill
    4 *fondas* (lodging places) attached to bars or stores
    2 restaurants (attached to bars or fondas), one with municipal dance-hall
    2 cake shops, selling local specialties (*sobaos* and *quesadas*)
    2 *estancos* (tobacco and stamp sales) attached to stores or bars
    6 drivers (of trucks and/or taxis, and one semi-weekly bus)
  Specialties
    1 carpenter-stoneworker
    1 carpenter
    1 stoneworker
    1 mason
    1 ladies' hairdresser
    1 seamstress
    1 barber
    1 *covanero* (producer of *cuévanos*, or carrying baskets) (produces small cuévanos primarily as toys or souvenirs)
  Other Facilities (excluding professional services)
    branch savings bank
    branch post office
    government trade unions office
    municipal government and judiciary offices and jail
    municipal slaughterhouse
    parish church, baptismal font, and cemetery (the latter technically in Candolías, just outside Casco: see map 5)
    stock-fair ground (*ferial*) (technically in Candolías, adjacent to Casco: see map 5)
    Sunday market (import items only)
Pandillo
  Businesses
    none
  Specialties
    none
Yera
  Businesses
    1 electrical supply plant
    1 bread bakery
  Specialties
    1 carpenter
    4 stoneworkers
    2 masons
    1 seamstress, specialized in work pants
    6 *almadreñeros* (producers of *almadreñas*, or wooden clogs)

TABLE 5—*Continued*

Viaña
  Businesses
    none
  Specialties
    2 stoneworkers
Candolías
  Businesses
    1 smithy
    1 general store/tavern, with *estanco* (tobacco and stamp sales)
    1 bread bakery
    1 mill
    1 trucker
  Specialties
    1 almadreñero
    1 stoneworker
La Gurueba
  Businesses
    1 general store and tavern ⎫
    1 mill   ⎬ single household
    1 trucker   ⎭
  Specialties
    3 covaneros
Guzparras
  Businesses
    none
  Specialties
    covaneros?

tracts dwellers of the barrio. The store in La Gurueba, however, also attracts many clients from San Pedro's barrios, as it lies near one of San Pedro's major points of access to the highway. The businesses—whatever their location, and with the exception of the mills, which grind animal fodder, and the smithy—all serve needs which are either common to the entire community or are explicitly external to it, that is, those that serve the tourist market. The barrios are marked primarily by the presence of specialties—enterprises from which families do not gain their only income—rather than by businesses. These specialties are for the most part related to the production of material items traditionally used in the barrios and not in the Casco: *almadreñas* (wooden clogs), cuévanos (carrying baskets), and stone for the construction of the cabaña, the barrio dwelling. With the exception of a single stoneworker, these specialists are not present in the Casco, nor are their products used in the Casco: the only *covanero* (cuévano maker) in the Casco produces souvenir-sized specimens for the tourist trade. Casco specialties are different and more varied. The only barrio whose specialists approach this variety is Yera—with a carpenter, two masons, and a seamstress, in addition to its stoneworkers and almadreñeros. In this case, again, the specialists in question live close to the highway, and their major clientele is not located in the barrio.

The distribution of commerce in Casco and barrios indicates where people must look locally to fill their daily personal and household needs. But table 5 in no way indicates where the majority of community income comes from, nor where the bulk of money is spent, for Pasiegos' transactional field in economics is farflung and there is no sector of the community which is subsistence-oriented or inward-looking. What the distribution does show us, however, is an essential difference between barrio and Casco which both reflects and produces contrasting lifestyles in those different parts of town. The barrios and the Casco are the spatial preserves of very different social traditions and different modes of livelihood, and their people project very different images of themselves. When inhabitants of either space encroach upon the other, the act catches the attention immediately and calls forth patterned responses. The differences contained within these opposed spaces are the focus of much of this study and will be described in a variety of contexts, but their first manifestation to the stranger is in the physical appearance of the different sectors of town (see plates section).

The Casco, with its commercial aspect and its clustered, urban-style buildings, defies the Pasiego stereotype; tourists express surprise to find this place where they had been led to expect a uniquely dispersed form of settlement in what Spaniards would consider "rural desolation." The image of a uniquely rural and a peculiar people is fostered, of course, by the omnipresent pasieguería in the literature and the press, both past and present. The notion that the Pas landscape is almost exclusively one of dispersed habitation is fostered, too, by the geographic literature on Spain. Many texts and sources on Spanish cultural geography make particular mention of the Montes de Pas, but they emphasize the landscape of the alpine barrios and make almost no mention of the variation present within the zone.[5] In fact, the peculiar atmosphere of "rural"—that is, barrio—Pas is due not solely to the dispersed settlement pattern, for in many zones the cabañas are not far apart by American, north European, or even Spanish standards. The point is that the cabañas

5. For example, Lautensach 1967; Terán, Solé Sabarís et al. 1968; Instituto Nacional de Estadística 1960: Nomenclator, Provincia de Santander.

are systematically distant, with less notable tendency to cluster
than exists in other regions, and a cabaña, even though it may
be fairly near its neighbors, may be empty for at least part of
the time its neighboring houses are inhabited. If we superimpose
upon these features the fact that virtually all business is concentrated around the center, the impression of "rural desolation" gains strength.

Communications, too, have the Casco as their center: the Entrambasmestas highway converges with the one from Carriedo
in the Casco neighborhood appropriately called "El Cruce" (the
crossroads). The telephone switchboard is located in one of the
Casco fonda/restaurants, and its lines serve no one outside the
Casco-Candolías business area. The bus which makes two round
trips per week to Santander, on Wednesdays and Saturdays, the
city's major market days, departs from the Plaza in the early
morning and returns there at nightfall; barrio dwellers must
come to the Plaza to board it.

Construction has not yet been completed on one line of communication which has tremendous potential for Pas. In two separate periods of construction—about 1940 to 1943 and about
1952 to 1961—a route was cut into the mountains and through,
by tunnel, to the Burgos side for the privately financed Santander-Mediterranean Railroad. This would, if terminated, be
Cantabria's only direct rail route to the eastern meseta and the
Mediterranean. To date, though the track bed, tunnel, and even
the station buildings (high on a side of the Yera Valley) have
been constructed, no tracks have been laid, nor is the completion
of the route foreseen. The Santander-Mediterranean functions
presently only between the levantine coast and the town of Vi-
llarcayo in Burgos. Were the line to be completed, enormous
changes would doubtless occur in Yera. Thus far, the railroad's
only effect has been to bring outsiders to town during times of
construction. The presence of these people widened local hori-
zons a bit, and some outsiders married Pasiegos; in most of the
latter cases, the Pasiegos took the opportunity to leave Pas with
their spouses for other parts of Spain.

As most of Vega de Pas' commerce and facilities are concentrated in the Casco, so too is its officialdom, which is dominated
by people who are not herders. The municipality is organized
according to the laws of local administration (*régimen local*)
and of local justice (*justicia municipal*), under the specific stip-
ulations for populations between 501 and 2000. The *alcalde*, or
mayor, is appointed at the provincial level (or at least a nomina-

tion originating at the local level is thus approved). The vice-alcalde (*teniente*) is selected by the alcalde. There are six coun-cilmen (*concejales*), one of whom is the teniente. The three pairs of concejales are elected by, and represent, distinct constituen-cies, in a system which in both Spain and Portugal is referred to as "corporative." Two concejales are *de representación familiar*, representing the constituent households of the municipality and elected by the official heads of family. Two are *de representa-ción sindical*, elected by all residents who have membership in trade unions, or guilds, the vast majority of whom belong to the farmer-stockmen's guild (Hermandad Sindical de Labradores y Ganaderos). The last pair, *de representación corporativo*, are representative of the ayuntamiento itself—the teniente alcalde always serves as one of this pair, and the first two pairs together select the second concejal corporativo.[6] The secretary of the ayuntamiento is specially trained and usually not native to the place he serves. The position of *alguacil* (aide or porter) may be solicited by war veterans with some disability, but if the post remains vacant it normally goes to a native of town. The post is the only one other than that of secretary which carries a salary, and it normally goes to a poor candidate willing and able to carry out its duties, which primarily involve serving as mes-senger, chief grave-digger, and ayuntamiento odd-job man.

The interlocking organization, the Hermandad Sindical de Labradores y Ganaderos, is the only trade union in Spain with a sufficiently large membership that towns such as La Vega have local offices. Likewise, there is an office of the Junta Local de la Seguridad Social Agraria (Agrarian Social Security Service). A single man functions as secretary of both of these organs in La Vega—a native of the Casco, he holds his positions by virtue of having passed the requisite examinations. Twelve *vocales* are elected every three years to serve the Hermandad (along with the election of the pair of concejales for the ayuntamiento). These twelve vocales themselves select six of their own number to serve the social security organ, and all twelve elect their head (*jefe local*), who serves both organs. Payment into the social security plan becomes compulsory at a certain age for anyone

6. Here, the local construction varies somewhat from the guidelines established in the published law: "[the third pair of concejales is] to be elected by the concejales of the two prior groups from among vecinos who are members of economic, cultural, and professional bodies present in the municipality, or if no such body is present, from among vecinos of recognized prestige in the locality" (Ley de Régimen Local 1968: art. 86–3).

practicing a guild-organized trade. Farmer-stockmen must pay between the ages of eighteen and fifty-five.

The town's judicial personnel are a justice of the peace (*juez de paz*, a position filled by the veterinarian); a secretary who is the ayuntamiento secretary; a treasurer (*fiscal*, a Casco resident); and the substitute or alternate justice (*juez suplente*), who handles cases when the justice is not available or when a case involves kinsmen of the justice. Serious cases pass from Vega de Pas to the *juzgado de instrucción* in Villacarriedo, the seat of the judicial district. The local judicial officials are aided in their tasks by the Civil Guard—the nature of these functions is discussed in chapter 5. In daily affairs the juzgado, through its secretary, functions primarily as the office of civil records.

The truly active official of the Sindicato system is its secretary, who opens his office daily. The active officials of the ayuntamiento and juzgado are the alcalde, the alguacil, and the secretary, and secondarily the justice of the peace; other officials meet only irregularly. Apropos of irregular meetings, I should mention two other officially constituted bodies of the town, the Junta de la Primera Enseñanza (Council on Primary Education)[7] and the Junta Protectora de Animales (Animal Protective Society)[8]: the former has met only once, when it was first constituted, and the latter has never met.

The ayuntamiento holds land—these are the only commonlands in Vega de Pas[9]—and in this case holds the cemetery, which in most places is Church property.[10] Most of the ayuntamiento property outside of the fairground, the Casco's plumbing facilities, and the electrical equipment serving town consists in hillside pasture (*pastizal*) and woodland (*monte*) and in local

7. This junta consists in the alcalde, one concejal of the ayuntamiento, one teacher, and one father and one mother (*padre* and *madre de familia*).

8. The junta's formal task is the imposition of fines on anyone willfully damaging animal property. Members are the alcalde, doctor, pharmacist, priest, and perhaps a teacher.

9. Lands are in some places held in the name of a corporation or *común* of vecinos, and these holdings are legally distinct from ayuntamiento lands. The former type is more likely to accompany a strong corporate tradition within a town (see Freeman 1968b, 1970a), and such a tradition is utterly absent in Pas.

10. No one could isolate for me the origin of this arrangement, but its peculiar result is that the cemetery is defined as civil rather than holy ground, so that each gravesite must be specially blessed before it receives a burial.

roads, paths, and bridges.[11] Waterways are by law in the public domain; watering stations, fountains, and other masonry facilities of the sort are ayuntamiento property but have minimal importance because surface water is everywhere plentiful and heavily used and, in addition, the Casco homes have enjoyed indoor plumbing for several years. The administration of at least some of these properties is subject to intervention by or requires permission of certain overarching governmental organs, the national forest service, the reforestation service, the hydraulic commission, and, of course, the provincial and national highway authorities.

Twelve vocales of the Sindicato organization are, by definition, herders, as are two of the concejales in the ayuntamiento. During my residence in Pas, a third concejal as well was a herder— all three herder-concejales were from barrios. But none of the active officials mentioned above was either a herder or a barrio dweller.

The ayuntamiento reaches out into the space of the barrios by way of two separate mechanisms. The town *junta*, or *junta del concejo*, is simply a town meeting for advisory purposes which is convened by the peal of the church bells after mass, normally on a Sunday when attendance is higher than during the week. When the bells peal for the junta, people gather around the stone "junta bench" against one of the old trees in front of the church (map 6). The alguacil, from the bench, announces the business at hand and those in attendance carry the news home to their barrios. This method is used to announce such events as the quarterly visits in the Plaza of the government tax collector, or the collection dates and procedures for ayuntamiento taxes, or for census enrollment, or to announce occasions requiring cooperative labor on public properties. The need for cooperative labor (*prestación*) activates a second mechanism, within the barrios, established for that purpose.[12] There is an *alcalde de barrio* (appointed by the alcalde) in each barrio and in the

11. Areas with electrical service are most of the barrio of Candolías, all of Guzparras, all of La Gurueba except for the branizas, the settlement of Gucimprún in Viaña, the Yera riverside cabañas from above the school to the Casco, and the Casco itself.

12. There is no specific term in use in Pas to designate corvée labor other than *prestación* (lit. "lending" or "borrowing") or, occasionally, *han echado a caminos* ("they've called up [labor] for roads"), which refers to labor on any property as well as on roads. Special terms are in use elsewhere in Spain—*cendera, facendera, fagina* (reviewed in Freeman 1968b).

Casco whose specific function is to call up the necessary number
of men required for a specific task on public properties. Each
alcalde de barrio is supplied with a list of all able-bodied men
in his territory between the ages of eighteen and fifty-five, and
the required number are called up, by rotation, for different
jobs.[13] The ayuntamiento's call to work is regarded as something
of an imposition from outside—the tasks are not considered
necessities by the barrio dweller, and the spirit in which the
duty is regarded is considerably different from that in cases
where labor on public properties is viewed as part of one's
neighborly commitment to the territory from which he makes
his living (see, for example, Freeman 1968b, 1970a). The sense
of commitment—the notion of neighborly obligation—is very
nearly absent from Pas. In the Casco, in contrast to the barrios,
there is, if not full commitment, at least a considerably larger
sense of involvement in the administrative workings and in making the administration of town work.

The notions of physical isolation and marginality to the center
of social action to a large extent characterize the barrio dweller's
own, as well as others', image of the territory in which he dwells.
The boundaries which set off town and country are, for everyone
in La Vega, the boundaries of the Casco. The Casco's peripheral
neighborhoods (among which roadside parts of Candolías must
be included) are filled with recent retirees from barrio life; the
Casco is La Vega's only candidate for urban living, and if urban
living is not sought there, it is sought in Santander, Torrelavega,
Madrid, or some other capital city. Living in any of these places,
including the Casco, is accompanied by great behavioral changes
—a general overhauling of the barrio image takes place and both
the content and style of daily behavior patterns are much altered.

The uniqueness in Spain of the settlement pattern and geographic mobility which characterize the Pas barrios suggests
that a quite different evaluation of spatial types might obtain
there than elsewhere in Spain. Instead, the atypical appearance
of Pas simply obscures the existence there of the most typical
Spanish evaluative patterns. There are within the barrios em-

13. It is probably significant that here, unlike many other known cases,
the call to corvée labor is by individual rather than by household. The
method here is an apparent bureaucratic convenience which does not
take cognizance of the household's traditional place as the basic unit in
the social structure. Cooperative labor has no traditional importance in
the barrios.

bryonic sedentary settlements which contain small nuclei of households whose heads have retired from transhumant herding. To the choicest areas among these—to those with mostly sedentary inhabitants and most favorably located—barrio Pasiegos apply the term *pueblo* (peopled place or town). This is a wistful application: neither the census nor any outsider recognizes in these areas even *caseríos*—the minimal official unit of nucleated settlement. Even Pasiegos who have grown up in the Casco, and who can afford to set their sights higher, fail to regard these tiny settlements in any special way: from the viewpoint of the Casco native, all the territory of any barrio is uniformly "countryside" (*campo*) rather than town, settlement, or pueblo.

If Casco usage is fully informed by standard Spanish attitudes, barrio usage reveals these same attitudes in a heavily frustrated state. Qualitative judgments distinguish the three basic altitudinal zones between which pastures are distributed: the higher the zone, the lower the esteem in which it is held. The *branizas*, the high summer pastures, are held to be almost frightening for the isolation which they impose—isolation not so much from neighbors, for ties between neighbors are perhaps strongest there—but isolation from pueblos, settled centers, which are in most instances at least two and a-half hours distant by foot.[14] The closer a *pradera* (meadow-cluster) is to a town center, the more habitable it becomes by Pasiego standards. Thus, almost all of the praderas selected for settlement by retired people, or by herders who for other reasons do not practice transhumance, are located in the *ribero*, or valley-bottom zone.[15] Only some of

14. For example, the Yera meadows at the head of the Mazón and the Pandillo ones at the head of the Rullemas are about equidistant from the Plaza and from Espinosa de los Monteros, at two and a-half to three hours' distance. The Viaña/Yera meadows at the heads of the Arroyo Bustalbaín (Viaña) and the Aján (Yera) are the farthest from the Plaza (about three hours) but are even farther from other towns. The above distances are for ascent without animals; descent is slightly more rapid, but the presence of animals can lengthen any of these journeys by as much as 50 percent.

15. The exceptions are the following hill-flank praderas: Pandeacebo (La Gurueba) and Gucimprún (Viaña), in which most inhabitants are sedentary and which will be described in chapter 4; los Cimientos (Yera), where there are sedentary inhabitants but almost no livestock; and Bircidío (Pandillo), where there is one nearly sedentary herder whose case is also discussed in chapter 4. In Guzparras, the pradera which gives the barrio its name contains permanent settlement, even though it is classed as low braniza. This is rather a special exception, because all braniza is lower in Guzparras than elsewhere and, further, there are only three ribero meadows (in a single pradera) in the entire barrio, and all the others are classed as braniza. Guzparras' special qualities relate to the

these, in turn, are referred to in daily parlance as pueblos, and the term pueblo is thus hardly applied outside of the ribero zone.[16]

Similarly, the distribution in Vega de Pas of *cabañas vividoras*, or dwelling cabañas, also clusters around the ribero zones, though it sometimes spills out onto favorable hillside areas. The features which qualify a cabaña for use as a vividora are that it be well located with respect to the town center and that the family in question be able to spend enough time in that single place to warrant the establishment of a vividora there. Neither qualification alone suffices; families who cannot stay long enough in otherwise favorable zones do not have vividoras there, and places where families do make long stops are not the sites of vividoras unless the zones themselves are also defined as favorable. Thus, even though the branizas are the site of the longest continuous visits by almost all herders, there are no vividoras there, and the branizas are, in the native evaluation, by definition desolate and unpeopled places. Truly, in this historical no-man's-land, the mountain meadows are a land for no man, and the transhumant life which involves their exploitation is borne as a burden.

---

geographic differences between barrios discussed above and further considered in chapter 4.

16. To my knowledge, there are three exceptions. Two are Pandeacebo and Gucimprún, referred to in note 15 above, which are called pueblos, and the other is Andaruz (Yera), which has no permanent settlement, but all fifteen herders who use meadows there visit the place simultaneously, which gives the pradera more of the qualities of a neighborhood than most other areas possess.

PLATE 1. A view of Pasiego settlement in a middle-altitude zone near the Luena border. Haystacks, as seen in left foreground, are atypical of the Montes de Pas.

PLATE 2. A Pandillo woman and her children pose for a photograph. The youngest child is in the carrying basket—the *cuévano niñero*.

PLATE 3. A *cabaña* in the high meadows, beneath the peak of the Castro Valnera. Both porch and chimney are lacking. The structure at the right is a *colgadiza*, or sheep barn.

PLATE 4. In a *cabaña* in the high meadows, a family gathers around a low stool, preparing supper. Children manage knives from the age of two or three.

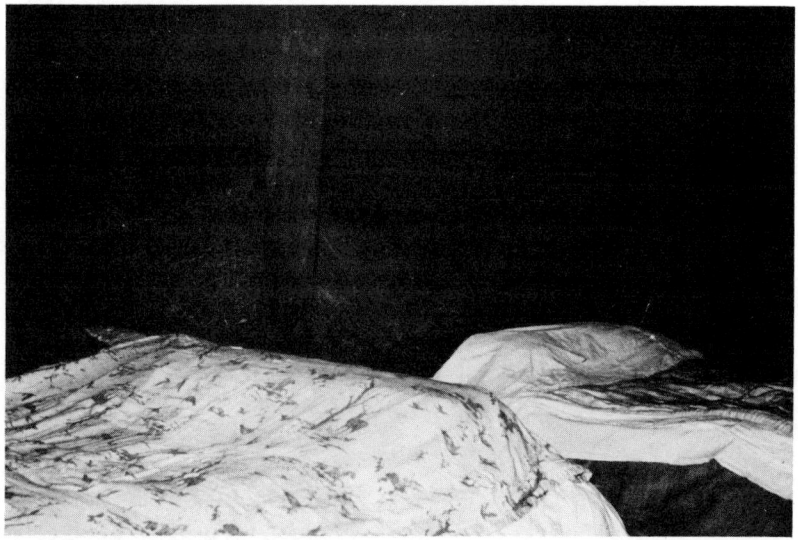

PLATE 5. In the *branizas*, beds are made in the dried grass in the loft.

PLATE 6. The valley-bottom *pradera* of Arejos (Yera), on the banks of the river.

PLATE 7. A retired couple sun themselves on the porch of their *vividora* in Arejos. This *cabaña* is entirely partitioned, contains no grass storage, and houses no cows at any season.

PLATE 8. Arejos: a bedroom.

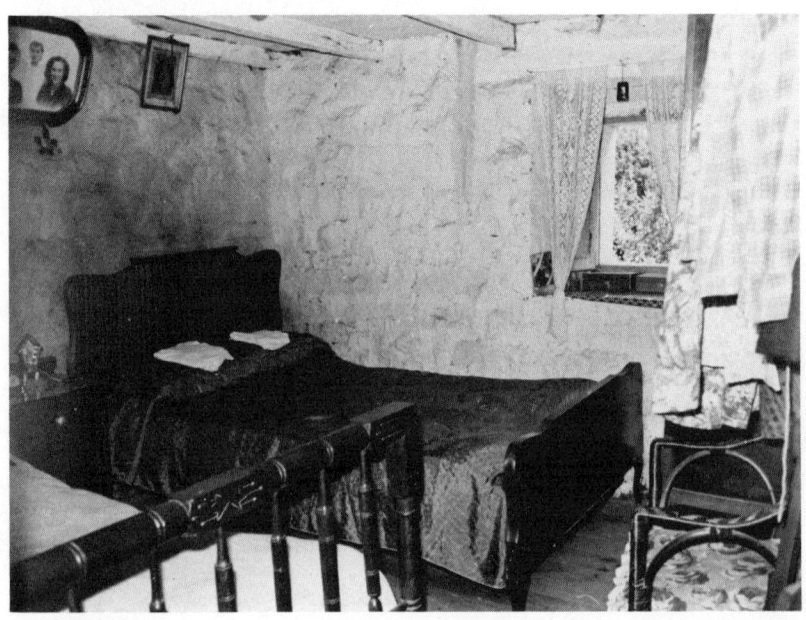

PLATE 9. An elegant house of an era past stands in the Calle Atrás on what is said to have once been the Plaza of Vega de Pas.

PLATE 10. A view of the modern Plaza. The church stands at left, the tree with *junta* bench at center, the entrance to the Pandillo road at right,

where people stand. The building next to the road was once a central point of distribution of contraband from France, bound for Santander and Asturias.

PLATE 11. Another view of the Plaza. Private dwellings with their glassed-in *galerías* rise above the street-level entries which, for the most part, house places of business.

PLATE 12. A mother shows off her baby in its *cuévano*, which stands like a crib and rocks slightly, like a cradle.

PLATE 13. *Picando el dalle*: cold-tempering the scythe.

PLATE 14. Holding both ends of the *belorta*, a man moves under a load of grass as his wife secures it.

PLATE 15. *Belorteando*: walking the grass into the *cabaña*.

PLATE 16. On the stock-fair grounds, a young man poses with his prize cow.

PLATE 17. In the Plaza, sold cows are loaded for travel.

PLATE 18. The tiny Sunday "market" draws customers largely from the barrios and outlying neighborhoods of the Casco.

PLATE 19. Herders play their afternoon card games in a Plaza tavern.

PLATE 20. A Casco girl places batter for *sobaos*—butter cakes—in paper forms for baking and for sale to Sunday tourists.

THREE

The Barrio Livelihood: The Past

Land: of poor quality but good for timber . . . Roads are local . . .
Products: maize, beans, pasture; stock-raising; large and small game;
trout, eel, and some salmon fishing. Industries: some grain mills,
and the traffic in woolen cloth, linen, and other effects.

Madoz, on Vega de Pas (1849)

When Don Sancho granted the dependencies of Oña rights to
enter freely with their livestock to graze and pasture in that
broad area which included the Montes de Pas, he named their
animals: cows, mares, goats, and pigs (see appendix A). By the
time we first know these herders settled in the Montes de Pas,
we find also sheep and bees, and probably domestic fowl and
rabbits as well. Also, we find that they were cultivating grain
and pursuing what appears to have been a fairly typical alpine
livelihood.[1]

The whole of the Montes de Pas, as pasture, was defined at
base as commonlands. However, forest came eventually to be
cleared and land to be enclosed on private initiative. We do not
know when this first occurred, but legal proceedings beginning
as early as 1561 (see Escagedo Salmón 1921:78–83; Arroyo del
Prado 1958:406–7) dealt with the evident fact that the inhabitants of Pas had already cleared forest in the Montes. The decision, and most later reviews of the sentence, confirmed the
Pasiegos' rights to do so freely and rejected claims of both Espinosa and Carriedo to be able to impose fees on Pasiegos for these
deeds. The definitive decision, in 1586, in the Pasiegos' favor,

---

1. See Burns 1961, 1963; Honigmann 1964; Stancliffe 1966; Netting 1972;
Cole 1972; Cole and Wolf 1974; Friedl 1972, 1974.

gave the Pasiegos the right to "enclose royal and communally held commonlands and to reduce the land to bread and grass."[2] They received permission to clear trees as well, reducing forest to "pasture and grass" because, the sentence stated, the land would thus be of greater benefit to the Crown, nourishing the more than two thousand head of livestock which supplied the "butcheries of these regions all the way to very near to Vizcaya" (cited in Escagedo Salmón 1921:80). The decision goes on to cite the Pasiegos' role as purveyors of butter and cheese to the court and elsewhere, to which I have already referred, and stresses that the sentence is in support of the royal patrimony. Pasiegos' importance in these commercial respects will be considered at length later.

In 1648, when Carriedo had won rights to jurisdiction over the Montes de Pas, the question of clearing and enclosure there arose again. The Valley of Carriedo was itself charged with enclosing and alienating, by sale, lands within Pas. An example, cited by Escagedo (1921:82), is the case of Don Domingo de Herrera Concha, a royal official (*ujier de cámara*) and a native of Vega de Carriedo, who apparently had a role in gaining for Carriedo the favorable (1648) court decision regarding jurisdiction in Pas: when Herrera refused to charge Carriedo for his services, the Valley made him a present of three *brañas* (that is, branizas), one of which was "La Braquilla"—probably La Braguía, on the border between Vega de Pas and Selaya.[3] These acts caused the Pasiegos (*qua* Espinosans) to bring suit against Carriedo. Carriedo apparently made claim to enclosure rights by virtue of possession of jurisdiction of the Montes, but this was not upheld. The decision, handed down in 1650 and confirmed after an appeal in 1651, supported the Pasiegos' exclusive rights to clearing and enclosure in their mountains and ordered the

2. Cited by Escagedo Salmón (1921:80) as follows: "*poder cerrar exidos* [read modern *ejidos*] *reales y comunes y reducir la tierra a pan y yerba . . .*" Spanish usage often applies the word *pan* (bread) descriptively to lands or facilities (such as threshing floors) pertaining to the cultivation or handling of bread grains, whatever these may be in different times and places. Grain itself is sometimes referred to as bread, as in the statement of rents as a certain number of "bushels of bread."

3. The *ujier de cámara* was not a legal official but, rather, was in the personal service of the king. The "services" rendered by Don Domingo may therefore have been primarily in the exercise of persuasion in the right quarters. He was a businessman of influence in Madrid and in his native province: a biographical note has been published (Solana 1957), and his correct name appears to have been Herrera and not the Herrero given by Escagedo.

responsible Carriedo officials to dismantle all enclosures they had made in Pas.[4]

The clearing of brush and the cutting of timber were explicitly for two purposes: the former for the care and feeding of the animals (and also doubtless for fuel) and the latter for the construction of cabañas. Thus, we know that the construction of dwellings within Pas was certainly under way by 1561 (and probably much earlier) and that by that same date some cultivation —the conversion of land into bread—was at issue within the Montes. We do not know, however, for that date or for a long time to come, what grain or grains were cultivated, in what proportions various kinds of animals were raised, or how they were herded. It is fully two hundred years later, in the era of the 1750s, that we learn, from the Cadaster of the Marqués de la Ensenada, some details of the Pasiego livelihood.[5]

The Ensenada cadaster volumes for Vega de Pas have, unfortunately, been lost for at least two decades, and it is possible that they were destroyed by an archive fire in Santander which claimed much material. None of the scholars writing on Pas has had reference to them. The complete cadasters for both San Pedro and San Roque are preserved, though San Pedro's responses to the initial general questionnaire are missing, and I have studied both of these for an overview of the livelihood of those two towns and to understand which generalizations might be applicable to Vega de Pas as well. This overview from the mid-eighteenth century combines with older informants' statements about Vega de Pas in the late nineteenth century to give some notion of the town's livelihood before the occurrence of the critical changes which I shall detail later. The following paragraphs attempt to bridge a gap of more than a century for which there are no documents, and while surely this was not a changeless period, there is no evidence for changes in that period which could even approach the magnitude of those of the late nineteenth century. Older informants' portraits of the economy around 1880 replicate much of the picture yielded by the cadaster of the 1750s.

4. This review of enclosure litigation depends almost entirely on Escagedo's work. I have not read the cases nor found reference to them in the archives I have seen. Escagedo is the only secondary source I know to treat the subject in any detail.

5. This property survey, for purposes of tax assessment, covered most of Spain. It was conducted during the regime of the Marqués de la Ensenada as Minister of Finance (Hacienda), beginning in 1748. García-Badell (1963:241–46) gives its history. Volumes cited here are listed in appendix B.

The bottomlands of Vega de Pas were, at the end of the nineteenth century, planted almost in their entirety in maize, the
only grain of which informants have any memory. The cadaster,
too, in the previous century, makes reference only to maize. Two
centuries earlier, however, in the era of the first enclosure litigation, the grain in question is unknown. Whether maize might
have arrived in Pas as early as the mid-sixteenth century is
doubtful, and I am not familiar with archives documenting its
arrival. On the other hand, the province of Santander and its
capital city, with Castile's only port, have always been at the
vanguard of contact with the New World (as well as with northern Europe), and the relatively early introduction of maize there
is to be expected.[6] It was apparently established by the first part
of the seventeenth century: Christian (1972:4) notes its cultivation in the Nansa Valley in 1626 and Ortega Valcárcel (1974:164)
in the Pasiego zone of Espinosa in 1630. The case is complicated
by the fact that the common bread grain prior to the introduction of maize was millet (*mijo*), which also bore the Spanish
name *borona*, a reference both to the grain and to the bread
made from it. Borona is the word which also came locally to
apply to maize, as it still does in the Santander countryside.
Thus, when Maza Solano (1957b:376) cites reports from the last
third of the sixteenth century quoting the value of the bushel of
"borona y mijo," it is unclear if the reference is only to millet,
perhaps to more than one variety of same, or also to maize, and
the source he cites is perhaps equally unclear. Occasionally we
see references to "mijo *or* borona," and it is possible that in

6. There was and is massive exchange via emigrants to the New World,
of which this region has supplied many. On a different level, Santander
coastal populations have important and historically deep ties with certain
Andalusian centers which, in turn, are or were involved in massive exchange with the New World. The port of Cádiz itself, the second major
departure point (after Seville) for "the Indies," was ordered repopulated
by Alfonso X in the latter half of the thirteenth century by three hundred
families from the Santander coastal cities of Castro Urdiales, Laredo,
Santander, and San Vicente de la Barquera. The intent here was to establish people with know-how in commerce, shipping, and shipbuilding. While
González y González remarks (1951:204) that records show a lower percentage of Montañeses in Cádiz than some have claimed, nonetheless
there is still today much population movement between the two provinces (though the Montes de Pas participates little in it), and this is
largely in commercial enterprise. From the sixteenth century on, some of
the "Andalusians" who set sail from Seville and Cádiz for the New World
were actually emigrés from Santander towns. Christian (1972 and pers.
comm.), for example, has studied the records of families of the upper
Nansa Valley who have traveled this route.

many instances historians of the period cannot tell to which grain documents refer.

The province of Santander had long depended heavily on the importation of Castilian wheat,[7] which was also by the eighteenth century being milled in the province for export to the Americas. The traditional breads of the region were not wheaten; millet was probably very important as a bread grain, and there is also record of breads made of such things as chestnut flour. We do not know what bread, or breads, the Pasiegos may have consumed in addition to the millet bread I suppose they ate, but after maize took hold, the ubiquitous element of the diet was the maize hearthcake, or *torta de borona*, prepared at every meal.

The significant point for the Montes de Pas is that any grain at all was once cultivated there, for today there is little cultivation of any kind: in the alpine barrios of Vega de Pas, there is virtually none. With the bottom lands under cultivation, the proportion of the municipality dedicated to meadow was comparatively small, and so was the number of cattle maintained.

The local breed of cattle, now extinct, was known as the Pasiego breed, typically referred to in the feminine singular form as *la vaca pasiega*. The center of the distribution of the vaca pasiega was indeed the Montes de Pas, and the remainder of Santander province was dominated by the Tudanca breed, heavily used for draft and insignificant in terms of dairy production. The Campóo breed (of the Reinosa area, adjacent to Pas) had similar characteristics and uses. The vaca pasiega, on the other hand, was exploited in particular for its milk, which, though not abundant, had an especially high (8 percent) butterfat content.[8] The cattle were not bred for sale so much as maintained for their milk, though they may eventually have been sold for meat. (The 1586 court decision cited above, in naming Pas as a source of meat, probably refers primarily to sheep and

7. Though it is a part of the kingdom of Old Castile, the province of Santander is most commonly referred to as La Montaña, in contradistinction to Castilla, which refers to the arid parts of the kingdom on the meseta, south of the Cantabrian range. For residents of the coastal plain and provincial historians, the Montes de Pas are located in La Montaña. Pasiegos themselves, however, further distinguish the Montaña as the zone which corresponds with those parts of the province below 200 m. (map 2), and other parts of the province are carefully designated by other names: Pas, Campóo, Soba, Liébana, Cabuérniga, and so on.

8. Madariaga (1970) summarizes the distribution and characteristics of Santander's native breeds of cattle, in addition to other stock traditionally maintained in the province, and summarizes the history of livestock importation into the province.

goats, secondarily to male calves, and thirdly, if at all, to aging cows, for even today beef is not a favored meat in Spain.) The milk was used for the nourishment of calves, for cheese, and, skimmed of its butterfat, for human consumption. The cream was churned into butter and was both consumed at home and sold in markets: in Vega de Pas, at least, butter rather than cheese appears to have been the primary export; San Roque seems to have produced, in the eighteenth and nineteenth centuries as now, more cheese than La Vega.

Informants report that, in the latter days of the vaca pasiega, a family normally kept no more than two or three cows (*con cría*—that is, in calf or with small offspring). They also maintained considerable flocks of sheep and goats, though without reference to the cadaster we cannot judge the normal size of these flocks. For San Pedro, according to the cadaster, a typical family holding in livestock was two cows (con cría), two pigs, nine or ten sheep, and about thirty goats.[9] In San Roque, there were typically more cows—about four (con cría) per family—and smaller flocks of goats and sheep, of approximately equal size, perhaps three or four of each. In neither town in mid-eighteenth century were there many horses or mules. We might interpret the differences between San Pedro and San Roque to reflect (1) differences in choices made in allocating herding labor of different kinds for the three chief types of stock, (2) differential interest in the products of these animals, and (3) local differences in availability of meadow, sheep pasture, and browsing areas for goats, differences which are in part geographic and in part the artifacts of human choice. In Vega de Pas, and one assumes in the other towns as well, goats and sheep were traditionally herded separately, on different tracts of land. We cannot know, for Vega de Pas, the relative numbers of the different animals, but there might well have been more sheep and goats than in San Roque, reflecting the much larger territorial extent of La Vega (as well as San Pedro) compared with San Roque.

While sheep traditionally provided meat and wool, and goats also provided meat, there is no contemporary or documented tradition of the use of goat's or ewe's milk in cheese. The typical Pasiego cheeses of printed reference are all of cow's milk. And San Roque, particularly known for its cheeses, kept fewest

9. I should emphasize that I was unable to extract all statistics on land and livestock holdings from the several thousand pages of available cadaster. This and following statements about such holdings are based on a scanning of both cadasters in their entirety.

goats! But informants confirm that—at least in Vega de Pas—both goat's and ewe's milk were mixed with cow's milk in the production of cheese. It is also possible that goat's milk was used to supplement the diets of weaned calves and was perhaps consumed by humans. Data collected by Penny (1969) support the former suggestion.[10]

The cadasters for both San Pedro and San Roque yield an interesting datum which may well reflect the relative value placed on different sorts of animals (and animal products) and the types of herding they require. In both towns, when an individual with cows kept in addition only one sort of smaller stock, he almost invariably kept sheep rather than goats. It appears to have been people with more than the average number of cows who made this selection for sheep; in some cases, individuals with numerous cows kept neither sheep nor goats. Since the possession of cows and the necessary meadow for their sustenance represent personal wealth, the abandonment of goat and sometimes sheep herding can be seen as a luxury of the few. On the other end of the economic ladder, in both towns, we find some people who kept only sheep, or sheep and goats, or just goats, and I have listed the phenomena in what appears to have been descending order of their desirability and correlated with decreasing degrees of wealth in land and other properties. Sheep and goats, of course, could be herded exclusively on commonly held pasture and low brush and required no privately owned meadow. The scale of values evidenced here is fully corroborated in Vega de Pas today (see chap. 4). It is also true, however, in light of the use of goat's milk in cheese, that the abandonment of goat herding by larger holders of cattle was not merely a luxury for them:—goat-herding may also have been redundant: the greater the number of cows kept, the less the need for goat's milk as a supplement in cheese, for there were always limits to the amount of time and labor which a family could dedicate to cheese production alone, and thus the total production was limited. This might explain why the San Roque herds contained at

10. Penny (1969:266) states: "Goats were even less important than sheep . . . Their milk has not been used in a long time . . . , and it served only for young animals. No one remembers that it was ever consumed by people or entered into the production of cheese." For reasons detailed in the Introduction, this citation must for our purposes be used with caution. Further, appearances are not necessarily a good guide to the past, for goats were in some respects probably not less important than sheep, and the Pasiego memory is sometimes short, so we cannot be sure what varied uses goat's milk had in addition to its confirmed use in cheese.

once fewer goats and more cows than those of San Pedro. Sheep, however, because of their wool yield, were abandoned less quickly.

In addition to sheep, goats, and the vaca pasiega, most families kept one or two pigs for slaughter, poultry, occasionally rabbits, and often beehives, which are rarer today and less evenly distributed throughout the population than the San Pedro and San Roque cadasters indicate for the 1750s.

In reference to the size of herds, the system of *aparcería* must be mentioned. Aparcería is literally sharecropping, but in Pas it, and sometimes the term *calda*, refer primarily to the maintenance of animals (especially cows) and to sharing of the profits they earn, rather than to the working of land and the sharing of crops. I have found no reference to aparcería in cultivated lands in Pas. Aparecería is known in two forms, both of them obsolete in Vega de Pas today. I shall review both forms here so that they may be compared, though one takes us momentarily out of the eighteenth century. The apparently older form, known only from archives, saw Pasiegos maintaining cattle in Pas on contract with vecinos from towns outside Pas, and these outsiders were not apparently Pasiegos. This system is in evidence in the Ensenada cadaster for both San Roque and San Pedro. In a fair number of instances, Pasiegos grazed animals of other owners with their own small herds—these appear to have been the less well-off people with very few or no cows of their own. They did not necessarily own the meadows they exploited, either, but it is unclear if some of the owners they rented land from were also the owners of the cows they held in aparcería. (This would be unlikely if the outsiders, indeed, were not descended from Pas.) For aparcería in San Roque, the contractants were often from Soba; for aparcería in San Pedro, they were most often from the Valley of Toranzo (a sector of the main Pas Valley, downstream from Luena). But the cadaster, of course, gives no details of the terms governing aparcería arrangements. Historians acquainted with the archives for neighboring zones, however, have given some details uncovered in those archives: vecinos from the Valleys of Toranzo, Luena, and Carriedo frequently gave herds into the care of Pasiegos in Pas on a profit-sharing basis (apparently half for each party) and yielded to the Pasiego caretaker the use and proceeds of the milk itself.[11]

11. Here I gratefully acknowledge personal communications from M. C. González Echegaray (1969 and 1974) and Agustín Rodríguez Fernández (1974).

The system outlined above may have persisted into the nineteenth century, but there is no mention of it in the notarial archives (1838–66) preserved for La Vega from that century (see appendix B). It is possible that aparcería contracts were not normally notarized; it is also possible that they were drawn up, notarized, and filed exclusively in towns other than Pas if, as before, one of the contractants lived outside Pas. The only aparcería documents which I found in the nineteenth-century notarial files were of a rather different form. One (for 1846) was between a Pasiego father and his son. The son was serving in the court in Madrid and had sent his father money. The father gave the son two cows and one *jato* (a weaned and grazing calf under breeding age) for a three-year period, after which the son was to receive possession of the cows, whatever their condition; the father and son would share the offspring and the price brought by the calf, but the son would not share in milk proceeds. Later in the year, the same young man bought twenty goats and placed them in his father's care for three years. In the next year, 1847, two vecinos of La Vega who had a business in Zaragoza left a diversified herd to be cared for in Pas.

These arrangements between Pasiegos resemble the form of aparcería arrangements which informants remember but which does not appear in archives.[12] The more recent, remembered system apparently involved, most of the time, Pasiego contractants from the same town. A person who owned meadows and chose not to exploit them personally bought cows and let another care for them on his meadows, with no charge for rent. The caretaker party, in turn, returned to the owner fifty percent of all profit from the cows, and this included the price of cows sold, the offspring both kept and sold, and milk. The sharing of milk in this system may have something to do with the fact that both parties to the contract lived near where the herd was kept.

For the caretaker contractants, who were inevitably not large holders in either land or livestock, the benefits of either system of aparcería are evident. For the stock owner, the aparcería in force in the eighteenth century was primarily a way of owning

12. Notarial records do not become accessible for public perusal or placement in archives until one hundred years after the date they bear; thus more recent notarized aparcería arrangements, if they exist, cannot be studied. I learned about the existence of aparcería in Pas late in my fieldwork and did not have the opportunity to request details from as many informants as I would have liked. Throughout my work in Pas no one made spontaneous mention of the system.

stock without necessarily owning land, and without living in Pas. We would have to know more about these outsiders—their chief occupations, their places in the social structure—before we could tell in precisely what ways they were benefited by owning stock maintained in Pas. In the more recent arrangements, it is interesting that one of the chief benefits to the stock-owner, who is also a land-owner, is that he is freed from the transhumant regime. That people seek such opportunity is still very much the case, though today they use methods other than aparcería to gain this end.

Let us now return to the Ensenada cadasters to consider other aspects of the herding regime. The cadaster shows that San Pedro families normally held no more than three or four cabañas. The number appears to have been slightly higher in San Roque, and this is possibly related to the greater number of cows in the typical herd there. The cabaña today is inalienable from the meadow on which it stands, and while this appears also to have been the case two centuries ago, there were also more meadows without cabañas than there are now (at least in modern Vega de Pas there are only perhaps three meadows in the entire municipality without attached cabañas). It was also common then, apparently, for two or more families to share cabañas, each owning a portion. We do not know the old cabaña's size, but the modern size and ubiquity of cabañas may date only from the period of expansion of the cattle population in Pas— that is, from the very end of the nineteenth century.

Informants in La Vega cite the numbers "three or four" when they speak of the number of cabañas and meadows they used to exploit for the vaca pasiega. They do not speak of cabañas and meadows separately, nor do they speak of having shared cabañas, but they are referring to a later period than does the cadaster.

Transhumance was evidently more attenuated in the past than it is today and consisted primarily in the movement of animals vertically, from one altitude zone to another, on a seasonal basis. In the cadasters, respondents normally specify that one of their cabañas is a *casa-cabaña* (that is, dwelling or house cabaña) or "the one in which I live." The usage is, of course, parallel to today's reference to vividoras. We cannot tell from cadastral material whether entire families actually moved from one cabaña to another, as they do today, for periods of time. Informants say that late nineteenth-century transhumance in Vega de Pas was less demanding than today's, in that a family using three or four meadows moved no more than seven or eight times a year, but the whole family generally moved together, except at harvest time, when groups of family members moved separately.

Only the oldest residents of La Vega have planted maize and been involved in its harvest, but even younger people remember (with great pleasure) the hearthcakes they ate, and there was evidently importation of high-quality maize into Pas for human consumption even after its cultivation in Pas ceased. The older informants give much more detail on the annual cycle of agricultural and pastoral activities than can possibly be gleaned from the cadaster. I have cross-checked data from several informants and combined them below to give a composite picture.

Pumpkins, turnips, and beans were planted amid the maize, for home consumption. After the maize fields were cleared and planted in May, when families worked together as much as possible, part of the family went up to the branizas with most of the herds to spend the entire period until after the grass harvest in August. It was customary to supplement the grass available on the high meadows and extend the stay in the branizas by sending the cows into the monte or—as brushland is sometimes called—the *sierra*. This was occasionally done at other altitudes as well, where possible, and permitted a longer stay in those localities. At least one informant pointed out that, because fertilizer was scarcer and less general care was lavished on the meadows, the quality of grazing in the enclosures was not much better than in the monte. The August grass harvest was carried on much as it is today, except that more hired hands, called *agosteros* (lit. Augusters), were used. October was the season of the maize harvest, when people had come down from the branizas.

The maize harvest also brought with it some of the memorable events of the old barrio social life—husking bees (*deshojas* or *deshojes*) and, when the corn had dried, shelling bees (*pelas*)—which occasioned the gathering of friends to accomplish these tasks for the host family, with partying to accompany the work. There was no binding principle of inclusion other than friendship. Other acts of mutual assistance between friends, or simply the desire to be together, also occasioned evening gatherings in one or another cabaña. They were simply called functions—*funciones*—and they and the bees were the only systematic social gatherings that took place in the barrios. (Events which brought barrio people to the fairground and the Casco will be described later.) Private functions were marked by the consumption of wine, probably, and by the playing of the tambourine (*pandereta*) in accompaniment to song and dance.

With the maize in, the winter months were spent caring for the animals, with occasional moves, and in whatever cottage industries and trading activities (including peddling excursions) a particular household engaged. (Some people, of course, were dedicated to peddling and trade the year round, or in summer in particular, while the rest of their families carried out the agro-pastoral tasks, and some peddled on a day-to-day basis, alternating with the agro-pastoral routine in Pas.) The maize fields required sporadic care, and there were always the chores of hauling firewood and bedding for the animals to each of the cabañas used. The bedding consisted traditionally in fern (*helecho*), heather (*brezo*), and furze (*árgoma*), which had to be collected in wooded areas, and in poor-quality cornhusks. One of the prime reasons for collecting plants for stall bedding was that the vegetable matter enriched the manure used to fertilize the fields. The best cornhusks were used to fill mattresses for use in the vividoras. Cornstalks, which were often left standing in the ground for several months, were eventually burned; corn cobs were favored as fuel for the baking of hearthcakes.

The daily diet reflected production. In addition to cornbread, its main elements were eggs and milk; butter and cheese (fresh curd); turnips, beans, and pumpkin from the maize fields; and some cabbage and kale. Meat was a luxury, as it still is today, and included the products of the pig slaughter or, occasionally, lamb or goat, which were normally slaughtered privately. I have been told that excess lamb or goat was dried into *cecina* (a word applied to dried meats other than pork) and saved for stews. Pork products were also used sparingly in this way. Veal was available from the butchers, who purchased male calves for slaughter and sale, but was a true luxury. The favored legume was, and is, white beans—in general, Pasiegos' tastes in legumes, like their production, are more limited than those in surrounding areas. Pumpkin, turnips, and chestnuts were all used in stews, as were cabbage and kale, but these things are not used in cooking today, and traditionally pumpkin, turnip greens, cabbage, and kale served as food for pigs as much as they did for humans. The major items in the diet in many cases were simply cornbread and milk products: with large families, and moving around as they did, Pasiegos were sometimes even short of eggs.

Even a century ago, some items were imported from outside Pas, and most of them have come to be used more and more in the barrios. Major imports were wheat—which barrio people ate only on special occasions but which served the Casco daily— and potatoes; and turnips, maize, and beans to supplement the local production. Potatoes are listed by Madoz (1849) as a local product of San Pedro, but informants in Vega de Pas make little mention of their cultivation and normally list them among the imports.

Imported items were sold both by the Casco's growing population of merchants and in the Sunday market in the Plaza, which was then a major locus of exchange. Pasiegos brought milk, butter, and cheese to the Plaza to sell; occasionally surplus eggs, lambs, and goats were sold there as well.

The marketplace in La Vega was visited by residents of both San Pedro and Pisueña, while residents of San Roque apparently patronized the market in Selaya. San Pedro and San Roque may have had diminutive markets of their own, but that of La Vega appears to have been much more important. One informant relates that, in his memory, La Vega was also something of a center for the manufacture of almadreñas. People from San Pedro tended to purchase these in La Vega and not to make them themselves, while in La Vega people manufactured them for sale as well as for home use.

In addition to almadreñas and cuévanos, certain implements —such as wooden rakes and cattle halters—were manufactured at home, as were some elements of the costume: the thonged leather *chátaras*, the traditional dress footgear for whose manufacture strips of cowhide were sold in the market, and the *escarpines*, cut from heavy wool cloth (*sayal*, an import), which fit into chátaras or almadreñas and gave warmth.[13]

By the end of the eighteenth century, coarse wool blankets were being processed at a number of rural fulling mills in the province. Barreda (1957:566) locates at least one of these in Vega de Pas; one informant offered the correction that the true location had been in San Pedro, in Vegalosvados (maps 4 and 5), near La Gurueba. In any case, various informants speak of the existence of blanket manufacture in Pas, though none exists today.[14] At least one document (VPA 1790), in an apparent ref-

13. The traditional Pasiego costume of which a few are preserved and which is represented in pictorial records of the last two centuries is the dress costume. This is described by Hoyos Sancho (1969).

14. The many references to blankets (as well as to capes) and the presence nearby of a fulling mill raise the question of the presence in the area of weavers, of which there is to my knowledge no documented mention and no confirmation by older informants. The question is, then, whether woven wool was imported from elsewhere; whether weavers were locally so common as to have been considered less than professionals and, along with almadreñeros and covaneros, went unlisted in such documents as the Ensenada cadaster; or, finally, whether blankets

erence to the year 1759, states that Pasiegos sometimes paid
fines imposed upon them for violating pasturage regulations
with blankets, axes, and capes. Axe blades were possibly imports, but blankets may well have been produced locally and so
might capes, of which there is no evidence one way or the
other. (The cape, of wool, was the single most important item
of men's dress until fairly recently and to wear it was, according
to informants, *de rigeur* at funerals; capes were lent for this
purpose to people who did not own them.)

In addition to whatever spinning and processing of wool there
may have been, and in addition to the other kinds of manufacture already described, some segment of the Pasiego population
was always occupied in trade—carrying into regional markets
any products, such as butter and cheese, that they could sell.
These activities will be considered more fully when we discuss in
chapter 9 the forms of migration (temporary and seasonal) and
emigration (permanent) from Pas, but I should emphasize that
commercial activities beyond the Montes de Pas involved people
on all rungs of the town's socioeconomic ladder. To be sure, in
many instances both the scale and the nature of their commercial activities differed, but it is safe to say that there was probably no one in town who did not produce for the market and
depend to a fair degree on the market (including exchange
within town) for his own needs.

Holstein-Friesian cattle, usually called simply "Dutch" cattle
in Spain, were being imported experimentally into Santander
province by 1870, when they first came to general attention and
were shown at stock expositions. Swiss cattle were also being
tested in the province at that time, and there was experimental
breeding of both imported types with the Pasiego stock with a
view toward increasing local dairy output. The Holstein adapted
better than the Swiss to the local circumstances, some say,
though Holstein are generally delicate cattle, or they were preferred perhaps for other reasons, and they became, by 1900, a
major import.

Santander, at the end of the "wool route" from Castile, had
been one of the North's major ports in the wool trade with
France, Flanders, and England. The continuing involvement with
Holland and Belgium in various kinds of trade, and today in

---

and other woolen items might have been felted rather than woven. We
do know that women spun wool in their homes in Vega de Pas until
fairly recently.

northbound migration, appears to have grown out of the older ties—political, economic, and cultural—from the days of the Empire. The trade relations are visible in certain Vega de Pas family histories; some Pasiegos were actively engaged in commercial activities in Spain and Holland, particularly in linens and other dry goods, in the middle of the last century, and some of these individuals became important in the ensuing cattle trade between the two countries. Pasiegos who had migrated to points outside Pas, and who perhaps were better situated in regard to news from abroad, also numbered among the first importers (see Madariaga 1970).

It is fairly certain that a few Holstein cattle were present in Pas by at least the mid-1880s, if not sooner, but they were not wholly adopted, to the exclusion of the vaca pasiega, until around the turn of the century. Thus, one of my informants, born in 1878, says that her family maintained the vaca pasiega until she was about fourteen, or until about 1882; a man, born in 1891, remembers only the Dutch cows, and not the pasiegas, but his family's herd was small and the frequency of moves unchanged from former times, and they still cultivated maize. On the other hand, one woman, who was born about 1899, remembers that her family practiced throughout her childhood a form of transhumance that was virtually identical with that of Tista's Year, moving between eight different meadows, and she never saw maize harvested in La Vega in her lifetime.

The vaca pasiega became effectively extinct in the first two decades of the twentieth century, perhaps even earlier, and though there had been some initial experimentation with crossbreeding, ultimately the stock bred in Pas was imported Holstein and not hybrid. The option for Holstein, as opposed to Swiss, Pasiega, or other cows producing butterfat-rich milk, was an option in favor of milk production and away from the labor-intensive production of butter and cheese. At first, families who kept very small herds and continued to cultivate maize did not create or face a serious problem of how to market surplus milk without first converting it into a preservable form—that is, butter or cheese. There persists even today the manufacture of some butter and cheese in private households. Pursuing this manufacture, and with both humans and calves to feed on milk, a family with a very small herd does not produce much surplus milk. But the ultimate motive in the change of cattle was not simply to substitute one small herd with another; it was, in fact, toward a more radical change, from a mixed agro-pastoral livelihood based on maize, sheep, goats, and cows, to a highly specialized and thus heavily market-oriented production based on dairy cattle alone. Thus, what ensued in Pas was intimately linked with the development of Spain's dairy industry and forms an important part of that industry's history—and so it is for my purposes unfortunate that this history is, as far as I know, largely unwritten.

We do know that, by the years of the large Holstein importation, there was in Santander some experimentation with milk preservation under varying conditions (see Madariaga 1970). The demand for fresh milk was great in Spain: the arid countryside depended for milk largely on locally herded goats, for dairy cows are hardly abundant in the Spanish countryside. Most urban areas depended on what little surplus emerged from their respective hinterlands and on the goatherds who wandered from town to town, stopping on the outskirts to sell the day's milk. Even in the lush northern provinces, most areas maintained draft cattle like the Tudanca and, while these were systematically milked, they did not support a diet rich in milk products or yield any appreciable marketable surplus. Santander stock men and entrepreneurs, recognizing the demand and having at hand the Holstein cows who could satisfy it, faced the problem of transporting milk to the areas in need. The Pasiegos had already emerged with one solution: the urban *vaquería*.

The vaquería is a small establishment, usually in the heart of an urban neighborhood, consisting in a cow stall (normally accommodating two or three animals at most) and a storefront where milk is sold daily. Madriaga (1970: 187) cites an 1882 report by a Santander writer that at that date there were already some 150 vaquerías in Madrid, mostly of Pasiego ownership and stocked with the vaca pasiega. In other words, just as the demand for milk antedated the Holstein importation, so too the first Pasiego moves toward supplying the need preceded the adoption of Holstein stock. But the real florescence of the vaquería business came with the Holstein cows. While parts of the vaquería tradition are appropriately considered with other forms of emigration, in chapter 9, its development is so intimately related to developments within the Montes de Pas that I shall refer to vaquerías repeatedly in discussing the economic life of La Vega.

Returning to the concomitants of the adoption of Dutch cows in Pas, it is important to repeat that the fact which wrought crucial changes was not the adoption of the new stock in itself but, rather, the fact that Pasiegos sought to become dairy specialists and thus to enlarge their herds. This endeavor brought about enormous changes in land use and, as we shall see, in transhumance. The changes are simply described if we understand first the apparent constraints on both the availability of land for clearing and on the size of enclosed plots.

There is no evidence that more land became enclosed for use as meadow for Holstein cows than was already enclosed by the late nineteenth century. Indeed, all privately owned land is enclosed today and this appears long to have been the case—it may well be that most enclosures date back to the period of the sixteenth and seventeenth centuries when they first come into written evidence. Maize fields and privately owned plots dedicated to woods and sheep pasture, as well as cow meadow, apparently were, and still are, enclosed by the low walls of loose stone which characterize the Pasiego landscape as well as that of the lower Montaña plain.[15]

Table 6, based on the modern cadaster, summarizes the major land types present in Pas today. The high proportion of pasture, low woods, and timberland, which together comprise 75 percent of all land in town, primarily, of course, reflects the vastness of the mountains which, the farther up one goes, come more and more to dwarf the clearings that men have made on their flanks. The ayuntamiento's monopoly on mountain holdings—especially in the category of pasture and secondly in high timber—stems from the traditional definition of these resources as commons and accounts for the fact that 71 percent of the town's lands are in common rather than private holdings.

Since the ayuntamiento holdings have apparently long been inaccessible to further enclosure—that is to say, there is no assarting whatever in Pas—any recent accommodation to increased herd size has come about through a rededication of privately held resources to new ends. In other words, the use

---

15. The Ensenada cadaster contains frequent references to parcels of land dedicated at least partially to grazing and carefully distinguished from cultivated plots and from meadows. Grazing plots were called "*de derrota*," the Spanish term in use for stubble-grazed crop areas in open field systems, but I suspect that the term's use in Pas may be abnormal, that the areas in question were not at times under cultivation, and that the term in this instance simply means "delimited territory open to entry by livestock." We know from informants that such plots were indeed enclosed. They persist today as *erial a pastos* (see table 6 below); sectors of enclosed plots in which there are stands of timber are not infrequent either. All of this is simply to say that pasture and woodland in Pas are not exclusively associated with common tenure.

of 29 percent of the town's land has been altered internally, but the amount of land available for and subject to such manipulation on private initiative has not increased.

One of the great changes which occurred in Pas in regard to land use was that, shortly after the introduction of Holstein stock, virtually all cultivation was abandoned. Maize has probably not been harvested during this century in the alpine barrios and Candolías; there is still a small amount harvested today in the downstream barrios—La Gurueba and Guzparras—but there, too, the crop is by all reports significantly diminished.

TABLE 6
PRIVATE AND AYUNTAMIENTO HOLDINGS, BY LAND TYPE[a]

Land Type	Total Hectares	Percent Total Land	Private Holdings	Ayuntamiento Holdings
Meadow (*prado*)	2,005	23	2,004	1
Gardenland (*huerta*)	5	—	5	—
Uncultivated (*erial a pastos*)	163	2	122	41
Cereal (*cereal*)	9	—	9	—
Low woodland (*monte bajo*)	367	4	230	137
Timberland (*monte alto*)	564	7	154	410
Pasture (*pastizal*)	5,491	64	8	5,483
Total	8,604		2,532	6,072
			(= 29% tot.)	(= 71% tot.)

[a]These figures are drawn exclusively from the modern cadaster for Vega de Pas, first surveyed and catalogued in the 1950s. Informants agree that the unenviable job of surveying a terrain like that of Pas and cataloguing it with informants as inaccessible and reluctant as were many Pasiegos was, on the whole, faithfully accomplished, though no one argues that it must contain inaccuracies. The cadaster includes all parceled and common lands but not routes of communication, waterways, and so on, so the total land surface dealt with here is necessarily slightly less than the 87.6 sq. km. (or 8,759 hectares) total listed on the official survey maps (cf. map 5). Land types listed on the table are cadastral classifications directly related to local uses of land. There are actually six official classes of meadow and three of cereal land within the municipality; their ranking is internal to the town. When ranked on the province-wide scale, La Vega's highest quality of meadow is only ninth, as is its timberland; low woodland is tenth; while first-class garden and cereal lands both rank less than twenty-third in the province. Only in pasture (*pastizal*) and the uncultivated *erial a pastos* does La Vega's absolute ranking rise, to eighth and third, respectively. The above table excludes only two categories, virtually negligible: land in poplars and "unproductive" land (such as cemetery ground), which between them total only 1.8 hectares.

The figures on table 6 give clear evidence of the relative un-importance of cultivation as opposed to meadows. Kitchen gardens are generally associated with areas of more sedentary settlement: they are fairly common among the houses of the Casco and the Candolías roadside area, and in the two downstream barrios, but they are virtually nonexistent in the alpine barrios. All of the riverside plots which once stood in maize are today meadows, and the general view of Pas today is dominated by such meadows at all altitudes, joined by woods and brush which belong to the ayuntamiento and, in these days, are little used.

Another change has been in the increased clearing of meadow at the expense of private tracts of pasture and low woods. The latter types were dedicated to sheep and goats as well as to cattle where necessary. Since the commonlands also provide sheep and goat pasture, people could clear more meadow without necessarily abandoning the herding of smaller stock (though this, too, eventually diminished). Thus, the private maintenance of brushlands (*monte bajo*) is associated primarily with the need for convenient sources of fuel and only secondarily with the herding of sheep, which are kept by fewer than half of the herding families in La Vega today;[16] the remaining hectares of privately held high timber (*monte alto*) are maintained by their owners as a valuable resource.

While individual Pasiegos adjusted the use of their personal resources to new circumstances as they saw fit, the overall availability of land was limited, and people with more land or more wherewithall to rent land were in a better position to expand their herds. Ultimately, when certain forms of emigration became common enough to release considerable land for rent, even relatively poor families found that income from a larger herd enabled them to bear the rental costs of the necessary land for the herd's maintenance.[17] Thus, increased average herd size is

16. People also gather fuel from ayuntamiento brushlands, which they are technically not free to do without some regulation, but the ayuntamiento has found no way to control the activity or to assess people appropriately for wood taken. The problem is not so much one of creating income for the ayuntamiento but, rather, of balancing the rights of all vecinos to common resources against the fact that some people use them more heavily than others. The concern with assessing differential use of commons in regions where their use is easier to control and assess is exemplified by a complex of traditions for that purpose (see Freeman 1970a:98–100).

17. The two forms of emigration which have proceeded directly from the barrios and affected them most are the movement into northern Spanish cities via the institution of the vaquería and the movement of Pasiegos

intimately related to increased emigration as well, and this will be considered further later.

Whenever we speak of private holdings in Pas, we speak of enclosures whose size was fixed in a time past and in response to past needs. Originally, the scattering of an individual's holding was in direct relation to variations in altitude, and the number of plots in the average holding certainly did not exceed the number of recognized zones of micro-climatic variation: three. Today, families who practice transhumance exploit a minimum average of five or six meadows, depending on the barrio, with the exception of Guzparras, where the number is lower (see table 7). Families have increased the number of meadows under

TABLE 7
NUMBERS OF MEADOWS IN USE BY TRANSHUMANT HOUSEHOLDS,
BY BARRIO[a]

	Transhumant Households	Meadows Used by Transhumants	Average Meadows per Unit
Pandillo	77	465	6.04
Yera	33	158	4.79
Viaña	29	174	6.00
Candolías	26	138	5.31
La Gurueba	8	44	5.50
Guzparras	4	14	3.50
Casco	2	12	6.00

[a]Data come from combined sources: town rolls, genealogies, and a field survey of transhumance routes. Note that the number of meadows listed in no way represents the total number in town, for they are *only* those exploited by transhumants. Further, the meadows used by individuals enrolled in a specific barrio are not necessarily located within that barrio or even, in some cases, within Vega de Pas.

exploitation without being able to consolidate them. The problems militating against consolidation are, of course, perennial and widespread, and the literature on them is voluminous in several disciplines: in Pas, they are exacerbated by the facts of altitudinal variation and abrupt topographic discontinuities. The result in Pas today is that almost everyone practicing transhumance is moving not only vertically, with the seasons, but also horizontally, from one to another meadow within a single altitude zone, as the small meadows are exhausted in turn by the large number of cows they support.

---

as sedentary herders onto the Santander coastal plain. These are discussed in detail in chapter 9.

FOUR

The Barrio Livelihood: The Present

The cow is a noble beast.

a barrio woman

Mama, we played cows, and Juan was the veterinarian and delivered my calf.

a Casco boy, returning from play

The meadows of Vega de Pas today support just over three thousand cattle. Some of the cattle listed on table 8 are nourished in part on meadows outside of La Vega, either owned or rented by their masters. In 1969, forty-four households were exploiting sixty-eight or more meadows outside their native town.[1] That three thousand cattle are sustained on La Vega's meadows owes to the fact that only a few cows are kept in full milk production and the rest are fed less. Today's adaptation is a complex one, oriented partially toward milk production but even more heavily toward the breeding of dairy stock for market.

Pasiego dairy cows are much appreciated by outside dairymen for their relative hardiness and their high milk yield once they

1. The data break down as follows: from Pandillo, eighteen households exploit twenty-six or more outside meadows, in San Pedro, Luena, the Valleys of Carriedo and Toranzo, Pisueña, and nearby parts of Burgos; from Yera, two households exploit a total of three meadows in Burgos; from Viaña, eight households exploit sixteen outside meadows, all in San Pedro; from Candolías, twelve families exploit at least fifteen outside meadows in San Pedro, Toranzo, Luena, Carriedo, and Burgos; from La Gurueba, three families exploit at least five meadows in San Pedro and Carriedo; and from Guzparras, three families exploit three or more meadows in Carriedo and Luena. The total number of hectares exploited in other towns is unknown.

TABLE 8
Livestock Census (July, 1969)[a]

Livestock	Barrio							
	Pandillo	Yera	Viaña	Candolías	La Gurueba	Guzparras	Casco	Total
Cattle								
Families with Animals	81	44	30	34	25	9	12	235
Cows	1,365	512	466	420	241	97	97	3,198
Average Herd Size (cows only)	17	11.5	15.5	12.5	10	11	8	13.6
Range in Herd Size (cows only)	2–28	1–41	2–35	2–35	1–28	2–20	2–29	
Herds of 10+ (cows only)	76	30	25	18	10	5	4	168
Percent Total Herds 10+	94	68	83	53	40	55	33	71
Bulls	71	26	26	18	10	3	2	156
Herds of 10+ with Bulls	71	26	25	18	10	2	2	154
Sheep								
Families with Animals	45	23	11	4	6	7	—	96
Sheep	1,117	539	248	70	128	132	—	2,234
Average Flock Size	24.8	23.4	22.5	17.5	21.3	18.8	—	23.3
Range in Flock Size	15–80[b]	15–40	12–40	12–20	15–30	10–30	—	
Goats								
Families with Animals	2	—	—	—	—	—	—	2
Goats	87	—	—	—	—	—	—	87

TABLE 8—Continued

Livestock	Pandillo	Yera	Viaña	Barrio Candolias	La Gurueba	Guzparras	Casco	Total
Equids[c]								
Families with Animals	82	47	32	23	20	9	6	219
Families with 2+ Animals	16	8	12	—	—	1	2	39
Horses	34	11	18	12	11	8	5	99
Mules	43	8	8	6	1	—	—	66
Asses	22	39	19	5	8	2	3	98
Total Equids	99	58	35	23	20	10	8	253
Beehives								
Families with hives	—	6	4	—	—	1	2	13
Approximate Number of Hives	—	34	22	—	—	6	72	134

[a]Standard holdings not listed here are one pig and about eight hens per house in the barrios, and also in some Casco houses; one dog per house in the barrios and often in the Casco as well; and house cats in the more settled areas. About forty households in the entire town keep one or two rabbits each. There are two cases—one in the Casco and one in Candolías—where households keep six pigs: these are raised for sale.

[b]Only one Pandillo flock exceeds thirty-five in number: this is the flock of eighty sheep.

[c]In most cases, equids of all kinds are females.

are put into full production. Most experts attribute their high milk production to the fact that Pasiego cows are bred relatively late in life and are not made to produce at capacity from a young age, and their hardiness is attributed to these facts as well as to the physical regime to which rearing in Pas accustoms them.

Pasiego herders often rationalize their cattle-breeding schedule in terms of the sale cycle: "we breed our cows so that they will have calved by September or October because that's when we sell them." Indeed, September, October, and November see La Vega's largest and traditionally most important *ferias*, or stock fairs. Also, this is the beginning of the season of greatest demand for milk in Spanish urban areas—the winter season of café life with high demand for milk and coffee rather than cold drinks. This aside, the high point of the sale cycle is really an artifact of the breeding cycle and could fall elsewhere in the year were the breeding cycle not affected also by the demands of the transhumance cycle. Thus, another given rationale for the breeding schedule which recognizes this is perhaps more accurate: "we breed our cows so that as few as possible will have to be milked while we're in the branizas and busy with the harvest."[2]

Whatever cows are not destined to calve by autumn are usually bred to calve sometime in spring so that households and young calves will not be without milk at any time. In much of La Vega, cows are milked for as long as eight months (in a few cases longer) after calving. In Viaña, the norm is to milk less—for five or six months only—and to allow the cow to go dry (*estilar*) as soon as she becomes pregnant again. Elsewhere in town, cows are let go dry during only the last five or six months of their nine-month gestation. (In regard to the length of the cow's gestation period, various Pasiegos have happily pointed out to me that "cows are just like people.") The normal life cycle of the cow in Pas until time of sale is summarized as follows:[3]

2. Yet a third explanation offered, in reference to the cow's salability, is that this improves with warm weather: *la vaca luce más* (the cow shines more) refers to the fact that the coat is glossier and the udder fuller in warm weather than in cold. But this hardly explains the fact that major sales are in fall rather than in summer.

3. By comparison, among Pasiegos and other herders on the coastal plain specializing in milk production, cows are first bred at eleven to fourteen months, are milked for about three months longer in each lactation, and are given only one month's rest before the next breeding.

Stage	Months duration
Birth to breeding	24–30
Gestation (1st)	9
Lactation	8
Rest (dry)	5–6
Gestation (2d)	9
Lactation	8 (or until sale)
Rest (dry)	5–6
Gestation (3d)	9
Lactation	until sale

About 40 percent of cows are sold after the second calving, at about five years of age, and 60 percent after the third calving, around age six. A cow is sold after her first calving (*de prime-rizas*) for the most part only when it appears that a second calving will cause the udder to hang down and lower the animal's price.

The standard practice, then, is to wean the new calf in its first two weeks (calves are then fed on milk and bread until three or four months of age) and to sell the mother soon afterward at an autumn fair. Thus, the mother will have been in full production (that is, on a maximal feeding schedule) for at most the last months of her pregnancy and the few weeks between calving and sale. And while about a third of a herd will be producing milk at any given time, only the cows which are near calving or being readied for sale are fed their fill; this approximately doubles their milk production. A cow who, having calved, is not for sale is reduced again to half production as soon as her calf is weaned.

A herder generally plans to sell about one-fifth of his cows each year. Herders with fewer than twenty cows sell three or four, herders with twenty to twenty-five animals might sell five, and herders with more than twenty-five might sell six or more. In addition to milk cows, a herder sells virtually all of the male calves born in a year. If by chance fewer females are born than a herder wishes to raise, he may purchase female calves from others whose cows have produced more female offspring than they wish to keep. Young females are thus exchanged within the herding community, while young males are normally sold to the Casco's butchers for slaughter. Whereas virtually every herder with ten or more cows also keeps a seed bull (table 8), the bull is not always raised out of his own herd but, rather, purchased from another herder. Thus, a few bulls reared for breeding also change hands within the herding community in transactions occurring in or out of the context of the stock fair. When a seed bull has been in use for two years, it too is sold for butchering, and there are no old bulls in Pas: seed bulls are reared from calves, relinquished to avoid inbreeding after two seasons, and destined for sale to butchers rather than for further use in breeding. (Sale of these beef animals is normally for export and slaughter outside Pas; beef is neither eaten nor sold in Pas and it is despised by most Pasiegos.)[4]

A cow reared in Pas and sold after her third calving does not have more than three or four productive years left in her. On the other hand, a cow reared on the coastal plain, exploited more fully at an earlier age, and perhaps not strengthened by the physical regime of Pas does not have a significantly longer productive life either.[5] The chief demand for Pasiego cows is in the urban vaquerías. Even though many of these have since about 1965 been zoned out of central urban areas, I use the word vaquería here to include the larger and less central milk-producing businesses which have developed out of or replaced some of the neighborhood outlets. The dairy personnel who serve urban markets are in many cases former vaquería personnel, and even if not, they know to seek the same qualities in the stock they purchase.

The vaquería tradition developed and continues to exist in symbiosis with the stock breeding practiced in Pas. Cows are brought into the vaquerías and continue to be bred there, with prize bulls from Pas, or now increasingly by artificial insemination, for their remaining productive years. Their calves are born in the city. Males are sold for butchering (as are their mothers when they cease to be productive), but it is normal to return female calves to Pas to be reared there. The descent of such

4. In days of worse roads and more difficult trucking, and especially in meadows with poor access to these, a cow who suffered an accident and had to be slaughtered was often simply buried. Today, such animals are usually sold to a butcher, whose business frequently takes him into the barrios in this way. The point is that a beef carcass was not consumed even when it could not be sold to a butcher. While the dislike of beef might contain some element of sentiment for the deceased animal, it is unsafe to stretch the point, for Pasiegos willingly eat veal from their own herds—sold for butchering in the Plaza and repurchased there for consumption. Veal is the most prized meat and today dominates festive meals to the exclusion of almost all other foods.

5. The high lime content of the soil in Pas as opposed to lower areas is also beneficial and is particularly important to pregnant and lactating cows in Pas, where their diet of grass is little supplemented.

calves is well known to their prospective breeders, and Pasiegos in 1969 were paying up to one thousand *pesetas* more per calf than the animals would have brought in other markets.[6] Stock dealers (*tratantes*), the important intermediaries of cattle exchange, thus have a dual role in bringing mature cattle out of Pas and in returning newborn females to be reared there.

Some years ago, the possession of calves of known descent was so important that when a Pasiego sold a cow in calf, the sale agreement (usually unwritten) required that the seller not only keep the offspring but also be called to the scene of its birth: this practice was informed by the fear that a calf of unknown and supposedly inferior descent might be substituted for the sold cow's true offspring. Thus, Pasiego herders frequently traveled to Madrid and other capitals to witness their calves' delivery and to bring them home to Pas, just as vaquería owners frequently traveled in the opposite direction to replenish their number of milk cows.[7] Today only about 15 percent of cows sold are sold before calving. This was done formerly because, since there was no veterinary service in Pas until around 1930, herders feared the complications of calving and preferred to have this take place in less remote areas. The reclaiming of calves is less frequent today and occurs mostly where cows have been sold into zones close to Pas. When a pregnant cow is sold (in any case not the most common practice), the price is usually augmented by the market price of a calf and the deal is closed before the calving. This change is probably related to the increase in available cash in Pas due to cattle and milk sales and to new estimates on the expenditure of time: most herders today would be unwilling to travel to Madrid and back for a single calf.[8]

A good cow in full production in Pas gives about thirty liters a day, and prize animals have given well over forty. The main-

6. In the 1969 exchange, the U.S. dollar was worth seventy pesetas. At that time, an average cow sold in La Vega for 30,000 ptas. (and sometimes for over 40,000) and an aging or unproductive one for around 20,000 ptas. Female calves brought 6,000 to 7,000 ptas. and immature males for breeding about 10,000 ptas.

7. Reference to this system is made by Ahumada, Diego, and Madariaga (1966). This brief article, incidentally, fails to distinguish field ownership from actual exploitation and thus gives a somewhat exaggerated impression of the number of points in the typical transhumance cycle: some owners may hold large numbers of meadows, but many if not all of these will be rented out, and no herder exploits as many meadows as the cadaster lists for the largest owners.

8. Milk sales may at any one time be a herder's largest source of ready cash, for cows are usually bought and sold on credit.

tenance of high production requires heavy feeding (20 kg. per day of grass and other fodder), and in the vaquerías the diet is often supplemented with beer as well. For sale, a cow is brought to the fairground without her morning milking, and her production is tested on the spot by a prospective buyer—the cow is milked in public and her yield made public. Many outside dealers employ the service of professional milkers (*ordeñadores*) on the fairgrounds, but there are no professional milkers within the barrio community, nor to my knowledge are such individuals employed in transactions between Pasiegos themselves. I refer here primarily to transactions between residents of La Vega and their kinsmen who have emigrated as herders. These people are themselves accustomed to milking. Pasiegos normally extend credit to one another in stock trading. Negotiations between them always become known and the practice of deception is extremely uncommon: public opinion has its sharpest cutting edge in these matters. Credit is also extended to outsiders brought into the system by established participants. The infrequency of default in stock payments is partly due to the force of public opinion but also to the fact that people do not strike deals with others of whose paying capacity they are not already aware.

The extension of credit is possibly one of the best measures of the size and limits of the collective network of herding acquaintances of Vega de Pas herders: it includes virtually all descendants of La Vega and many people from or descended from San Pedro, in addition to numerous non-Pasiegos, but it seems to exclude San Roque, most of Pisueña, and most Burgos Pasiegos. While some Vega herders have social contacts in these places, the community of mutual credit extension, of systematic information exchange, and of mutual sensitivity to public opinion in stock transactions is largely confined to people who patronize and people from towns which patronize the same local stock fair.

With one or two exceptions, barrio herders tend not to be large-scale dealers, although any one of them at some times is likely to function as an intermediary in sales between other Pasiegos and outsiders, who may also be Pasiegos: kinship and friendship foster such intermediacy.[9] About 25 percent of cows sold in La Vega are destined for owners on the coastal plain and 75 percent for urban areas. The dairy stock dealers in La Vega buy stock for resale largely within the province; dealers who

9. Because every herder is something of a stock dealer, this kind of enterprise is excluded from the census of specialties recorded in table 5.

systematically negotiate stock sales between Pas and urban dairy enterprises tend not to live in Pas, but they are often of Pasiego descent.[10] The dealer is, however, a familiar figure in town, both in and out of the stock fair. The reason is that the dairy-stock market in La Vega (and secondarily in the other two Pas towns, which are smaller and have fewer fairs) is a market primarily for dealers and is the ultimate purveyor of much of the stock which changes hands in the more publicly recognized fair of Torrelavega, Spain's largest marketplace for dairy cattle.[11] Many of the dealers who purchase in La Vega resell in Torrelavega in a much more public and less specialized market than exists in any of the Pasiego towns.

The household regime which turns on the care and sale of cows is, as I have told, one of frequent movement in the exploitation of sufficient meadows to keep the cows even at half production.

Tista Pelayo, the herder from Pandillo whose annual transhumance I have described, had in October of 1969 a herd of twenty-three cows and one bull. The herd's age structure and percentage of lactating cows are typical of most herds in La Vega, though his herd is somewhat more numerous than the average. It was composed as follows:

4 female calves (*becerras*) under three months (fed on milk and bread)
6 cows under breeding age, from six months to two years of age
6 cows in calf:
    4 for May delivery (three 1st and one 2d calving)
    1 for February delivery (3d calving)
    1 for October delivery (3d calving)
7 cows in milk:
    5 three-year-olds after 1st calving
    1 four-year-old after 2d calving
    1 five-year-old after 3d calving

10. This discussion does not consider the activities of butchers as dealers in meat stock. All of the Casco butchers are dealers, and one on a particularly large scale with a farflung transactional network.

11. San Roque has two fairs monthly; San Pedro has fairs only from the end of August through October, at the rate of three per month; while Vega de Pas holds three fairs every month, with the exception of most of June and all of July, the main harvest and braniza season. Many herders from San Pedro sell at the Vega de Pas fair: about 20 percent of the cows sold in La Vega originate in San Pedro.

Three to four of the older animals would be sold that year and at least one of the lactating animals was, along with at least one pregnant one, on a full feeding schedule.

A full feeding in La Vega consists of about 14 kg. of grass and 6 kg. of imported feed (maize, wheat bran, wheat and barley waste—*harinilla*—and fava beans). This diet produces in a normal cow about thirty liters of milk daily; cows fed solely on grass in the amount supplied in La Vega (14–16 kg. per day) yield only about fifteen liters daily.

Tista's meadows—all of which are in rent, mostly from his father-in-law—total thirty-five *obreros* (or 315 *plazas*) in area. These are traditional surface measures in use in the Pas villas and Luena. The obrero is equivalent to 2.772 hectares and contains nine plazas (each .308 ha.). Thus, Tista exploits ninety-seven hectares of meadow with his twenty-four animals. Herders estimate that a single animal requires two and a-half obreros, or almost seven hectares, in a year: this estimate takes account of altitudinal differences in yield (see table 9), of differences in rates of consumption of dried and of green grass, and of the proportions of cows in full and half production during a year. Thus, Tista exploits just enough meadow for fourteen animals. In 1969, he was for the first time about to apply chemical fertilizer to all of his meadows save the braniza, but he thought of doing this simultaneously with relinquishing one of his rented hillside fields, and this would lessen considerably his total gain in grass crop. To compensate for his low animal-to-meadow ratio, Tista had in 1969 purchased 9200 kg. of alfalfa in addition to the fodder on which full milk production is achieved, and on all these imports he had spent a total of 40,000 ptas. The alfalfa was used specifically to supplement the grass crop of Tista's lowest meadow and thus to permit a longer stay in the vividora. Otherwise, the meadow is sufficient to support Tista's herd during at most three of the four months he spends there yearly. In addition, while in the braniza, he grazes his cows in the monte to stretch the grass supply in the meadow and cabaña.

TABLE 9
MEADOW YIELDS: THOROUGHLY DRIED GRASS
PER PLAZA (.308 hectare) OF LAND

Meadow Level	Crops Per Year	Average Yield (manuring only)	Average Yield (chemical fertilizer)
Ribero	4	100 kg.	150 kg.
Ladera	3	50 kg.	75 kg.
Braniza	2	50 kg.	75 kg.

There are in Pas certain pasturage traditions which are at least in part concomitants of the low feeding schedule on which cattle are maintained. Cattle are grazed outside for a little over six months at most, as exemplified in Tista's transhumance schedule (see table 1). Whenever they are stall-fed, their masters control closely the amount of grass they are given: 14 to 16 kg. per day of grass only, except for cows in full production. Outdoor grazing is also carefully controlled, for the cows cannot be allowed to eat their fill: informants say the average cow would consume 16 to 18 kg. per day if left to herself. Cows are stabled whenever the ground is thoroughly wet (and Pas counts on heavy moisture at least one in every five days). While cattle are quite able to withstand rain, the retreat into the stable helps to control their feeding. (There is another reason: people say that the number of animals on the small meadows in wet weather is sufficient to churn and damage the earth beyond the extent of the simple trampling which is beneficial to grass growth.) Pasiegos do not pasture their animals at night, and again this helps to control grass consumption. On the precipitous mountainside pastures, of course, animals can get lost or hurt either at night or in the frequent heavy fogs which shroud the upper reaches of the valleys. But even in lower areas and on gentle terrain, animals are always stabled before their evening milking. These practices substantially reduce the time in which cows graze outside, and during a year there might be at least one month of stall-feeding beyond those indicated on table 1.

Cows are not pastured alone but are always cared for by someone. People explain this on grounds both that terrain is precipitous and that the stone walls are low and easily jumped. The latter fact, while true, is, of course, an artifact of tradition, and we must accept out of the realm of tradition the fact that in circumstances where other people might leave their cows to graze unwatched on a meadow adjoining a house, Pasiegos always keep company with their animals in the meadows. This, then, must be counted as one of the labor requirements of Pasiego herding. Further, where a number of sheep are kept, they must be herded separately on the pasturelands; individual households almost invariably herd their own sheep—there are no collective herds—and thus allocate another person's labor to this end. However, in households like Tista's where only one or two sheep are kept, these are grazed on the meadow with the cows and are called *ovejas vaqueras* (sheep of the cow herd).

Other daily labor needs relating to the cattle are in milking; in taking milk to collection points either once or twice a day, depending on the locality, with travel time (usually by horse, mule, or burra) also dependent on locality; feeding and caring for the calves which do not yet graze; and cleaning the manure from the stable and piling it in the meadow, from whence it is spread before each departure from the meadow. Water is hauled to the cabaña from the nearest source, usually more than once a day, and three meals are cooked and the few dishes washed, normally after each meal.

Periodically, household laundry is washed at the nearest running stream. Firewood, tinder, and a few wild grasses for the milk-fed calves are collected periodically, though perhaps not daily, and there is shopping to be done at the most convenient locality. When distance makes shopping or other business in the Casco difficult, these are combined with visits to stock fairs or to mass on days of religious importance. Shopping is a true problem from localities in the branizas, and in the summer season the bakers and a few others make some items available at milk collection points, not daily but at least once a week.

People busy themselves periodically with making repairs and occasional replacements for parts of the cabaña or implements. Manure spreading occupies some time on the last day of any stay in a meadow: the manure is distributed roughly about the meadow from a mule-drawn trough (*nerra*) and then is spread more evenly by human labor. The task is repeated before every move in the year. Finally, we must not underestimate the time spent in uprooting, moving, and resettling a family, its animals, and its living equipment twenty times a year. Sometimes, because of the limits of both humans and beasts of burden, moving a household may require two trips.

The grass harvest, lasting six weeks or so, requires a burst of labor and an allocation of as many hands as possible away from the cows and toward the meadows themselves. The grass is cut, immediately before its ripest stage, by scythe (*dalle*). The mowing is punctuated by numerous stops to cold-temper the scythe's edge (*picar el dalle*): this is done in the meadow by the harvester(s) on a small anvil. This and other parts of the harvest procedure are shown in plates 13–15. Mown grass is left spread out to dry and, in the two or three days that this requires in good weather, it is turned (by rake) at least once. Then it is raked into piles to be carried into the loft of the adjacent cabaña. While in most cases the grass need not be hauled farther than the distance from the cabaña door to the meadow's farthest corner, there are no wheeled vehicles to aid in the task: dried grass is piled (in loads of about 100 kg. for men and 50 kg. for women) across a long switch of green hazelwood. The person doing the hauling leans over, pressing his or her head into the center of the pile, and grabs an end of the hazel switch, the *belorta*, in each hand, bending the rod into a semi-circle while gradually rising to a standing position and bringing the load of grass up, essentially "strapped" on top of the head and shoulders by the belorta. The stack of hay thus "walks" into the cabaña for deposit in the loft. The hauling of loads of grass by belorta (*belortear*) often involves at least two people, the hauler and an assistant to help him straighten up, and the two alternate at these tasks. The tasks of cutting, turning, and hauling grass and waiting for it to dry are repeated up the slopes in every meadow. The harvesters usually keep with them two cows—a milk cow to supply their own needs and one to keep her company—and they keep house for themselves during the' weeks of the harvest. Rains, fogs, and heavy dews retard the drying process. In the threat of heavy rain, the spread-out grass is raked into larger stacks for protection from moisture, and then it must be spread to dry again.

In 1969 there were in all of Vega de Pas sixteen mowing machines: six of the owners were from Pandillo, one from Yera, one from Viaña, three from Candolías, two from La Gurueba, one from Guzparras, and two from the Casco. Some of the hindrances to mechanization include the nature of the terrain, fuel costs and availability, and problems of getting machines from one meadow to another.[12] There are access paths to only a few meadows and most must be reached circuitously, often by climbing the stone walls of adjacent meadows—once access to the pradera has been attained in the first place! Problems of transport and electrical service also militate against the use of milking machines, and there are none in town, but it is also true that the proportion of cows in milk at one time in even the largest herds does not make milking a great consumer of time, nor is time at a premium in Pas: the tendency is to seek relief from tasks requiring heavy labor, rather than simply from time-consuming ones.[13]

Tista Pelayo's annual family budget, presented on table 10, shows the narrow financial margin on which most barrio households operate, and the absence of any property insurance should

12. Despite these difficulties, the benefits of using mowers were increasingly recognized and by the end of 1974 there were said to be more than thirty in town, though I did not get a precise census of them.

13. After initial massage of the udder, a cow is milked in about four minutes. Tista spends a little over half an hour at each milking of eight cows.

TABLE 10
Breakdown of Sample Family Budget

The following itemization of income and expenses is for a family of two adults and three children utilizing ninety-seven hectares of rented meadow with twenty-four bovids, two equids, and one sheep. Prices are as of October 1969. Asterisks indicate items which are annualized from longer periods of time.

Income

Sale of 3.5 cows/year @ 31,125 ptas. average	108,938 ptas.
Sale of calves	31,500
*Sale of bull (.5/year)	12,000
Sale of milk (ca. 1,500 liters/month @ 6.50 ptas/liter)	97,500
Total income	249,938

Expenses

Foods and Supplies	ptas/month
Meat (6 kg.)	360
Legumes (4 kg.)	120
Wine (30–32 liters)	280
Bread (20 ptas./day)	600
Coffee (ca. .5 kg.)	65
Sugar (5 kg.)	80
Eggs (if no hens are kept) (3 doz.)	105
Fruit (15 ptas./day)	450
Oil (6 liters)	240
Potatoes (2 kg./day)	300
Vegetables	50
Paprika, garlic, condiments	60
Soup pasta (4 kg.)	65
Colacao (similar to Ovaltine)	104
Soap powder (8 boxes)	86
Soap cakes (8)	40
Lamp oil (4 liters)	22
Carbide fuel (4 kg.)	36
Batteries (4)	36
Monthly total	3099
Annual total food and supplies	37,188

Tools and Equipment	
Slates, scythe, rakes, scythe handle	500
Cuévanos	500
Ropes	150
Mule harness and misc.	300
Pots and pans, etc.	500
Total tools and equipment	1,950

Clothing	
Shoes and footgear	2,500
Clothing	5,000
Umbrellas (2)	300
Bedclothes	690
Total clothing	8,490

TABLE 10—*Continued*

Stock Purchases		
Pig (purchased for slaughter)		8,000
*Equid		1,000
*Bull (av. .5/year @ 25,000)		12,000
	Total stock	21,000
Rents, Services, and Other		
Veterinarian		2,000
Medical plan		740
House repairs		10,000
Chemical fertilizer		2,200
Fodder		40,000
Rents		80,500
Leisure (cigarettes, bar/restaurant, etc.)		3,650
School tuition (1 child)		15,000
	Total rents and services	154,090
	Total expenses	222,718
	Net income	27,220 ptas.

be noted. The budget is a fairly standard one for a family of five whose adult members have not yet inherited or been "given" meadows (see below). However, the five meadows which are rented from kin (at a total of 27,000 ptas. per year) are acquired at approximately half the rate a non-kinsman would charge. Tista's situation will be better when the older generation settles the meadows on the younger, and he then expects to buy out the shares of emigrants, placing himself temporarily in their debt. In Tista's case, he would then owe 200,000 ptas. each to two people, at 6 percent interest. (There are several large holders in town who lend money locally at 3 percent less than the current bank rates.) He would also be assessed a share in the annual support of his wife's parents—the couple whose donation was at issue. This arrangement was being discussed in 1969 but met with some opposition in the family. For the present, Tista was lucky to be able to rent as many as five meadows at half price. Some people fare much worse in this regard and either pay out more in rent or must be content to exploit less meadow and keep smaller herds. Tista, on the other hand, was even able to spend 35,000 ptas. to rent his ribero meadow and vividora from a non-kinsman. The value of the house and field at the time was about two million pesetas, and it was the largest first-quality meadow in La Vega. Tista gave high priority to the benefits of using this prize meadow; others might not have been willing or able to pay the price.

Two respects in which Tista's expenditures are higher than normal are in the purchase of meat, of which some families consume much less, and in the annual tuition payments for his son's schooling outside Pas. Tista's was the only Pandillo family in 1969 educating a child beyond the age of fourteen, when local and compulsory schooling ends, though there are a few cases in other barrios. In most such instances, the total cost of a child's further education is ultimately deducted from the amount of his inheritance. Finally, in the realm of income, Tista's milk sales are slightly greater than other families', as he tends to milk his cows for a full ten months after calving.

The diet reflected in Tista's expenditures shows certain changes in the degree to which imported items are today included in the barrio diet. All bread is wheaten, and virtually nothing in the diet other than milk, eggs, and some meat (chiefly pork) is homegrown. The variety of local production ceased with the abandonment of cultivation and the intensification of transhumance, and the consumption of vegetables in particular has probably decreased. Tista's family consumes more potatoes than most, and possibly therefore fewer legumes, but aside from potatoes and legumes the expenditure of only fifty pesetas a month for other vegetables where none are homegrown is typical of barrio patterns. Tista's family consumes about six liters of milk daily. (Milk-fed calves are also given six liters a day per animal.) Families spending less on meat consume more milk and perhaps more eggs. Even with numerous imported foodstuffs available through the Casco grocers, there are still families which, unlike Tista's, choose to live almost exclusively on milk, eggs, bread, and occasionally cheaper meat products such as blood sausage. However, even blood sausage and lamb offal, fried in the traditional *asadurilla*, are only occasional indulgences.

Tista, like most herders, has no income other than that from the sale of livestock and milk, and only 39 percent of his income is from milk. Large commercial dairy concerns which collect and process milk and market milk products have been established in the province since about 1915. That period saw the Swiss firm Nestlé build its first Spanish plant in La Penilla, in the Cayón Valley of the coastal plain, and within a couple of years a large dairy cooperative was formed in the province—the SAM (Sindicatos Agrícolas Montañeses)—with its plant in Renedo, in the Toranzo Valley. A third large firm today is Clesa. These are the area's major processors of milk and the three are, between them, responsible for all milk collection in Pas. Most of their business, however, comes from the sedentary herders of the coastal plain, among them the numerous emigrant Pasiegos who have become full-time milk producers rather than stock breeders.

In Pas, aside from the fact that there is not enough land to support at full production as many cattle as the present population would need to subsist on the sale of milk alone, the problem of access to collection points also inhibits fuller concentration on milk for sale. It is probably safe to say that for most families the time spent yearly in hauling milk for pick-up is as great as or greater than the time spent milking; from some points and in bad weather it may be as much as twice as great. Only a few sedentary herders of the Casco, none with more than six cows, can be regarded as dairy producers rather than stock breeders, and they sell milk to the commercial families of the Casco itself rather than to the large dairies; but these producers also follow occupations other than herding and do not live from milk sales alone. The Pasiego herder opts to be primarily a milk producer when he can, but he leaves Pas to do so and he becomes sedentary in the process.

Within Pas, though the desideratum of milk specialization is not achieved, there are ways of achieving a more sedentary life than the normal one, such as Tista's, of the alpine barrios. At least in the alpine barrios, most of these adaptations are achieved only by fairly well-to-do herders, but one is achieved by most herders simply with age, and that is the sedentarization at retirement to which I have already referred.

Retirement from herding is synonymous with sedentarization and, normally, with the "donation" of land and animal holdings to the younger generation. The so-called donation (I employ the term used by Pasiegos) consists in a contractual (and usually notarized) arrangement between a retiring couple (usually nearing age sixty-five) and their heirs. Title is transferred to heirs in exchange for annual support, to which all contribute, for the parents during their lifetime together and when widowed; ownership of the parents' herd is transferred to heirs active as herders, with compensation for non-herding heirs; and the parents settle down in a single cabaña in a preferred location.[14] Some people seek to purchase fields in choice locations precisely in preparation for retirement. In any case, areas preferred for retirement coincide with those in which vividoras are estab-

14. Donations are further discussed with other aspects of inheritance in chapters 5 and 6.

lished, as described in chapter 2, and often a couple simply retires in its own vividora. They might keep a cow on the attached meadow, but more often they simply rent out the meadow: when, as often, the rental is to an heir, the older couple is joined periodically in the cabaña by the heir's family as they move in and out with their cattle.

Aside from retirement, permanent or nearly permanent settlement requires capital and is in some cases the result of many years of planning. It must first be understood that land in Pas is a commodity with an active market whose exchangeability is subject to no sentimental constraints, whose value is assessed in monetary terms alone, and whose price fluctuates with demand. In this context, individuals are able, with capital, to acquire fields other than their inherited ones, to sell the fields of their patrimony and purchase preferred ones, and to set about strategically to amass meadows which are close together. In some instances, then, herders have been able to limit the distances over which they move and thus achieve a transhumance style which in some ways resembles that of the days of the vaca pasiega. While almost everyone has at least one braniza meadow, some have amassed lower meadows that are close enough so that at least part of the time cows stabled in one cabaña can graze that meadow and be cared for there while the entire family still enjoys life in its vividora nearby: people simply spend the day with the cows and return to the vividora at night and perhaps for meals. These families move to the branizas, and they sometimes move at other seasons as well, but their transhumance is much attenuated by the normal standards of the alpine barrios. There are such cases in all of the alpine barrios as well as in Candolías, La Gurueba, and Guzparras, and the attenuated transhumance is closer to the normal pattern in the latter three barrios. In La Gurueba and Guzparras especially, the occurrence of transhumance itself is diminished and the proportion of sedentary active herders is greater (see table 4 above).

Two major localities which are composed primarily of active herders who are permanently settled are referred to above (chap. 2, nn. 15, 16). They are not ribero praderas but they nonetheless assume the character of neighborhoods and are called pueblos: they are Gucimprún (Viaña) and Pandeacebo (La Gurueba). Of the twelve families with meadows in Gucimprún, only two do not reside there all year, and of the ten with year-round vividoras, six are active herders. Often, in some of these families, someone must spend the nights with the cows in cabañas located elsewhere, but whole families do not move. Gucimprún is on open terrain and is composed of twenty-three separate meadows; it is located not far above the highway and has electrical service. Life there differs sharply from life in the rest of Viaña. Pandeacebo is also composed of twenty-three meadows, belonging similarly to only thirteen owners. Three households are fully sedentary but not active herders. Three of the ten active herders move considerably but have vividoras in Pandeacebo. Four move little and live most of the time in their vividoras, and the remaining three active herders are indeed permanently settled. Pandeacebo, too, enjoys electricity. Two or three of the smaller praderas in La Gurueba and Guzparras follow the same pattern.

Most of the herders who are permanently settled in Gucimprún and Pandeacebo do not keep as many cows as does the average family in Pandillo or most of Viaña and hence do not require as much meadow, but there are exceptions. One Gucimprún herder has one of the largest herds in town—thirty-five cows and two bulls. He does move around, but nonetheless he manages a life-style that would be the envy of a Pandillo herder with the same number of animals.

In Pandillo, in contrast, the pradera called Portilla, which has the largest number of fixed residents and vividoras in that barrio, is nonetheless populated mostly by transhumants. There are thirty-three meadows belonging to twenty-one owners. Of the fifteen vividoras, six are permanently inhabited, but in five cases the settled residents are retired and without animals, and the sixth household keeps only two cows. To my knowledge, there are only two Pandillo families with sizable herds who are able to approximate on a nearly settled basis the life-style of Gucimprún or Pandeacebo. One Portilla family, with the best-appointed vividora in all of Pandillo, owns three Pandillo meadows and lives in its vividora most of the time except during visits to the braniza meadows, which are rented in San Pedro. However, the wife stays in Portilla with part of the family while her husband and three grown sons harvest and care for the herd. This particular family has more adult manpower than most. The second instance (see chap. 2, n. 15) is of a Pandillo herder who is settled almost permanently in a hillside pradera where there are no other vividoras. He owns four or five meadows in the pradera and, with twelve cows, a bull, and a small flock of sheep, stays almost permanently in his vividora there except during occasional visits in the Casco, where he rents one meadow. However, he, like Tista, imports fodder in order to be able to stay longer in a single place. Other herders might instead spend the price of fodder, if they have it, on the rental of another

meadow, and this accentuates rather than alleviates the problem
of making frequent moves.

There are, then, aside from retirement, various strategies of
sedentarization, and they often occur in combination. One is the
reduction of herd size, and this is common mostly in the downstream barrios and near the highway in Yera, where there are
more non-herding occupations practiced and (in La Gurueba
and Guzparras) more land under cultivation and less high
braniza. Another strategy, which may or may not accompany reduced herd size, is the amassing of meadows in contiguous zones.
This is most frequent in La Gurueba and Guzparras. In the alpine zones, most people are unsuccessful in eliminating the trip
to the branizas in this way, but this is partially because they are
loathe to reduce their herd size at all—Pandillo and Viaña in
particular are barrios in which there is almost complete dedica-
tion to stock breeding, though it is impossible to say whether
this is more the cause or the result of the way choices are made.
At any rate, the ultimate strategy is to spend money on imported
fodder for the maintenance of cattle in a fixed place for a longer
time than the size of any single meadow will permit. This practice, which is at best a partial solution for any large herd, is to
be found primarily in the alpine barrios in association with the
exclusive emphasis on stock breeding.

None of these strategies has produced the perfect result: a
situation in which a large herd is maintained exclusively in a
single place for the entire year. Even the largest ribero meadows
in La Vega could not support more than three or four cows for
a full year. Only a tremendous increase in emigration could permit the effective consolidation of meadows for the families remaining, and problems of terrain and altitude might prohibit
extensive consolidation in any case. All of the strategies which
meet with partial success have drawbacks as well: herd reduction reduces capital income; amassing meadows in contiguous
praderas requires both capital expenditure and often years of
waiting; and the importation of fodder is not only costly but, in
the physical setting of Pas, it is feasible on a large scale only in
zones fairly close to the roads. Even where herders are able to
maintain vividoras the year round, their lives are not always as
settled as they may seem. In precisely the parts of the barrios
where fixed residence of active herders is most common, the
maintenance of a permanently occupied vividora comes to mean
that household members are not always together. Since cows are
always stabled in the cabaña whose meadow they are grazing,
and since no one's meadows are all contiguous and many are not

even in the same pradera, there is a high incidence of periodic residential separation within families. This is particularly true in Guzparras and La Gurueba, at the mouth of the Viaña valley in Candolías, and in roadside areas of Candolías and Yera, where numerous families keep fairly large herds and send some members off with the cattle while other members maintain an open vividora throughout the year. This does not happen only in families with much manpower, such as the Portilla (Pandillo) family described above; there are also frequent cases in which a husband and wife, with or without small children, live separately much of the time, one in a vividora and the other moving with the cattle. Thus, even the existence of what Pasiegos proudly call permanently inhabited vividoras belies the fact that the demands of transhumance are often still in force and working their effects on family life.[15]

Inevitably, as some families acquire meadows as close together as possible, others are left with the less select holdings: meadows which are widely dispersed, poorly located with respect to the center, and/or of poorer quality. Though it affords less physical comfort, the exploitation of some of these holdings can be as profitable as any herding in La Vega. Many families maintain large herds on meadows which are dispersed, poorly located, and sometimes of low quality (though no cowherd in the alpine barrios lives solely in the branizas). Some families move between two or more barrios, in addition, or spend part of each year on meadows in other municipalities. It is less the herd than the family that suffers. Pasiegos sometimes describe themselves or their neighbors as "living badly": this phrase is applied not only to the recognized poor but also to that minority of families who are so continually on the move that they haven't even a vividora, though they may own substantial land and large herds. These people are working their way toward an easier life, and many have the means to succeed. Tista, for example, only recently came out of the recesses of Pandillo to rent the large ribero meadow where he has a vividora for the first time. One Viaña herder exploited ten fields as a newlywed and recalls the grim business of moving more than thirty times a year; he is now a nearly sedentary herder and large landowner. Such improvements are continually in the making.

---

15. The areas in question, particularly those near the highway, are precisely those where houses are most improved, externally as well as internally for use as vividoras, and are sometimes even new constructions rather than the modified cabañas found elsewhere.

The sedentarization sought by all Pasiegos is fully achieved by a few people with large fortunes in land and cattle, and these people then tend to give up their cattle to become landlords. Similarly in the past, with the form of aparcería or sharecropping documented in the nineteenth century, Pasiegos with sufficient land let others herd cattle on it. There has been a continual process of amassing wealth by people who cease herding and eventually move out of the barrios, either into the Casco or out of Pas altogether. This phenomenon is discussed in chapters 7 and 9; it remains here to examine the less fortunate members of barrio society.

A person's lot in life is influenced not only by the amount and quality of land he or she is bound to inherit, or by the circumstances of his or her spouse in this respect, and not only by the number of animals settled upon him by his parents, but also by the number of siblings who decide to relinquish rather than exploit their inherited shares and thus increase the availability of land for rent at the low rates offered by kinsmen. Two heirs to a small number of inferior meadows may ultimately be as well off as the members of a larger sibling group who between them stand to inherit superior and more numerous meadows. Because of barriers to their mobility in places outside Pas (see chap. 9), Pasiegos have often tended to stay within Pas even when their prospects are worse than were those of their parents, or else they have migrated on a temporary or seasonal basis, making a full life neither within Pas nor outside it. These marginal adaptations were more common a generation or two ago than they are now, but there are still cases today in all of the barrios. The principal adaptation to poverty—and also poverty's principal indicator—among people who make their living within Pas is to turn away from cattle herding and toward the herding of sheep and/or goats. These animals require no meadow, and many of the people who spend their lives herding them have access to little or no meadow.

One man, now in his sixties, grew up entirely in the branizas: his parents made their living herding sheep and goats. As a young adult with no land to inherit, the man moved into the Plaza and apprenticed himself to one of the bakers, and so he lived until his retirement.

Today there are four families in La Vega who keep sheep and no cows. In Pandillo, two women, one a widow and one a spinster, live high up the Pandillo Valley herding only sheep—one keeps about thirty-five and the other eighty. In Yera there are two similar cases, again involving women. One is the widow of a Yera laborer, living with her daughter, her daughter's son, and her own young son: they possess a single meadow on which they live, and they keep twenty sheep. The second woman, a sister-in-law of the first, is an elderly spinster living on her one meadow with her son and his wife and children: the son supports himself by occasional manual labor and as a handyman. There is in this family a history of both illegitimate births and marginal occupations.

What, if any, is the significance of the fact that all four of the above cases involve women living without spouses? There are other widows and spinsters in La Vega who, just like a number of single or widowed men, keep cows. However, those who keep cows, men or women, do not normally live alone; they live with their offspring or with siblings. Although all the tasks of cow-herding and harvesting and most of housekeeping are carried out equally by men and women—the sexual division of labor in Pas is very weak—cowherding and related tasks appear almost always to be carried out by units larger than single individuals, be they composed of women alone, of men alone, or of both sexes, and an adult of either sex may head a unit otherwise composed entirely of children and still herd cows. There are, however, two or three cases of either men or women who live and herd cows alone. Only one of the widows or spinsters who keep sheep lives alone, and we see nothing in the statuses or household sizes of any of them to prevent them, theoretically, from keeping cows. Instead, these four cases appear to represent adaptations to poorly endowed widow- or spinsterhood rather than to those statuses *per se*: men whose lot in life is poor have options in manual labor and commercial apprenticeship—options which are not normally recognized for women. Sheepherding and peddling, on the other hand, are open to women. The four women in question live fairly if not wholly sedentary lives, and this holds advantages over both peddling and cattle transhumance. Finally, I cannot say if any personality factors influence these cases or result from them or what importance the illegitimate births may have for the cases in which they occur: the spinster sheepherder of Pandillo who lives alone is considered strange and a recluse; the other women are viewed as normal socially and marginal only in economic terms.[16]

16. The bearing of children out of wedlock is not looked upon askance. Over 11 percent of the 215 single adult women in recorded geneologies (appendix C) had illegitimate children; many women with natural children eventually marry men other than the fathers of their first children. See chapter 6 for the context in which many conceptions occur.

The two cases where households keep goats are entirely different. Both herds, of about forty goats each, are in Pandillo, kept by full-family households. But one family, though it has twenty cows, also has nine children to feed. The other has only five cows and an invalid male head. These are among the poorest cowherding families of the barrio and, lacking capital, they seem to opt for the more diversified herding of times past—and they keep sheep as well as goats. This is an option which is quite out of style.

The distribution in town of goat and sheep herding (table 8) indicates that all mixed herding is going out of style. Goats are already few in number and kept by a negligible proportion of families. Sheep are more widely kept, but still by only 40 percent of the number of families with cows. These data indicate a pattern in the abandonment of different kinds of herding which is closely parallel to the one already in evidence in San Roque and San Pedro in the eighteenth century.

A life spent in the sheep pastures is by all local standards an unfortunate one: it is spent away from social contacts and beyond the radius of permanent settlement and produces little income. All of barrio culture's strain toward permanent settlement and location in a population nucleus are doubly frustrated in the life of the shepherd or goatherd. Happily, many who have taken up that life have had to do so only temporarily. Though the pattern appears to have disappeared today, perhaps with the existence of more alternatives outside Pas, until fairly recently newlyweds occasionally took up sheep or goat herding until their parents retired and settled property upon them, or until the young couple acquired enough money for pasture rental and the purchase of a cow. Then the young couple descended into the meadowlands and the shifting centers of barrio social life.

FIVE

The Barrio Social Life:
Family and Community
on the Mountainsides

Yes, I know what you mean about cooperative work and joint herding. Other people do them, but not here. Maybe those things have been lost here.

a barrio-born Casco resident

For whores I don't wear mourning.

a barrio man, on hearing read the
sealed will of his mother-in-law, who
had left a prize meadow to another heir

The people who unite to form a barrio household with a persistent identity through time are not necessarily united in daily affairs. We have seen that in some cases, from day to day, different household members may inhabit different cabañas and eat separately, and the membership of such sub-units may itself be in flux. The notion of household thus does not imply continual cohabitation, commensality, or habitation in a particular place. A household in the barrios of Pas is, rather, a group of people who move spatially in the exploitation of the same properties and recognize the same vividora, if they have one. In most cases, since kinship and marriage define access to property, households are groups of kinsmen and affines. But the extent to which a domestic economy is necessarily shared by all household members is still in many cases questionable: while most households are composed of members of single nuclear families (some of these fragmented by death and emigration), many contain "adjunct" members who do not in all cases have jural access to the properties exploited by the household head, do not necessarily share in the full range of agro-pastoral tasks, and are

91

sometimes effectively "boarders" by contract rather than by virtue of their inherent status in a nuclear family.

One group of adjuncts found in many barrio households is often temporary, sometimes only seasonal, and does not enter the official rolls. These are children who board with relatives for some length of time even though their parents usually live in the same barrio. Their cases fall into two types. First, while children are of school age, if their parents care about their school attendance and wish it to continue even when their movements take them out of easy range of the school, children may periodically be sent to stay with relations who are closer to the school. It is my impression that these arrangements are normally between lineal relations (that is, a set of parents and one or another set of their child's grandparents) and less frequently between collaterals (such as a set of parents and the household of a sibling of one of them). There is, I believe, some accompanying notion of recompense due the child's hosts, but this appears to be variable. The second, longer term boarding of children might in some cases be classed as fosterage or quasi-adoption. This is most usual for children whose parents are active herders with a number of offspring and where there are also in the barrio close lineal or collateral relations (as above) whose children are grown or who are childless or, often, who are retired or otherwise sedentary. When economic pressures in the child's natal household encourage and the size of the family labor force permits the removal of the child to another receptive household, this is often effected at an early age and on a relatively permanent basis. The degree of welcome in the receiving household may vary: in some cases, grandparents who were happily retired are constrained to take on grandchildren as an aid to their own children's families even when they would rather not. I have known some who grumbled openly and reluctantly fulfilled what they conceived as a parental and grandparental duty. In other cases, an old or childless couple would rather not be alone and welcomes a youngster or two into its home. In the latter cases, the foster child will probably receive part of the couple's property, especially if they are childless, the collateral relationship notwithstanding. In none of these cases, however, are adoptions legally effected; legal adoption is virtually unknown.

We can regard the nuclear-family household as the basic type in Pas precisely because Pasiegos tend to define as adjuncts any household members who do not stand in the relationship of offspring to a head couple. But it is also true that all household members, including adjuncts, are generally kinsmen or affines rather than unrelated individuals such as servants. Thus, Pasiegos refer to what I call households as "families," for their members are with very few exceptions bound by kinship and affinity.[1]

Pasiegos do not distinguish household and family by separate terms;[2] rather, "the family" in the narrowest sense *is* the household, while "family" in the broader sense refers to all individuals, living or dead, in or out of town, who share common descent and even, for some purposes, just affinity. Descent, as in all of Spain, is reckoned bilaterally, and kin-based associations are ego-focused. Pasiego reckoning and terminology are in no major respects distinct from those in use elsewhere in the country. As in most other areas, the notion of kinship beyond the nuclear family is not bounded in geneaological space,[3] it often extends to individuals linked by affinal ties only,[4] and it does not imply mutual rights or obligations beyond those that bind parents and their children and, secondarily, siblings.[5]

1. There were on the Vega de Pas rolls for 1965 forty-eight households (over 12 percent of all households) with a total of fifty-four adjunct members. Six households had two adjuncts each, the rest had one each. Of the forty-four adjuncts in the thirty-nine households headed by married or widowed people, sixteen were relations of the wife (eight parents, six siblings, one aunt, and one illegitimate child); fourteen were relations of the husband (seven parents, three siblings, two children from prior marriages, one niece, and one aunt); and eleven were lineal descendants of both spouses, in all cases grandchildren, three of them illegitimate; in two of the cases the relationships were either unclear or unspecified; and in only one case was the adjunct a hired hand unrelated to anyone in the family. In the eight households composed either of siblings or unmarried people living without siblings, there were nine adjuncts: three were illegitimate children of spinsters; one was a spinster's nephew; one bachelor housed an aunt, one a male servant, and one a female servant (actually his longtime mistress); and one spinster housed two double first cousins—the three were related both paternally and maternally in a wealthy Casco family marked by a high incidence of spinster- and bachelorhood and consanguineal marriage. The last household was normal in that it was composed of a couple and their children but the anomaly lay in the fact that the woman, a widow, had borne her children out of wedlock in cohabitation with her deceased husband's father. Ten of the forty-eight households with adjunct members were of the Casco rather than the barrios.

2. The word *casa*, or house, is occasionally used in reference to a household group, but it is not in frequent use in any context. This contrasts with its extensive use and more embracing connotation in other parts of Spain (see Lisón 1973a, 1974:61–97).

3. Compare Freeman 1970a; contrast Basque usage described by Douglass 1969.

4. Cf. Freeman 1970a:chap. 5.

5. Compare Pitt-Rivers 1971b and Freeman 1970a; contrast Douglass 1969.

Households are large, but their size is in most cases due to the size of nuclear families and not to the number of adjuncts. Genealogical data on families residing in Vega de Pas show that out of 325 documented households, 61 percent have three or more children, and 34.7 percent have five or more; as many as 6.5 percent of the total have eight children. Families are normally larger in the barrios than in the Casco, and while some people relate this to the need for a large labor force in the barrios, many barrio informants vehemently deny the extent of this need.[6]

Barrio households whose members are related by kinship or marriage (and thus are members of the same family in the term's broader sense) are in no way bound socially to one another. Because there is a high rate of marriage within barrios, most households are related to many others in their barrio, but kinship is, as Pitt-Rivers has told us, "a facultative rather than a firm bond" (1971b:106). This is a familiar truth in Spanish society, but it is accompanied in Pas by a striking absence of any other strong bonds and by a fluidity of social contacts in general.

There is no indigenous strain toward corporacy in Pasiego social organization, or even toward informal cooperative action. In many other Iberian communities, great pains are taken to regulate relations between households both in their personal dealings and in their management of material resources, and this accompanies strongly bonded associations based on village and/or neighborhood membership, and often on the basis of age

6. Many people insist that the costs of rearing large numbers of children are far in excess of the assistance children render to the household effort. Observation seems to corroborate this view. The chief function of large numbers of children might, rather, be sought in another context and perhaps helps to explain the persistence of large families in poor and marginal strata in many societies of the world. Where formal insurance systems and social security are relatively new, perhaps viewed with suspicion, and require cash contributions, children offer crucial support to their parents in old age and in case of need. This is among the explicit provisions of the donation of property in Pas, for example. The couple without children had no way of retiring in this fashion until the Sindicato's pension system went into effect for all farmers and herders. The persistence of large families today may be attributed to a time lag in adjustment to both the pension and health-care systems and the lowered mortality rate, but it is also positively related to the continued absence of property insurance and probable insufficiency of other kinds of benefits. While the obligations of siblings to support each other or their parents in case of loss is extra-legal, it is encouraged by strong sanctions, and there are no similar sanctions to support mutual aid between kinsmen of different nuclear families.

and marital status or other shared characteristics as well. The existence and functions of such groups are usually invested with sociable, ceremonial, and economic importance, and much of public community life centers on the groups' joint actions. Not all communities are tightly corporate to the same degree, and large populations are usually less so than smaller ones, but Pas, by almost all standards, stands at the far end of the continuum.[7] The only corporate administration of resources and collective labor is guided by the ayuntamiento and takes the form of administrative impositions upon otherwise independent households—this is how the community views them.

Beside the realm of formally organized social action lies that of more informal cooperative arrangements. Here, too, the barrio households stand far apart from one another and leave to individual labor, luck, and sentiment the tasks and the resolution of problems which traditionally in many other communities in Spain and elsewhere have been dealt with collectively and defined as matters of community-wide responsibility. Thus, there is in Pas no collective herding of animals of any kind—even of the sheep and goats which elsewhere often form communal flocks, or of cows in the high meadows during the harvest. There is no communal regulation of the use of resources such as timberland and the high meadow and pasturelands.[8] Households may hire services (usually harvesters) on their own initiative; otherwise no one but household members systematically labors on the properties of that household. There are no traditional mechanisms in use ensuring mutual aid and constraining people to contribute for the benefit of others in cases of major loss.[9]

This is not to say that Pasiegos do not help one another, but simply that there are no consistent constraints upon them to do so unless they wish to. In other words, constraints must be conceived in terms of friendship and facultative ties between kins-

7. On corporacy in village life, past and present, and on the social bonds fostered by membership in sharply demarcated small territories, see especially Costa 1898, 1902; Costa et al. 1902; Brandes 1973a; Dias 1948, 1953; Freeman 1968b, 1970a; and Lisón 1971. On comparative questions of population size and corporacy see especially Freeman 1968a and b.

8. On communal herding and/or control of high pasture resources, contrast cases from the Alps (for example, Netting 1976; Friedl 1974; Cole and Wolf 1974) and the Catalan Pyrenees (Stancliffe 1966). On regulation of use of timber land and wood land (for fuel) contrast Kenny 1962a and Freeman 1970a, respectively.

9. Contrast the indigenous insurance systems in other localities which variously cover losses of buildings, crops, and livestock, either formally or informally (see Costa et al. 1902; Freeman 1968b, 1970a).

men rather than as obligations attaching to the relationships of "neighbor" or "kinsman" *per se*; specific categories of relationship do not by their nature alone constrain individuals from different households to cooperate with one another.

The major areas of cooperation are several. I have already mentioned the bees of the past, for husking and shelling maize. Individuals who joined in these efforts were normally drawn from the same pool of friends, neighbors, and kinsmen who today might occasionally lend each other tools and equipment, assist in major house repairs or in the construction of a new house, or exchange the services of a seed bull without charge.[10]

Harvesting involves a smaller pool of potential assistants, for inevitably most of one's friends, neighbors, and kinsmen in town have their own meadows to harvest. Thus, leaving aside hired hands and newlyweds (see chap. 6), those who help in the grass harvest are normally kinsmen who are retired or otherwise in situations in which they have little or none of their own harvesting to do.[11] Not all families enjoy the benefits of such assistance, but it is by no means rare. In some instances, when a sedentary person rents a meadow to a herder who is not a kinsman, the owner assists the tenant in the harvest of that meadow, but only if the two are friends, and not always even then.

A wider than normal pool of assistants is sought in cases of major property loss—when a cabaña burns down or when a significant number of animals is lost (the most frequent destructive agent being lightning). In these cases, the affected owner might actively solicit financial subscriptions from a large number of households to help him recover his losses. While there is no organized response to bring people automatically to another's aid in such cases, losses are often covered by subscription, out of sympathy, from households which may not have strong ties of any kind to the affected person(s). For example, in the year prior to my fieldwork, a herder from the Burgos side, using a meadow in Vega de Pas, lost seventeen cows in an electrical

10. Informants estimate that herders charge their fellows for a bull's services in only about 5 percent of all cases. Access to seed bulls is consistently required by all of the small-scale herders who do not keep their own bulls and by any herder who requires a mate for the cow which has mothered the bull of his own herd.

11. However, this normally excludes kinsmen who are non-herders, resident in the Casco, and were not themselves reared in the barrios: at a generation's remove from the herding life, relations between Casco people and their herder-kinsmen tend to be asymmetrical. Born Casco dwellers do not usually know how to harvest and haul grass, for example, but loss of know-how is not the only cause of the relationship's imbalance (see chaps. 7, 8).

storm. He requested subscription in Vega de Pas and San Pedro as well as elsewhere and his loss was amply repaid. Major property loss is greatly feared, and while people do not buy formal property insurance and cannot count on automatic, village-wide aid, it is clear that Pasiegos assist others in cases of catastrophe and that even a person who is roundly disliked could probably recover the value of lost property. However, not everyone requests support in such cases: the Burgos man was actually criticized for "going out begging" when he allegedly had enough remaining stock to survive his misfortune without enlisting support. I was told of at least two cases in which natives of La Vega suffered losses (the largest involving eight cows and a cabaña) in which the injured parties did not solicit aid and, therefore, received none. Nevertheless, support has normally been rendered in cases where it was solicited. It is, in part, the notion of random catastrophe which inspires genuine mutual support; in cases where individuals or families are continually in bad straits and their situations can be attributed to personal or family characteristics (stupidity, indolence, passivity, and so on) rather than to random fate which might have struck anyone, their plights do not evoke much sympathy or assistance.

Informal social contacts in daily barrio life are confined largely to the immediate neighborhood, or pradera. Thus, daily contacts between any two given families are limited to the periods in which they simultaneously occupy the same pradera. A Pasiego family moves along its transhumance route, gaining and losing neighbors from one pradera to the next. Its contacts with specific neighbors achieve constancy only if and insofar as both of their strategies of sedentarization are operative and successful. However, we should not overestimate the amount of flux in the contacts of even the most transient family, for it does visit its meadows as often as four times yearly and sees each set of neighbors as often, even if different families do not arrive at and depart from a pradera at exactly the same time. Since relations between households are often unfriendly, simultaneous visits to a single pradera can foster as much mutual avoidance among some residents as they do contact between others. The peculiar form of Pasiego transhumance, in which families follow idiosyncratic routes even within a barrio, denies year-round expression to amities and at the same time ensures that specific enmities do not constitute a year-round plague. Transhumance simultaneously curtails both social pleasures and social ills.

Individual barrios, and even the town as a whole, are sufficiently small and stable demographically to partake of all of the qualities of community life. Crucial among these are the quali-

ties described by Arensberg (1961) and Pitt-Rivers (1958) centering upon the facts of families' interaction (as equals or
otherwise) in a shared social arena and their shared historical
knowledge (including memory and myth) of one another. The
strengths of community life are its frustrations as well: there
are on the one hand the social and economic benefits of belonging which are denied outsiders; on the other hand, people become entrapped by others' conceptions of them and are com-
pelled to perform according to specific expectations and by the
general rules, even when they would rather not.

In Pas, long mutual acquaintance and action upon the same
stage, before the same critical audience, foster the same effects
in the realm of social control that they do elsewhere. The primary mechanism of control is, as elsewhere, the flow of information (via gossip) within the community, serving to guide
behavior before the fact and to support or condemn it afterward. In Pas, public opinion has its most obvious force in the
economic sphere—in questions regarding the extension of credit,
the payment of debts, and the control of chicanery in major
dealings. Credit is almost always extended, for no one asks for
more than he can reasonably expect to receive from creditors
who know him; debts are almost always paid for exactly the
same reason; and chicanery is rare in dealings involving goods
of any significant worth. The fact that private dealings become
public knowledge assures that such dealings are usually honest.

If we turn away from the sphere of large transactions and
from the simple question of default in business dealings to examine instead the style of personal interaction, the contrast
with other communities becomes sharper. Relations between
households may everywhere be fraught with suspicion and hostility (see especially Brandes 1973a and Lisón 1973b). Nonetheless, interaction among many Spanish villagers is controlled and
politic (Brandes 1973a, Freeman 1970a), and mutual suspicion
and the guards against other households' retaliation in many
cases has the ultimate effect of cementing the community together (Lisón 1973b). In Pas, where the lack of corporate organization or formal mutual supports for members of the community offer fewer rewards than do other Iberian social settings
(Dias 1948, 1953; Freeman 1970a), the style of interpersonal
dealings is often rude or even overtly hostile. The Pasiego case
shows that the constraints of community living, however active
in important transactions, are not necessarily accompanied
everywhere by the practice of dissemblance between persons
and households.

The volatile nature of interpersonal relations in Pas is obviously more than simply a question of style: the frequency of social ruptures, feuding, and even violence is a symptom of the low efficacy of mechanisms of control beyond the economic sphere. Even further, it brings into question the need for strong social controls in a mobile and fluid setting such as that of the barrios. Like the Alorese (DuBois 1944), for example, the barrio Pasiegos appear to dwell in a social and physical universe which is capable of supporting a high degree of social disharmony, and, correspondingly, social rupture is accepted as a fact of daily life and not discouraged. The anthropologist properly asks not only "Why are social controls not tighter?" but also "Why should they be?" Let us, accordingly, examine some of the factors which systematically provoke social ruptures and perpetuate old ones and review the ways in which these ruptures are absorbed into daily experience.

While major transactions involving goods of worth are normally made honorably, petty chicanery, thievery, and bad-faith pranks are part and parcel of daily dealings. Many barrio women, for example, lament that they cannot keep more household equipment in each of their cabañas. Some have tried to stock each dwelling permanently with such items as chamberpots, mirrors, or kitchen equipment. But it is apparently inevitable that such items are stolen (even from locked cabañas), and families thus learn to content themselves with the use only of the items that they can move around with them. Systematic petty theft from the cabañas is attributed almost exclusively to bands of boys (*niños*) and young men (*mozos*) of the same barrio—the neighbors' sons and sometimes one's own! The marauding activities of youths are widespread on the European scene, past and present; before marriage, youths exercise a certain license to engage in such activities. A Spanish term widely used in reference to groups of young males of certain ages is *rapaces* (sing. *rapaz*), or "rapacious ones."[12] In Pas and in adjacent zones of Santander, youth groups are not corporately organized on a territorial basis; in Pas, rather, they are shifting groups of friends, usually from a single barrio, but the principles of mem-

12. On the activities of such groups in Spain, see especially Costa et al. 1902; Freeman 1968a, 1970a. Elsewhere in Europe, the license given bachelors is especially obvious in parts of modern Hungary (Fél and Hofer 1969), and the age-group organization there is exemplary of a widespread type. See also Boissevain 1965. On the traditional special license of young men in France in particular, see Davis 1971, and on young men as students, see Ariès 1962.

bership and exclusion on the basis of age and/or bachelor status
are not as closely defined as they are elsewhere. In this zone, the
license elsewhere attached to the status of bachelor youths
sometimes extends to, or is extended at will by themselves to
older and married men as well. In some such cases, "license" is
simply group drinking accompanied by the assertive group behavior in public which is elsewhere associated with bachelors
alone.[13] These groups of adults, however, do not normally steal
from or play tricks upon others: this sort of behavior continues
to characterize only the relations between youths and their
elders. On the other hand, adult Pasiego men, as individuals, in
the course of leisure activities practice petty trickery upon each
other within the groups of drinkers and card players. If a bar-
tender places some cash change next to a man after he has paid
for his drink, his companion at bar or table might try to cover
a coin with his elbow and work it into his lap and pocket without being noticed. People who have invited others to a drink or
coffee, or who owe drinks or coffee after losing at cards (where
the stakes are often drinks), may attempt to leave the game and
the tavern without paying. Inevitably, the guests instruct bar-
tenders to place the proper number of items on the host's bill.
The point here is not that individuals get away with much
(though filched coins are not returned and there is a real attempt to escape without paying small bills), but that behavior
between adult men often has an overt taunting quality which is
in marked contrast with the cautious and even overly courteous
manner in which the representatives of different households
may interact in other Spanish communities. While the behavior
of youths toward various households is informed by an opposition of age groups, the behavior of adult men toward each other
reflects the extent to which they conceive themselves and their
households to be opposed and symbolizes the competitive qualities inherent in this opposition. In daily affairs, acts of opposition are held at levels which are accepted as symbolic rather
than substantive offenses, but they always constitute a sub-
stratum of interactions which can become subject to interpretation as true aggressions, and these sometimes lead to lasting
quarrels and physical violence.

Physical violence tends to break out primarily among youths,
and only rarely do injuries result.[14] Many of the fights between

13. Contrast Hungarian men's groups which meet in the stables (*tan-
yázás*) and are private gatherings rather than performances in public
space (Fél and Hofer 1973).
14. However, five of the six homicides of which I have heard involved
adults rather than youths (though one involved youths as well) and grew

youths seem to occur in the May and October periods when herders are concentrated in the valley bottom meadows near the Casco taverns: both liquor consumption and social contact are then greater than at other times of year. Some of these conflicts are resolved without recourse to any authorities; some are dealt with locally by the Civil Guard and/or the alcalde (both are empowered to impose fines and jail disputants); only when there are injuries are cases referred to the court in Villacarriedo. But any of these occurrences, however small, as well as many which involve no violence, lay the foundation for lasting grudges between the opposing parties and sometimes their respective supporters as well. People harboring grudges may explode one day, under further provocation, or antagonisms may lessen with time; but occasionally major antagonisms, such as those resulting from incidents involving violence, fester for years and assume the proportions of feuds between individuals, families, or larger groups of people. It is difficult for an outsider to count accurately the number of ongoing feuds at any given time or to identify the number of parties to a single feud. Opposing constituencies change with time even though the antagonism persists, and apparent lessening of sympathy or changes in loyalty can create new antagonism between people who were formerly allies.

Other disputes which may form the basis for long-term enmities are those arising from disagreements regarding land rental. While conditions of rental are usually indisputably clear (though normally informally contracted), one recurrent problem revolves about the definition of the starting or terminal dates. Although rental arrangements are traditionally made or renewed in autumn and technically become effective with the new year, in January, occupancy in fact begins when the cabaña is empty (*con cabaña limpia*)—that is, when the stored grass from the previous harvest has been consumed, by May. The retoño crop is then at the disposition of the new occupant and the harvests are his to store and use until the following May. Change of occupancy is often a problem, even though it is effected by law and in practice with a year's notice and allows the prior tenant first option on continued occupancy. The out-going tenant is

out of deep antagonisms: in three, the victims and their murderers were close kinsmen. The sixth murder was the sudden act of a half-witted youth who shot a mozo from another town without real provocation, and the case is not properly classified with the other five. Only one of the six murders was recent and occurred while I was in town; the most recent of the other five occurred more than twenty years earlier.

often still using the last of the stored grass while the new renter is ready to move in to exploit the new grass crop. Like all disputes in which no violence occurs, most rental disputes are settled out of court, but a few, upon formal denunciation of one party by another, become the subject of litigation.

Trespassing, too, is a frequent problem: it is often tolerated, and people who wish to avoid trouble carefully skirt the properties of those who are least tolerant. The offense is worst, of course, when it involves animals, and this is infrequent; usually trespassing consists in people's climbing stone walls and crossing others' meadows for quicker access to some location. For the most part, this is tolerated, and most people do it all the time, taking detours only around properties whose owners are known to be particularly sensitive or with whom there are already bad relations. When some other circumstance imperils a relationship, antagonism can be brought to a head by making an issue of trespassing which was previously tolerated. Mutual tolerance or intolerance of trespassing across meadows is a useful index of good and neutral versus bad relationships between parties in other spheres of life. When relations worsen, trespassing ceases, except for cases of accidental entry by animals or (infrequently) willful provocation by their owners.

The office of the justice of the peace in Vega de Pas handles cases of trespass, disturbance of the peace, or other minor damage (*juicios de falta*) if a denunciation by one party leads to litigation and if damages are assessed below the sum of 500 ptas. and no injuries result.[15] Otherwise the litigation is referred to the higher court. Very few conflicts result in formal denunciation: there had been only one case, involving youthful brawling, in the three years prior to my residence in La Vega, though conflicts were and are numerous.

Disputes over rental and land use which normally involve separate households and which are not settled out of court are litigated in *juicios de conciliación*. (Disputes within families, over inheritance, are in the same category and are discussed below.) This type of litigation is more frequent than the *juicio de falta* but is still not commonplace. When disputes cannot be settled out of court, the parties formalize their complaint and each seeks an *hombre bueno*, or referee, to act as negotiator in seeking a settlement. Negotiations take place out of court, but the settlement, or conciliation, is recorded in court and placed on file

15. Two assessors (*peritos*) are named by the justice when a denunciation has been made.

there. If no agreement can be reached, a case is taken to the higher court.

Rental cases, as stated, usually concern dates of changes in occupancy. Water and land-use cases, usually between field neighbors, involve actions by one party which the other alleges to be damaging, such as the alleged diversion of a stream.[16] Disputes on such issues are very frequent; as with *juicios de falta*, it is only the formal litigation which is infrequent. Cases which cannot be settled locally and must be referred to the higher court are rarer yet, and they lodge in the memories of all villagers.

Whether or not they lead to litigation, conflicts both reflect and perpetuate tensions with which people continue to live, often for years. Antagonisms between youths tend to be short-lived: they are considered appropriate to the years before marriage. Antagonisms between individuals who, as adults, represent established households are slower to die. These are very common, and there is no one who does not bear hard feelings—on his own or his family's account—against someone else in town. These circumstances are widely characteristic of town life. Small communities have been likened to theaters in which all inhabitants are both actors and chorus of observers. While the theatrical quality inheres by definition in what we call a community, we, of course, find differences between communities. In Pas we find not one stage but many on which daily life is played, and the level of responsiveness of the actors to their critics—their audience—is relatively low. This is only to repeat what I have said earlier, that the social and physical universe in which Pasiegos dwell supports a high degree of conflict. To this we must add that the way in which social contacts are distributed in time and space helps to minimize the degree to which conflicting parties are constrained by each other's continual presence. In other words, while the level of conflict is high, the possibilities of avoidance are equally so, and Pasiegos live with their many animosities away from constant contact with the people who inspire them.

In this light, it is important to reiterate that, in Pas, the use of public space and of common properties is individual rather than collective: in order to exploit common pasture or wood-

16. There is no artificial irrigation in the Montes de Pas, and this entire realm of potential regulation and dispute is absent. The lush meadows are watered by the abundant surface streams and springs, by heavy dews and fogs, and by frequent rains. The porous soil and karst topography do not facilitate irrigation, nor do climatic circumstances necessitate it.

land or the common water supply, the Pasiego herder is not constrained to cooperate with anyone else. The absence of collective herding traditions has already been mentioned. I should also point out that households' sources of water—either for hauling into the cabañas or for washing laundry—are individually selected and may shift from day to day if circumstances encourage change. Women do not visit as they launder at the streamside unless they choose to, nor do they launder in the same place unless they wish; animals are watered similarly; and thus patterns of water use do not themselves establish, as they do elsewhere, central meeting points where people from different households are forced to interact. Surface water is plentiful; the many streams and arroyos offer lengths of banks for people to use. The nearly ubiquitous role in village social life of the town or barrio fountain is absent in the barrios, for the fountain itself does not exist. There is neither public fountain nor central plaza within the barrios, nor any other public meeting place whose functions in daily communication and social control correspond with those found in Iberia's more nucleated and less transient communities.[17]

The public places in which barrio dwellers have their principal social contact are all located in or near the Casco. Large-scale public interaction occurs primarily in the contexts of trade, ceremonial, or leisure.

Trade, at market, shops, or stock fairs, does not unite herders but simply concentrates their individual activities in a common locus—the Plaza and the fairground, respectively. In the sale of cattle, much significant activity does not even take place on the fairground. Particularly in the months of the largest fairs, in late summer and fall, when most cows are being readied for sale, the town is filled with dealers, who lodge in the Casco or barrios and spend their days visiting prospective sellers. Many sales, if not closed outside the context of the fair, are at least near closure when herders bring animals to the fair to see if the offer of the highest bidding dealer cannot be bettered. If so, the herder may sell to the new high bidder or renegotiate with the dealer with whom he was already dealing. In cases where mutual acquaintance is an important consideration, a herder may sell at the fair to an acquaintance at a lower price than he was previously offered by a dealer whom he knows less well. In any

17. Contrast the importance of central water sources in much of Spain (Pitt-Rivers 1968; Freeman, n.d.).

case, during at least two or three months of the year, livestock dealings burst the confines of the fairgrounds and invade the space of the barrios, increasing some of the tensions between herding families. It is a season when, with the calving of cows which are sooner or later to be sold, the veterinarian is most frequently needed, but now his visits constitute a particular threat. When a delivery presents any difficulty, as, for example, when the placenta is not expelled normally and must be removed surgically, the cow's worth is lowered by nearly a third (by 8,000 to 10,000 ptas. in 1969). Since a herder's enemies as well as his friends are aware when his cow is ready to deliver, he is loathe to have it known that he had to call the veterinarian, for fear that someone will pass this news to the dealers. Thus, the veterinarian makes most of his visits at night, if possible. The season of most frequent calving is also that of close social contact in the valley bottom, following the late summer descent from the branizas, and neighborly relations are complicated by the additional worries of healthy calving and maintenance of high asking prices for cows. Trade, whether its locus is in public or private space, is never an activity which promotes harmony in the herding community.

Despite the divisive character of trading activities, fairs themselves are the events which most closely approximate community-wide festivals. Even outside the peak season, they bring together in a central place people who are otherwise out of contact, at least temporarily, and all fairs have the quality of secular fiestas. People attend fairs even when they have no business to transact, and they use the occasion to eat, drink, and socialize in the taverns of the Plaza. It is from fairs that taverns gain their major income and at fairs that herders spend more consistently and in greater annual amounts than in any other leisurely or ceremonial context.

Certain fairs are traditionally associated with saints' days, though the modern schedule simply places stock fairs on the ninth, nineteenth, and twenty-ninth of each month. Today, the last fair of September, which coincides with the final descent from the branizas, marks the beginning of the peak sale season. Though this falls on San Miguel, 29 September, it is not universally associated with the saint. Later in the peak season, 20–21 November traditionally saw the celebration of a two-day "fiesta of the ferial"—a stock fair, exposition, and *romería* (outdoor festival).[18] The entire month of November is called "the month

18. Romerías are most often celebrated at shrines or at least associated with occasions of religious significance. There is in this case no shrine

of San Andrés" for the day of the apostle on 30 November. (The day of San Andrés Avelino on 10 November is not important.) The thirtieth is the traditional date for the payment of rents and the finalization of other contracts for the coming year.[19] In addition to the continued importance of the thirtieth and the identification of the entire month as that of a saint, the month of November today is marked only by the celebration of three of the season's important fairs, but there is no celebration of the saint himself, and none of the fair days (or other days in the month) is associated with an important mass. Likewise, March is called "the month of San José," and the fair on that date (19 March) is a large and important one, marking the secondary calving season in Spring, but there is no further association of the fair with the saint or with church celebration.

Indeed, none of the important collective events of barrio life is oriented primarily toward celebration in church, and I shall turn now to place the discussion of stock fairs in the larger context of the ceremonial life of Vega de Pas and, specifically, the barrios. The official major fiestas of Vega de Pas are the Ascension of the Virgin (usually in May), Corpus Cristi (usually in June), and the day of the local virgin, Santa María de la Vega, on 8 September, the day dedicated to the celebration of local virgins throughout Spain. These three dates are important throughout Spain. In many instances, their elevation to major status comes through parish priests and in deference to Church preference. Saints' days of some traditional importance in Vega de Pas are San Isidro (15 May) and San Antonio (13 June), and these appear to have been replaced by the celebrations of the Ascension and Corpus Cristi, respectively, as fiestas which fall in the same periods and sometimes even on the same dates. Barrio people do not consistently attend masses on these dates, although it is customary for many to confess on the Ascension and for first communions to be celebrated then. The afternoon and evening dances held on those dates, however, are traditionally attended by barrio people in great numbers. Some informants mention these as the principal dates, aside from fairs,

---

and—at least today—no vestige of association with a saint, except for the fact that the entire month of November is associated with the apostle San Andrés.

19. Autumn is traditionally the crucial season for closure of contracts and rent payment: important dates in various other regions of Spain include San Miguel (29 September), San Martín (11 November), Todos los Santos (1 November), and Santo Tomás (21 December).

for coming down to the Plaza, and they refer primarily to the dances and not to the masses and processions.

Even the saints' days which appear to have had some importance in the past seem to have passed from fashion. San Antonio was mentioned by Madoz in 1849 along with Nuestra Señora [Santa María] de la Vega and the Cármen, to whom the chapel in La Grueba is dedicated. San Antonio is no longer celebrated, though the other two are (the Cármen on 16 July locally in La Grueba only). In the Casco, the schoolhouse is said formerly to have been a chapel dedicated to San Antonio, and the Casco neighborhood in which it stands is known as the barrio de San Antonio. But the saint's day itself is not observed at all today, though there is a statue of San Antonio in the Plaza church and the church archive holds accounts of a cult dedicated to him in the seventeenth and eighteenth centuries. Similarly, we know, Santa María del Porrato is no longer honored in Viaña, nor does her chapel stand (see chap. 1). San Isidro was not mentioned by Madoz and appears to have come into fashion not earlier than the early years of the twentieth century; there is still a procession of the saint on 15 May but there are no associated festivities. The barrio of Pandillo celebrates, on 8 May, the Virgin of the Desamparados. The celebration, which does not have high attendance even within the barrio, takes place near the schoolhouse, but there is no shrine there. There are in the outskirts of the Casco, at the entrance from Pandillo, at least two wall niches which once housed images of saints or virgins and where, at least in one case, funeral processions normally halted on their route into the Plaza. However, neither niche now houses an image and there is little recollection of which saints were there.

It seems reasonable to generalize from these facts and from barrio behavior that foci of collective religious identity in barrio life (shrines and saints) are not usually historically very stable nor, at least today, is their role very important. The object of general devotion (to the extent that any devotion is general) which has been most stable historically is Santa María de la Vega, to whom La Vega's first church, like the present one, was dedicated and from whom the town originally took its name. Even in this case, the devotion is more general in the Casco than in the barrios. An object of equal if not greater personal devotion is the Virgin of Valbanuz, whose shrine in the Valbanuz sector of Selaya municipality has become, since the first apparition, the site of a massive romería (on 15 August) attended by many Pasiegos. Valbanuz, however, draws devotés from a wide region within the province; within Pas, devotion is far from universal.[20]

Private devotions themselves are far from universal in the barrios, and in no case should their objects be confused with the foci of collective (territorial) identity to which I have referred. The latter, while they have a shifting existence in Pas, are not the objects of the pronounced collective observances that they are elsewhere, and their general lack of importance appears to correlate with the relative unimportance of collective activity of other kinds.[21]

Dates whose importance is universally recognized in barrio culture—those of the fairs—have minimal relationship to symbols of religious importance. It is true that important fairs occur near the vernal and autumnal equinoxes (March and September) and further that the peak fair season occupies almost the entire period between the vernal equinox and the winter solstice (from September to December), and there may well be archaic religious significance in this—but, in fact, it is archaic and should not be overemphasized. On the other hand, the importance of the two solstices along with the equinoxes is still reflected in the barrio traditions of specially naming the solstice months— San Juan (June) and Navidad (Christmas; December)—as well as the equinox month of March (but seldom September). San José and the Ascension in March, like Christmas Day (Navidad), still occasion special baking and household celebration in the barrios. San Juan (24 June) is still important as Midsummer's Day and is the subject of many beliefs, and Juan, or Juan Bautista, also ranks among the most popular male names.[22]

Ceremonial events of another order which bring barrio families together are weddings and funerals. Collective observation

20. Valbanuz is frequently designated in the province as "the virgin of the Pasiegos," but this is simply another example of the application by outsiders of the term "Pasiego" to rural zones outside the Montes de Pas (see chap. 1). Pasiegos do not claim the virgin as "their own." In Vega de Pas today, devotion to Valbanuz is said to be most concentrated among Pandillo people, but it is far from universal there or elsewhere in town.

21. For the opposite case—the correlation of intensive observance of collective symbols with tight corporate social organization—see Freeman 1968b. For an intermediate case, and a study whose author has paid unique attention to the nature of personal devotion in a context where symbols of collective identity are also important, see Christian 1972.

22. For example, many subscribe to the belief that people—especially children—may be cured of hernias if, on the eve of San Juan, at midnight, the afflicted individual, naked, is passed by two men named Juan Bautista through a split oak sapling. (*cajigo*).

of marriages and deaths also occurs in public space in or near the Casco and outside the barrios.

Barrio weddings today have lost much of their folk quality and simply involve a heavy meal (and sometimes dancing) in one of the Casco taverns after the wedding mass.[23] Deaths evoke a show of support for the bereaved family on the part of friends and close kin, and this begins with the vigil during terminal stages of illness or with the vigil over the corpse from the time of death until burial. Today burials involve the gathering of the funeral party at the cabaña of the deceased (corpses are usually brought to conveniently located cabañas even if death occurs farther away), procession with the coffin to the church for the burial mass, and further procession to the cemetery for burial.[24] Traditionally, the bereaved family hosted a special banquet after the burial. This was served in one of the taverns and consisted of traditional foods (salt-cod with rice, or veal stew; fresh curd; wheat bread; and wine); funeral banquets were among the largest feasts of traditional barrio social life, ranking with weddings in scale and in the investment involved. Such banquets are no longer held and only weddings remain. However, neither traditional weddings nor funerals appear to have involved whole barrios or entire territorial collectivities of any kind, even on a symbolic level; there was and is neither collective representation at the associated masses nor a token attempt on the part of the hosts to include the entire collectivity in the subsequent festivities.[25]

23. In the past, wedding meals were typically served in a cabaña of the bride's family, and the intrusion of the wedding meal into public space is quite recent, probably reflecting the increasing amount of cash available for such expenditures.

24. Until about a century ago, people were interred under the church floor. No living informant remembers seeing this or can offer enough detail to permit comparison, for example, with the Vizcayan practices reported by Douglass (1969).

25. Contrast Freeman 1970a: chap. 4. Lasaga Larreta, in 1865 and 1934, refers to a variety of funerary customs in Pas and adjacent zones (all of which he considers "Pasiego"). Among these is the offering of wine and bread or biscuits "to the public" at the church door after a burial. Depending on the exact nature of "the public," this tradition might have paralleled those of other regions in which some token of participation is extended to a collectivity larger than the funeral party itself. However, no one I asked recalled such a practice, though Lasaga's latest reference was to the year 1902. (His 1934 article is the publication of a previously unpublished manuscript dated 1902.) Lasaga also made reference in both works to the heartier meals offered in the taverns by bereaved families and implies (1865) that it was primarily men who attended these, wearing capes, while women returned home after burials.

Wedding and funeral parties alike are composed only of friends and kinsmen who are able to attend (or, in the case of weddings, those who are invited) and who wish to: even attendance at a burial is not considered obligatory for a kinsman who is not on good terms with the bereaved family, but general sentiment often outweighs personal animosities in such cases, and most close kinsmen who live in town attend the funeral of a deceased relative. Here, kinship ties to the deceased are active collaterally in ego's generation at least through first cousins and also especially among collaterals in ascending generations.[26] Active ties can unite more distant kin as well, but primarily by choice and not systematically.

Baptisms and first communions are celebrated by barrio families primarily in the church and there is no systematic occurrence of entertaining after the associated ritual.[27]

As I have said, the objects of private devotions vary, as does the incidence itself of personal devotion. The people with most obvious active devotion, both men and women, appear to have overarching religiosity as well as more particular devotions to specific saints or virgins. However, the majority of these active devotés are to be found in and around the Casco; the isolation and transiency of barrio life seem to discourage overt expressions of devotion if not also its essence. All barrio dwellers are baptised and all receive sufficient instruction—at least today, and primarily through the schoolteachers—to become communicants by the ages of six to eight years, but the exigencies of the herder's life do not leave much opportunity for elaborate observance or involvement in church activities. Retired and sedentary herders within the barrios do not differentiate themselves from active, transhumant herders in the ways in which they spend time. They neither develop new forms of leisure nor spend more time in the Casco than is customary for other barrio herders—the church, then, is not a center for any sector of barrio society.[28] The barrios have none of the pagan aspect which some local writers have tried to see there, but it is also certain that they do not participate in organized religious activity or the

26. I would not offer a more definitive statement on the limits of kinship in funeral attendance; since fixed limits are not recognized, the ties which are activated are variable, and I did not study this variation in detail.

27. Modern treatment of first communions, usually celebrated en masse once a year, is interesting for other reasons and is discussed in chapter 8.

28. The maintenance of uniformity in barrio life-style is explored in chapter 8.

celebration of symbols of collectivity to the extent which characterizes more sedentary and nucleated populations.[29]

Where in traditional Spanish village life leisure and ceremonial often converge, they generally do not in Pas. Leisure is principally associated with stock fairs rather than with other collective events of the social life, and otherwise leisure is pursued privately, either in public or private space. In the confines of the barrios, leisure is pursued entirely in private space—that is, in the cabañas. Daily life in the cabañas was traditionally punctuated by *funciones*, or private gatherings, some of them arising from husking or shelling bees and the like, and by weddings. Today, with the disappearance of most private gatherings and the removal of weddings to the Casco, there is only informal visiting among friends and the evening visiting related to courtship, which is more fully described in chap. 6.

Visiting is casual and can be frequent for some people; for others it is rare, and there are a number of people in the barrios, usually living alone rather than in families, who are regarded by their fellows as truly reclusive. Herders say that they generally cultivate closer relationships with their neighbors in the branizas, for the need for mutual support is greater in isolated praderas than farther down. Otherwise, even gregarious people may spend entire days without visiting, and the pace of a single

29. There is some tendency—particularly with such writers as Lasaga—to seek in Pas in traditions like funeral banquets a larger pre-Christian residue than exists outside Pas. In actuality, many of the "pre-Christian" elements are very widespread in the North (as are funeral banquets) and elsewhere. The Pasiego zone is distinct only in that all observances are attenuated in form and not in that pre-Christian beliefs are less thoroughly amalgamated with Catholic practice than elsewhere. In 1952, Miguel Cascón edited and published a manuscript of Luís Valdivia, written probably between 1618 and 1624, reporting a Jesuit mission to the Montes de Pas prior to that period (Cascón 1952:21–22). The object here was simply to preach the doctrine rather than to convert persons to the faith: Pas was already apparently fully Christian, even as a marginal zone in a larger area that itself was only Christianized between the sixth and ninth centuries at the earliest (J. González Echegaray 1969). Thus, the Valdivia manuscript says simply that the Pasiegos "were gathered to hear sermons of the Christian doctrine, of which many of them had had no news for many years" (Cascón 1952:22). However, Valdivia refers to the fact that prior to meetings in two churches, meetings were held "in a cabaña or next to a great oak" and that Pasiegos commemorated the death of one of the early missionaries at an altar raised next to the oak. This invites special emphasis on the pre-Christian importance of trees, but the Pasiego traditions today are less distinct in this feature than are traditions of many other Spanish populations whose ceremonial life in general is richer than that of Pas.

family's interactions with others over the years varies from
pradera to pradera, depending on who the neighbors in residence may be and on the proximity to special friends (including
kin) in nearby praderas. Contacts across household lines within
praderas are most frequent among children. The pursuit of companionship from one pradera to another, usually within single
barrios, is most common among unmarried youth of courting
age (beginning at age sixteen or seventeen), and it is usually
young men rather than young women who travel through barrio
space exclusively for social ends; young women travel freely (and
also extensively) in the context of work but stay at home to receive social visits from young men.

Friendship often binds young people whose parents do not
get along together. Similarly, there may be at least casual friendship between women whose husbands do not get along, or vice
versa. In other words, at some level enmities, at least the less
serious ones, are dyadic and not necessarily shared by all members of the concerned households. In the case of two adults, one
of whom has bad relations with the spouse of the other or
whose spouses do not get along together, casual friendship is
possible between the two primarily because adult men and
women pursue many of their leisure activities separately. Thus,
men may cement friendships with other men, and women with
other women, even in the face of animosities between their
spouses. There are also cases in which cross-sex relations may
be cordial—for example, between an adult man and a woman of
another family who is on bad terms with the first man's wife—
but cordiality between married adults of opposite sex is never
expressed in the common pursuit of leisure or visiting and is
confined to exchanges upon chance meeting in public space.
When adults of opposite sex visit in private space, it is always
in the company of their spouses: married couples do occasionally visit other cabañas in the late afternoon or evening.

The pursuit of leisure by adult women is generally confined to
visiting in the cabañas or to such activities as laundering or
going shopping together. The demands of caring for children
and cattle and the preparation of meals and other household
tasks typically occupy women's time and discourage extensive
socializing. While men may perform all of the household tasks,
cook, and care for both livestock and children—standard household management, child-care, and often much caring for cattle
as well are frequently left by married men to their wives while
they themselves gather to play cards.

Men socialize in large groups in the taverns of the Casco. Their leisure hours typically begin after the noon meal, and perhaps after a brief siesta, sometime after one or two in the afternoon. Most return home in the late afternoon, around milking time, and barrio families eat their supper and retire early, especially in areas without electricity. Many men enjoy their afternoon leisure even when they must walk to the Casco from considerable distances. Men who live either permanently or momentarily close to the Casco may return there after supper to pass some time with their cronies. When distances are too great, daily socializing is curtailed and gatherings take place primarily on fair days.

Within the larger praderas there may be enough friends to gather, but the tendency is for men to prefer to gather in public places away from the cabañas. Most of the largest praderas are in any case not very distant from a public establishment, while many of the distant praderas are not large enough to support more than casual, small-scale visiting. Whether men spent more of their leisure time in the barrios in an era when they had less spending money is hard to say, for the Casco has been important as a place of enjoyment for as long as anyone can remember.

Many Casco tavern keepers in the past maintained bowling greens on their premises to attract patrons. Bowling (skittles) was a male sport associated with tavern visits. It is not played frequently today, though one Casco restaurant still maintains a green which is in occasional use. Young men as well as their fathers today spend more time (and money) inside the taverns and do not seek the kind of entertainment that bowling provided.

Traditionally there was weekly dancing in the Casco, sometimes outdoors in front of the church or inside one of the taverns. Today, in accord with the law of local governance, one of the tavern keepers holds the municipal franchise for maintaining a large hall for the weekly dance; previously, at least at some periods, there were at least two dances. Dances were and are popular with barrio youth and are the chief social functions for which young girls come to the Plaza; even some married couples attend when they can. Three or four dances a year are larger than usual: they are the afternoon dances on fiesta days, and attendance from all sectors of town is high. For these special dances, in the past, musicians paid by the ayuntamiento performed on pipe and drum (*pitu y tambor*). Folklorists identify these as the chief traditional instruments of Pasiego music-making. In actuality, they were associated with a few fiestas only, and weekly dances, weddings, and private gatherings in the cabañas all normally featured only singing and tambourines, played by the girls present. Today, ballroom dancing has replaced the old, individual dance style, and a hired dance band usually plays even for the weekly dances. Barrio and Casco youth alike attend the dances, which, like stock fairs, cease only during the harvest season.

For barrio people, the pleasures offered by the Casco cease when their periodic moves take them beyond the range of easy access. Young people, especially men, continue to be most mobile in seeking out social contacts, while others in their families keep company largely with one another.

Within households as well as between them, relationships may be strained or overtly hostile, and people do not feel constrained to maintain the appearance of family harmony where there is none. Just as bad relations between households are mitigated by spatial and temporal remove, so the spatial distribution of a single family's holdings permits members to escape one another when pressures mount. We have seen that members of seemingly sedentary families are in fact separated at times by the needs of their herds. So, too, in transhumant families, moves are frequently undertaken in stages and entail momentary separation of family members. Sometimes parents will move down from the branizas with the main herd when the grass is almost consumed and an older child or two are charged to stay with a few animals for one or two days until the remaining grass is gone. The general weakness of the division of labor by sex and age, combined with the fact that most people are experienced in fending for themselves at least periodically, makes individuals potentially independent from an early age. This potential independence is actualized not only when circumstances require but also when tempers flare. Again, the anthropologist must ask not only why households do not achieve greater unity but also why they should be expected to. We find various examples of husbands and wives who form a single official household but take the opportunity not to cohabit regularly; of groups of adult siblings who maintain separate hearths while exploiting the same holdings; and of individuals who, in temporary pique, stalk out of their households to seek solitude in another of the family cabañas, even though they may be constrained to return in the daylight hours to perform their share of the day's tasks. In other words, people make regular use of the dispersed nature of the holding and of its number of cabañas to get away from each other when they so desire.

It is primarily property—land—which tears families apart just as it holds them together. The field of relations between individual family members and between theirs and certain other households is dominated not only by concerns of estate partition but also by the problems of welding new estates—that is, of making marriages. The two sets of related concerns are consciously regarded as dominating social relations in the barrios, and the bulk of bad relations within families and between related households is attributed to "troubles" arising in one or the other of these areas.

Spouses are dependent on each other for what the other has brought to the holding and continues to contribute to it, and children are dependent upon their parents' holding. These dependencies promote both cohesion and resentment. The fact that the holding will undergo division at some future time lives in the minds of adults and children alike. Pasiegos are hardly unusual in this, but they are also perhaps more dependent upon their land than many other rural peoples in modern Spain and elsewhere who do not suffer from the problems of illiteracy and ethnic stigma and who, as a result, find the outside world more welcoming as a place in which to seek a living away from the soil. In Pas, the possession of a single poor meadow may permit a person to eke out a living and keep him from being forced permanently into the difficult and sometimes hostile world outside.

The transmission of property is governed by the Spanish civil code (Ministerio de Justicia 1968) and the Castilian customary law which the code most closely reflects. This permits the free disposition of one-third of a person's inherited property, while two-thirds (the *legítima*) must be transmitted to the legal heirs. Only one-half of the legítima need be divided equally among the heirs, and the other half may go to favored heirs. By law, men and women inherit equally. In Pas, they inherit equally various types of property; there is no tradition of transmitting property of a specific kind, such as land, to heirs of one sex in particular. A woman may bring into her marriage as much land as her husband does, or more. When a couple has no surviving children or grandchildren, the bulk of each spouse's estate reverts at his or her death to his or her surviving parents or, lacking these, to siblings, though something other than the legítima may be willed to chosen heirs in cases of quasi-adoption. Pasiegos tend to handle earnings (*gananciales*) accruing to their inherited estates as part of the latter, though this is not required by law. The number of parties interested in the disposition of an estate, having either blood or affinal ties to its owners, may be very large.

In the barrios, most married couples with children, especially when some of the children are herders in Pas, transmit the bulk of their estates to their heirs before their deaths in the tradition of the "donations" which I have mentioned. In other instances, as, for example, when the terms of donation cannot be agreed upon, or when none of the heirs is a herder in Pas and retired parents rent their meadows to non-heirs, estates may not be transmitted until the death of one or both parents. Often in Pas, as elsewhere in Spain (see Freeman 1970a), a widowed person will relinquish his or her control of an estate to the heirs by means of a contractual arrangement which is essentially the same as the "donation."

The equality of shares in an estate is of great concern regardless of the form of the estate's transmission. Extraordinary expenditures in the name of one child, such as educational expenses, will be deducted from his share; inequalities in the marriage portions (see below) given different offspring are also usually equalized in this way. If both parents are deceased before title is transmitted and there is no testament willing specifically otherwise, the heirs as a group are themselves responsible for combining all types of property into lots whose equivalence is agreed upon by all. The distribution of the lots among the heirs is then normally accomplished by lottery, a tradition which is widespread in Europe, unless heirs agree privately without the aid of this mechanism. In some instances the bulk of an estate is divided in this way even though a testament directs the disposition of a few specific pieces of property. For example, individuals sometimes bequeath something extra (land and sometimes livestock) to unmarried daughters, mentally or physically disabled children, or favored individuals who would otherwise inherit nothing and who have perhaps rendered some service to the deceased in his lifetime. Extra bequests to heirs are known as *mejoras* (lit. betterments) and tend to be reserved as mentioned for the disabled or for single females. Groups of heirs often agree that specific co-heirs should receive mejoras, though this may also be cause for contention. When parents are alive to argue the case with contentious heirs, mejoras of any kind may be problematic and are usually confined to the kinds of cases mentioned. In general, there may be more contention when parents are alive and susceptible to persuasion, and arrangements to donate estates may drag on for long periods.

The question which normally gives rise to dispute is the true equivalence of so-called equal shares, and this is a common issue in cases both of donation and of transmission after the owner's death. Meadows are not usually divided physically; rather, the total number of meadows in the estate is divided among the heirs, and so some lots contain worse or smaller meadows, whose defects are compensated by the addition of cash and other items. Lots which have equivalent cash value are not, however, valued alike by their potential owners. For non-herders, the issues are less crucial, but herding heirs must also evaluate their potential lots in terms of how well or badly certain meadows fit into their strategies of sedentarization: the competition for meadows which are in these terms choice may be very keen. These problems of assessment plague all sibling groups as they face the partition of an estate, regardless whether their parents are dead or alive. No partition is accomplished without hard feelings. Worse, some must be negotiated locally in *juicios de conciliación*. A few, oft-cited cases are taken to higher courts, and in these it is not uncommon that the cost of legal fees ultimately consumes the better part of the contested estate: prime meadows are auctioned to raise money for legal debts and everybody loses.

The only manner in which owners occasionally avoid bringing the issues before the heirs is by effecting a partition in sealed testament. This may involve only rough equivalence of lots, but enough to meet the demands of law, and takes the bulk of the matter of estate division entirely out of the hands of the heirs. This is not frequent among herders, who prefer to donate estates in their lifetime, nor does this method prevent contention among co-heirs. Co-heirs almost always adopt something of a contentious stance toward one another, especially as their parents age and economic pressures in their own, expanding families mount. Relations within households and between related ones are ridden with these schisms, waxing before partition and later gradually waning: parents and their children, siblings, kinsmen whose households are in any way affected—all are caught in their grip.

The making of marriages also creates both new schisms and new unities. Property is a prime concern and affection is not, and people sometimes enter voluntarily into matches deemed important for them while their affections lie elsewhere. The *mariage de convenance* is a thing of the past in many parts of rural Spain, but it still lives in Pas. I shall leave the question of barrio courtship style for the next chapter, but here I should say that courtship activities may involve a girl with more than one man over time and that marriage is not always the result of long courting. I have recorded cases in which girls who had long been courted by particular men abruptly decided to marry men who had been courting only briefly and announced banns with the latter to the complete surprise of the former. Family pressures as well as individual volition govern such actions.

There are no matchmakers or go-betweens in Pas, and the atmosphere in which marriages are made is somewhat anarchic, particularly because there is no single firm basis for assessing potential matches. Affection can be important, other things being equal, and parents do not have the sole recognized authority in choosing marriage partners. Young people can indeed rebel against their parents' preferences and cause their matchmaking attempts to fail, but elopement is nonetheless rare because affection is not an over-riding consideration, especially if it threatens to jeopardize the marriage portion which children expect from their parents. But since the marriage portion is in large part negotiated after rather than before marriage, the question of jeopardizing it is moot: there is always room for persuasion.

The marriage portion, consisting of livestock and the opportunity for meadow rental, is discussed before banns are announced, but its full extent is not determined, nor is it handed over to a new couple, until they have completed the traditional term of co-residence in one or both of the parental households (see chap. 6).[30] The marriage portion is given by parents to male and female children alike (with inequalities recorded for later adjustment when the parental estate is partitioned) and becomes the joint property of the new couple when they establish themselves as an independent unit. There are frequently differences in the amounts brought in by the two spouses, but these imbalances are usually foreseen before the match is made and are accepted by all parties, though sometimes resentfully. No party

30. The marriage portion is called *dote*, which is often translated as dowry, but I have avoided this English term because it is so often associated with property settled on the bride alone by her family. The marriage portion is not to be confused with the *ajuar*, or trousseau, which only the bride brings with her and which consists in domestic equipment —primarily bedding and other linens, sometimes also the bed, and sometimes kitchen equipment. The minimal trousseau in Spain generally includes both bed and bedding; in the Pas barrios, where furniture has little importance, the minimal trousseau contains bedclothes, including blankets, and a mattress, but it may contain the bed and other items as well.

—neither set of parents nor the contracting spouses—has total control in questions of the marriage portion. A couple marries without firm parental commitments regarding their portions. By the time a couple establishes itself independently, some months after the wedding, one set of parents may for some reason give a smaller portion than was originally expected of them, and this can cause open ruptures between themselves and the new couple and also the other pair of parents, who feel cheated on behalf of their child. Hard feelings thus arise after as well as before weddings, since the economic adjustments focusing on the new couple extend over this time. There is often sufficient antagonism before a wedding to influence the new couple's choice of the parental household in which to co-reside.[31] The antagonism may result from negotiations or be considerably older: in any case, informants define "how people get along" as an important factor determining the locus of co-residence, and not occasionally it is a newlywed and his or her own parents, rather than in-laws, who prefer to live under different roofs.[32]

The fact that marriages are often more firmly based in economics than in mutual affection helps to account for the frequency of effective separation of spouses. Since, in addition, each owns property, spouses may differ on details of marriage settlements for their own children and may effect property transmission separately. This creates in some households camps of opposed sentiment, dividing family opinion and promoting the disharmony which has set its stamp on barrio social life.[33]

31. Some statistics of co-residence are given in chapter 6.

32. Other considerations are also important influences on residence decisions—principally herd size and the size of the labor force in the respective households. The variety of considerations is parallel to those first outlined by Pehrson for the Lapps (1954).

33. The foregoing discussion of social control contains no reference to the figure of the witch (*bruja*) because witches, as defined in Pas, are quite peripheral to questions of harmony and disharmony in the community at large. Their existence should be mentioned, however. Locally, the bruja is a woman whose casual curses, in contrast to those of other citizens, are believed likely to be effective, but this belief is not universal among barrio people. Barrio sceptics assign the bruja's reputation to historical coincidence: if in ire a woman once said "may your cow break a leg" and subsequently the other's cow did suffer an accident, believers began to fear the woman's curses. Cursing in itself is not uncommon and is regarded in most cases as a simple expression of anger without causative power. However, where a woman's curses are reputed to be effective, people deal with her cautiously so as not to incite her ire: a bruja's trespassing, for example, is fully tolerated, even with animals, and conflict that might erupt with other people is here carefully avoided. I knew of only two women who in some quarters were believed to be brujas—

and, indeed, the qualities of the bruja are attributed only to women. Both women lived in Pandillo. One was the spinster-recluse living high up the valley with her large flock of sheep; the other was the widowed mother of a large family, settled in an attractive pradera and apparently fully participant in its social life and in the lives of her children and their families: there seemed to be little similarity between the women except, as was said, that their curses had been known to have effect. The local notion of *brujería* in the first case helped primarily to classify and deal with mild deviance; in the second case, the notion counseled caution in personal dealings but did not appear to affect seriously the social personality or relationships of the alleged witch. Local notions exist alongside the widespread but far from universal belief that certain individuals have efficacy in the realms of curing and clairvoyance: some Pasiegos have been known to patronize male or female professional witches, as curers and seers, but these are located outside Pas, serve patrons from large areas, and have only minute followings in any single community. Their effects in the realm of local social dynamics are nil.

SIX

The Barrio Social Life:
Elements of a Stereotype

If in their ancient costume, as we have seen, they were perfectly distinct from the inhabitants of neighboring zones, so they were no less distinct in their customs.

Escagedo Salmón 1921

Upon the whole, had I daughters now, I would venture to let them bundle on the bed, or even on the sofa, after a proper education, sooner than adopt the Spanish mode of forcing young people to prattle only before the lady's mother the chit-chat of artless lovers.

The Rev. Samuel Peters, cited by Stiles (1934)

The cabaña, the barrio home, lends to the distinctiveness of barrio dwellers, which marks them in material as well as in other ways. Folklorists have made much of the material distinctions, and because they and their effects on personal bearing and habits, along with other barrio traditions, also have great semiotic importance within Pas, they indeed require exploration.

The most distinctive feature of the slate-roofed, two-storied cabaña is the proximity of people and animals within it. Living quarters for animals and people are often, in Spain, contained within the same structure, but stable and home are normally well insulated from one another. In the cabaña, by contrast, the coexistence is deliberately close. Humans depend upon the warmth, rising through the floor timbers, of the animals beneath them. The animals' noises rise likewise, and humans are sensitive to them as to children crying. Further, the family's living space is shared with the animals' food supply—the stored grass—and hence the amount of space available for the family's use varies with the season, being least in summer just after the harvest and increasing as the grass is consumed during the year.

Thus, accumulation of household goods and personal effects is affected not only by the demands of transhumance but also by a cyclical diminution of storage space simultaneously in all cabañas.

There is probably no active herding family save the most sedentary few which has bedsteads in all of its cabañas, so for almost everyone, at some periods, the cows' food supply serves as bedding. The accumulation of furnishings varies directly with the degree of sedentarization and, among fully transhumant families, with the extent to which they are able to enjoy a vividora, which becomes the only cabaña to contain room partitions, perhaps, and more furnishings, as well as more furnishings of standard style. The only furnishings to be found in the non-vividoras might be the low, three-legged milking stools (*tajos*) fashioned at home out of sections of tree trunk, and these often double as tables (see plates 4, 7). Some but by no means all cabañas may contain a low rectangular table or a standard-sized chair or two. Standard-sized chairs and bedframes are not made at home, and it is frequent that cabañas contain nothing but homemade furniture, often nothing more than a few stools.

Equipment other than furniture is similarly kept at a minimum. The few implements involved in cleaning stables and collecting and spreading manure are normally homemade (they are wooden) and are made in sufficient numbers that they are left behind in each cabaña. The same may be true of wooden rakes. Scythes (neither blades nor their wooden handles are homemade) are normally transported from one cabaña to the next during the season of their use. Likewise, cooking and eating utensils and milk cans are moved with the family, along with bedding supplies (blankets and sometimes sheets) and clothing. Accordingly, all of these items are kept at a minimum. When I moved into a braniza cabaña with a family of five, we shared our food from two soup plates. The six of us made use of five spoons, two sharp knives, and one fork, which had been borrowed in my honor. With the exception of two of the children, we each had a drinking mug.[1] In the way of cooking utensils, there were in use two (or possibly three) deep pots, for stews and for heating milk and water, and one frying pan.

1. A note on commensal styles which are general to the Spanish countryside (and which intrude into some urban situations as well) should help to place these data in their proper context. Many of these styles were even more widespread formerly than they are today. Certain foods are normally eaten from a common plate—examples are paella and other rice dishes, some legume dishes, salads, and dishes based on breadcrumbs

In cabañas where people sleep in the grass, only blankets are absolutely necessary. However, many people take care to make "beds" as correctly as possible—following national norms—with bottom and top sheets as well as blankets, and with extra piles of grass forming "pillows" at the head (plate 5). Degrees of concern for Spanish correctness may vary from person to person and family to family, as do standards of cleanliness and attention to such things as changing into nightclothes for sleeping. (There is a range in the latter instance from sleeping in daytime clothes to sleeping in underwear or changing into nightclothes.) In general, Spaniards from elsewhere and even Pasiegos bred on the Plaza find the barrio styles of homemaking and personal habits deplorable.

Barrio dwellers are visually identifiable in a variety of ways but foremost by their different costume.[2] The contrasts between barrios and Plaza will be more fully considered in chapter 8; generally, modern barrio styles are highly conservative, with the result that we see in them clothing traditions from the past and of a general style which was once more widespread, while Plaza

---

(*migas*), which are a classic element in rural cookery. The foods generally shared in this way are dishes composed of discrete and separable pieces and not normally containing liquid. Thus, individuals eat from the portion of a platter nearest them, and food does not "swim" from one place to the next. Gerald Brenan (1963:158), writing of Andalusia, describes an elegant sharing style in which narrow walls are actually left standing between the various commensals' portions of a paella, but I have never observed such formality among commensals. Nonetheless, the hygienic disadvantage of sharing soupy foods is widely recognized, and Pasiegos are somewhat embarrassed by their own recourse to the sharing of soups and stews from common plates. Sharp knives, for both cutting and spearing foods, and spoons, for liquids, are everywhere sufficient for most needs, but forks are also widely in use. Normally, each commensal has his own utensils and both the sharing of utensils and the scarcity of forks are also recognized by Pasiegos as extremes. Everywhere, bread serves partially as plates and even napkins, and Pas is no exception.

2. The use of dialect also distinguishes many barrio dwellers from most Casco people and from outsiders. It is spoken by fewer people now than in the past, but it is probably more striking to outsiders now than it was in earlier times when standard Castilian had not penetrated the countryside to as great an extent as it has today. It is important to note that the use of dialect in Pas was not counted among the remarkable characteristics by the earliest writers; it has become an object of interest largely in the twentieth century. Penny's 1969 monograph is the major descriptive work. It was preceded in 1954 by two essays of Ramón Menéndez y Pidal, who argued on philological grounds alone that the Pasiego and Vaqueiro presence in Spain might be the result of colonization from southern Italy.

people are sensitive to modern fashions and reflect them in their dress.

There is marked age-grading in female costume style within the barrios. The most distinctive costume is associated with adult women, married or not, whose dress is invariably black and—at least for the older ones—involves long skirts. Aprons and head-scarves are part of this attire and are of a standard printed material, usually predominantly blue. The donning of black aprons and head-scarves signalizes mourning. Women usually begin to wear this costume around age forty to fifty, or at their first mourning period as adults for a close kinsman—a parent, husband, or child. This is when they forsake the slightly more colorful and less standardized skirts, sweaters, aprons, and scarves of their younger years. The wearing of the scarf is less standard for younger women, whereas older women are almost never seen without them and sometimes even wear them in bed.[3]

Men's styles are not so strikingly distinct from national ones, at least in cut and materials used. Standard clothing are trousers and jacket, both of dark corduroy for dress, with blue cotton trousers for work, and shirts of standard cut. The wearing of the *boina* (beret), however, is age-graded (as in most of Spain), being worn habitually only by bachelors and adult men but not by boys. While the boina does not distinguish herders from manual laborers (or the farmers of other regions), it does distinguish most of the former from the commercial and professional males of the Plaza who were not born in the barrios.

One element of male costume which distinguishes herders of most ages from all other males is the *palo*—the long staff which is central to the Pasiego stereotype prevailing outside Pas. Elegant versions of this are carried today to the stock-fairs (see plate 16), even occasionally by outsiders, but the traditional herder's staff is (or was) much heavier, and its owner was inseparable from it. The staff is no longer so omnipresent. For example, rows of staves could once be seen standing by the tavern doors at the entrance to the dance hall, to be picked up by

3. The extent to which today's younger barrio women will, in their fifties, be wearing this costume is to me questionable. In the barrios, as elsewhere, styles change. A younger woman in mourning may—as the one shown in plate 12 with her baby—wear shorter skirts of more modern style. Thus, the sharp stylistic difference between costumes of older and younger women visible today may actually die along with the older generation and give way to a lesser distinction.

their owners after cards, drinks, or dancing. This is no longer the case, and the staves are normally used only in the barrios, where they are aids in walking, testing terrain, jumping gulleys, and driving cattle. But they still hold their place in the stereotype, and have given rise to the "Pasiego" sport of pole-vaulting which is sometimes a fiesta attraction in towns surrounding Pas, where elements of the Pasiego stereotype are often imported— even invented—and exhibited for tourists.[4]

Finally, two accessories are in use by all barrio people, regardless of age and sex. These are the cuévano, used for most transport, and the almadreñas, wooden clogs, which are worn over slippers for entry into stables and muddy areas and removed for entry into the dwelling areas of the cabañas. These items are seldom visible in the Plaza except when barrio people pass through. The cuévano is little used even at the edges of the Casco, for roads and streets are paved there and there are other means of transport. The use or abandonment of barrio footgear by people who move to the Casco will be examined later.

There is in the barrios a further distinction, in addition to the conservatism and sameness of dress in the herding population. This is that people do not own many clothes, for the same reasons that all material accumulation is avoided, and they practice a tradition of mending and remending (especially men's clothes) often to the point of producing the effect we call patchwork[5] (see plate 13). The patchwork tradition cannot be ascribed to a general inability to purchase new clothing. Rather, in addition to reflecting a rather sensible effort to make maximal use of material, there is a tendency for people to maintain—and even to advertise—a modest style regardless of their purchasing power (which can vary greatly) so long as they are living in the barrios. This can best be analyzed in contrast with the opposite

4. Primary among such occasions is the fiesta of the Virgin of Valbanuz, in Selaya, where the proximity to the Montes de Pas is heavily exploited. The *salto pasiego*, or Pasiego vault, is one featured event. Another is Santander folk dancing to the music of *pitu* (Sp. pito, meaning whistle or pipe) and *tambor* (drum), which are in many quarters supposed to be reminiscent of Pas. Actually, the only traditional instrument played by Pasiegos themselves in any Pasiego's memory is the tambourine; for them, as for others in the province, the music of pipe and drum was imported for special occasions.

5. The Spanish term *remendado*, like the English "patchwork," implies random patching and, often, variety of shades or colors. The term is applied locally to the barrio clothing; it is often used critically in Spain, in nicknames and in farce.

tendency, toward ostentation, among Pasiegos of the Casco; I shall deal further with the problem in analyzing the interaction between these two sectors of Pasiego society in chapter 8.

In addition to the material indicators of barrio origin, a variety of barrio traditions have caught the attention of local ethnographers and folklorists and have led them to proclaim the Pasiegos peculiar and distinct from other Spaniards. The barrios truly stand apart from the long-settled Plaza area in respect to these practices—a fact not much appreciated by the ethnographers—and most of the customs I am about to describe are abandoned by herders who become sedentary in the Casco. This process will be detailed later; now let us review some of the traditions of barrio life as they are practiced in the barrios themselves.

Distinctive barrio traditions cluster heavily about the events of courtship, marriage, and the initial stages of residence of a new couple, and about the later retirement of their parents. Certain funerary traditions have also caught ethnographers' attention. By contrast, traditions surrounding birth do not differ substantially from those obtaining in the Casco or in much of the rest of rural Spain. Let us look briefly at the latter before turning to courtship.

Women give birth at home, as they do also in the Casco, and seek professional medical assistance both at birth and in difficulties of pregnancy—though there is doubtless more frequent consultation of the doctor by Casco women than by those of the barrios. Beliefs and attitudes surrounding pregnancy and birth do not seem to vary significantly between the two communities and are, in general, fairly "modern." Some Pasiegos have spoken to me about other, more "backward" zones where old beliefs and practices still prevail.

A mother accompanies her child to its baptism, a few days after its birth. The post-partum quarantine from the church observed in some parts of Spain—which prevents mothers from attending the baptisms of their own children—is in this zone regarded as archaic.[6] Godparents are normally selected from among close kinsmen, usually of the parents' generation. Later in life, their roles as godparents are almost totally eclipsed by their roles as kinsmen, but they can be quite important in the naming of the child. Sometimes parents settle on a name for

6. The status of the quarantine in Spain is varied, and it is not necessarily associated with "backward" areas—see Freeman 1970a:142n.

their child, but often they ask the godparents to choose it. Often a child is named for one of its godparents, by parental choice, or for one of its own parents. Even where parents or godparents choose names other than one of their own, naming is often after some other individual. Naming for others (usually for living people) frequently crosses sex boundaries, as virtually all names have both feminine and masculine forms. The custom of naming after people who, when they are not parents or godparents are usually kinsmen nonetheless, produces a great repetition of names within family groups. I know of one case in which two brothers bore identical names.[7] This phenomenon distinguishes the barrios from the Plaza, at least in degree—the prevailing tendencies in the Plaza population are described in chapter 7.

Courtship, and much of pre-marital social life in general, is carried out in the complex of traditions known as *la rolda* (Spanish variant of the term *ronda*).[8] This is partially comparable to the complex of traditions called in English "night-courting" (including "bundling"), which is or has been widespread in Europe from the British Isles, across north-central Europe, into the Baltics, and farther south as well (for example, in the Alps).[9]

In Pas, the rolda seems to be—at least today—more frequently an individual than a group activity for bachelors. It consists in

7. The repetition of names fosters, in the barrios, a great variety of modes of shortening or altering individual names. For example, all of the following versions of Manuel are current, and no individual is called by more than one of them: Manuel, Manolo, Manolín, Manín, Nelo, Lolo, Lele, Lile, Lilil, Lilín. There is also a greater use of nicknames in the barrios than in the Casco, and almost every family, if not its individual members, has one.

8. Aranzadi wrote in 1910 that a Pasiego once told him that "the couvade was said to have existed in the Valleys of Pas (Santander) and Pozas (Burgos) until the parish priest of that time succeeded in abolishing it, just like the 'rolda' of the youths with the maidens" (Aranzadi 1910:777). The couvade, of which there are no modern traces, has been the subject of much discussion in Spanish ethnography. Caro Baroja (1943) reviews and extends this discussion. The rolda, on the other hand, despite its persistence—for it was *not* abolished—has excited almost no comparative attention. Aranzadi's and other ethnographers' references to it are minimal, and the tradition is often assumed to be limited to a simple *ronda* or group serenade.

9. Aspects of this complex are reviewed by Wikman (1937), and by Sarmela (1969) and Löfgren (1974). Stiles's amusing treatise (1934) deals with bundling in Colonial America and its antecedents in the British Isles and the Low Countries, in particular. R. T. and G. Anderson (1962) deal with some Ukrainian night-courting traditions.

the young man's paying an evening visit to a young girl, who receives him in her "kitchen" (that is, by the hearth of the cabaña), where they visit together, usually in the presence of her family. Sometimes, two friends may make such a visit together without significantly altering its style. A full group rolda, however, is not kindly looked upon in Pas: these night-time excursions of groups of bachelors to women's houses easily assume a ribald character and are often taken (and intended) as affronts to her and her family.[10] There is also a tradition of calling to a girl from outside her cabaña *hablando en garavía*—that is, employing falsetto or some other vocal guise—and this, too, is considered offensive. Informants insist that rolda visits of friendship and affection are frank and individual, not group visits and not characterized by singing, noise-making, or vocal disguises.[11]

Bundling—the tradition of the young couple, fully clothed, sharing the same bed during nocturnal visits—is apparently not a part of the rolda, at least today. There is, in other words, no convention which openly permits a couple to lie together and governs the style in which they do so. Rather, the nature of the visits may be described in the words of one informant who set about summarizing it for me:

The mozos go off on the rolda at night, after supper, and the rolda takes place in the cabaña kitchens. If the parents of the girls don't like the mozo much, they send their daughter to bed before it gets late, but if the mozo is well regarded by the parents, they themselves go to bed so that the courting of the boy and girl can be more agreeable. At the same time, the sooner the marriage the better, because parents—especially mothers— take pride in marrying their daughters between the ages of sixteen and nineteen. If the mozo who goes courting is surprised by bad weather and he's come a long way to court, the couple stays in the kitchen until dawn, but under no circumstances can they lie down together.

The precise conventions of bundling are absent and are replaced by other conventions (which in neither case always prevent the

10. Groups of males do, however, roam through the barrio together, leaving individuals alone to enter the houses of their destination.

11. I had little opportunity to observe the rolda firsthand because I never stayed with a barrio family with girls of courting age. If I had, I wonder if night-courting would have been permitted in my presence. Pasiegos are extremely sensitive about some of their traditions, the rolda above all, since their practice stigmatizes them in the eyes of all Spaniards.

consummation of relationships).[12] For the rest, the rolda is not unlike night-courting elsewhere.

The ease with which a man gains entry to a woman's house and the informality and duration of his visits there, in addition to the number of men who may pay such visits, contrast sharply with the pattern prevailing in much of the nation, where entry into the woman's house indicates a firm commitment and constitutes a formal step in engagement.[13] On the contrary, a Pasiego girl may receive rolda visits from more than one youth during the same period.[14] One older woman related to me her situation just before becoming engaged. One young man had been visiting her for about two years when a second one began visiting. At this time, the first was about to enlist for military service. Though the first man considered the girl committed to him, she was unwilling, she says, to marry someone about to

12. The data on illegitimacy are relevant to the failure of these conventions. Twenty-four (11.2 percent) of the 215 unmarried women in the genealogical sample have borne at least one child out of wedlock. Of the married women in the sample, seven had borne one or more children out of wedlock before marriage; their husbands were not the fathers of their first children. One woman bore an illegitimate child after marriage; she is long dead and I know of no details of the case. There are probably a large number of cases in which girls have been pregnant at the time of posting of banns or marriage to the father of the child, but these are difficult to document. Women who have borne children out of wedlock are almost invariably from the barrios or from the geographic fringes of the Casco which are the receiving grounds for new emigrants from the barrios.

13. On the more formal courtship patterns of other regions see Pitt-Rivers 1971b, Lisón Tolosana 1966, and Price and Price 1966 a, b. The barrio pattern described here is strongly affected by the simple lack of public meeting places within the barrios. While barrio youth may first become attracted at the dance in the Plaza, they literally have no place to meet within the barrios except the homes. The general distribution of night-courting traditions does appear to correlate with areas of dispersed settlement and low density of public meeting places, as well as with situations in which a man may have to walk long distances to court a woman, making the return journey at night inconvenient at best. There is also some correlation with dwelling situations in which beds are scarce and, in some cases—as, for example, in Finland (Sarmela 1969)—where at least some family members habitually sleep in the stables.

14. García-Lomas, in his brief discussion of the rolda, misunderstands this point, which is common in night-courting traditions. He speaks of visits between "promised" parties (1960:342). However, his mention of the rolda in Pas is almost the only one after Aranzadi's (except for Caro Baroja's reiteration of Aranzadi's comment), and his acknowledgement of overnight visiting there is possibly unique.

leave town for two years: "God knows who he might have attached himself to in two years away." So, she and the second
youth, who had already done his military service, announced
banns one Sunday, after he had been *roldando* for only about
two weeks. The announcement took the first suitor by surprise
and he was so angered that, meeting the girl in the barrio shortly
afterward, he struck her. She married her new suitor, however,
and the first one did his military service and, ultimately, emigrated from town. This is not an unusual story.

The contrast in courtship customs between barrios and Plaza
is accompanied by a different manner of beginning cohabitation,
as well as by a different kind of residential arrangement in the
first months after marriage.

In the barrios, an engaged couple begins married life in the
weeks when banns are being announced; the wedding usually
follows in a matter of a few weeks.[15] When cohabitation has begun, before the wedding, the couple is referred to as *un matri-
monio*—a married couple.

The wedding, when it takes place, follows the standard pattern. A wedding mass is said in the church.[16] After mass, invited
guests (as described in chap. 5) join the families of the new
spouses for a meal in one of the taverns of the Plaza. The menu
for these meals is quite standardized and is composed almost
wholly of meat dishes which are rarely eaten in the barrios
themselves: there is normally a chicken broth, a ragoût of veal,
and then veal steaks. These are followed by two traditional des-
serts—*sobaos* (butter cakes) and *quesada* (fresh curd pudding)
—which are produced commercially today by various families of
the Casco but are rarely made by barrio women at home. The
meals which barrio people order on special visits to the taverns
—on fair days, for example—tend to follow this pattern. The
milk, eggs, and legume-based dishes of daily barrio fare are

15. Banns are announced on three consecutive Sundays and/or Church
holidays. The bedding before wedding, at the time of a trothplight, is
again a familiar European custom (see, for example, Homans 1941), but
is in most places archaic. Forms of trial marriage were widely recorded
in parts of northern Spain (cf. Caro Baroja 1946) but are also now obsolete in most regions.

16. Under civil law, there must be a civil ceremony as well, and in many
parts of Spain this is performed at the church door before entry for the
mass. Barrio couples usually separate the two and appear sometime after
their wedding day at the ayuntamiento for civil nuptials. The mass is
considered the important ceremony; some couples apparently fail to go
through civil marriages for long periods unless they come to need civil
documentation of marital status.

shunned, veal is favored over lamb or fowl, and most vegetables are avoided in the Plaza just as they are at home.

Weddings have their appropriate season, and this is closely related to the traditions governing residence. Most newlyweds eventually form separate households, independent of both sets of parents, but it is customary that a period of co-residence of up to a year, or slightly longer, follow the beginning of married life. Most barrio marriages are between members of the herding community and usually between residents of the same barrio, and the norms described here refer to this majority of cases. If they are to be herders, a new couple needs its own livestock, access to meadows and cabañas, and dried grass in order to support themselves.

In Pas, as was also traditional in other parts of Spain, young people only begin to earn rights to their marriage portions from their parents after their marriage has become a social fact.[17] The process of establishing economic independence begins after the posting of banns and lasts until the newlyweds have given to their families the labor considered to be sufficient return for the marriage portion. The full establishment of an independent household must begin with empty cabañas, *con cabaña limpia,* in the same way that new rentals begin. Cabañas are empty just prior to the grazing or harvesting of the retoño crop, in May. In order to begin on their own in May, a couple may marry as long as twelve to fifteen months earlier, in winter or spring of the previous year. Thus, they contribute their labor to their parents during the harvest season of the year prior to their independence.

This long period of co-residence seems to be disappearing—only thirteen of the sixty-four most recent Pandillo marriages I studied involved co-residence of this length.[18] The long period of co-residence saw young people working for their parents as agosteros—harvest hands—during the season prior to their separation; the second harvest of their marriage was gathered in by them alone, or with paid help. Today, all informants agree, the hiring of agosteros is disappearing. The cost of hiring help is prohibitive—in 1969, a harvester asked 30,000 to 35,000 pesetas, plus room and board, for the season. Simultaneously, people have begun to harvest earlier, when the grass is less ripe and less prone to become over-dry, and this permits a more extensive,

17. Cf. Ateneo 1901; Freeman 1970a: 75–76.
18. In six of these cases, the couples were still co-residing in late 1969, either as recent newlyweds still, before eventual separation, or in some cases after the passage of a few years and evidently with notions of permanence.

less desperate harvest period, manageable by family members without outside help. The additional burden of the maize harvest is, of course, gone. Finally, people say that there is simply a more modern attitude toward the beginnings of marriage. A young couple is aware of its earning power on the labor market outside the family and outside Pas; emigration of youth is increasingly popular, and newlyweds are no longer content to relinquish all independence and all cash income in following the tradition of lengthy co-residence. Further, this co-residence was not all gain for the parents in question, who took on all of the young couple's expenses, including medical ones, for the youngsters had no economic resources whatever.

Nowadays, with more cash in the economy, parents may help their children become established through new purchases or rentals. In fact, the modern period of co-residence is greatly reduced and tends to exclude the harvest season. The season of marriage is still in winter and early spring, but co-residence lasts for from four to six months only and ends by May. When newlyweds plan to emigrate as herders to towns of the Montaña, they separate (*apartarse*) from their parents as early as March or April, for this is when the spring grass ripens in the Montaña and legal tenancy on rented meadows begins.

There is still a strong tendency to co-reside for a period, and this may be related to the process of finalizing the marriage portions of the new spouses, which usually occurs in this period. In the cases where couples separate from their parents immediately, the finalization simply takes place earlier.[19] The settlement of the marriage portion, as noted earlier, proceeds separately in each parental household with respect to that household's newlywed child, but the arena of interested observers, of course, widens and now most crucially includes the family of new in-laws.

The factors governing a couple's choice of mode of co-residence are varied and, as noted earlier, good or bad personal relations may play a large part in the decision. So, however, do other factors, such as the size and composition of the labor force in the respective households or the size of their herds. Taken together, all of these factors produce a pattern which shows no marked tendency to favor, a priori, either bride's or groom's family. I studied details of sixty-four recent marriages of couples in the Pandillo rolls whose wedding dates, residential arrange-

19. One informant says, "You have to be rich to do this." However, I wonder if one has to be richer to settle property on one's child at marriage than to do so six months later.

ments, and ultimate places of settlement were recalled by one Pandillo informant. Of these, newlyweds resided with the groom's family in twenty-five cases; with the bride's family in seventeen cases; alternately with both sets of parents in four cases, and in two of these, residence was more often with the bride's family than with the groom's. Newlyweds resided separately (that is, natolocally) in eight cases. Eight couples established their own households immediately, six of these outside Pas. The informant was uncertain of the place of residence in two cases, but believed it to have been with the bride's family. Finally, in some cases, while newlyweds dwelt with either bride's or groom's family, the other spouse spent considerable time in his or her natal household, in effect almost alternating between the two families.

All of these temporary co-residential arrangements are part of the spectrum of rural Spanish traditions, but in most parts of the countryside they have been obsolete for at least a generation. Modern Spaniards look upon them as rustic and old-fashioned at best, and, at worst, as primitive traditions whose presence on Spanish soil requires special explanation.[20]

In some parts of Spain, the natolocal arrangement was considered ideal in that bride and groom each contributed to his or her own family in return for the marriage portion expected from each side. In Pas, many of the more unilateral arrangements are the results of personal and/or economic factors favoring something other than a bilateral solution. In such cases, where one newlywed may have worked harder for his or her parents than did the spouse, the spouse still expects a marriage portion. This portion might be less than that given a sibling who worked harder for the parents. Such inequalities in siblings' marriage portions are ideally compensated when estates are ulti-

20. It is not at all unusual for newlyweds to establish residence within or very near to the parental household of one of them, even in urban settings, but modern newlyweds are not held economically dependent upon their parents after their marriage. Traditions of long dependency at least until the moment of marriage if not also afterwards are, of course, common in parts of rural Europe. But the increasing importance of cash in rural economies, the fact that younger people can now earn salaries which their parents could not have, are everywhere affecting domestic power structures. In Spain, emphasis on attaining the ideal of independence for young couples is interestingly illustrated, in Ávila, in a form of wedding donation (*el ofrecijo*) which allows newlyweds to amass capital on their own at the moment of their marriage (Brandes 1973b, 1975). This tradition appears to have enough extension in the area to have preceded the modern era of cash surpluses: it is the way some Spaniards have devised to avoid the co-residence described above.

mately transmitted by parents to their children. If the compensation is not considered adequate, the resulting animosities are among the factors which complicate estate transmission in Pas. Differences in the marriage portions of two spouses, on the other hand, even though they may provoke ill feeling, are not subject to later adjustment by the respective families.

Marriage for the children does not initiate retirement for the parents. People generally marry young in the barrios—far younger than in the Plaza—and their parents may remain active for many years.[21] These facts alone contribute to the pressure on resources and, as described in chapter 4, force many young couples to begin their married lives at the economic margins of the herding community. Parents do not normally begin to "give away" their meadows to their children until they are in their sixties. Donation of property—variously called *donación de bienes, alargación de bienes,* or *cesión de bienes*—is an old tradition. At least eighty donations are recorded in the legible notarial archives for 1836–66, and it is possible that many more went unnotarized. Historians familiar with notarial archives throughout the province indicate that donations of the Pasiego type are uncommon outside Pas. That is, title to lands is not usually relinquished by able-bodied couples, though usufruct may be relinquished, or title also, by widowed and/or disabled parents. Writers expounding on Pasiego distinctiveness have made much of this (see, for example, Lasaga 1889). Again, the Pasiego case has been lifted out of its Spanish and European context and made to look peculiar. In fact, donations of property by individuals to their children, in exchange for support, are common. They are sometimes but by no means everywhere reserved for widowed people, particularly women, and for the handicapped. Donations may involve actual title to lands or only usufruct, but the contracts are widely similar in form throughout rural Europe.[22]

21. Most barrio people who marry do so by the time they are in their early twenties. The pattern among Plaza families, and the Casco population in general, is the more familiar one of marriage around age twenty-five for females and thirty or later for males.

22. I have described support contracts between widows or aged parents with their children for central Castile (Freeman 1970a), where disabled children are given special allotments by testament. Lisón (1971) describes at length issues of parental support in the Spanish provinces of Galicia. Bernard (1969), using notarial archives from the last half of the eighteenth century, describes a wide variety of contracts for the Gévaudan region of France from that period: these pensions were established in men's wills

Pasiego funerary customs, too, are well within the European and northern Spanish spectrum. Their most striking element has been the associated feasting, for standard usage in modern Spain separates events involving death from events of major food-sharing. In Pas, too, the banquet is a thing of the past, but local folklorists' (particularly Lasaga's) attention to it has nonetheless influenced outsiders' attitudes toward Pasiegos. The features stressed by Lasaga in his various references to Pasiego funerary customs (1865, 1934) are the post-burial banquets in the taverns and the distribution of wine and breadstuffs at the church door, which I have already cited (chap. 5, p. 109 and n. 25). He also mentions the wearing of capes as if it were somehow unique to Pas, which it was not. The feasting tradition and the distribution of a "charity" (wine and breadstuffs) in association with burials are (or were) widespread in Spain, as was the use of paid mourners (*lloronas*) which Lasaga also notes with special interest for areas adjacent to Pas.[23]

Beyond the traditions described already, two trivial features of barrio custom have attracted attention and contributed to the Pasiego stereotype. One of these is the *guceo* (dial., v. *gucear*; Sp. *vocear*, to shout). This calling, or loud whooping, is in use especially in the upper reaches of the barrios to initiate communication between farflung meadows and to announce people's arrival at new locations. Unlike the yodel, the guceo does not to my knowledge involve the alternation of chest-voice with falsetto. Its communicative functions are extremely limited and it

---

for their widows, in marriage contracts for the future necessities of the parent(s) of one or both of the spouses, and variously for the maintenance of disabled individuals. Löfgren summarizes data from all over Scandanavia, where, in his words, "inheritance, in reality, became a premortem transaction" in which an aging couple "set up a retirement contract with one of their children . . . giving him or her usufruct rights to the farm in exchange for ample provision" (1974:40–41). Similar arrangements are detailed for Upper Austria (Khera 1973), for County Clare, Ireland (Arensberg and Kimball 1968:chap. 7), and widely for medieval England (Homans 1941), to give but a few examples. By contrast, the tendency of a father to remain active estate manager for as long as possible, subjugating his heir(s) well into adulthood, as documented for parts of the Italian Alps (Cole and Wolf 1974) and in parts of Hungary—even when heirs have married (Fél and Hofer 1969)—seems to be less frequent.

23. For reviews of the distribution of such funerary customs see Ateneo 1901, Caro Baroja 1946, and Foster 1960 (chap. 12). Douglass's 1969 monograph on the Basque town of Murélaga focuses specifically and in detail on funerary ritual, including the associated banquets.

does not evolve into song, but singing groups of mozos often punctuate their song with whoops.

Second, writers on the Pasiegos usually remark on the importance in the diet of skimmed milk, and Lasaga (1889) comments also on the consumption of whey (presumably fresh) and buttermilk (dial. *trebejos*). Pasiego consumption even of standard dairy products is unequaled in most other regions, but whey, skimmed milk, and buttermilk in particular are deprecated by modern Spaniards. Butter is often regarded by Spaniards as difficult to digest, so small wonder that a people which is known to consume *sopas de manteca*, or butter soup (melted butter with bread floating in it) is regarded as at best "curious." But most unusual in rural Spain is the consumption of soured or sour-tasting milk products, other than certain cheeses, and buttermilk evokes expressions of horror.

For the rest, the stereotype of the Pasiego held and published by outsiders rests heavily upon images derived from Pasiegos outside Pas, plying the trades which have characterized their emergence from the Montes into the rest of Spain. Sedentary Pasiegos of the Casco, to the extent that they are able to shed the traditions and the physical habits of barrio life, are not—to strangers schooled in the stereotype—identifiable as Pasiegos at all.

SEVEN

The Casco

When people come here on excursions, they even seem surprised
that we've got bathrooms. "Oh, I thought the Montes de Pas was
uncivilized," they say. What do they think we are?

a Casco girl

Local legend tells that long ago, before La Vega became a villa,
the inhabitants met together on community business in the
Pandillo pradera called La Bara (or La Vara), and that the
pradera is named for the staff of office (*bara* or *vara*) of the community's leadership.[1] La Bara lies high in the branizas of Pandillo, near the crests which face Espinosa. By local accounts,
this was the first seat of the Pasiego community within the modern territory of Vega de Pas, across the crests from Espinosa.
This is one of the few items of local history which I heard repeated in the barrios themselves, where people otherwise do not
cite the facts reviewed in chapter 1 because they are largely unaware of them. In La Bara itself, there is no evidence for or
against the place's one-time function as a meeting ground. Eventually, however, centers of importance in the community became distinguishable stylistically—architecturally and in their
internal spatial arrangements. Such architectural distinction
may once have come to the riverside pradera of El Porrato, when
it housed its chapel, but there is no longer evidence of this;
similar distinction has today come to roadside areas where

---

1. A wooden staff is a common trapping of local office in Iberia. Sometimes, a staff might be passed from house to house as office or assigned
duties rotated from one household to another (see, for example, Dias
1953).

sedentary Pasiegos pursue livelihoods in commerce. But in all of Vega de Pas there is no more than a single zone whose truly distinctive style permits it alone to be regarded as something other than "countryside" and defines it as the center of town: the Casco, with the Plaza at its heart.

The Plaza was not always located where it stands today. Within the period of genealogical history of some contemporary residents, the Plaza was located in the Casco neighborhood now known as the Calle Atrás (the Back Street), and the important families in town had their homes there. The architectural character of the place today is sharply different from that of the barrios, yet rustic and antique in comparison with the modern Plaza (see plates 10, 11). At least one of the houses of the old center still has an imposing name, and in this zone are located the niches which formerly housed images to be venerated as processions passed. The modern church, on the modern Plaza, bears the date 1697. I doubt that the present church or the Plaza itself are really of that age, but there are no traces of an earlier church in the Calle Atrás. However, the Calle Atrás does encompass the site of a former cemetery, on a riverside spot called La Piriría.

In the barrios, social distinctions have their primary basis in the relative size of landholdings and degrees of sedentarization, but they are architecturally invisible. Barrio people do not seek to distinguish themselves visibly from their neighbors: rather, social difference is ultimately expressed by ceasing to be a barrio person, by quitting the space of the barrios and living differently. There is no herder living in the barrios whose landholdings are great enough to have permitted his retirement from herding long ago: such people (if they do not emigrate) remove themselves immediately to the center of town, or to one of the adjacent roadside areas, where they are to be found today. These people and their immediate ancestors represent that sector of the population whose strategies of sedentarization came to full fruition, who amassed enough holdings at the valley bottom to become landlords of the richest meadows, or whose other holdings were so extensive as to produce enough income to support their removal to the Casco. These people have left herding to others; they collect rents and, very often, pursue other business as well. In many instances, most of their relatives have already left Pas for other parts of Spain.

From early times, people of substance, social position, and, presumably, greater literacy and *savoir faire* lived in the valley bottoms. In the 1530s we find there—in Viaña, with his private chapel—the King's porter. In 1689, the man who was named first alcalde of La Vega was a native and an educated man—Don Joseph Conde Pelayo, a *licenciado* and lawyer. Being, evidently, from the Plaza, he appointed alcaldes of the various barrios, and while these are each named with the title *don*, a possible embellishment on the part of the scribe, none apparently had academic degrees or official positions in the world outside Pas.[2] A century later (VPA 1789), one vecino of La Vega was serving as a montero at the Court, and various other monteros were also named: they are listed as being from the villas, probably in the narrowest sense of the term, as distinct from the barrios.

Today, non-herding occupations among barrio dwellers, as detailed in chapter 2, are only supplementary to herding and comprise a category of pursuits which are considered more lowly than most of those pursued by Casco residents. They are the production of material items associated with barrio life—cuévanos, almadreñas, cabañas—and petty trade, pursued on a part-time and largely itinerant basis outside the barrios. People with full-time commercial pursuits are concentrated in the Casco, and along adjacent roadside areas, leaving the barrios entirely to herders.

To move to the Casco is, in most cases, one step in a family's emigration from the Montes de Pas. Family histories make this clear. Table 11 combines a variety of data on the Casco and focuses particularly on the genealogical remove from the barrios of the various Casco residents. Table 12 completes the data on house ownership in the Casco, and the data on ownership in both tables show the extent to which property ownership in the Casco is a monopoly of Casco dwellers or emigrants, to the exclusion of barrio people. Except for the siblings who occupy structures 8, 21, 107, and 108, to be discussed presently, there is only one household (number 25) whose members may have been out of the barrios for more than four generations, and one other (number 22) whose residence out of the barrios probably has four generations' depth.[3] In both of these latter cases, the

---

2. San Pedro's new alcalde was similarly designated simply as *don*. In San Roque, the king's officials left the naming of alcalde to be decided locally, stating the position reserved for whomever appeared most meritorious; they themselves, as outsiders, apparently knew of no members of a local elite with outside connections.

3. The owner of structure number 10 possibly has greater remove from the barrios, but is only a very occasional resident, even in summer. She is the grand-niece of the famous Doctor Madrazo (Enrique Diego Madrazo), a native of Vega de Pas, possessor of the chair of surgery at Barcelona;

TABLE 11
OCCUPATION AND OWNERSHIP OF CASCO DWELLINGS,
BY NEIGHBORHOOD[a]

Structure Number	Occupant Owns/Rents	Remove From Barrios[b]	Occupant's Occupation[c]	Owner's Relation to Head[d]	Owner's Residence[e]
La Plaza (map 6–A)					
2	rents	0	retired worker	—	emigrant
3	rents	1	butcher	—	Plaza
4	rents	1	baker	WF	Plaza
5	owns	0	genl. store; landlord		
6	rents	0 + vaq.		—	emigrant
7	rents	?	summer resident	—	B. San Antonio
8	owns	4 + ?	bar-restaurant		
9	rents	3	store	—	emigrant
10	owns	?	summer resident		
11	rents	0	peddler; ret. barrio	—	emigrant
12	rents	0	income	B	emigrant
13	owns	0	bar		
14	owns	0	ret. herder		
15	rents	3 + ?	store; ret. worker; carpenter	FZ	emigrant
16	rents	1	veterinarian	F	Plaza
	rents	0	ret. barrio		
	rents	0	ret. barrio		
17	owns	2	butcher; genl. store		
18	rents	1	municipal secretary	—	emigrant
19	rents	0	ret. worker	—	emigrant
21	owns	3 + ?	butcher; genl. store		
	owns	4 + ?	sindicato secretary; postal official		
22	owns	4 ?	income		
23	owns	3 + ?	bar-tobacconist; bus-driver		
24	owns	3 + ?	income		
25	rents	4 + ?	income	double first cousin	emigrant
27	owns	3 + ?	income; cake shop		
28	owns	3 ?	bar; cake shop		

TABLE 11—*Continued*

Structure Number	Occupant Owns/Rents	Remove From Barriosᵇ	Occupant's Occupationᶜ	Owner's Relation to Headᵈ	Owner's Residenceᵉ
La Cuesta (map 6–C)					
31	owns	0	bar-restaurant		
34	rents	3+ ?	ret. teacher	ZH	emigrant
35	owns	0	bar; transport		
El Cruce (map 6–D)					
37	owns	1	baker		
	rents	0	ret. barrio	—	Cruce
38	rents	0		DH	Yera
	rents	1		ZS	Yera
39	rents	0	ret. worker; herder	—	emigrant
40	owns	0	income		
41	owns	1	bar-restaurant; dance-hall		
43	owns	0	carpenter-mason		
44	owns	0	transport		
46 (La Calza)	owns	0	herder		
48	rents	0	income	FBD	emigrant
49	owns	2	bar-restaurant		
50	owns	2	dry-goods and genl. store		
51	rents	2+ ?	transport	F	La Gurueba
52	owns	0	herder-tratante		
53	owns	1+	herder		
55	owns	0	income		
58	rents	0	herder	—	Plaza
61 (Tocino)	rents	0	herder	—	emigrant
La Calle Atrás (map 6–B)					
62	owns	0	ret. herder		
	rents	0	ret. barrio	B	Calle Atrás
63	rents	0	herder	—	Plaza
64	rents	0	alguacil	—	Plaza
65	owns	0	ret. barrio		
66	owns	0	income		
67	rents	1	transport; peddler	—	Plaza
68	rents	0	herder	—	Calle Atrás
69	owns	2	income		
70	owns	2	income		
72	owns	2 ?	income		
73	owns	3+	income		
74	owns	2+ ?	income		

TABLE 11—*Continued*

Structure Number	Occupant Owns/Rents	Remove From Barrios[b]	Occupant's Occupation[c]	Owner's Relation to Head[d]	Owner's Residence[e]
75, 77	owns	0	herder		
76	rents	2+ ?	income	—	Calle Atrás
79	rents	0	herder	—	emigrant
	rents	0	herder	—	Plaza
80	rents	0	ret. barrio	—	emigrant
81	rents	0	herder	—	Plaza
82	owns	0	ret. barrio		
83	owns	0	income		
85	owns	0	herder		
86	rents	0	herder	—	emigrant
87	owns	3 ?	summer resident		
90	owns	2+ ?	summer resident		
92	rents	0	herder	—	Plaza
93	owns	0	ret. barrio	—	Plaza
94	owns	2 ?	servant		
95	owns	0+ vaq.	herder		
96	rents	0	ret. barrio	—	Plaza
97	owns	0	ret. barrio		
98	rents	0	herder	—	Plaza
99	owns	0	ret. barrio		
101	owns	3 ?	ret. worker		
104	owns	0	ret. herder		
105	rents	0	herder	—	emigrant
106	owns	2+ ?	income		

El Barrio de San Antonio (map 6–E)

Structure Number	Occupant Owns/Rents	Remove From Barrios[b]	Occupant's Occupation[c]	Owner's Relation to Head[d]	Owner's Residence[e]
107	rents	4+ ?	summer resident	M	Plaza
108	rents	4+ ?	provincial employee	M	Plaza
110	rents	0	ret. herder	—	emigrant
112	rents	0	herder	—	Plaza
113	owns	3+ ?	herder		
114	owns	0	income		
115	owns	0	ret. barrio		
116	owns	3+ ?	ret. herder		
117	rents	0	herder	—	Plaza

[a]Structures listed are occupied dwellings. Unoccupied dwellings are listed in table 12. All other structures shown on map 6 and its insets A–E are either public buildings owned by the ayuntamiento, the parish church, or structures dedicated to non-residential uses, such as garages and storehouses. None of the resident outsiders (non-Pasiego professionals) is listed, but Pasiegos occupying apartments in the same structures are. Where Pasiego residents are married to outsiders, the households are listed as Pasiego-occupied and the Pasiego spouse's genealogy alone is under consideration in column 3, unless the outsider is also ultimately descended from Pas.

[b]Genealogical remove from the barrios has been calculated for household heads, male or female, and for the spouse, if the head is married. Adjunct

TABLE 11—*Continued*

members of households are excluded, and in the few cases of compound families, only the head couple's status is considered. Thus, the table in no way presents a census of the Casco. For each household, a maximum of four family lines was considered—male heads' father's and mother's lines and female head's father's and mother's lines. These were documentable in all but two cases of emigrants who are now only summer residents. The number in this column records the *highest* number of generations' removal from the barrios which emerged in any of the lines considered, and this reflects the maximum length of contact with the Casco of that household. Generations of removal from the barrios are recorded as follows:

    0 householder born in barrio
    1 householder's parents born in barrio
    2 householder's grandparents born in barrio
    3 householder's great-grandparents born in barrio
      etc.
    0 + vaq. notes cases where individual was raised in a barrio and an
      urban vaquería

Obviously, at greater remove from the barrios, informants are less able to give precise information on their herder forbears, and some of the recorded figures express uncertainty. For example, "3?" indicates that two generations' remove from the barrios can be documented but that further data suggest that the number might be greater; "3+ ?" indicates the possibility but not the certainty that an individual is removed from the barrios by as many as four generations.

c"Worker" is a translation of *obrero* and indicates a manual laborer, usually semi- or un-skilled, and not self-employed.

"Ret. herder," distinguished from "herder" (active), describes men or couples who have retired from herding, usually on contract with their heirs.

"Ret. barrio" distinguishes barrio women, single or widowed, who have entered contractual relations with their siblings or heirs, respectively, and retired to the Casco. In the case of single women, these were often not fully active herders in the barrios, but retirement in all of these cases is supported by the income gained from shares of the average herding enterprise—a meadow or two—and not large accumulations of property. These incomes may be described as humble and did not normally in 1969 exceed 60,000 ptas. annually.

"Income" describes those individuals who live from the income on larger accumulations of property than those which characterize most of the herding community: many of these include family income from urban vaquerías or other non-herding activities pursued in the family over a generation or more. The incomes thus described vary from modest (estimated at around 70,000 to 100,000 ptas. in 1969) to very large (in the millions of pesetas).

The individual listed as "ret. barrio" or "ret. herder" often supplements his income through petty commerce—for example, the sale of eggs within town or the sale of cakes once or twice a week in one of the market towns of the province. Individuals listed as having "income" do not normally supplement it actively.

dRelationship of owner to occupant, where it exists, is abbreviated as follows: W = wife; H = husband; F = father; M = mother; B = brother; Z = sister; S = son; D = daughter. The kinship term uses household head as referent—for example, "WF" signifies that owner is head's wife's father. Dash signifies no kinship between owner and occupants.

eOwner's place of residence is not listed if he occupies the structure in question.

households are composed of pairs of unmarried sisters whose nearest relations all live in other parts of the province or the nation. These women were all born outside Pas—two are daughters of a doctor and the other two of a successful businessman—and most of their contact with Pas, before they decided to settle there, in at least one case, I believe, during the Civil War, was during summer visits to their properties. For all these women, this was a choice from a number of alternatives; the women's primary contacts are outside town; they do not spend much time outside of their houses, which are the most elegantly appointed in town, nor do they socialize much with other Plaza families. Their close kinsmen have all emigrated before them and their income comes from family fortunes which were made primarily outside Pas. They are the upper class of the Plaza and of all of La Vega.

Household number 8 runs a highly successful bar-restaurant, located on property which belongs to the restaurateur's wife. She was the daughter of a man from outside Pas who married a Pasiega and settled in the Casco as its pharmacist. He died young, leaving his wife and children, one of whom ultimately inherited the tavern which had been her grandmother's. Her siblings all emigrated into urban areas and hold middle-class jobs. She married Facundo López, who now runs the restaurant, and stayed in town. López is from a family which, on his mother's side, is as far removed from the barrios as any other on the Plaza but which fell on hard times. Facundo's maternal grandfather and great-grandfather were both pharmacists and natives of the Casco. The grandfather married a woman from a Yera family which had accumulated prime meadows near El Cruce; he himself in his professional position amassed considerable capital. He was, however, a compulsive gambler and

founder of the Madrazo Clinic in Vega de Pas, which was later moved to Santander; liberal man of letters and advocate of progressive education. Besides his clinic, which is today administered by his grand-niece, he also founded a private, secular school in Vega de Pas which functioned in the early years of this century. The school and other projects which he envisioned for La Vega became embroiled in both local and family politics. The school was closed after a rather brief existence (some of its last pupils still live in the Plaza) and plans for a fodder cooperative were apparently foiled by competing local interests before they bore fruit. Madrazo himself died some years after the Civil War, under house arrest, and is buried in Vega de Pas. His history of opposition to the Franco regime colored most people's memories of him in one way or another and made his works difficult to assess locally, while there were, of course, no official appreciation of him or significant writings about him.

TABLE 12
OWNERSHIP OF UNOCCUPIED CASCO DWELLINGS[a]

Sector/Number		Owner Resides
Plaza	20	Plaza
	29	emigrant
Cuesta	30	Cruce
	33	emigrant
	36	Cruce
	42	Yera
La Calza	46a	La Calza
El Cruce	47	Candolías
	54	Cruce
	56	Cuesta
	57	Cruce
	59	emigrant
	60	Yera
Calle Atrás	71	Calle Atrás
	73a	Calle Atrás
	78	Calle Atrás
	84	emigrant
	89	emigrant[b]
	91	emigrant
	100	Plaza
	102	emigrant
	103	Plaza
San Antonio	109	emigrant

[a]Table excludes non-dwellings, all of which are facilities attached to dwellings whose owners are already listed. Public buildings, not otherwise listed, are the following: 1—parish church; 26—ayuntamiento, judiciary, and jail; 32—municipal slaughterhouse; 88—Civil Guard headquarters; 111—school for boys and girls.
[b]The only owner listed who is neither a Pasiego nor married to one, this former servant was bequeathed a house by her employer.

brought catastrophe to his family, losing much of its fortune in a single night of cards which many villagers can still describe from hearsay. As a result, his children did not make the kinds of careers and marriages they otherwise might have. His son emigrated to France and opened a fruit shop; one daughter married a Casco grocer, and one—Facundo's mother—married a man from a Yera herding family who had entered the lumber business at a time when there was some local exploitation of timber near the highway in Yera. Facundo entered the lumber business with his father and later constructed a sawmill of his own in the Casco, but this was closed when Facundo took over his wife's family's tavern. Problems of access and transport made timbering in Pas a less-than-profitable business and uncompetitive in modern terms. At least one of Facundo's six children will probably succeed him in the tavern and raise his family in Pas. The others will probably emigrate. Facundo's siblings in town—two brothers and a sister—have with one exception married people of modest means; most of the emigrant siblings also are modestly employed. Despite its long history in the Plaza as propertied and professional people, Facundo's mother's family can no longer be counted in the exclusive circles of the Plaza, where money, conspicuous leisure, material display, and high-status occupations are the only accepted marks of high social class.

Many of the families of three generations' remove from the barrios will not leave descendants in Pas: their children are already in professions or business careers and reside elsewhere. The process of arrival in the Casco can be detailed by a few cases which help to exemplify the character and diversity of the Casco and the manners in which one-time barrio families prepare their members' ultimate departure from Pas.

The heads of households 5, 19, and 35 were all born in the barrios of parents of differing fortunes, and their lives in the Casco have differed accordingly.

The head of household 19, Simón Abascal, is from Candolías. His mother, Consuelo, is from a land-poor family there. Consuelo's family kept two or three pasiego cows and sold butter locally; her father supplemented the family income by doing odd jobs within the community. Consuelo married a young man, Matías, from a land-poor family in La Gurueba. Matías's father died young, leaving him and his two brothers to earn their livings by doing odd jobs and working as agosteros. At the age of about twelve, Simón's father and his brothers began seasonally to go to France under the aegis of a man from La Gurueba who ran a business vending butter-wafers and chestnuts. After marrying Consuelo, Matías returned at least once to France. At this time, their first child was four and one-half months old. Consuelo decided that she, too, would go off to work—to Madrid, as a wet-nurse. She left her child with a Yera woman, who nursed him. Consuelo spent two years with a noble family in Madrid, sending money back to La Vega for the maintenance of her child and for her family. She was taught to read and write by the cook in her employers' household and became acquainted not only with Madrid but also with San Sebastián, where her employer spent the summers with the Court and Parliament. After returning to Pas and bearing her second child, Consuelo went to Zaragoza, this time in the family of an architect, kinsmen of her Madrid employers. This time she left her children with her sister-in-law, who nursed local children for pay. She was away for about a year and summered in the Guadarrama mountains and San Sebastián. Meanwhile Matías had returned from France and was again working at odd jobs. He wanted to apply for a position as highway construction worker—roads were being laid in Pas at this time—but had difficulty because he had not done military service, a standard prerequisite. Consuelo related these difficulties to her former employer in Madrid, who arranged the job for Matías and had the necessary papers forwarded to Santander.[4] And so for thirty years, until his retirement, Matías was a tenured *caminero* (road worker). The couple left their rented house in Candolías and purchased one of their own in the barrio, where their eight children were raised. Their sons worked with their father a great deal; as adults, two of them acquired positions as road workers and one daughter married a road worker—all of these remained in La Vega, one of the sons in the Casco. Simón, another son, also remained in the Casco, working in one of the bakeries until his retirement. Another son remained as a herder in Candolías, one stayed there as a laborer, and another opened a vaquería in Logroño. One of the girls married a vaquería owner.

Consuelo's two sons in the Casco, Simón and his brother José, have six surviving children between them. José's son works in a Casco bakery, one daughter is married to a factory worker, and two daughters still live at home. Simón married a Candolías girl; they have a daughter still at home, and their other daughter is married to one of the Casco butchers. Recently, Simón's only son, who was employed in a French factory, died in an automobile accident in France.

Household 35 is headed by Pío Revuelta, a man from a La Gurueba family which had actually moved into Candolías by the time of Pío's birth. Considerable property was amassed in roadside areas of Candolías and La Gurueba before any member moved to the Casco; most of Pío's collateral relations emigrated from the barrio, according to patterns detailed in chapter 9, without ever residing in the Casco. Pío's ancestors on both sides, from La Gurueba, were land-poor and earned much of their living in the pursuits by which Pasiegos became known outside Pas—itinerant or sporadic petty commerce. The maternal grandfather fished the River Pas and sold his catch; he peddled cloth and meat (lamb and goat); he also sold meat and cloth on a

---

4. It was to the woman of the house, whom she considered her true employer, that Consuelo appealed. Wet-nurses approached their male employers largely through their wives, it seems; the wives, in turn, were indeed largely responsible for contracting wet-nurses.

regular basis in the Sunday market at Entrambasmestas, on the mainstream of the Pas. Pío's mother was the only one of her father's seven surviving children to remain in Pas.

On his father's side, Pío's great-grandfather was known as "the Devil," and his descendants in Pas are still known as Los Diablos. The original Devil ran contraband between Bayonne or Hendaye and Oviedo, by way of Vega de Pas. He was an independent runner, though a considerable amount of the smuggling business was organized under bosses. Reportedly, the Devil acquired his name for the speed with which he made the trip between La Vega and Bilbao, for he "ran like the devil."[5] He also had some agro-pastoral holdings in La Gurueba and sometimes, in summers, sold butter-wafers in Bilbao. One of the Devil's three sons settled in Asturias, where his father had had contacts; the other two remained in Pas. One of these, Pío's grandfather, had six children. The three daughters—two of them married—remained in La Gurueba. But the three sons all spent considerable parts of their lives in Paris, selling either ice cream or wafers there. Pío's father was born in 1871 in Pas but did not come to live there as an adult until 1918, upon his return from Paris, years after his marriage to Pío's mother and shortly before her early death. He opened a small tavern in Candolías, and this Devil established himself as a carter. One of his first cousins had also become a carter, working out of La Gurueba.

Pío himself was the tenth of twelve siblings, eight of whom lived to adulthood. The first eight children were born and/or raised in Paris. Pío was born in Candolías two years before his father settled there permanently. Pío and two of his brothers, like their father, went into the transport business, but now with motorized vehicles. Pío married the daughter of a land-rich family from Yera and Viaña. Pío today is one of the Casco's two largest truckers—his brother (head of household 44) is already retired, and the third brother works out of Candolías. The chief items of transport are, of course, cattle. The oldest of Pío's seven sons have worked with him. One now is in partnership with one of the butchers' sons and together they are both stock dealers and truckers. Pío and some of his sons also offer taxi service.

5. The smuggling route ran from the Yera-Pandillo branizas toward Espinosa and through the upland Mena Valley into Bilbao. Considerably shorter and gentler than the more traveled coastal routes, the modern automobile road measures ninety-one kilometers from the Estacas de Trueba to the center of Bilbao. Pasiego smugglers normally traveled on foot, carrying only their cuévanos, and appeared no different from their more innocent fellows going to and from market centers.

Pío is one of the only people in the Casco—indeed, in all of La Vega—who keeps cows for the sheer love of them. He maintains four cows on two meadows which he has acquired in the Casco itself; he has help in their care and in the care of the meadows, but he spends some time with the cows almost every day.

There are few rags-to-riches stories to be told of people who have lived out their lives within Pas. There are a few more about emigrants. However, one man living on the Plaza has moved from barrio beginnings to the top of La Vega's economic ladder. This is Andrés Pelayo, the head of household 5. He was one of nine children of a herding family from the pradera called La Maza, in Candolías. His parents were from adjacent zones in Candolías and both from herding families, though both grandfathers had supplemented their incomes by other activities: one peddled goods between the various market centers of the region; the other was a stoneworker. Andrés was the third child; his six brothers all became herders and his two sisters married herders. One sister and two brothers remained in La Maza as married adults; all of the rest participated in the migration of Pasiego herders to the towns of the coastal plain.

Andrés's parents were hardly rich, but they were lucky in having access to meadows in contiguous zones, even though some were held only in rent. When the children were little, they had only fourteen or fifteen cows and were able to move these between various meadows while themselves remaining in their vividora most of the time. Later, Andrés remembers, when the children were older, the herd size was expanded to about twenty-five and the family rented a braniza in San Pedro, near the Puerto de la Matanela. However, while the parents were still under the pressures of feeding a large family of youngsters, Andrés left home for the Plaza. It is typical in the larger families that elder children strike out early on their own, or occasionally that they are given in fosterage; younger children are better assured of support in the parental household. Thus, at the age of twelve, in 1903, Andrés went to work for a Plaza man who was a baker and storekeeper, selling grains and *ultramarinos*. (This term technically applies to imported groceries but in fact refers simply to canned goods and other imperishables.) Andrés remained with the baker-storekeeper for about four years, then went to work on the construction of Dr. Madrazo's schools (see n. 3 above). After two years he was sought out by a baker from Selaya who needed a helper. He was in Selaya for about four years before being drafted into the army at age twenty-one.

Military service at that time lasted for twenty-six months. Andrés served near Bilbao. He had left school at the age of twelve and, by his own account, "didn't know much and forgot some of it." He volunteered for schooling offered by the army and now says that his most important schooling came from there rather than from his early, sporadic, and prematurely terminated career in the Casco school.[6]

After his military service, Andrés returned to Selaya for a little more than two years, and then he returned to La Vega, to the Plaza, to establish his own bakery. He bought an old house and built an oven next to it. After a few years, he bought an adjacent building and modernized the complex which is marked on the Plaza map as numbers 5 and 5a–c. Andrés married a woman from a commercial family in Selaya. A general store and fodder depot were soon added to the bakery. These are rivaled in extent today by only one other Plaza enterprise with a different specialization (butchering). With his profits, Andrés bought prime meadows in the riverside areas around the Casco —in both Pandillo and Candolías—and became a landlord. He is one of the two most active moneylenders in town. The other is also his chief rival in general business. In 1969, Andrés held at least seventeen and one-half hectares of meadowland, all of it in ribero zones, and all of it was held in rent by herders. He had also bought one of the fine old Plaza houses which, until the death of its commercial tenant in the late 1950s, housed the café patronized by the Plaza's upper class and professional population. The elegant apartment above it has always been rented to a professional family and is today inhabited by the veterinarian, one of Andrés's sons.

Andrés has three daughters and two sons. One daughter is married to the owner of a factory in Madrid. The other two have stayed in the Plaza, where their husbands are in business with Andrés. One, from the Montaña, runs the bakery; the other, a Pasiego raised in France, runs the general store. The daughters' families live with or next to Andrés and his wife in the complex of dwellings above the store and bakery. The veterinarian, married into a well-to-do Yera family, lives across the Plaza, and the other son, still unmarried, was in 1969 studying to become a pharmacist.

In its history, the Casco has offered different kinds of opportunities, and their range reflects the changing economic times.

6. Candolías children have always attended the Casco school.

The early legal documents do not give systematic data on the Casco's composition or on its commerce and industries, and unfortunately the crucial volume of the 1750 cadaster of the Marqués de la Ensenada is lost. Thus, our earliest document is Madoz's 1849 *Diccionario Geográfico-Estadístico-Histórico*, but even the few data provided there help to sharpen the contrasts between the modern era and the times prior to the importation of Holstein cattle.

Enumerating the products of Vega de Pas, Madoz only lists maize, beans, pasture, livestock, the presence of large and small wild game, and of fish—trout, eels, and some salmon—in the local streams. The only locally established industries he mentions are "some flour mills," in addition to the "traffic in cloth, linen, and other effects" (Madoz 1849, 15:625). The textile traffic apparently included woolen as well as linen fabrics, or perhaps mixtures thereof, and the reference is apparently not to contraband silks.[7]

For San Pedro, Madoz adds potatoes to the list of products, removes the emphasis on game, and mentions no local industries whatever (Madoz 1849, 12:744). For San Roque (Madoz 1849, 13:568), the list of products includes only maize, pasture, and livestock, but here alone, for 1849, there is a discussion of the dairy industry:

. . . there is abundant milk for the working of cheese and butter [or cream?], which the inhabitants take to Santander and other places. They also make a butter known as 'pasiego,' highly regarded in Burgos, Bilbao, Zaragoza, and the Court: in 1843, Don Sisto del Diestro, a Santander businessman, established a factory for cheese and Holland-style butter, but because the operators weren't technically skilled, they failed to give it the correct color and quality, for which reason the work was suspended to be continued later.

The term "Holland-style" refers to salt-butter, which of course is much less perishable than the unsalted product; extended to cheeses it means cured cheeses as opposed to fresh curd. The Pasiegos apparently marketed both types of cheese in Madoz's time (1849, 16:102); today, only San Roque is known for cured cheeses.[8] The milk surplus and local industrial elaboration of

7. Madoz notes that flax was under cultivation in Santander towns adjacent to Pas and was woven industrially in Villacarriedo (Madoz 1849, 16:101–3).

8. For the most part, these are exported to nearby markets. None of the villas produces salt-butter today, and the product marketed is always the more perishable sweet butter. A half century after Madoz wrote, San-

milk products in San Roque, then, antedated the arrival of Holstein stock. So, too, did the regular sale of dairy cattle, as well as the role of tratante, or stock-dealer, probably in all three towns, for as early as 1689 a witness giving testimony certifies his knowledge of "these [three Pasiego] towns" because he "buys cattle in them to take to the stock-fairs" (VPA 1689:305a). Madoz makes no mention of stock-fairs within Pas in 1849.

If Madoz paints an accurate picture, the procurement of most essentials in his day was left to individual Pasiegos as traders in markets outside Pas or in dyadic exchanges outside the marketplace. Madoz says, for example, that Pasiego cheeses were sold "in all the markets of the province, where [the Pasiegos] buy the grain [probably wheat] that they cannot gather from their own rocky mountainsides" (Madoz 1849, 16:102). There is no mention in Madoz's writings on the towns of Pas of stores, taverns, or bakeries, nor of markets, stock fairs, or any factories other than the defunct one listed for San Roque. There was, obviously, cottage industry, but even though he mentions the marketing of woolen cloth, Madoz gives no hint of the fulling mill we know to have existed earlier or of weavers or commercial dry-goods establishments in Pas. While Madoz's data might well be deficient—for even the Ensenada Cadaster listed one tavern each in San Roque and San Pedro a century earlier—it is unlikely that a Casco with significant commercial development would have escaped his attention.[9]

La Vega was the chief redistribution center for contraband in the Montes de Pas. Indeed, runners from France and Bilbao stopped at the house which Andrés Pelayo bought before their departure for Asturias, and when Andrés remodeled the house he found caches in its walls. Smuggling was at its height when Madoz wrote, and he acknowledged this, but it cannot be said that the Casco's commercial activity was necessarily enriched by the fact that it was a way-station for smuggled goods. The ultimate destinations of most of the silks and tobacco were surely outside Pas, and profits were concentrated locally among the few bosses who organized the traffic. Further, some of the organizers might well have been non-Pasiegos, but we have few reliable data on them or on the organization of smuggling in general.

---

tander writers were lamenting the perishability of the Pasiego butter and urging experimentation with the Holland type. The impetus in this appears always to have come from outside Pas, while Pasiegos themselves have been more interested in abandoning butter production altogether.

9. See appendix B and Maza Solano 1956.

Following the importation of Holstein stock, beginning about fifty years after Madoz wrote, the Casco flourished. The changes in land-use which accompanied the expansion of the bovine population made a variety of enterprises profitable. One was the large-scale importation of wheat to supplant the decreasing maize production; hence mills and bakeries were also established. Importation of other food items, such as potatoes and greens, which were never produced in quantity in Pas, and of such items as beans, whose cultivation was now being abandoned, continued. The demand for fodder grew, along with the number of cattle, among those who could afford to keep more animals than they could pasture; and the market for clothing produced outside the home doubtless grew as the flocks of sheep grew smaller. Finally, the increasing amount of cash in the local economy, deriving from milk sales, eventually supported a demand for all kinds of goods produced outside Pas. For example, today virtually all Pasiego women do most of their daily cooking with olive oil, which they prefer to butter, but this can hardly have been the case a century ago. In addition, of course, butter production has decreased sharply.

It is from the early years of Holstein importation that we have our first evidence (from informants) of the active weekly market in Vega de Pas described in chapter 3. It is also from these years that commerce of an entrepreneurial scale is evident in the Casco. I have mentioned feed stores, bakeries, and general stores. Butchers, too, became established: meat has become somewhat more affordable for people with some cash income, at the same time that the flocks of sheep—the major meat animal—have diminished in size. Finally, there was a period—before the establishment of Nestlé and the dairy cooperative—in which the processing of surplus milk became the basis of local enterprise. There were two cheese factories operative in Vega de Pas prior to the arrival of Nestlé. Their founders were two first cousins in a family which later went on to make its fortune at milk wholesaling outside Pas.

With the Holstein importation, the resulting increase in the value of pasture, and the growing commerce of the Casco, families made fortunes in transport, as landlords, in stock dealing, or in the kinds of commerce dealt with above. The Casco—and particularly the Plaza—came to contain an increasingly large stratum of wealthy people whose life-style and educational level diverged sharply from those of the barrios. While there is evidence, cited earlier, for social differentiation of this kind in the Casco centuries before, the upper stratum was probably larger than ever in the early twentieth century. The Casco itself was probably larger as well, though the current official data on census changes do not permit the analysis of population shifts within town.

Andrés Pelayo, who came to the Plaza as a baker's apprentice in 1903, paints the following picture for that period. There were three full-fledged taverns, and a few other establishments also sold wine. There were a few stores in addition to the market, four bread bakeries, and one butcher. The taverns, as I have said earlier, had bowling greens. In the way of other entertainment, there were in those days two weekly dances in the Plaza—one, for barrio people, in one of the large taverns, and another, for "the *señoritos*" (people of "good family"), in the café which Andrés later came to own. (This distinction no longer exists.) There was also the café itself.

In the period which Andrés describes, at least one of the cheese factories, founded in 1888, was in operation, and it did not close until 1935. The second cheese factory had a briefer existence during this period; some chocolate factories lived and died during the period also.[10]

The *Nueva guía de Santander y la Montaña*, published by Blanchard in 1892, listed for Vega de Pas two pharmacies (in the Casco and Candolías) and—in the Casco—the presence of a doctor and notary, the latter known to have served from outside Pas. At least some of the schools still in existence today are listed (Casco, La Gurueba, Pandillo), and omissions are not necessarily absences, since the authors of the *Nueva guía* obviously suffer from unfamiliarity with Pas and its remoter subsections. For example, the very existence of the barrios of Guzparras and Yera is ignored.

The date of establishment of stock fairs within Pas is unknown to me, but by the 1930s there were already two monthly fairs in Vega de Pas. In 1934, Andrés became alcalde (a post he

10. Family-run chocolate factories are fairly common in northern localities. There were as many as three in the Casco in the period prior to the arrival of Nestlé, but since these do not generally produce milk chocolate, their establishment is tied to factors other than the existence of a milk surplus. In parts of Basque country, where chocolate factories are common, they seem to be related to experience gained by families with histories of migration to the New World. The Basque town of Oñate, for example, recently had as many as eight chocolate factories in simultaneous operation—by families with New World connections. Vega de Pas' chocolate factories were small and short-lived. There are very few New World contacts in Pas (although parts of Selaya have many) and the impetus for establishment of these now defunct enterprises is unknown.

held only until 1935 and the upsurge of pre-war animosities in town). It was during his brief administration that the number of fairs was increased to three per month. By 1974, an increase to four monthly fairs seemed imminent.

The development of much of the Casco's commercial activity has been intimately tied to the improvement of the roads into Pas from adjacent zones. Even the existence of cheese factories, or the lack of them, can be related to improved communications, for most surplus milk had to be processed locally before the era of motor transport and better roads permitted the extensive pick-up operations of such organizations as Nestlé and SAM. Local processing plants then gave way to larger, regional ones as soon as conditions favored their development. Conversely, the increased production of milk and dairy stock in Pas, combined with outside demand for these products, stimulated the improvement of communications which made possible both the regional milk pick-up systems and the systematic, long-range trucking of cattle. Interestingly, however, Pasiego entrepreneurial activity has always remained small in scale, local, and in the long run, has inevitably given way when faced with competition from establishments based outside the Montes de Pas. This is not to say that Pas has not produced its own entrepreneurs, but they have flourished ultimately as emigrants living in zones outside Pas and—in the traditional spheres of production—have capitalized on close ties with Pas and on the use of Pasiego labor.

Today, with the disappearance from the Casco of the intermediaries dealing in milk products, the largest enterprises are the general stores, butcher shops, and feed stores which serve local needs. The truckers and cattle dealers systematically serve both local and outside demands and have prosperous businesses, but these are challenged in scale by similar enterprises in adjacent, better connected zones—particularly those along the national highway in the Toranzo Valley or around the great public stock fair of Torrelavega.

Recently, since about the mid-1960s, the Casco has come to serve a new kind of public—Spanish tourists. Correspondingly, there is a new flourishing trade in certain local products which earlier were produced by individual households largely for their own consumption: the more-or-less traditional baked goods, sobaos and quesada. Sobaos, probably more than quesada, are eaten in the barrios as well as the Casco, and they were standard fare for weddings held in the barrios, as they still are for family holidays and occasions where visiting is involved, such as Christmas or special stock fairs. However, neither sobaos nor quesadas are baked in the barrios, where the only traditional baked food was the maize hearthcake and the ashes of the hearth constituted the only "oven." (I know of one or two houses with attached ovens in all of La Vega, but only one of these, in a roadside area, is still occasionally used. I do not know of any cabañas deep in the barrios that have ovens.) Pasiegos, like many other Spaniards, depend upon a large commercial or communal oven in the town center for baking the dough they prepare at home. In the Pasiego case, the only dough prepared at home, for special occasions only, is that for sobaos; bread has been purchased ever since maize hearthcakes passed into history, and I doubt that any barrio woman would know how to make her own wheat bread.

The term sobao is from *sobado* (inf. *sobar*), meaning kneaded, worked, or handled, and the traditional name for the cakes is actually *pan sobao* (worked bread). The dough is rich in eggs and butter, today combined with bread flour but formerly made with bread dough leavened with yeast starter. The bread-dough sobaos do not stay fresh as long as the modern ones. The development of the modern sobao recipe is generally attributed to a woman from the province of Ávila who married a Candolías man who ran the mill in the Casco's Barrio de San Antonio. She was Eusebia Hernández; collateral relations of her husband still live in the Casco; she is designated by them (and others) as baker's wife, cook, and inventor of the modern sobao; during the time when I was recording the data, one of the woman's daughters was working in Madrid as a cook. Eusebia Hernández's invention made the sobao less perishable but did not necessarily widen the market for it. While some cakes may long have been transported to market centers for sale outside Pas, the sobao's popularity has come chiefly with the increase in automobile traffic in Spain and thus with internal tourism—most of this development came only after 1960. Today, the Plaza is a center for tourists, mostly Sunday excursionists from within Santander province, who come to lunch or picnic, to purchase local products, and occasionally to wander a few meters into one of the nearest barrios. (A much smaller number of equally dedicated pursuers of leisure come this far to fish the local trout streams, but the mainstream of the Pas, in the Toranzo Valley, and the lower Miera are more heavily fished by tourists.)

Most of the Plaza's stores and taverns do some business in sobaos and quesada. Quesada is a sweetened milk pudding which has a shelf life of a week or more. Sobaos are better known outside Pas, however, and the sale of quesada is limited to the larger establishments, nor is quesada normally transported for sale outside Pas. One Plaza business is exclusively an outlet for both items; one of the bars specializes heavily in them, and both of these houses ship on a large scale to points as far away as Madrid. A third bar-restaurant sells only on the premises but on a very large scale. Other stores and taverns do a regular but smaller business in these items. Sobaos and quesada have long been available in Santander and other major towns of the Montaña, but since about 1974, they have also been sold and appreciated in the cafés of Madrid. Two or three houses in Vega de Pas are alone responsible for much of the Madrid business, and the rest seems to come mostly from Montaña families who are either of Pasiego descent or have simply imitated Pasiego products for sale along the highways of the province and have now joined the Madrid export trade. Here I should point out that gold cakes of butter, lard, or oil are common local bakery products in Spain and are often distinguished by special local names, and one of these types (made of lard and called sobao or sobado) from Pas' neighbor zone of Soba is even the subject of published description (Sáiz Antomil 1954).[11] Nonetheless, dealers in butter cakes in the province of Santander invariably designate their product as "Pasiego," and the traditional square casing of specially folded white paper is retained even by manufacturers who live outside Pas, are not Pasiegos, and are accused by purists of severely altering the recipe.[12]

In addition to the large-scale manufacture and sale of sobaos by the Casco's larger places of business, several women regularly produce sobaos for sale outside town. This must be counted among the modern-day varieties of petty commerce supplementing the income of certain families (often retired) and of single women. There are at least eight women who vend sobaos of their own making—mostly in Santander and secondarily in Torrelavega—both in the marketplaces and on contract to shops and cafés. All of these women live in the Casco itself or near the road in Candolías, in easy range of the commercial bakeries whose ovens they use. In other words, the manufacture and sale of

11. Common designations are *mantecado* and *mantecada*, and cakes of these names are local specialties in the provinces of both Soria and León.

12. A similar phenomenon occurs in the area around Astorga (León), where mantecados are associated with the Maragato population, whose status in León's provincial history is similar to that of the Pasiegos in Santander (see chap. 10).

local baked specialties is again, like most other commerce, concentrated in the Casco and offers a viable opportunity only for people who live in or near it.

The Casco's sobao production has stimulated, at least in a small way, the continued production of butter by a few barrio herders, for the most careful sobao producers insist on fresh, local butter and pay well for it. Likewise, the producers of milk-based quesada are steady customers of a few of the herders—particularly Casco-based herders—who are happy to sell the bulk of their entire surplus locally; small-scale herding around the margins of the Casco is thus stimulated. Egg production around the Casco may receive a similar stimulus, but the demand for eggs is generally too great to be met by local surpluses and eggs are imported by the largest users.

Aside from the sale of bakery items, tourism itself quickens the pulse of the Casco's economy simply through the sale of drinks, coffee, meals, and sundries to outsiders. The season of weekend and feast-day excursions extends from Holy Week through October, or longer with good weather, and the month of August brings the largest number and variety of vacationers, including some non-Spaniards, through town. The steady business of the summer months helps to underwrite the decline which comes with winter.

What has been said of the household and of family relationships in the barrios may also be said of the Casco, except that Casco families (aside from the few full-scale herders there) possess only one dwelling and inhabit it continuously throughout the year. Since they do not move about town, the first form of temporary fosterage described for the barrios—that facilitating school attendance—does not exist. (Simultaneously, Casco school attendance is good and literacy high.) The more permanent fosterage of children with childless kinsmen, however, is fairly common and generally involves the eldest children of struggling young couples. Casco families, as I have said, tend to be somewhat smaller than those of the barrios, and Casco residents of long standing also have larger incomes and better acquaintance with formal personal and property insurance systems and less suspicion of them—factors which may ultimately be related to the reduction in number of children per family.

Continual occupation of common space in a nucleated setting creates in the Casco the close atmosphere of true town life which contrasts sharply with that of the barrios. The concentration in space of the arena of social interaction plus the omnipresence there of audience and actors produce at full strength the pressures of community living which are so much more attenuated in the barrios. That there are also social benefits to be gained by living in the nucleus is evidenced by herders' readiness to retire there, but the social pressures are well recognized; it is mostly the physical comforts which are sought after, and urban crowding is not valued. It is my impression that Pasiegos and other Santander herders make poorer neighbors in urban settings than do people from rural areas of compact, nucleated settlements. The adjustment to Casco dwelling and proximity to others is the greatest problem for new arrivals from the barrios.

Since there is an important difference (detailed in the next chapter) between new arrivals and longer-term residents of the Casco, I often refer to the Plaza dwellers (the home-owners there) as representative of the most developed Casco traditions, that is, the traditions visible at farthest remove from the barrios. The following portrait, then, is of Casco traditions expressed in "the Plaza" and not necessarily by new arrivals.

Casco people are able to meet casually in Casco space in the course of their daily activities. Men and women alike (but separately) visit casually in the public places of the Casco; they do not have to depend upon specific events to bring them together in the way that barrio dwellers must do. The more formal Casco social life does not center, as in the barrios, on stock fairs and other trade. The events of social importance are, rather, events in the local church calendar, Sunday masses, family celebrations (as in the barrios also), and the weekly Sunday dances (attended by the youth only).

Most Casco families attend mass weekly (though masses are also said on all week-days), or at least women and children do.[13]

13. My discussion of church attendance and the celebration of fiestas focuses, as for the barrios, on the patterns of collective observance. The community of people delineated by participation in these events, or observance of the weekly mass, is not necessarily coincident with the community of the faithful. While few people, if any, profess to be faithless, not all of the settled population attends church. The especially pious, on the other hand, practice their devotion with much more frequency than my description of the general pattern indicates. They may worship daily, visit shrines of importance to them outside Pas, and live by vows to favored saints or virgins. Piety of this sort is cause for comment by the rest of the community, not always with admiration alone—it is often regarded as excessive. Generally, in Spain it is possible to describe, in contrast to collective community patterns, forms of individual devotion which are often locally regarded as deviant but are not negatively sanctioned—they serve as partial models for religious expression. See Chris-

Many men who would have attended did not, while I lived there, because they found the leftist politics of one of the priests intolerable, and he allowed his views to figure in his sermons. (The priest was eventually given a different parish, but only after public physical assault by one of the outraged Casco wives, following a sermon, had created a province-wide scandal.) Sunday mass is the weekly occasion for dressing up, and Sunday afternoons are the prime occasions for casual socializing—for adults and youth alike—either in public (in the taverns) or, in the extended family and among close friends, in private homes. There is a well-developed tradition among adult women as well as younger, unmarried ones of gathering for coffee or a glass of wine in one of the taverns in the afternoon or evening, especially on Sundays but on other days as well. Men, in groups segregated by relative age, do likewise.

The town's official feast days, the Ascension, Corpus Cristi, and the local virgin, are celebrated with varying degrees of public display: festival masses, processions (except for the Ascension), afternoon and evening dances. The year's first communions are celebrated en masse during mass on the Feast of the Ascension. San Isidro, too, is marked by a processional mass and an afternoon dance. A dance is held on All Saints' Day (Todos los Santos), 1 November. On the following day, All Souls' Day (Día de los Difuntos), many Casco residents visit the cemetery. In addition to these events, Christmas (normally celebrated with a midnight mass) and Holy Week (with most intense observation concentrated from Holy Thursday through Easter Sunday) are other Church holidays accompanied by heightened activity (visiting, festive meals) in the homes. There are almost no local traditions associated with any of the feasts (save the door-to-door begging by youths on Epiphany, 6 January), and some of the content of observances in church (particularly during Holy Week) change at the will of the parish priest, whose design is implemented by the unmarried girls of the Plaza, who help organize many such activities.

The *mozas*, or unmarried young women, are socially the most active group in the Casco, rising to the call for participation which normally comes from the priest rather than from within the community itself.[14] It is they, for example, who sing choral

---

tian's discussion of hermits and *beatas* (n.d.) for an important historical overview of the phenomenon.

14. The mozos, in contrast to most of the rest of Spain, are much less organized than the mozas. They do not assume responsibilities in the community; rather, their association is primarily leisure oriented and their chief activity is carousing together.

masses. It is they who help most to prepare the town for its major fiestas. They have the most active social conscience and collective social life, and on occasion they have prepared dramatic performances to be played in La Vega and once—mostly for their cohorts—in a nearby town of the Toranzo Valley, where they have many of their social contacts. But most of their activity is indeed organized at the bidding of the priest(s).

The observances of Holy Week in 1969 provide examples of several of the phenomena under discussion. First, some of the substance of the observation was new that year and was introduced by the priest himself. Normally, beginning Thursday evening and throughout Good Friday, there is a wake in the church, with the body of Christ represented in the church's Pietà. In 1969, the priest decided to prepare an elaborate layout replicating the table of the Last Supper, placed before the altar for the contemplation of the people keeping vigil. For this he called upon the girls, and he made them responsible for assigning the turns by which the vigil would be kept. (He also asked them to wash the church windows, but they refused.) The girls prepared an impressive Last Supper table. The task of assigning turns was less simple but instructive for the outsider. The half-hour turns were scheduled for two to three people simultaneously. People of like sex and age would take turns together, but they must be people who would do so willingly—that is, who normally attended mass and "cared" about community affairs. Thus, assignments were confined to members of the sedentary community and concentrated among families of the Plaza area and people of long residence in the Casco. The assignment list clearly demarcates the socially active community, in which both political and religious participation is most intense.[15] The most difficult goal, however, was to find people from among the active core who were on speaking terms to keep the vigil together. This problem, along with the lack of an infrastructure to deal with the community's needs, and, indeed, the absence of a consensus defining those needs, all serve to underline the competitive nature of relationships in Casco society and its fragility as a sentimental community.

The primacy of family concerns to the exclusion of village-wide celebration for weddings and funerals in the Casco are the same as in the barrios, but the style of these events differs. After

15. The existence of this active core of the community corresponds closely with that documented—and similarly bounded—for the *bourg* of Chanzeaux (Anjou). The *bourg-campagne* opposition in Chanzeaux and other parts of France finds closer parallel in Pas than in most other parts of Spain. (See Wylie, ed., 1966.)

a wedding mass in La Vega (if the bride is from there), Casco families often host their wedding feasts in restaurants of coastal towns rather than in the more rustic and familiar establishments of La Vega. Casco wedding parties are normally larger, clothing more stylish, food more sophisticated. There is a greater proportion of friends, as opposed to relatives only, in wedding parties, and many of these may be from outside Pas. Funerals, too, may bring mourners from outside the family and from a wider area, a reflection of a different network of social contacts and a greater number of relationships with non-kinsmen. There is no feasting tradition associated with Casco funerals, though everyone recognizes historical descent from the barrios, where the tradition was most recently observed. Funeral feasts were actively discouraged by the Church in centuries past, and Casco people may have responded to official will long before the feasts became obsolete in the barrios.

Casco courtship style, also, reflects "centrist" patterns—those which have been distilled out of regional traditions and come to be identified as the national patterns and imitated as such. The standard Spanish courtship pattern, which I have commented on earlier and which is most familiar to readers, keeps couples in public—forbidding them entry into private space—until their engagement is formal and their marriage imminent. Cohabitation does not begin until after the wedding ceremony,[16] at which time the newlyweds are financially independent and responsible for themselves; they tend not to reside with either set of parents, and if they do, the terms of the co-residence are governed by a financial contract between independent parties.

Finally, in further contrast to the barrios, the common form of estate transmission by Casco families differs markedly. The donation of fields so common in the barrios is, after all, a way for parents to retire from herding, and Casco parents do not have to retire from herding. Estates are transmitted by testament—often sealed testament—at the time of the death of a parent. Land, residential, and commercial properties are portioned out to the heirs on an essentially equal basis and sometimes undivided, to be administered by them jointly. Widows seem generally to retain control over their estates after their husbands' deaths rather than relinquish that control by contract to children. Thus, frequently, a set of co-heirs will inherit twice, once at the death of the first parent and again at the surviving par-

16. I refer to open cohabitation. Many couples may have had sexual relations before marriage; the state of a bride's virginity at the time of her marriage is not a serious issue in this region.

ent's death. All of the concerns regarding inheritance and the making of good marriages, which can revolve primarily around property considerations, are as intense in the Casco as in the barrios. While hostile parties must live at closer quarters in the Casco, physical and unveiled verbal expressions of antagonisms are not as well tolerated there, and the drama of interpersonal, interfamilial contention is played out on other levels—the economic and political and the symbolic, that is, in conspicuous display.

Since the Casco businesses serve a population which is finite and even decreasing in size, there is a spirit of intense competition for local patronage. None of the larger businesses is without contacts and channels of exchange outside town as well, but the in-town business in most cases brings in the bulk of income. There is some tendency for businesses to specialize differently and thus not to duplicate one another exactly. One butcher, for instance, deals more in lamb than the others; one baker transports bread into the barrios more systematically than another; one grocer does the same with other provisions, while the others sell mainly on their premises. Some dealers import products from inland Castile; others from coastal regions. Some storekeepers deal more heavily in clothing, others in feed, in combination with other specialties. People keep a sharp eye on others' activities and jealously pursue their own interests. Relationships between people who are conceived to be in competition are fragile. Recent arrivals from the barrios are on the fringes of this competitive arena and are often minimally involved in it, except sometimes as satellites to people who are their employers or landlords. The longer a family has been settled in the Casco, the more embroiled it becomes, the more pitted against others. Great economic success, such as that of Andrés Pelayo, brings isolation from most others who are not involved by kinship in the enterprise. The richest are the loneliest. On the other hand, there are cases where true friendships spring up despite these obstacles, and they tend to be lasting and fruitful companionships. Further, the more successful a Casco businessman is, the more conversant he is in the world outside Pas, travelling in it often and forming friendships there. Hence the greater proportion of personal friends to family members at such events as weddings and funerals of Casco Pasiegos.

The economic field is inseparable from the political one. Economic issues are crucial in the formation of allegiance and alliance, faction and schism. Plaza society has been rent, since the 1930s, by two great disputes which I have been able to document, and by several others on which I have less information. None of the disputes is unrelated to the ones which preceded it, for the contending personalities are the same and influence the sides taken in each new affair. The first dispute, in the early 1930s, centered upon the struggle between two medical doctors to obtain the title of official town doctor (*titular*). (Dr. Madrazo, with his clinic in Santander, did not to my knowledge enter the contention.) It was possible at that time for an additional doctor to establish a private practice in the town; a private practitioner who was already established would not be removed by a diminution in population size which would prohibit the establishment of a new private practice. Thus, the issue of the 1930s was which practicing doctor would receive the title to a state-guaranteed practice and which would be relegated to the sidelines, competing for patients while setting his own prices. Large blocs of Plaza families, each for its own reasons, became engaged on the side of one or the other of the doctors. Simultaneously, the political turmoil of the end of the Republic and the beginning of the Civil War added a wider political dimension to what was in essence a dispute based on local issues. The tug-of-war is often described today in terms of the liberal-conservative issues of the time, but most informants agree that the basic issues were local and personal. However, the politics of the war provided a rationale for more drastic acts than would have been possible in peace: parties to the dispute denounced others and a few political assassinations ensued.

Prior to the dispute concerning the doctors, the activities in town of Dr. Madrazo appear already to have engendered much taking of sides. Madrazo's progressive views and his relative national visibility doubtless sharpened all of the sentiments about him, and people's stances toward him ultimately became interpreted politically as well—in terms of the issues plaguing the nation at the outbreak of the Civil War. The snarl of relationships and motivations has been difficult for me to untangle, especially because many of the hostilities are still active and still have their political colorings, but there appears to be some identity of personnel in the factions formed regarding Dr. Madrazo and those formed in the dispute over the doctors. The time period was much the same and the issues could hardly have been kept entirely separate.

The second well-documented dispute, of the 1950s, again revolved around competing interests in scarce resources—in this case the franchise to operate the town's one and only authorized dance hall. The franchise, in effect, went with the physical plant already equipped to handle the dance. This was inhabited and maintained by a family who leased the place. When the ten-year lease ran out, the emigrant family, who meanwhile had inherited ownership of the property, returned to La Vega to take possession of the business and the premises. The lessee refused to move, and the owner sued. After two and a half years of litigation, a higher court (in Burgos) ordered the immediate eviction of the tenant. The tenant's case may have been weak, but he had powerful relatives on his side. So had the owner. Numerous households became involved and the hostility between them persists today, in veiled form.

When Plaza people speak about their fellow villagers, they often refer categorically to their fellows as members of one or another interest group. This they do in terms of families, first, and secondarily in terms of issues, which change, and the characterizations follow these lines: "Oh, Manuel is one of the Pérezes—the ones who sided with the dance-hall tenant and were so brutish about things— . . . you know how they are. He married an Alonso but she keeps to the background and his in-laws don't cut much ice with him—he's still a Pérez."

As commercial people, and because their businesses deal heavily in imported goods, Plaza families have important relationships with non-Pasiegos outside the Montes de Pas. Business relationships form a basis for social relationships as well; some of these are asymmetrical in nature, with families of superior status, but most are probably with equals in socio-economic terms. Plaza people marry outsiders and non-Pasiegos with much greater frequency than barrio people do. Short of marriage, they display their outside contacts with pride and often seek to strengthen them through ritual kinship. For the youth, the focus of pre-marital social life is as much in nearby towns of the Toranzo and Carriedo valleys as in the Casco itself; the barrios lie largely outside the social field of Casco youth. Thus, Sunday dances, feast-days, and weddings see a significant movement of Casco people and non-Pasiegos in and out of the Montes de Pas, and this movement has increased with the growth of automobile traffic. Differences in style—from the naming of children to forms of leisure—between Casco and barrios are, thus, reflective of true differences in social field, sharpened by the Casco's better access to means of transport. On Sundays, the Casco's taxis are heavily engaged.

A few people from long-time Plaza families say, wistfully, that "today there is no *señorío* left in La Vega." They lament that most of the moneyed families who once peopled the Casco's upper class no longer inhabit their Plaza homes and, in many cases, have even sold them. Indeed, prior to the Civil War of 1936–39, the number of old Plaza families was greater and practicing professionals were more numerous among them. Their exodus was in many cases apparently related to the animosities which grew out of old disputes and were fired by the events of the war. The ones who remain are single women or retirees and, for the most part, those whose personal politics did not alienate them from what is today a community of predominantly conservative cast —when it is not apolitical. The emigration from rural zones of moneyed and educated people, however, is hardly a function of local politics alone—it has been a widespread movement during at least this century and probably much of the last and would doubtless have taken its toll in Pas anyway.

The result of the diminution of Plaza society is that the remaining "old families" have not the power of numbers to maintain some of their traditions of exclusiveness, and these have broken down. No longer do they enjoy their own meeting place— the café—but must mingle with herders in the taverns. No longer are there two dances, one for barrio people and one for Casco society. And no longer do the members of old Plaza families have reserved for them specific seats in the church. Aside from these losses, or perhaps particularly because of them, Plaza people seek in every other way possible to differentiate themselves, behaviorally and materially, from the barrio people with whom they share descent and by whom they are surrounded.

EIGHT

Encounter in the Casco

... esteem is awarded only on evidence.

Veblen 1899

... we don't even know if we're speaking with the right words.

a barrio woman

The architectural diversity of the Casco is a sound guide to the diversity of its people—diversity, that is, in terms of length of residence out of the barrios and rate of adoption of national styles. Stylistic diversity within the Casco falls along a spatial continuum beginning in the "fringe" neighborhoods (among which we might include adjacent roadside parts of Candolías and Yera, along with the Barrio de San Antonio and the Calle Atrás) and proceeding through the Cruce, up the hill (La Cuesta), and into the Plaza itself (see map 6 and insets). The stylistic continuum in space has its beginning in the barrios themselves. Within the Casco, certain barrio usages are still visible, but largely in the fringe neighborhoods, and national usages prevail increasingly as we approach the commercial, social, political, and ceremonial center. The correspondence between length of residence in the Casco and movement toward the center is not perfect—table 11 shows a number of families of three and four generations' remove from the barrios who live in the Barrio de San Antonio and the Calle Atrás, but these people conceive of themselves as being on the fringes, willingly or not, and some would opt for Plaza dwellings if they could; they are not strong economically, however. Conversely, on the Plaza, where there is a tight real estate market, there are only two owners (of structures 5 and 14) who were born in the barrios, living among the old families who concentrate there.[1] One of these is Andrés, whose years outside La Vega, money, and Selaya-born wife have helped him to close the behavioral gap which others close more slowly. His personal style is intermediate between that of the old families and that of new arrivals. The other barrio-born home-owner is a wealthy retired herder, the only such individual to become a property owner on the Plaza, and the intrusion into the Plaza of his barrio habits is a cause of constant mirth to others. I shall return to him later.

The cause of mirth is a congeries of habits which people normally shed long before, if ever, they become Plaza home-owners. Normally, the fringe neighborhoods are the territory in which such shedding, and the adoption of new styles, take place. In those areas (as well as among some of the tenants living on the Plaza) we find people—whole families—in varied stages of transformation.

People who have moved out of the barrios no longer live in cabañas. There are a few very old cabaña-like structures in the Casco, but they contain no stables; their porches, if any, and entrances are not as rigidly placed as in the barrios; their internal floorplan is altered; and they are fully partitioned and appointed with standard kitchens and chimneys. Their chief claim to being "cabaña-like" (a native term) is their exterior façade of rough stone (no masonry or whitewash) and slate roofs. No one builds such homes today; the remaining few are among the Plaza's oldest buildings. The Calle Atrás, on the other hand, is composed almost entirely of these modified cabañas or of true cabañas. (Non-herders living in a true cabaña on a meadow either convert the stable to new uses or rent it—and the meadow—for a herder's use.)

The majority of Casco homes have been—or are being—constructed in various imported styles. There are classic country homes, from modest to elegant, that use elements of the traditional woodwork and trim of the *casa montañesa*, the country home typical of other parts of the province. There are new-style houses, also free-standing, with wrought-iron trim. There are multi-storied buildings faced by the glassed-in *galerías*, or galleries, typical of the urban centers of the province. These often house more than a single family. And there are new-style apartment buildings with galleries of masonry rather than wood or with no galleries at all. There is a variety of décor and furnish-

1. I exclude the owner of structure number 13. In fact, it is the owner's wife who is barrio-born, and the husband/owner is from Espinosa—a butcher by trade who had his business in La Vega before his retirement.

ings, all of them imported, and a taste for the traditional "Castilian" or "rustic" carved wooden furniture is only one among many displayed by Casco dwellers.

While former herders in the Casco begin immediately to accumulate furniture and other household belongings to complement their sedentary existence, they learn the subtleties of style only gradually. Thus, concern with styles *per se* is evinced most perfectly on the Plaza and among other old Casco families. The same is true of clothing.

Clothing has crucial semiotic functions, both among Pasiegos and between them and outsiders. Most new arrivals from the barrios dispense with patched clothing and also accumulate more clothing than they had before, but its style changes little. Old families have achieved a degree of stylishness, in national terms, that renders them indistinguishable from outsiders and urbanites. This they flaunt, and retired herders can only hope that their children or grandchildren will achieve such stylishness.

Footgear is very important for personal images. The almadreñas which are so well suited for use on stone paths and in mud and dung are easily taken on and off at the house door and are one of the most distinctive trappings of barrio life. They would not be badly suited to use in the Casco, many of whose streets are not paved, though they do not keep out heavy rain. However, most Casco people avoid using almadreñas because they are so clearly associated with the barrios and might stigmatize their wearers. They resort instead to rubber, leather, or vinyl boots of standard design; these are much less easy to take on and off and tend to inconvenience wearers who go in and out with frequency.[2] Indoors, herders wear footgear which fits easily into almadreñas—soft felt slippers or, formerly, socks (*escarpines*) of heavy homespun wool (*sayal*). Leather shoes (*zapatos*) are rarely seen in the barrios; they are imports, purchased and worn only for special occasions in the Casco or outside the Montes de Pas. While felt or carpet slippers are also worn indoors and for daily purposes by some Casco people (especially in winter, for warmth), Casco people also own and use (in some cases exclusively) leather shoes. This is one of their distinguishing marks and it, too, is flaunted.

The importance of Casco styles to barrio people is evident, for example, in the fact that when barrio dwellers come to the

2. I have seen barrio people wearing high rubber boots or rubbers for walking in bad weather, as when changing house, but almadreñas are still indispensable to them in close range of house and stable.

Plaza for a special event, such as a church function or a dance, they usually rise to the occasion by wearing shoes. I have heard it told, at least of past times, that often, in order to save wear on their leather shoes, herders would not put them on until they were about to enter the Plaza. Then they would sit down, shed their almadreñas and escarpines, and don shoes for their first appearance in the Plaza. Plaza streets are mostly cobbled or paved and main roads to the barrios were until recently of dirt, as all barrio paths still are. Plaza people have to change or cover their shoes only in severe weather and after snow. Barrio people, on the other hand, are consistently condemned by the conditions in roads and stables to use footgear that is deemed inappropriate to Plaza life, so their habits must change if they wish to begin the process of integration into the society of the Casco.

Footgear is, indeed, one of the first elements of costume to change—even among adults who do not change clothing habits in most other respects. New Casco residents wear leather shoes more often and otherwise wear soft shoes (*zapatillas*) for casual wear. They are circumspect about the use of almadreñas, and some abandon them altogether in favor of store-bought boots. The symbolic importance of these choices is clearly recognized and footgear is often consciously manipulated in the transformation of the barrio image.

The use of the herder's staff and the cuévano are abandoned even more completely than almadreñas. The staff disappears entirely among Casco dwellers, though most men continue to sport lighter sticks on the fairgrounds and this is adopted even by outsiders or returned emigrants—they function as pointers and cattle prods. Cuévanos are occasionally seen in the fringe neighborhoods, especially among people who carry goods to market, but people are quick to adopt more standard carrying equipment in the Casco, where they are not burdened by the tasks of herding and where, in addition, streets permit the use of wagons or wheelbarrows.

Men and women born in the barrios who came to the Casco as adults rarely abandon the head coverings worn in all of their waking hours, indoors and out. These are for women the square head scarf and for men the beret. (The beret is, of course, in use throughout the nation among manual laborers of all kinds, rural and urban.) Young women, however, abandon scarves, while young men continue to wear berets unless they change occupational status, becoming students or running businesses. There is some latitude for choice of personal style in use of the beret, and Andrés Pelayo, for example, continues to wear it, but his sons do not, nor do most other business owners in the Casco.[3]

Some elements of the barrio image are less easy to manipulate and change than are the elements of costume. Among these are the body habits which come of cabaña living and use of cabaña furnishings, and food and eating habits. These are not simply styles, easily changed, but deeply ingrained physical habits and tastes which are not easily unlearned even when alternative styles are highly visible. In these respects, barrio families remain "barrio people" and it is only their children who begin to break the mold. After a generation or two in the Casco, food habits become broader, as they are among old families (though the Montes de Pas as a whole is characterized by fairly narrow tastes), and table habits conform to the national standards in which only very few foods are eaten from common plates and each commensal manipulates fork, knife, and spoon of his own.

In contrast to personal habits like grooming, carriage, tastes, and table manners, the traditions surrounding courtship and marriage change immediately when the family moves from the barrios. Parents who received rolda visits to their daughter cease to permit these upon settling in the Casco. Courting assumes the national style. The transformation is quick and easy.[4] Similarly, the custom of beginning open cohabitation at the posting of banns is abandoned as soon as the barrios are left behind. So are the initial co-residence with the parents and the donation of fields, which are closely linked to the beginning of active herding and retirement from it, respectively.[5]

The segments of the Pasiego population which appear as distinct types are in actuality only at different positions with respect to achievement of the ideals which they hold in common. The entire culture places high value on outward-looking, on living amidst other people, on a sedentary way of life, and on certain forms of leisure, eschewing at the same time certain forms of labor (herding and agriculture). The very mobility which mo-

3. This is even true in the Basque country, where the beret is seen among many urban men of means and states for them a certain pan-Basque identity in which rural traditions figure heavily.

4. The rapidity and ease of this transformation reveal the dominant character of Pasiego courtship customs as simple stylistic strategies easily dispensed with where alternative styles become preferable.

5. This and many other elements of the transformation from barrio to Casco traditions are directly comparable with those characterizing the shift from Fur to Baggara traditions of domestic style and management as described by Haaland (1969).

tivates the vast bulk of the population at the same time generates in some parts of the system the reactive responses, such as conspicuous display, which help to give the various segments of the population the appearance of being so utterly distinct. The achievement of the particular kind of distinctiveness associated with the Plaza is, indeed, one of the chief objectives of the whole social movement out of the barrios.

It is in the Plaza, where many of the superficial distinctions begin to disappear and social encroachment accompanies physical encroachment, that sedentary Pasiegos react to the least clue of barrio provenience to build social barriers between themselves and those who came to town just a while later. Those people who leave the Montes de Pas directly from the barrios choose, perhaps, more comfortable avenues of relative anonymity.

The attainment of "old family" status and a house on the Plaza are, of course, achievable goals for families from the barrios. All of the old families have made that journey and the same path is open to others. However, it is important among old families to try to close to barrio people the avenues of success, the entry to the Plaza, as thoroughly as possible—in other words, in the interests of remaining exclusive, they build around their small society barriers intended to be insurmountable by herders. These barriers are largely in the form of imported styles—material and otherwise—of which herders are generally ignorant and which they are hard put to imitate with much success. The preserve of the old families is thus one whose breach requires a generation or more of learning and imitation, built upon a sensitivity and concern for fashions which are foreign to the barrios.

It is impossible to consider the life of the Casco and not take serious account of Veblen's ideas (1899). In the Plaza we see the culminating local expressions of conspicuous leisure (especially in public forms of leisure for females and in church-related activities) and conspicuous consumption (particularly in architecture, furnishings, and female dress). There is the invidious strain in social relationships which informs all of the local concepts of social status and the emulative process which underlies the choice of objects for display and the style of display. These things are particularly striking because it is possible, as I have said, to define their occurrence in Pas in both spatial and temporal dimensions. In a ten-minute walk starting from a barrio cow pasture they make their first appearance in the fringe neighborhoods and they flower in the Plaza. When we then add the genealogical dimension of different families' histories, we discover that property-owners' proximity to the Plaza generally correlates with length of time out of the barrios and the degree to which display behavior is in evidence.[6]

Veblen would have explained most of the emulative, conspicuous display of the Plaza dwellers as expressive of "the master's ability to pay." Though it is true that Pasiegos employ pecuniary measures of worth to the exclusion of most other measures, the situation is really more complex: in a community where everyone knows everyone else's worth, such expressions are redundant if "ability to pay" is really all they communicate. They are more completely understood if we also regard them as ways of reaching outside the local scene to import material and behavioral styles which form barriers to access by people who have as yet less familiarity with phenomena foreign to the barrios. Spanish national culture, as it is communicated to the Plaza and interpreted there, is a weapon wielded by Plaza people against encroachment from the barrios.[7]

An example shows the extreme to which Plaza families can go to render themselves inaccessible. One old family has an elegant house with a marble staircase leading from the ground floor entrance to the living quarters. There was a period during which the owners required visitors to remove their shoes at the entrance (as in a cabaña!) and to don felt slippers, much in the style of some Continental museums, in respect for the marble stairs. Needless to say, the number of visitors this family received from within town was not great; even members of other old families found this obstacle, and those who built it, forbidding. The family no longer requires the removal of shoes, but the number of visitors has probably not increased.

Outsiders can find the material display on the Plaza, and the discomfiture of barrio people in the face of it, appalling. Recently, the disjunction of barrio and Plaza clothing styles for the children taking their first communion together became too great for one of the priests. He enlisted the young ladies of the Plaza in sewing white tunics to be worn by Plaza and barrio children alike so that barrio children could not, on this special and public occasion, be put to shame by their Plaza counterparts. This is the only attempt at leveling of stylistic differences of which I am aware, and of course it came from an outsider.

6. Indeed, old families who live outside the Plaza do not display to the extent that Plaza families do.

7. When Plaza families of the same degree of sophistication wield this weapon against outsiders, the fight assumes more of the meaning Veblen would have assigned it. Also, as I have suggested, it provides one of the fields in which hostilities may be played out politely.

In this context we can review the position of the one retired herder who purchased a Plaza home and has become the laughingstock of Plaza society. His intrusion threatens the integrity of Plaza society, and the old families see to it that this man's stylistic failures are a focus of constant attention. Thus, an outsider like myself is regaled with stories of the herder's inadequacy for his physical surroundings—his ignorance of the properties of electricity and how to use it; his cabaña-like furnishings (or, better said, general lack of furnishings); his use of almadreñas even indoors, and particularly on the wooden floor of the house gallery, whence his steps echo loudly across the Plaza; his ancient clothing; his general suspiciousness of strangers and of new ways, evincing an utter lack of sophistication about the larger world.[8] The entry requirements for the status game are rigid, and "pretenders" are made constantly—even sometimes painfully—aware that they do not measure up.[9] Wealth alone is not quite sufficient to make one a member of the Plaza elite, while wealth and stylishness are; and lost wealth—as described in chapter 7—reduces a family's status, even if it is an old family, simply because they can no longer indulge in conspicuous display and leisure.

Many other aspects of Plaza life-style appear as exaggerated contrasts to barrio style. The commercial community is generally the latest-rising community I have come across anywhere in Spain—many people do not arise until eleven or twelve in the morning and a few are notable for arising much later. The town waits longer than most for its morning bread, for bakers, too, keep a late schedule. There is a correspondingly late nightlife in the taverns, but the youth, particularly young girls, display an extravagant preference for travel, for dining out elsewhere in the province, for associating with friends from outside Pas whenever possible. They are also obsessed with displaying the latest fashions in clothing, jewelry, and makeup. Makeup, the least expensive element of personal adornment, is sometimes applied in a ridiculously exaggerated way. Outsiders are struck with wonder by its garish use.

8. I am not sure if the man actually wears almadreñas indoors or if this is apocryphal, for it is not even done in the barrios. Unfortunately, however, if this individual is caricatured by Plaza people it is in part because he lends himself to it exceedingly well.

9. I myself came under fire, especially from the Plaza's young ladies, for not dressing up more and not displaying jewelry—habits which would seriously have impeded work in the barrios. Aware of my purchasing power, they could not tolerate in silence my failure to display material possessions.

I also noted in some homes what I felt to be an exaggerated refusal by one family member to taste liquids from another's glass—a sharp contrast to the sharing at barrio tables. A cautionary statement I heard made to a child being urged to eat his food cited a barrio family of four children and the "fact" that its children had to share a single egg between them daily—a tale which exaggerates barrio poverty and casts sharing in a negative light. A similar story tells that in a family of legendary size— more than twenty children—there were not enough clothes to go around and children could only leave the cabaña by turns in order to appear outside in a clothed state. There is some tendency here to relate food sharing as well as sharing of clothes to poverty. In the case of food, this is a false correlation, but it is telling that Plaza people see it that way.

There is, finally, in many quarters of the Plaza a profound ignorance of the details of barrio life. Some of the Plaza youth I asked, for example, were unaware of the frequency with which barrio families move around, and the facts surprised them. Some of their fathers are far better informed. Barrio personalities stand out for Casco people largely when they are "characters" about whom anecdotes may be told; the people, their cows, and their stock fairs are viewed largely with condescension. Kinship does not mitigate these attitudes. Plaza people venture little if at all into the barrios, except for a few whose business or properties take them there. They enter with some apparent trepidation, surrounded and overpowered on the home ground of their inferiors: there is a sense of adventure, but not always a positive one. It is not unfashionable, of course, to go for walks, especially on Sundays, and Plaza people take walks in groups. Occasionally the youths will play a prank or two, or just make noise, but are ready to flee at any sign of hostility. Their intrusion is not necessarily greeted with innocent acceptance either. In 1969, a group of Plaza bachelors organized a walking expedition to San Roque via the mountain pastures of Pandillo. Half-way up the barrio, where both the path and the river fork, they had to ask which turn to take. They were given wrong directions, apparently deliberately, and their journey was prolonged by a couple of hours' walk toward Espinosa. If the misdirection was indeed deliberate, barrio guile was matched only by shocking Casco ignorance of the most basic geography of the municipality.

Barrio people, in their turn, maintain a jealous mistrust of the Plaza dwellers and are quick to cite hurts and slights suffered at their hands and to spread malicious gossip about them. One barrio woman whose *vividora* is in easy reach of the Casco school sends her children to the barrio school instead because she doesn't want them scorned, though she recognizes the superiority of learning conditions in the Casco and wants her children to continue their schooling beyond the village school. The woman with whom I stayed in the branizas questioned me carefully before I left, in deep concern for the way in which I would present the facts of barrio life at its worst—in the high pastures.

Mutual antagonism is explicable in terms of the antagonisms which traditionally obtain in Spain—at least in some contexts— between distinct territorial entities (see Freeman n.d.), but also as a response to the condescension and veiled scorn which herders habitually meet in the Casco. Mutual antagonism and mutual ignorance of the other party's ways are most pronounced between herders, on the one hand, and long-time Casco residents on the other. Relations are much softened between barrio herders and Casco people of recent barrio extraction; time and genealogical remove widen the gulf between them.

There are a few successful Plaza men who freely cross the boundaries, both territorial and stylistic, between the barrios and the Plaza and who shun display. They are businessmen who deal heavily with barrio people. One of them, Andrés Pelayo, was himself born in a barrio and has never tried to minimize his origins. He treats all of his customers alike and his style is modest. Another man of similar fortune but of an old Plaza family is equally accessible and unassuming. These characteristics are personal and yet also politically strategic; it is no accident that these two people have enormous power bases within the municipality, and that power in town tends to correlate with humility of style and general accessibility. In many cases, businessmen's wives are more aloof.

In sharp contrast to the Casco, conspicuous display and stylishness are anathema in the barrios. Display is discouraged, national fashions eschewed, and uniformity of style rigidly maintained. There is no architectural variation, except in roadside areas, and the true cabaña is ubiquitous. I have been told that when new cabañas were built (there is little new cabaña construction today), even after the advent of Holstein cattle, their traditional style was strictly adhered to despite the fact that the traditional stable doors are too low for Holstein cows. In areas near the major roads, many herders whitewash the exteriors of their vividoras; in Pandillo and Viaña this is rarely done. Everywhere, whitewashing and some degree of interior partitioning represent the extent to which vividoras are made "stylish": there is no special attention paid to the style of furnishings other than the fact that different families use factory furniture in different proportion to homemade items. A few people in roadside areas lavish care on their vividoras in all of these ways—they are mostly retired or semi-sedentary herders.

I know of only one active herder whose vividora is extraordinarily appointed—largely the doing of his wife. She lives in the stylistically conservative Pandillo yet has whitewashed the cabaña's exterior, painted the doors and window frames, and filled the porch with potted flowers. The ceilings and walls inside are plastered and whitewashed. She has made her kitchen as modern as the more traditional ones of the Casco, with an iron range, a masonry sink rigged with a hose to supply water from outside, cabinets, factory furniture, and linoleum floor covering. This woman also dresses her family with extraordinary neatness and firmly resists patching clothes. For all these things, she is criticized sharply by all of her neighbors, yet she persists. I do not know whether her cabaña has been subject to the vandalism which other women complain of: perhaps not, because one or another family member inhabits it most of the time.

In view of herders' explicit distaste for their own way of life, and in view of their demonstrated willingness to change such elements as clothing style, house style, and courtship style as soon as they leave the barrios, why do they not change as many of these things as possible while they are still in the barrios? We cannot say that it is impossible in a barrio to achieve enough awareness of alternatives, because some degree of awareness is always present and is partly what motivates the movement out. And it must be remembered that there are in the barrios numerout people who have lived parts of their lives in Spanish or French towns and cities, or who have close kinsmen outside, and that even lacking these experiences, the Casco itself serves them as a model of stylistic alternatives. The answer lies not in any lack of awareness of alternatives but rather in the realm of ideology and meaning, where the maintenance of uniform barrio styles can be seen to serve some positive purpose. Let us review a few pertinent facts.

First, while social control is generally weak in the barrios, controls appear strong and effective precisely in the stylistic realm, forcing the preservation of a uniform barrio appearance despite internal economic diversity and undeniable motivations to achieve a different life-style. Very few people demonstrate any interest in stylistic display. No sanctions other than gossip are brought into play against nonconformists, and people appear to be positively committed to conformity without the existence of fearsome sanctions. The maintenance of barrio style is a focus on which there is near unanimity among barrio people; it can indeed be viewed as a rallying point for the positive expression of a pan-barrio identity. There are many points of agreement about barrio identity, but few of them are in any sense positive; the elements of style, therefore, have special importance. They are viewed not as being better or worse than someone else's customs but uniquely "our own." There is a tendency to use national styles as measures of local ones in discourse with outsiders, a self-deprecatory attitude,[10] but this disappears when barrio people deal with one another. The styles in which uniformity is maintained are symbols of a shared culture and social position, a common way of life. In this there is at least defiant pride.

Second, barrio people display a virtually unanimous negative attitude toward the people of the Casco, especially those of the Plaza. Herders share a sense of hurt at the scornful attitudes Plaza people show toward them. This serves to reinforce the general mistrust of the political power—real and imagined—lodged in the Plaza; it creates a general concern with why people have to become "like that" just because they have stopped herding cows. Again here, as in the reverse direction, these attitudes are not affected by the existence of kinship ties between barrio and Plaza families.

It is useful to view the persistent contrasting styles of barrios and Plaza at least partially as effects of one another—of mutual contact—in a schismogenic system of complementary differentiation (Bateson 1935, 1936). That is to say that Plaza behavior evokes contrasting behavior in the barrios, and vice versa; each mode is intensified by the continued presence of the other. Defiant pride accompanies rejection of the other's image. There are two respects, though, in which Bateson's model of complementary differentiation requires qualification in application to the Pasiego situation, and these points are crucial to an understanding of cultural dynamics in Pas. First, Bateson states that complementary differentiation characterizes cases in which "the behavior and aspirations of the members of the two groups are fundamentally different" (1935, par. 17). In Pas, while the behavior of the two sectors of the population is different, their aspirations are fundamentally similar. The life-style displayed by Plaza people is sought by barrio people as well, and emigrants

---

10. This is quite notable in regard to the dialect, which, in self-deprecation, Pasiegos refer to as "bad Spanish."

begin to assume the trappings of that life-style—including the display behavior described for the Casco—as soon as they leave the barrios for points outside Pas, where they are usually able to adapt more quickly than in the Casco, where they are held back by those who arrived there first. It is not the life-style of the Casco which inspires adverse reaction in the barrios; it is the style of interpersonal behavior—the expression of social superiority—which is deplored and renounced. This renunciation continues for as long as a person stays in the barrios but in large part ends with emigration.

Second, Bateson states that "this schismogenesis, unless it is restrained, leads to a progressive unilateral distortion of the personalities of the members of both groups, which results in mutual hostility between them and must end in the break-down of the system" (1935, par. 17). If Bateson's assessment is correct, we must seek in Pas some restraining factor which has prevented breakdown, for there is evidence of stylistic divergence between Plaza and barrios for several centuries, though it is difficult to compare it in detail with what is observable today. The evidence, some of which I have cited earlier, is from documents and such material features as architecture and indicates internal social differentiation in Pas by at least the early sixteenth century. That behavior has become "distorted" in the eyes of Spaniards from other zones is borne out by their reactions to the ostentation of the Plaza in relation to the barrios—in short, they find the contrasts in Pas bizarre.[11] But there is no evidence whatever of past breakdown in the system, nor does any seem imminent today. For all of the same centuries through which social differentiation has progressed, barrio people have been using the escape routes presented by the forms of seasonal migration and permanent emigration which have come to be associated with Pasiegos. It is reasonable to assume that the

11. I found it instructive, gratifying, and somewhat amusing that Spanish friends, colleagues, and students from diverse regions of the Peninsula experienced culture shock in Santander province, and particularly in Pas itself. As Spain's largest dairying region, much of the province has a unique aspect, marked by relative dispersion of settlement, a pronounced dominance of meadowland with very little cultivation of any kind, and correspondingly different traditions regarding work. One of my visitors, a working-class man from neighboring Asturias, scanned the coastal plain from the Braguía Pass and—noting that there were almost no orchards or vegetable gardens or stands of maize—declared, "My God, these people are lazy!" Friends from the city of Santander were shocked by the exaggerated styles of the Plaza's young women, particularly their use of makeup.

knowledge of these escape routes has permitted the situation at home to remain stable. It is hard to imagine the oppressive quality which barrio existence must assume without them. In fact, the barrios have consistently been deserted by people at both ends of the economic ladder (as well as by many at the middle): the most successful foresake herding and move either to the Casco or directly out of Pas; the least successful foresake herding and move into the traditional trades which have taken them directly away from Pas, in most cases entirely bypassing the Casco. Any herder, in any economic position, can look outside Pas and follow the footsteps of someone of similar means who has left before him.

I have said that the strict maintenance of barrio styles is a rallying point for the expression of pan-barrio identity and that this is one of the more positive elements of that identity. The existence of this focus may be crucial for the persistence of barrio culture. It is difficult to imagine barrio society, with all of its divisive qualities, without some positive sense of identity. Uniformity of style creates among herders a sense of community; there is no other respect in which a sense of community is positively—rather than negatively—defined. Because style is in so many of its manifestations material and highly visible, the barrio community advertises itself continually. Style marks the boundaries separating the barrio community from outsiders and announces publicly the fact that there is a consensus of herders which subsumes personal differences between them. This would be less necessary if there were no challenge from the Plaza.

One other feature of barrio culture has similar positive functions in maintaining the community—the low evaluation of education shared by most herders. This keeps more people in the barrios and slows somewhat the exodus to non-herding professions and the outside world. The flow into barrio consciousness of new information and models for emulation—the progress of literacy, sophistication, and connectedness with the outside world—is also impeded by a curious disinterest in television within the herding community. This is anomalous for rural Spaniards, but it is only one aspect of the more general lack of curiosity which I found so dismaying in Pas. The barrio women who come into the taverns on errands, the men who play cards there all day, are virtually oblivious to the telecasts. First encounters with television have in a few cases brought reactions which have become legendary in town. For example, one barrio woman is said to have remarked: "Imagine! Now you can have a baby even if you're here in Candolías and your husband's in

France!" (Someone else is said to have responded that the old way was better.) Reactions like this fuel the hilarity with which Casco people view barrio people. Far more important, however, is the extent to which barrio people's "immunity" to mass media cuts them off from the substance and style of Spanish national culture. Attitudes toward education are part of this larger phenomenon. When barrio people have become settled in the Casco, they begin to enjoy television—or their children do. Then, also, they recognize the value of education as a social tool. There are a few families—distributed through all of the barrios—who are educating some or all of their children. None of these students expects to return to live in La Vega, nor do their parents want them to. The herders who consider themselves and are considered by others to be most forward-looking are insuring their families' future outside of Pas, the place where no one wants to be.

Pasiegos from different sectors of the population hold differing views of what it is to be a Pasiego, or at least they emphasize different aspects of Pasiego identity. For herders, Pasiegoness is defined primarily by the transhumant life of the zone; transhumant herders and those descended from them are Pasiegos. Thus, barrio people include among Pasiegos the transhumant herders (and their kinsmen) who live adjacent to the three municipalities, on the slopes of Selaya, Soba, and Espinosa, immediately across the mountain crests which form the political boundaries of the modern Montes de Pas.[12] In other words, Pasiegos—in the herders' view—are the inhabitants of and descendants from an ecological zone. When I questioned barrio people on whether their neighbor-herders were also Pasiegos, they would say, "Of course! They live just as badly as we do." For them, the boundaries of Pasiego country lie at the boundaries of the zone in which transhumance is practiced, and there is frequent marriage between Pasiegos of the "official" barrios and the "unofficial" Pasiegos on the other side of a mountain crest—those with whom they are most likely to share zones of summer pasturage.

Emphasis upon herding and relationship to herders is inimical to the Plaza's self-image, and its people's view of Pasiego identity relies upon a different set of facts: the documented history of Pas and secondary sources about it—on Pasiego history and

12. See chap. 1, n. 2, concerning the inclusion of Luena among these territories.

Pasiego lore. First and foremost, the very fact that there are archival and published sources in Plaza people's view speaks for the importance of Pasiegos in the history of Spain. Further, the emphasis upon documented history is made only by a literate population with knowledge and appreciation of the written word, and thus again the Plaza people distinguish themselves from the herders. For the purists of the Plaza, the only Pasiegos are the inhabitants of the three Pasiego villas and their kinsmen —those who share a common legal history—and the herders of Soba, Selaya, and Espinosa do not count. Although it is impossible for anyone born of Pasiego parents in the Plaza (or elsewhere) to disclaim descent from the herding community, kinship with herders is deemphasized. Instead, old families and those imitating them emphasize the eminence which has been won outside Pas by certain emigrants. At the time I lived there, two or three civil governors of various provinces, a Cardinal (then deceased), one or two bishops, a prominent notary, and a businessman in France were most frequently cited.[13] With one exception, these people did not have close relations left in Pas nor were most of them born there. The French businessman, who was born in La Vega and has relatives there, began his career as a goatherd in Viaña, migrated to France vending wafers, and eventually founded a large wafer factory in Lille. He was decorated by the French government shortly before my arrival, apparently for exemplary factory conditions in his family-run firm. The other rags-to-riches story is that of the Cardinal, who was also born in La Vega, but I know no details of his career, which evolved long ago. For the most part, however, Pasiegos who arrived at eminence were born outside Pas, to families which had already emigrated, established themselves outside, and begun to intermarry with outsiders. There is a paucity of models closer to Pas which people find worth citing and imitating. The road to eminence is long—usually measured in generations rather than years. It is an unhappy truth that the people in Pas who present the Pasiego image to outsiders have been left behind by their enterprising brethren who have emigrated.

I have written in chapter 1 of the noble status of most Pasiego families. Today, barrio families evidence no consciousness of the one-time status of their ancestors in the lower nobility. Noble or not, life is as bad in the barrios as it ever was. Various older houses—including some cabañas (but generally those close to

13. Dr. Madrazo is properly a member of this group but, for political reasons, rarely cited.

the town centers)—bear inscriptions stating the identity of some former owner, if not a coat of arms.[14] Most of these contain some reference to family line and suggest a one-time pan-Pasiego concern with these matters, in barrios and town centers alike. However, their style varies greatly, ranging from full coats of arms with statements such as "nobler than the King" to simple statements of family name, and intermediate examples like the one reported to me by La Vega's veterinarian, who found it in the settled zone of Bustalejín (San Pedro): *Soy el Pedrero. Hice esta casa con mis ahorros y dineros. Soy de la villa de Espinosa y lo mismo mis padres que mis abuelos son monteros. Año 1711.*" ("I am the Stoneworker. I made this house with my savings and monies. I am from the villa of Espinosa and my parents and grandparents alike are monteros. Year 1711." The rude rhyme is lost in translation.) It is interesting that the Plaza people show little more concern for the question of noble status than do the herders. To emphasize a status which was so widely shared would enhance the image of the barrios along with that of the Casco, at the expense of the Casco's uniqueness. But the reasons may be less perverse: most people who are not themselves historians seem to lack the sense of what the nobility was, or why; it left them no material rewards, and many families are in ignorance of their own ancestors' legal status. In fact, the inglorious nobility of the Pasiegos has been glorified by only a few—the amateur and professional historians and genealogists of Santander province who derive much of their business from emigrants to America seeking their roots after many generations out of rural Spain.[15]

Emigrants who are successfully established outside Pas are the Pasiegos who can afford the broadest vision of Pasiego identity; they are not threatened by the peculiarities of barrio style for it does not impinge upon their lives and self-images. Many of

14. I have not included these inscriptions and carved shields (*piedras armeras*) in my consideration of stylistic differentiation for the following reasons. (1) I have not studied them myself and do not know their precise distribution. (2) Since they are moveable, their original meaning and placement may have been lost with centuries of rebuilding cabañas. (3) There is enough variation in the content of the inscriptions that, were their original distribution proven, the simple categories of stone shields and inscription stones might be shown to be too gross.

15. Examples of the works of local historians which have fired the curiosity of the province's upper classes and its emigrants abroad are Maza Solano (1953, 1956, 1957a, 1961), Arroyo del Prado (1957, 1958), Pereda de la Reguera (1968), various works of M. C. González Echegaray (for example, 1969, 1970, 1972, 1974), and Banco de Santander (1957: sec. 5, art. 3).

these people maintain property in Pas and visit there at least once a year. Some make short jaunts to Pas from the more fashionable vacation resorts of the province. When they visit, they plunge with obvious pleasure into Pasiego life, mixing with herders in the taverns, attending the stock fairs, taking leisurely, solitary strolls through the barrios; they enjoy the landscape, the dialect, the cows, the diversity of style and companionship. These people don the beret, change their leather shoes for soft shoes, sometimes use almadreñas, and visit the fairgrounds carrying the customary staves—expressions which Plaza people do not feel they can afford. To be sure, there is an element of *noblesse oblige* in this broad acknowledgement of everything Pasiego, but it demonstrates that with release from the tight little world of Pas, Pasiegos can come to terms with their own history and appreciate the peculiarities of their homeland. It is noteworthy that theirs is a highly positive vision of Pasiegoness and sad that theirs alone is positive and unfettered.

NINE

Marriage and Emigration: The Community of Pasiegos

A Pasiega carrying in her cuévano, amid cheeses and butter, an infant: "We'd be better off anywhere else."

Picture and legend from a wine jug
in the ceramics museum at Oropesa,
described by Gutierrez Solana (1920)

At all levels of Pasiego society, the ideal lifeway is one of leisure. By leisure I mean in most cases what we would call idleness—a release from work which gives the freedom to do nothing at all. Casco people—and particularly the old families—are in many ways in a better position to achieve the ideal than are the herders, for they are often able to live comfortably on rents. But many herders also realize something of the ideal in that they may choose to live idly (but very modestly) on the rents from one or two meadows rather than exploit them themselves. Quite a few of the herders who move to the Casco do so on this basis, sometimes before they are of retirement age. Some of them do little more than sit in their doorways all day long, watching the world pass. Many retired herders in the barrios do likewise. Some of these people enjoy company in one of the taverns in the afternoons; others do not seek out company at all. There are reclusive people in the Casco as well as the barrios and at all levels of Casco society.

I speak of idleness because, indeed, this is what one sees most of in Pas: it is the poor man's style of leisure to do nothing. The pursuit of leisure activities in the company of others (largely card playing and other visiting) does not occupy a major portion of the free time of most barrio people, and solitary pursuits (such as hunting or fishing or even taking walks) are quite rare among herders. What we—and also most Spaniards—call leisure activities, either solitary or in company, are pursued at levels of society which are poorly represented in Pas: they are seen only among the older families in the Casco. Here, hunting, fishing, strolling, picnicking, socializing in private and public space are common. So, too, are travel and other forms of purchased leisure. Obviously, the ways in which people fill their free time are related not only to their purchasing power but also to the degree of people's integration into Casco society, with its patterns of ostentation, or into the contrasting, stylistically conservative barrio society. Most of the people of Vega de Pas have not learned the habits of leisure which distinguish it from idleness. Indeed, much of the herding community does not engage in many "productive time-fillers" either—by these I mean such activities as house-painting, furniture repair, general property maintenance—those things which country people do in slow seasons and spare moments. The conditions of barrio life do not encourage such concerns. To the extent that barrio conditions are extreme, so, too, are the styles engendered by them.

Where the life of leisure is not attainable, different kinds of work are esteemed according to both their physical demands and the attached benefits—salary and pension plans—which make the attainment of leisure possible when retirement age (as young as possible) is reached. Within Pas, transhumant herding is the most demanding occupation, and sedentarization is an ideal. Some people sacrifice income (in the form of larger herds which would require moving between different meadows) for smaller-scale herding, a sedentary life of little work, and a poor cash income. Many of these people, settled on single barrio meadows or at the fringe of the Casco, did not have sizable holdings to begin with, and the turning of a reasonable profit in herding would have come, in many of their views, only with immense struggle and physical sacrifice. A humble, early retirement into semi-idleness often seems preferable. The attainment of leisure in this way does not reflect an accumulation of means which can be passed on to a younger generation and it brings none of the social recognition brought by moneyed leisure. People with large numbers of children cannot afford to give up their economic struggle in this way, and the cases of early retirement are found mostly among those couples with few or no children and among unmarried people. Theirs is in some sense a hopeless withdrawal from competition by people who are able to manage it within town but find themselves unfitted to seek ways to the more highly esteemed release from work—the leisure which, supported by wealth, brings with it social recognition.

Esteemed work is salaried work with good security or commercial enterprise of a scale to permit comfort and some leisure, a good retirement, and the passage of financial benefits to the next generation. The purchase of higher education is generally regarded as an expensive way in which to achieve goals which might be more cheaply attained by other means. Positions requiring education and training are esteemed, but a good deal of attention is paid to the fact that success in them requires a prior investment of money—in education and training—and this is viewed as a drawback to clerical and professional occupations. For this reason, perhaps, careers in commerce have been sought far more than clerical or professional careers. The purchase of professional training is in most cases, then, a form of conspicuous display engaged in by only a few old families; it is far more current, and more often affordable, outside the Montes de Pas.

I wrote earlier of a regard for education as a social tool. Most education and professional training are viewed in Pas as just this: neither work nor learning is enjoyed for itself, but both are appreciated as tools for acquiring complete leisure. Genealogies yield a number of examples of individuals who, having acquired professional training and wealth, cease to pursue their careers. There are also people who, because they earned pensions for minor disabilities at a young age, never worked again, and died after a modest, lifelong retirement. These attitudes toward work and education are not peculiar to Pas: they characterize other parts of Santander at least. However, they are not found in all parts of the nation and Spaniards who visit Pas from other regions are shocked by them.

Esteemed kinds of work and the achievement of a stylish freedom from work are better sought in the Casco than in a barrio, but all potential is more limited in Pas than outside it, so emigration is even more desirable. For people who have no real economic foothold outside Pas, even though they may have kinsmen outside, escape through marriage is a great ideal. The best possible match is with an heir or heiress whose fortune would support both eternal idleness and an escape from Pas. There are a few such cases in genealogies and they were all regarded by my informants with envy.

Attempts to attract desirable spouses are materially most visible among the young women of the Plaza. Verbally, too, the girls are explicit about their aims: to catch well-paid husbands and move away. The young men of the Casco's commercial community are frequently passed over, and the result is out-marriage by both sexes. Barrio people do not have so many options, for their close acquaintances beyond the community of herders are few and, as herders, they do not make desirable mates for non-herders. I thought first that barrio women might be less entrapped than barrio men, that they might marry upward in the occupational hierarchy with greater frequency, but this is not the case. Just as Casco men and Casco women marry out with about equal frequency, so barrio men and women stay within the lower reaches of the social order with equal frequency.

I noted in chapter 2 that Spanish ideals regarding residential space are held by barrio people but that their actualization is frustrated by the conditions of barrio life. The same is true of ideals of marriage, residence, and occupation. The herders are less able and Casco people are more able to actualize ideals which, in fact, they all hold in common. As a result, the actual patterns of marriage and the degrees of social mobility displayed by the two main sectors of Pasiego society give them a widely different appearance and obscure the fact that people's strivings are the same in both cases. What the data analyzed below illuminate, then, are the differing degrees to which Casco and barrio people approach their dreams. When viewed with respect to Pasiego ideals, these data provide a concrete and detailed reflection of the obstacles which Pasiego herders encounter in the world into which they would like to move. The boundaries of this other world lie at the boundaries of the Casco itself, and because they are hard to breach, much of the herding community turns inward. Thus, the social world of the barrios is in most ways narrower than that of the Casco, even though barrio people can be the more mobile geographically. The inward turning of barrio society is reflected in the types of marriage most contracted and in the slow rate of entry by emigrants into any but the lower ranks of the Spanish society around them. But the barrio world is not uniform in these respects, as most of the statistical data illustrate.[1]

The 1,625 marriages in the sample were broken down into a number of types and by generation, as shown in table 13. Nearly 60 percent of all marriages are contracted between resident natives of Vega de Pas (table 14). Two-thirds of these—or nearly 40 percent of all marriages—are of people from the same barrio. When spouses are from the same barrio, more than half of the couples—and in Viaña as many as three-quarters of them—have

---

1. Appendix C is a companion primarily to this chapter; it outlines the nature of the data and of the analysis upon which generalizations in the text are based and explains the terms used in the text and tables.

TABLE 15

MARRIAGES IN GENEALOGIES

	Generation							Total	
	1	2	3	4	5	6	7	Number	Percent
Vega Male, Outside Female								213	13.11
Number	10	54	98	43	7	1	—		
Percent gen.	11.76	10.82	16.67	13.03	6.25	10.00	—		
Vega Female, Outside Male								301	18.52
Number	27	119	115	33	6	0	1		
Percent gen.	31.76	23.85	19.56	10.00	5.36	—			
One Spouse Vega,								69	4.25
Number	7	32	18	10	2	—	—		
Percent gen.	8.24	6.41	3.06	3.03	1.79	—	—		
One Spouse desc. Vega								27	1.66
Number	—	2	6	9	6	4	—		
Percent gen.	—	0.40	1.02	2.73	5.36	40.00	—		
Vega, One Spouse's Barrio Unknown									
Number	—	—	—	—	—	—	—		
Percent gen.	—	—	—	—	—	—	—		
Vega Origin of One Spouse Questionable								41	2.52
Number	1	1	12	16	9	2	—		
Percent gen.	1.18	0.20	2.04	4.85	8.04	20.00	—		
Within-barrio Marriages								640	39.38
Number	21	173	225	149	69	3	—		
Percent gen.	24.70	34.67	38.26	45.15	61.61	30.00	—		
Inter-barrio Marriages								334	20.55
Number	19	118	114	70	13	—	—		
Percent gen.	22.35	23.65	19.39	21.21	11.61	—	—		
Total	85	499	588	330	112	10	1	1,625	

TABLE 14
BREAKDOWN OF MARRIAGES WITHIN VEGA DE PAS,
BY LOCALITIES (ALL GENERATIONS)

Inter-barrio	Number	Within-barrio Marriages	Cousin Marriages	Percent Cousin Marriages
Pandillo		287	83	28.92
with Yera	55			
with Viaña	12			
with Candolías	18			
with La Gurueba	5			
with Guzparras	—			
with Casco	17			
Yera		114	18	15.79
with Viaña	47			
with Candolías	49			
with La Gurueba	11			
with Guzparras	—			
with Casco	33			
Viaña		75	17	22.66
with Candolías	16			
with La Gurueba	5			
with Guzparras	1			
with Casco	9			
Candolías		94	14	14.89
with La Gurueba	18			
with Guzparras	4			
with Casco	28			
La Gurueba		21	—	—
with Guzparras	—			
with Casco	6			
Guzparras		2	—	—
with Casco	—			
Casco		47	8	17.02
Total	334	640	140	

usually resided in that barrio (table 15), although neolocality has been increasing during the recorded period.

Nearly 17 percent (163) of all 974 marriages contracted within La Vega, by people from the same or different barrios, are cousin marriages. (This figure is probably low, as some cases surely went unidentified.) The recorded cases include 103 alliances between first cousins, thirteen between second cousins, and forty-five of unidentified degree. One hundred forty of all cousin marriages were among contractants from the same barrio. The frequency of cousin marriage in this category for each barrio is shown in table 14. Although the Casco is farthest from the alpine barrios in many other respects, the frequency of cousin marriages there is relatively high, and I attribute this to the efforts of the old families of the Plaza to remain exclusive and to keep their properties intact. The rates of consanguineal marriage in other parts of the Casco population do not seem as high as among the old families.

TABLE 15
RESIDENCE IN CASES OF WITHIN-BARRIO MARRIAGE

| | Total | Resident in Barrio | | Neolocal[a] | |
		Number	Percent	Number	Percent
Pandillo	287	160	55.75	127	44.25
Yera	114	65	57.02	49	42.98
Viaña	75	56	74.66	19	25.33
Candolías	94	61	64.89	33	35.11
La Gurueba	21	10	47.62	11	52.38
Guzparras	2	2	100.00	—	—
Casco	47	26	55.32	21	44.68
Total	640	380		260	
Percentage of Total			59.38		40.62

[a]This category includes a few cases in which couples resided for a period in the barrio but ultimately left, or in which a considerable period of neolocal residence was followed by a return to the barrio, but in an occupation derived from outside experience.

Cousin marriage is not the only form of consanguineal or other kinds of marriage in practice which require Church dispensation. The parish priests estimated that at least 20 percent of all the marriages they registered in La Vega required dispensation. Important among these are affinal marriages, largely of the sibling-exchange type, of which I recorded numerous cases in the barrios. The Pasiegos are hardly unique in these practices, for cousin and affinal marriage are widely practiced in the Spanish countryside (and in urban areas, too). Nearly 19 percent of marriages I recorded for Valdemora, in central Castile, required some form of dispensation. In Vega de Pas, however, the different sectors of the population display these measures of "closure" (if they can all indeed be called that) to differing degrees; the variation itself is what holds interest. The marriage of Pasiegos with outsiders shows this variation—this differential openness and closure—as well. Detail on marriages with outsiders is given on tables 16a, b, and c. Tables 17 and 18 summarize for specific uses statistics taken from previous tables.

The Casco stands at one extreme in most of the trends the tables illustrate and Pandillo, usually accompanied by Viaña, stands at the other. Between them range the other barrios. Yera

TABLE 16A
MARRIAGE WITH OUTSIDERS: VEGA MALE, OUTSIDE FEMALE, BY MALE'S BARRIO AND GENERATION

| | Generation | | | | | | | | | | | | | | Total |
| | 1 | | 2 | | 3 | | 4 | | 5 | | 6 | | 7 | | All Gen. |
	Number	Per cent	Number	Per cent	Number	Per cent	Number	Per cent	Number	Per cent	Number	Per cent	Number	Per cent	
Pandillo	—	—	5	9.26	8	8.16	9	20.93	2	28.57	—	—	—	—	24
Yera	1	10.00	4	7.40	19	19.39	11	25.58	1	14.29	—	—	—	—	36
Viaña	1	10.00	6	11.11	14	14.29	8	18.60	—	—	1		—	—	30
Candolías	1	10.00	16	29.63	22	22.45	4	9.30	—	—	—	—	—	—	43
La Gurueba	2	20.00	7	12.96	8	8.16	2	4.65	—	—	—	—	—	—	19
Guzparras	—	—	—	—	1	1.02	—	—	—	—	—	—	—	—	1
Casco	5	50.00	16	29.63	26	26.53	9	20.93	4	57.14	—	—	—	—	60
Total	10		54		98		43		7		1				213

TABLE 16B
MARRIAGE WITH OUTSIDERS: VEGA FEMALE, OUTSIDE MALE, BY FEMALE'S BARRIO AND GENERATION

| | Generation | | | | | | | | | | | | | | Total |
| | 1 | | 2 | | 3 | | 4 | | 5 | | 6 | | 7 | | All Gen. |
	Number	Per cent	Number	Per cent	Number	Per cent	Number	Per cent	Number	Per cent	Number	Per cent	Number	Per cent	
Pandillo	3	11.11	18	15.13	18	15.65	5	15.15	—	—	—	—	—	—	44
Yera	7	25.93	26	21.85	28	24.35	9	27.27	3	50.00	—	—	—	—	73
Viaña	—	—	21	17.65	14	12.17	4	12.12	—	—	—	—	—	—	39
Candolías	3	11.11	14	11.76	20	17.39	8	24.24	1	16.67	—	—	—	—	46
La Gurueba	3	11.11	3	2.52	13	11.30	—	—	1	16.67	—	—	—	—	20
Guzparras	2	7.40	2	1.68	—	—	—	—	—	—	—	—	—	—	4
Casco	9	33.33	35	29.41	22	19.13	7	21.21	1	16.67	—	—	—	—	74
Barrio Unknown	—	—	—	—	—	—	—	—	—	—	—	—	1	—	1
Total	27	—	119	—	115	—	33	—	6	—	—	—	1		301

TABLE 16C
MARRIAGE WITH OUTSIDERS: COMBINED TOTALS
FROM TABLES 16A AND B

	Vega Male	Vega Female	Total	Percent Total 514
Pandillo	24	44	68	13.22
Yera	36	73	109	21.21
Viaña	30	39	69	13.42
Candolías	43	46	89	17.32
La Gurueba	19	20	39	7.59
Guzparras	1	4	5	1.00
Casco	60	74	134	26.07
Barrio Unknown	0	1	1	
Total	213	301	514	

and Candolías, often accompanied by La Gurueba, show marked similarities to the Casco in certain respects: all three share, with the Casco, in the passage of the major roadways which have brought greater ease of travel, more contact with outsiders, and better opportunity for commercial development (particularly in the Casco and Candolías). Thus, Pandillo and Viaña show the lowest rates of marriage with outsiders and the Casco the highest (tables 16a–c); Pandillo shows the highest rate of marriage within the barrio and the Casco the lowest (table 17).[2]

The patterns, reflected in marriage, of the Casco's relations with other barrios differs generally from those of the barrios with one another. As shown in table 17, the Casco has the lowest rate of intermarriage with other barrios of all save Pandillo, whose case is affected by the very high incidence of marriage within the barrio. The rates of other barrios' intermarriage with Casco people are shown in table 18. The Casco, more than any other barrio, looks outward, while Pandillo more than any other looks inward, at least in questions of contracting marriage. The specific patterns of interbarrio marriage also distinguish the Casco from other sectors of La Vega. In general, barrio people—when they cross barrio lines in marriage—marry people from adjacent barrios. As shown in table 14, the bulk of Pandillo's interbarrio marriages are with the adjoining territories of Yera,

2. I have omitted from consideration here and at various other points the barrios of Guzparras and La Gurueba, for which the samples are smaller and statistics less meaningful. Pandillo is often represented to outsiders, by people from various parts of La Vega, as the "most Pasiego" of the barrios. The frequency of marriage within the barrio is also noted often. There is in general good recognition by natives of Pandillo's position at one end of the continuum of variation in town.

TABLE 17

PERCENTAGE BREAKDOWNS BY BARRIO OF THREE MARRIAGE TYPES:
WITH OUTSIDERS, INTER-BARRIO, AND WITHIN-BARRIO

	Total Three Categories[a]	Total Outsiders		Total Inter-barrio[a]		Total Within-barrio	
		Number	Percent	Number	Percent	Number	Percent
Pandillo	462	68	14.72	107	23.16	287	62.12
Yera	418	109	26.08	195	46.65	114	27.27
Viaña	234	69	29.49	90	38.46	75	32.05
Candolías	316	89	28.16	133	42.09	94	29.75
La Gurueba	105	39	37.14	45	42.86	21	20.00
Guzparras	12	5	41.66	5	41.66	2	16.66
Casco	274	134	48.91	93	33.94	47	17.15

[a]The sums of totals in columns 1 and 3 do not bear any relation to the true totals of marriages studied as the above analysis requires that each inter-barrio marriage be counted twice, once in the barrio of each spouse.

TABLE 18

PERCENTAGES OF INTER-BARRIO MARRIAGES INVOLVING CASCO CONTRACTANTS

	Total Inter-barrio[a]	% Casco
Pandillo	107	15.89
Yera	195	16.92
Viaña	90	10.00
Candolías	133	21.05
La Gurueba	45	13.33
Guzparras	5	—
Casco	93	—

[a]The sum of totals in column 1 does not bear any relation to the true totals of marriages studied, as the above analysis requires that each inter-barrio marriage be counted twice, once in the barrio of each spouse.

Candolías, and the Casco, in that order. For Yera, the bulk are with Pandillo, Candolías, and Viaña, in that order. (Yera's boundary with Candolías is very small, but the presence of the highway intensifies contact.) For Viaña, most interbarrio marriages are with Yera and Candolías. For Candolías, most are with Yera, the Casco, and Pandillo and La Gurueba equally. (Candolías is perhaps the most catholic of the barrios.) Casco people who marry outside the Casco's boundaries, however, do so mostly with people from Yera and Candolías, and not from adjacent Pandillo: the Yera and Candolías marriages generally unite Casco people with others of non-herding occupations; such potential spouses are not available in Pandillo. The Casco itself contains a herding population, of course, and their marriages follow the patterns of the other barrios; these cases account for the Casco's various marriages with Pandillo people. The asymmetry of the Casco's relations with its neighbor barrios is governed by the evaluation placed on different occupations and on the relative desirability of the different areas as places to live. Casco men and women of herding families do marry other herders and go to live in other barrios. But I have heard of no case in which a member, man or woman, of a non-herding family from the Casco assumed the life of a herder and moved into the barrios.[3] Casco men of non-herding families have not infrequently married herders' daughters from the barrios, but they do not go to the barrios to live. Rather, the wife moves into a new occupational stratum either in the Casco or entirely out of town. Occasionally Casco women of non-herding parents have married the sons of barrio herders, but almost invariably such marriages are associated with a change in occupation—and often with emigration—for the man.

The asymmetrical relation between Casco and barrios is replicated on a larger scale between Vega de Pas and zones outside Pas. This fact is made strikingly clear by the data on residence given in table 19. Here, I take residence in the place of a spouse from outside Pas to be a good "index of escape" from Pas. Indeed, as the table shows, for marriages of Vega people with outsiders, residence is heavily in the wife's town when the wife is the outsider and heavily in the husband's when he is the outsider. This pattern is strong in a setting in which symmetry otherwise prevails:[4] residences in wives' and husbands' localities are essentially equally frequent when both spouses are from La Vega (as they also are in the cases of within-barrio marriages discussed in chapter 6).

Among the marriages with outsiders documented in table 19 are a number with spouses from San Pedro, San Roque, Pisueña, and the Pasiego zone of Espinosa. The residence patterns of these couples are shown in table 20. Table 21 shows the pattern indicated on table 19 to be even more dramatic when inter-Pas marriages are excluded. However, the inter-Pas marriage sample, though it may seem a small one, shows significant trends which are not shared by the larger sample. Many fewer husbands from

3. One case is exceptional in all of Pas: an Andalusian man from a landless family who came into the area as a construction laborer on the railroad married a barrio woman and became a herder in Pandillo.

4. Chi-square for this comparison is 35.96. With one degree of freedom, such a value has less than one chance in 1000 of being due to random sampling error.

TABLE 19
RESIDENCE PATTERNS IN THE MARRIAGE SAMPLE[a]

	Husband's Locality	Wife's Locality	Both Spouses' Localities Simultaneous[b]	New Locality	Other[c]	No Information	Total
Desc. Vega	20	17	3	20	2	7	69
Vega Male + Outsider	30	71	6	75	5	26	213
Vega Female + Outsider	94	42	4	108	16	37	301
Inter-barrio	66	59	7	182	17	3	334
Total	210	189	20	385	40	73	917
Percent Sample	22.90	20.61	2.18	41.98	4.36	7.96	

[a]This breakdown excludes categories in which one spouse's place of origin is questionable or unknown. Within-barrio marriages are also excluded, as explained in appendix C.

[b]These are cases in which residences are maintained and property exploited in two places simultaneously—localities in which spouses have acquired access to property either directly through their parents or through their familiarity with opportunities available in the localities where their parents reside.

[c]This category primarily includes cases in which residence changes frequently and is governed by occupation—for example, by the military or educational systems, the police or medical services, or by the ambulatory nature of certain trades.

TABLE 20
RESIDENCE PATTERNS IN INTRA-PAS MARRIAGES: VEGA DE PAS PEOPLE WITH SPOUSES FROM SAN PEDRO, SAN ROQUE, PISUEÑA, AND PASIEGO ZONES OF ESPINOSA.

	Total n	Husband's Locality	% n	Wife's Locality	% n	Simultaneous	% n	New Locality	% n	Uncoded	% n
♂ from Vega	55	16	29.09	5	9.09	2	3.64	29	52.73	3	5.45
♀ from Vega	85	20	23.53	23	27.06	—	—	40	47.06	2	2.35

TABLE 21
SELECTED RESIDENCE PATTERNS (FROM TABLE 19) EXCLUDING INTRA-PAS
MARRIAGES (FROM TABLE 20) AND DEMONSTRATING ESCAPE FROM PAS

	Husband's Locality	Wife's Locality
Vega male + outsider	14	66
Vega female + outsider	74	19

Note: Chi square = 66.3 with df = 1. $\alpha = < .001$.

La Vega reside in the other Pasiego towns of their wives than would be expected from the proportion of Vega women residing in the other Pasiego towns of their husbands. There is less than one chance in twenty that this difference is due to random variation.[5] This suggests that, because La Vega's commercial development is greater than that of the other two villas, men from La Vega are not likely to find the spectrum of occupations available in the other two towns attractive if they are not herders. Occupational data bear this out for men from La Vega who marry into other Pas towns. Fully 50 percent of those who remain in La Vega are either non-herders or herders with a subsidiary occupation. In contrast, only one of the five individuals living in the Pas town his wife is from is not a full-time herder. Women are perhaps less affected by such considerations; their marriages with Pasiegos from other towns conform to the overall patterns of interbarrio marriage within La Vega. Occupational data for the group residing in the husband's town (outside La Vega) show that eighteen of twenty cases are herders and for those remaining in La Vega, nineteen of twenty-three cases are herders. None of the herders marrying women from La Vega is identified as having a subsidiary occupation. This also suggests that, much as men from the other towns might like to pursue subsidiary trades in La Vega, access to such opportunity is controlled by Vega families and this limits the chance for occupational mobility of outsiders who marry into herding families in La Vega.

As significant as the patterns of residence in husband's or wife's towns are, the fact still remains that in the sample of inter-Pas marriages, as in the larger one, neolocality is by far the most frequent choice, for everything except the grass is considered greener outside Pas than within it. Factors affecting residence, and even the prior choice of marriage partner, are closely related to questions of occupational opportunities and aptitudes of one or both spouses. Since there is at least a rough hierarchy of occupations in terms of their attractiveness, in local as well

5. Chi-square is 5.08, with one degree of freedom.

as in national esteem, and transhumant herding ranks very low among these (along with all herding and all itinerant lifeways), it is easy to see that any element of leverage—either financial or in terms of aptitudes and skills—is used to facilitate a departure from Pas. Even if the occupational alternative for an unskilled and illiterate individual is still one of low esteem, there is some advantage seen in moving away from Pas to live—or to let one's children live—in a less confining world from which emergence may be easier.

Prior to the epoch of Holstein breeding, the dominant mode of exit from the Montes de Pas was via petty commerce, often itinerant, often seasonal. The precise inventory of trades which Pasiegos plied, predominantly as peddlers, has varied with the times. Perhaps the one constant has been the vending of the Montes' own products, butter and cheese; I have indicated in chapter 1 that this activity was probably already of recognized importance by the last quarter of the sixteenth century. Another systematic effort—best documented in the nineteenth century— was the smuggling of silks and tobacco from France into Castile, across Basque country, and on into Asturias. The peddling of cloth—which was not confined to contraband silks—was apparently far more extensive than the Pasiego involvement in smuggling alone, and many Pasiegos settled into the villages and towns of northern Spain as dealers in dry goods. The figure of the Pasiego cloth dealer, itinerant or settled, is perhaps most familiar in the Basque provinces, but it is by no means absent from the Castilian and Aragonese meseta.

The vending of hydromel by Pasiegos in Madrid cafés was apparently a common summertime venture in the nineteenth century and perhaps earlier. Other summer peddling centering upon urban areas or popular spas involved ice cream and wafers (*barquillos*). Ice cream and wafers were sometimes sold by different people, but the activities responded to the same demand. This trade—at least in the period for which I have been best able to document it—was plied most commonly in France, in the southwestern area and all the way to Paris. It is still active, though more industrialized. Indeed, some Pasiego genealogies make it seem that all of the ice cream vendors of Paris must be Pasiegos. A history of the ice cream trade as a whole would dispel such a notion and reveal numerous other peoples with similar involvement, but Pasiegos were a strong contingent and were often organized under entrepreneurs, many of whom were themselves Pasiegos. As the demand for ice cream diminished with the onset of cool weather, most venders returned to Pas for the winter. Some people, however, stayed away in winter as well; there was apparently a close relationship between the peddling of ice cream and wafers in summer and of roasted chestnuts in winter; many Pasiegos did each in its season.

More limited attempts to supplement the living made from land and livestock have been documented for recent years; such activities have not been described in documents of the past but comparable ones presumably existed. There was the sale of snow from the peak of the Castro Valnera to bathing places in the Valley of Toranzo. This resource was free to whomever had the desire to collect it. Free, too, and used for the making of charcoal, were the remains of trees felled during the recent period of railroad construction. (The felling of trees now requires permission and would not normally be permitted for charcoal production alone.) The individuals who traded snow and charcoal were from the town's poorest strata. So, too, are many of the people who today sell butter and sobaos in markets outside Pas.

The poorer Pasiegos also sought (and still seek) employment as domestic servants outside Pas and, occasionally, in the Casco. Among these we must count the special cases of the *nodrizas, amas de leche*, or wet-nurses—hardly an attractive circumstance for a woman who could afford to stay at home and care for her own child. Picturesque as they may have been, characteristic as they came to seem of Pas itself, they represented only a segment of Pasiego society. This form of temporary migration of women grew, flourished, and diminished in approximately one century, beginning in the 1830s if not slightly earlier. But it was preceded, accompanied, and survived by an internal trade in mother's milk, in which women of the poorest stratum took on the nursing of other Pasiego children who for one reason or another could not be nursed by their own mothers. Among these, of course, were the infants of the women who left Pas to sell their services as wet-nurses elsewhere.

With the end of the nineteenth century and the switch to Holstein breeding in Pas, two forms of massive occupational emigration came to involve Pasiegos in numbers which had not previously characterized the movement into any single trade. One of these forms was urban and characterized by the establishment of the vaquerías, the cow stalls where milk is retailed; the other is rural and characterized by the establishment of milk-specialized dairy farms on the Santander coastal plain. Both together escalated the pace of emigration and created large, concentrated communities of Pasiegos outside Pas who maintained systematic relations with their home town. Information available from genealogies is heavily concentrated in the era following Holstein importation; thus, we have considerable documentation of these two important movements out of Pas. Tables 22 and 23 summarize the data on all forms of emigration in the entire span of the genealogies. Table 22 shows the preponderance of urban (44.22 percent) and Montaña (35.51 percent) emigration in the total spectrum, while table 23 suggests—particularly in the last six rows—the extent to which people from different sectors of Vega de Pas emigrate according to different dominant patterns. Again, the Casco and Pandillo show opposed tendencies.

By no means all of the emigration to urban areas is related to vaquerías—particularly today, when much is in unskilled or semi-skilled factory work, sedentary small commerce, or in low-status service positions. However, there are 183 emigrants with vaquería connections documented, and all but thirteen of these are in capital cities—none is strictly rural but some were classified as not strictly urban. A very few of these individuals enter joint ownership of a single vaquería or are employed in vaquerías in which they have no ownership interest, but for the most part each emigrant (single people or married couples) establishes an independent business. I estimate, therefore, that the total of 183 probably includes at least 165 or 170 individual vaquerías. These are heavily concentrated in Madrid (73) and Zaragoza (42), followed by other provincial capitals of the North —Valladolid (18), Logroño (17), Barcelona (9), Burgos (6), Palencia (3), Bilbao (2)—with thirteen cases scattered in northern provincial towns apart from the capitals (9) and in larger towns of the Montaña (4), outside of Santander itself.[6] I have no record of vaquerías in Santander capital, whose dairy needs are served by the large dairy plants located outside the city which collect, process, and market milk from the rural areas. Vaquerías sprang up precisely in those areas which were worse served by large intermediary institutions and without easy daily access to sources of milk such as Montaña people enjoy. The especially

6. Remember that these distributions exist through time and do not reflect the numbers of vaquerías operating simultaneously. On the other hand, not all of the simultaneously operating vaquerías are part of our sample. There is no way of assessing, from the genealogical data, the number of vaquerías operating at a given moment in a given city.

Table

Types of Emigration

	Gen. 1	Gen. 2	Gen. 3	Gen. 4	Gen. 5	Gen. 5+	Total All Gen.	Percent of Total n
Urban								
n	26	122	220	87	12	—	467	44.22
Percent Gen.	40.00	32.45	51.28	52.41	60.00	—		
Montaña								
Pas								
n	27	188	120	40	—	—	375	35.51
Percent Gen.	41.54	50.00	27.97	24.10	—	—		
Luena								
n	2	11	15	2	1	—	31	2.94
Percent Gen.	3.08	2.93	3.50	1.20	5.00	—		
n	—	1	4	2	—	—	7	0.66
Percent Gen.	—	0.30	0.93	1.20	—	—		
Other Rural Areas								
n	2	18	19	3	1	—	43	4.07
Percent Gen.	3.08	4.79	4.43	1.81	5.0	—		
Professional								
n	2	3	4	5	2	—	16	1.52
Percent Gen.	3.08	0.80	0.93	3.01	10.00	—		
International								
n	5	17	34	20	—	—	76	7.20
Percent Gen.	7.69	4.52	7.93	12.05	—	—		
Ambulatory								
n	—	—	1	2	1	—	4	0.38
Percent. Gen.	—	—	0.20	1.20	5.00	—		
Probable Emigrant, No Details								
n	1	16	12	5	3	—	37	3.50
Percent Gen.	1.54	4.26	2.80	3.01	15.00	—		
Gen. Totals	65	376	429	166	20	0	1,056	

TABLE 23
FREQUENCY OF EMIGRATION TYPES (BY GENEALOGICAL FILE CATEGORIES)

Category	Percent Urban	Percent Montaña	Percent Pas	Percent Luena	Percent Other Rural	Percent Professional	Percent International	Percent Ambulatory	Percent Probable Emigrant?	Total n
Single Male	52.94	17.65	1.96	—	1.96	3.92	13.73	1.96	5.88	51
Single Female	62.50	12.50	1.56	—	1.56	1.56	9.38	—	10.94	64
Vega Male, Outside Female	56.25	21.02	3.41	0.57	3.98	1.14	11.93	—	1.70	176
Vega Female, Outside Male	42.86	27.38	7.94	1.19	7.14	3.57	5.16	0.40	4.37	252
Vega Origin of One Spouse Questionable	70.00	16.67	—	—	3.33	—	—	—	10.00	30
One Spouse Desc. Vega	32.00	48.00	—	—	6.00	2.00	10.00	—	2.00	50
One Spouse's Barrio Unknown	75.00	25.00	—	—	—	—	—	—	—	12
Inter-barrio Marriage	42.44	41.86	0.58	0.58	4.07	0.58	6.40	—	3.49	172
Within-barrio Marriages										
Pandillo	10.66	88.52	—	—	—	—	0.82	—	—	122
Yera	57.14	36.74	2.04	—	—	—	—	2.04	2.04	49
Viaña	33.33	38.89	5.56	5.56	—	—	11.11	—	5.56	18
Candolías	34.37	40.63	—	3.13	9.37	—	12.50	—	—	32
La Gurueba	20.00	—	10.00	—	—	—	60.00	—	10.00	10
Casco	77.78	11.11	—	—	5.55	—	—	5.55	—	18

favorable areas were, thus, urban centers outside of dairying regions—that is, in arid Spain.

The concentration of Pasiegos in the North and their virtual absence until quite recently in cities south of Madrid reflect Pasiegos' strong preferences for those zones and, doubtless, for the other opportunities which they offer for alternative employment of emigrants or their children. When one man told me that the northern focus of emigration showed that Pasiegos "know where their fortunes lie," he was not saying that vaquerías would not have thrived or been welcomed in the South, but that Pasiegos were looking beyond the moment and demanded that their new locations offer more than just the demand for fresh milk. Even so, Pasiegos' progress up the social ladder in Spain's cities was often painfully slow, as we can see in the study of emigrants' children (below) and also from the fact that vaquería people sometimes returned to live in Pas at or even before retirement. It was in the very nature of the vaquería—in its symbiotic ties with the barrios as described in chapter 3— that its owners were in many ways in the city but not of it, and they did not feel at home there.

I have said little so far of the movement of Pasiegos to the Montaña of Santander, but burgeoning as it did with the coming of Holstein cows to Pas, that movement has much to compare with that to the vaquerías. Just as Pasiegos brought a milk supply to the cities, so they brought dairy stock to the coastal plain and made the province the nation's chief purveyor of both milk stock and milk products. Both the vaquerías and the coastal plain were peopled with Pasiego herders from the barrios who became sedentary by moving directly out of Vega de Pas rather than by settling first in the Casco. Just as vaquerías were present in cities like Madrid before the Holstein era, so were Pasiego herders already present on the coastal plain before then. We know of their presence, for example, from documents in the Montaña towns, where they appear in censuses, aparcería agreements, and the like, under the designation "Pasiego," which sets them apart from the natives of the places where they lived. They lived, for the most part, as far as I can tell, in upland sectors of Montaña towns, often on rented land and beyond the fringes of settled areas. Just as the movement into vaquerías took a quantum leap in the Holstein era, so, too, did the Pasiego settlement of the Montaña.

The coastal plain, the Montaña, offers larger continuous areas of pasturage on gentler terrain than can be found in Pas, and winter conditions do not prohibit the use of any part of a family

holding.[7] There are in some zones up to nine grass crops per
year, as opposed to the maximum of four upon a ribero meadow
in Vega de Pas. The common holding in the Montaña is a single
meadow larger than any single meadow in Pas and, indeed, more
comparable to many of the praderas in Pas. Many of these
meadows have been cleared by Pasiegos themselves and made
productive by them in new ways; previously these areas stood in
woodland or heavy brush and lay, as I have said, at the margins
of the Montaña settlements.[8]

The economy of the coastal plain at the end of the last century
was one of mixed herding and truck gardening, combined in
places with local industry and commerce, or with fishing and
maritime activities along the coast itself.[9] There was no commitment to specialized herding (or, indeed, to other specializations
either) to approach that which the Pasiegos were to develop
with Holstein stock. The Pasiegos moved into what were defined
as marginal zones associated with marginal activities—timbering and herding of pigs, sheep, or goats—and their rental or
sometimes purchase of these lands, which they rededicated to
their cattle's needs, became an important new element in local
economies. So did their cattle themselves, and the milk they
gave. The clearing of timber and brush eliminated the possibility of extensive maintenance of animals other than cattle and
affected timbering as well. The Montaña was transformed into
Spain's most specialized milk-producing area.[10] The scenery was

7. I should repeat (from chap. 3, n. 7) that my use of the designation
"Montaña" follows the Pasiegos' own rather that the more general Spanish
usage. While Spaniards use "la Montaña" synonymously with "province
of Santander," the Pasiegos refer only to the coastal plain, whose towns
all fall into the zone below 200 m. above sea level (shown on map 2). The
correspondence between this zone and the Montaña designated by Pasiegos is, as far as I can tell, perfect.

8. I say that these lands were made productive "in new ways" because
they were, of course, productive of income before also, but were not inhabited or consistently involved in food production. They were important
for timbering and timber-dependent industries and for the occasional
grazing of animals—particularly of pigs in areas covered by oaks.

9. For a portrait of the province's economy prior to the Pasiego expansion see Barreda 1950.

10. Spain's leading producer of cow's milk is Asturias (the province of
Oviedo), which in 1970 produced 12.37 percent of the nation's total with
439,541,000 liters, and Santander is second, with 10.32 percent of the nation's total in 1970, or 366,423,000 liters. Oviedo's bovid census is also
higher (355,549 head in 1971)—second only to Lugo (which slaughters
more meat)—and Santander's is third in the nation (280,593 head in
1971). However, Santander's cattle are maintained in a province only half
as large as Oviedo (10,565 and 5,289 sq. km., respectively) and both their

transformed as well. In some parts of the Montaña, Pasiegos can point to named hillsides, describe their former appearance, and name the Pasiegos who cleared them.

On the coastal plain, Pasiegos became primarily milk producers rather than stock breeders (see chap. 4, pp. 70–73). They became fully sedentary producers for the large dairy concerns;[11] their milk is collected at points of easy access and their life is comfortable in most of the respects in which it is not in Pas. They are still labeled "Pasiegos," however, and considered outsiders in the places where they live—particularly in the first and second generations and as long as they remain herders. Many Pasiegos on the coastal plain continue to live in unmodi-

---

exploitation and the destination of their milk are different. Asturias slaughters almost twice as many animals for meat as does Santander (103,-724 head, or 29.17 percent of the census, versus 55,938 head, or 19.94 percent of the census, respectively, in 1970). The official milk production figures for Asturias include 253,000 liters of sheep's milk and 648,000 liters of goat's milk, yielding a total milk production of 440,442,000 liters, while the official figure for Santander, given above, is exclusively of cow's milk—there is no significant production of goat's and sheep's milk. Oviedo, a producer of esteemed cheeses, dedicated, in 1970, 57,389,000 liters of milk to cheese production (13.03 percent of its total, and probably including most of the sheep and goat milk). Santander in the same year produced only 10,508,000 liters, or 2.87 percent of its total production, for cheese. Two-thirds (66.35 percent) of Asturian milk (292,230,000 liters) was consumed directly—that is, without industrial processing—a good indication of the extent to which milk production is based on very local demands and not integrated into a wider market. Only 90,823,000 liters, or 20.62 percent of the province's total milk yield was given over to industrial processing other than cheese manufacture. By contrast, only 133,732,000 liters, or 36.50 percent of Santander's total was consumed directly, while 222,183,000 liters, or 60.64 percent of the total yield, was processed industrially for purposes other than cheese manufacture. By contrast, Lugo, with more bovids than either Asturias or Santander, slaughters proportionally more head than Asturias, consumes 45 percent of its lower milk yield directly, and dedicates a full third of it to the making of cheese. (All of these calculations are based on data for the closest comparable years from relevant sections of the *Anuario estadístico* of the Instituto Nacional de Estadística, 1972.) The industrial milk products in question are primarily bottled, powdered, condensed, or evaporated milk, products for infants, and butter, and represent the chief products marketed by such Santander concerns as Nestlé, SAM, or Clesa. Nestlé, in particular, distributes these products nationally.

11. A few practice limited transhumance, in that they maintain some meadow in Pas and keep cows on it seasonally. They move many fewer times each year than most herders in Pas. There are a handful of families in this situation, some of them enrolled outside Pas; in some cases the exploitation of meadows in two different towns is continued in the second generation.

fied cabañas (vividoras), but probably just as many modify the cabaña's basic style or build or purchase houses of entirely different style. One of the crucial factors of continued marginality, however, is their residence on the fringes of settlements, on the meadows where their cows graze, and this is part and parcel of their commitment to herding. Thus, isolated residences in hilltop or hillside meadows outside of town centers are likely to belong to Pasiegos, whose meadows are further identifiable to the practiced eye by the absence of haystacks, which Pasiegos do not normally build; they store dried grass instead in the stables, as is done in Pas. And while most Montaña Pasiegos do not—need not—sleep in the grass, people *say* that they do, borrowing a stereotype most appropriate to the branizas of the Montes themselves.

Table 24 summarizes information on the occupations of all emigrants and of the number of emigrants' descendants—one, two, and three generations removed from Pas—about whom I was able to learn something. Some general comments can be made regarding certain occupational categories besides those with which I have just dealt in detail. Herding-related occupations are, for example, negligible when we separate them from such categories as vaquerías, other milk-related trades, and cattle-herding itself. The chief trade here is stock dealing, which rarely exists apart from other occupations in the list. Skilled trades are those which require some sort of apprenticeship, whether or not the individual comes to own his own establishment; salaried manual labor is less skilled and consistently more frequent. Transport callings are primarily of two types. First, many herders or vaquería owners have gone into trucking, for the demand for cattle transport makes this an obvious opportunity for them. Second, since many vaquerías have had to close recently due to new zoning laws, a fair number of their personnel have become taxicab drivers, and I believe this, along with trucking by Montaña dwellers, explains the increase in transport among emigrants' grandchildren (E–D2).

Both clerical employment and professional training (that is, training beyond the *bachillerato*) increase dramatically with time out of Pas.[12] Though it is hard to connect in detail the patterns shown on table 24 with specific parts of La Vega, it is clear that emigrants from the Casco are the first to gain such employ-

---

12. The *bachillerato* itself requires more than the compulsory education and is held by only a tiny percentage of people in the main sample.

ment, and the ranks are swelled in later generations by the descendants of herders, but not by people who have themselves been herders.

Such lowly occupations as those of domestic servants or peddlers are in low proportion among emigrants in the epoch covered by the genealogies, but this proportion is increased when we add the cases of ice cream and wafer peddling, which I have treated as a separate category. All peddling and domestic service would have been more frequent up until the end of the nineteenth century, but they were eclipsed, in most sectors of the population, by the emigration forms associated with Holstein herding and milk production. It is the very poorest people, those with few cattle or none, who still become ambulatory tradesmen or servants in the modern era.[13] Most of the ice cream vendors and other itinerant traders listed in genealogies originate from the downstream barrios, Guzparras, La Gurueba, and parts of Candolías—precisely those where the economy is most mixed and transhumance most attenuated, and where the Holstein cow has had less overwhelming impact (see pp. 29–31). In these areas, the Holstein-related emigration is much less and, instead, emigration follows patterns which are older and were probably more widespread in the past. On the other hand, the emigration to the Montaña and into vaquerías is heavily dominated by people from the alpine barrios—Pandillo, Yera, and Viaña.

Today there is a clear dominance among emigrants and their children (E–D1) of individually owned commerce. Here I include vaquerías, milk products, and other businesses, including those of entrepreneurial scale. These alone account for 25 percent of emigrants' occupations and over 30 percent of E–D1 occupations. They decrease to just under 20 percent in the E–D2 group, where they are eclipsed particularly by increases in clerical and professional work.[14]

Many Pasiego establishments—and, indeed, whole Pasiego communities—have grown up in areas where Pasiegos had prior dealings and some prior familiarity. Ice cream and wafer vending, for example, are most heavily concentrated in areas where both smuggling and some of the cloth peddling were concentrated: this includes much of southwestern France and also

13. Single women today dominate the category of domestic servants. It is hard to tell if they would have done so to the same extent in earlier times.

14. These percentages are low, for they exclude the categories of skilled trade and transport, in which many individuals also run their own enterprises. So, of course, do the vast majority of herders and peddlers.

TABLE 24
OCCUPATIONS OF PAS-BORN EMIGRANTS AND THEIR DESCENDANTS

| | Emigrants | | | | | | | Emigrants' Descendants[a] | | | | | |
| | | | | | | | | E-D1 | | E-D2 | | E-D3 | |
Occupation	Total $n=1056$	Per-cent Total n	Per-cent Gen. 5 $n=20$	Per-cent Gen. 4 $n=166$	Per-cent Gen. 3 $n=429$	Per-cent Gen. 2 $n=376$	Per-cent Gen. 1 $n=65$	$n=603^{b}$	Percent n	$n=119$	Percent n	$n=9$	Percent n
Vaquería	183	17.33	35.00	22.29	19.81	12.77	9.23	50	8.29	6	5.00	—	—
Herding-related Occupations	14	1.33	—	1.81	1.86	0.53	1.54	4	0.66	1	0.84	—	—
Skilled Trades	47	4.45	—	1.81	3.96	5.85	7.69	37	6.14	7	5.90	—	—
Salaried Manual Labor	101	9.56	—	7.23	9.09	10.11	18.46	75	12.44	16	13.40	—	—
Transport	22	2.08	—	1.20	3.03	1.33	3.08	18	2.99	7	5.90	—	—
Clerical	21	1.99	—	1.20	1.86	2.66	1.54	35	5.80	12	10.10	—	—
Farming	6	0.57	—	0.60	1.17	—	—	2	0.33	1	0.84	1	11.10
Professions	46	4.36	15.00	6.63	4.43	2.39	6.15	54	8.96	20	16.80	4	44.40
Own Commerce (Excl. Vaq. + Milk Prod.)	45	4.26	10.00	8.43	4.43	2.66	—	54	8.96	13	10.90	1	11.10
Milk Products (Own Commerce)	17	1.61	—	2.40	2.10	0.27	4.62	6	9.95	—	—	—	—

Entrepreneurial-scale Commerce	19	1.80	5.00	4.80	1.63	0.80	—	21	3.48	4	3.40	1	11.10
Domestic Service	25	2.37	—	2.40	2.56	2.66	—	2	0.33	—	—	—	—
Ambulatory Trade and Seafaring	6	0.57	5.00	1.20	0.47	—	1.54	2	0.33	1	0.84	—	—
Ice-cream and Wafers	40	3.79	—	4.22	4.43	2.66	6.15	21	3.48	3	2.50	—	—
Herding	355	33.62	5.00	19.88	25.87	49.47	36.92	113	18.74	7	5.90	—	—
Income from Rents	—	—	—	—	—	—	—	10	1.66	—	—	—	—
Other	5	0.47	5.00	0.60	0.47	0.27	—	7	1.16	—	—	—	—
Unknown	104	9.85	20.00	13.25	12.82	5.59	3.08	92	15.26	21	17.60	2	22.20

[a] Generations designate removal from emigrant, not generational designation for individuals, and hence do not block out chronological periods.
[b] There is one more case here than there are individuals in the sample, as in one case a remarriage involved a change of occupation.

Paris itself and the Belgian border region.[15] Many of the people
who peddled ice cream and wafers in France settled down and
established retail fruit stores, general grocery stores, or—in a
few cases—stores dealing in canned goods and dry groceries
(*ultramarinos*). I do not know how to explain these choices, but
it may be significant that they require no special training. France
is, further, the country of chief concentration of Pasiegos who
are employed in foreign industry today—employment which,
along with "own commerce," accounts for most of the contemporary movement of Pasiegos into Europe.[16]

In the north of Spain, early peddling of butter and cheese was
first supplemented by cloth peddling before both gave way to
the wave of migration into the vaquerías. Many cloth vendors
(the more recent and documentable of the early groups) settled
into commerce—often still in dry goods—in the areas which
later became the focus of establishment of vaquerías. Vaquería
owners, in their turn, have frequently established retail milk
businesses (the neighborhood *despachos de leche*) or, in a few
cases, creameries (*mantequerías*) or more generalized food
stores. Now a greater percentage of the youth is going into white-
collar or professional work.

When Pasiegos marry outsiders, including descendants of
Vega de Pas emigrants, the regions of origin of the outsider
spouses are largely the same as the foci of emigration. Outside
of Pas, Luena, and Burgos, which together account for 32.07
percent of the 583 outsider spouses, and the 28.30 percent from
the rest of Santander province, the distribution of spouses'
places of origin is as follows: Madrid (9.09 percent), Zaragoza
(5.49 percent), Europe (mostly France) (3.26 percent), Valladolid (2.57 percent), Basque Provinces (2.40 percent), Logroño
(1.72 percent). No other single area produced more than 1.5 percent of the total.[17]

15. Here one thinks of the old ties with Flanders, of the fact that some
Pasiego entrepreneurs were engaged in the Dutch linen trade, or of the
more modern cattle trade with Holland, which precede and perhaps
strengthen Pasiego presence in the zone north of Paris.

16. Of the seventy-six cases of emigration outside Spain in the main
sample, sixty-five were to France, two each to Holland and Switzerland,
one to Germany and six to Spanish America.

17. The Andalusian provinces as a group produced 1.72 percent of outsider spouses, but most of these couples became acquainted in Vega de
Pas in the period of railroad construction, and the marriages do not reflect any prior contact with Andalusia itself. There were no data on places
of origin for 5.49 percent of the sample.

Pasiegos' progress in the world outside Pas, considered in relation to such factors as continued intermarriage, continued economic ties with Pas, and slow occupational mobility, suggest that Pasiegos as emigrants find themselves encapsulated apart from the wider society rather than able to mingle freely in it. Some of this encapsulation is, of course, the result of positive choice: it is quite natural for emigrants to cling to some extent to the familiar—to people they know and to places where they know people. The role of kinsmen, in particular, in paving the way for new emigrants is well known.[18] Most new emigrants are, as outsiders in their new locations, somewhat encapsulated. Encapsulation deserves attention as a special phenomenon, however, when it continues through the entire lifetime even of people who emigrate young and when it appears to affect their children as well. In this sense, the emigration experience of Pasiegos (and other marginal peoples) seems most comparable to that experienced by other Spaniards when they migrate out of Spain, to strange countries whose languages are often strange as well, into the lower echelons of the social order.[19]

The degree to which communities of emigrant Pasiegos are encapsulated is difficult to measure for want of cases with which to compare other Spaniards on comparable questions. For example, I know of no study of emigrants' occupations which is comparable in detail to the material presented on table 24, nor do I know of any systematic study of emigrants' descendants, aside from my own very small one for Valdemora (1970a:148). This is partly explained by the fact that the genealogical method

18. Works which focus directly on internal migration for inland northern communities are Pérez Díaz 1971, on Tierra de Campos (in parts of Old Castile, León, and Zamora); Pérez Díaz 1972, on a town in Guadalajara (New Castile); and Brandes 1975, on a town in Ávila (Old Castile). I report some data on the topic for the Sierra Ministra, on the Soria-Guadalajara border (Old and New Castile) (Freeman 1970a), and again specifically in comparison with the Pasiego case (1976a). Douglass's work in two Basque communities focuses on the various—internal and international—forms of emigration to which their inhabitants have been attracted (Douglass 1971, 1975, 1976).

19. Anthropological work on migration into other European countries is being done by Gregory (1976a,b: Andalusia and Germany) and by Buechler and Buechler (1975: Galicia and Switzerland), among others. Spanish migration to Spanish America and remigration into Spain are studied by Kenny (1962b, 1973, 1976). Kenny's work shows that encapsulation can occur even where Spanish is the only language in question, but, of course, not all Spanish experience in Spanish America is best characterized this way, nor does it always occur in the lower ranks of society.

has not been used in comparable fashion in the other studies I have cited, so that data on migration are of a different order and differently organized. Thus, the portrait of Pasiegos' encapsulation in the following pages must necessarily be suggestive rather than definitive and rests heavily on my own comparative experience (Freeman 1976a) rather than on that of other scholars.

The comparative data cited here are from Valdemora, an agrarian village in a zone whose economic and social organization are well representative of the traditions obtaining in Spain's agrarian countryside before modernization. Her people share with millions of other Spaniards the positive attitudes toward city life and the desire for upward social mobility which have been widely documented in the countryside. Further, they consider themselves to be at the top of the rural social structure, and their calling, settled farming, an honorable one; few Spaniards would disagree with their self-assessment. Valdemorans share with millions of other Spaniards the disdain for herding, for wandering, which has brought the nation to sit in judgment on life-styles like that of the Pasiegos.

The children of emigrants from the farm village of Valdemora who, like many Pasiegos, concentrate in Madrid and Zaragoza, marry within the same area from which village residents choose their spouses in 27 percent of cases (ten of thirty-seven); they marry spouses from other places slightly more often (eleven cases), but in sixteen, or 43 percent, of cases, village informants cannot even give data on E–D1 marriages, which shows that ties have loosened. In contrast, Pasiego informants were uncertain of the same data in only twenty-nine—or just under 5 percent—of the 591 marriages contracted by emigrants' children, grandchildren, and great-grandchildren. The possession and retention of such information reflects the persistence of active communication within the community of Pasiegos in and out of the Montes de Pas, and this is not equaled by the Valdemorans for the same length of time or for the same range of purposes. Valdemorans move from their village into blue-collar jobs at the very least; emigrants themselves are fully literate and set about exploiting the opportunities for further education for their children and sometimes also for themselves. Their level of literacy and familiarity with the national culture, of which they feel and are felt by others to be fully a part, make their integration into urban neighborhoods and urban jobs smooth. They are at worst "country cousins" if they emigrate as adults, but no one views them—or treats them—as a breed apart.

Pasiegos of barrio origin are indeed seen as a breed apart when they move out of the Montes. Their experiences in different zones differ substantially, but in no place are they unmarked by their origins—not simply as "country cousins" but as true curiosities, refugees from a remote and unknown Spain. It is a matter of language and speech; of clothing, accessories, and body movement; of the association with a life of wandering or spent with animals; of unfamiliarity on the part of the newcomer and, for the old city dweller, unacceptance.

The substance of the Pasiego's distinctiveness is in the eye of the beholder. In the Montaña itself, where the literature or mythology of pasieguería is part of every consciousness, "Pasiego" is a truly ethnic designation, implying a differentness that puts Pasiegos (when they are visible as such) beyond the pale of Spanishness. The image is kept alive in every marketplace and stock fair, or on the streets of major market towns, where barrio people appear with staves or cuévanos and their generally rustic appearance is accentuated by the sound of their speech. I have heard older barrio women exchange tales of their experiences as they wandered through the Montaña, vending their wares, and sought places to rest at night. The occasions on which they remarked especially were those on which they were not treated as animals, were given a clean place to sleep in an outbuilding, or even sometimes a bed, and were offered even token amounts of food. Normally, Pasiegos carried some food with them when they traveled and expected to be left to sleep in the open, against haystacks, or in any shelter they could find. They were, for the most part, tolerated, but were sometimes chased away and were most often the objects of suspicion as well as disdain.

The presence of Pasiegos in the towns of the Montaña, first as peddlers and later as herders, has led non-Pasiegos of the province to produce a large inventory of "Pasiego jokes" which stress a combination of craftiness in money matters with rustic ignorance and suspiciousness of others. These are never repeated in the Pasiego community—many Pasiegos are probably unaware of them—and their repetition in these pages would be wholly inappropriate. But because they have become part of Montaña culture, these jokes keep attitudes toward Pasiegos much alive and deepen the stereotype.

Two well-traveled men from La Vega, one an artisan and one a stock dealer, show their understanding of the Pasiego's situation beyond his native Montes. One, discussing Pasiegos as traders, says: "The tratante is a well-dressed Gypsy." He recognizes that the Pasiego and the Gypsy are distained in much the same way; while the Pasiego is one notch above the Gypsy and considered not quite so different, both are pressed in their dealings in the wider society to make the best of every bargain, bargaining as strangers and not as friends or neighbors,[20] and both communities are made to suffer from exaggerated notions of their success in so doing. The second man remarks on the question of ignorance and suspiciousness of the outside world: "They talk here about people who are 'foxy' [*zorro*]. That means they swallow up information but give no response, because they think a response would commit them to something. They don't know enough about the world to *lose* their suspicion." Pasiegos do not always associate foxiness (being *zorro*) with ignorance. The term is applied to members of the community who, like the man I quote here, have had financial success in dealing with the outside world precisely through educating themselves to its ways. Foxiness in the speaker's sense—suspicion stemming from ignorance—is an important element of the stereotype of Pasiegos held by non-Pasiegos, but a different term is normally used to describe it: *recelo* (adj. *receloso*), timidity or fear combined with suspicion. Far from being an unwarranted part of the stereotype, this word accurately describes the attitudes of many barrio Pasiegos, and it is important to emphasize the element of fear along with innocence.

Images of the Pasiego deriving from contact in the marketplace and from his behavior there are widespread in the north of Spain, but outside of the province of Santander, beyond the orbit of the Santanderino's historical and ethnographic consciousness, the mythology of non-Spanish origins of Pasiegos is, as far as I know, absent. Rather, Pasiegoness is, as I have said, associated with a pronounced general rusticity, a sense of their remote (yet Spanish) homeland, and an association with the trades they ply. Associations with particular trades often become bound up with notions of ethnicity in Spain and elsewhere. Pasiegos of the North, as cloth traders, milk retailers, ice cream vendors, are not generally assigned non-Spanish origins by the people they deal with, but the term "Pasiego" can become almost synonymous with different trades in different regions, just as in some circles "Pasiega" signifies wet-nurse without exception.[21]

20. In much of Spanish tradition, friends and neighbors must not bargain at all with one another: bargaining is only for outsiders. Traditional attitudes toward commerce are considered briefly in chapter 10.

21. There are numerous such associations in Spanish usage—involving various trades and Gypsies, Gallegos, Jews (historically), and many

The vaquería owner, to be sure, is particularly distinct, living as he does with his cows in the middle of the city. In this more recent context, the Pasiego is again identified with a calling but not, generally, with non-Spanish origins: but being accepted as Spanish does not much help a man who lives with cows in mid-city to move upward in city society. It is this problem—for the herders of the city and those of the Montaña—which is reflected in the fact that Pasiegos do not loosen their economic ties with Pas any more than they loosen their social ones. In this they differ from the Valdemoran, who typically maintains close social ties with the village but relinquishes his share of his inherited land by selling it to the kinsman who works it relatively soon after he finds his footing in the city. Well before a Valdemoran farmer dies, he normally owns—through such purchase and through his own inheritance—all the land his father worked. Emigrants do not figure heavily in the census of the village's land holdings. In Vega de Pas, on the other hand, the cadaster is a register of Pasiegos in and out of Pas—some of them are descendants of emigrants who maintain their holdings even in a town in which they were not born.

The retention of property by emigrants is notable in Casco and barrios alike. Members of old families retain title to homes largely for summer use—not because they need economic security; many of these homes stand empty much or all of the time. In areas like the Calle Atrás, houses are often leased out, as are their meadows. This is the standard case in the barrios, too, where herders often rent cabaña and meadow from absentee owners. The reluctance of emigrants to sell their holdings worsens conditions for resident Pasiegos, many of whom must pay rents all their lives on some of the meadows they use.

A plot in the cemetery, too, is a thing to hold onto: the cemetery is a burial place for people born in La Vega. Regardless whom they have married or where they die, their bodies are returned to La Vega for burial whenever feasible, from all over Spain and Europe.[22]

Living emigrants also sometimes return to La Vega. Indeed, it is hard to determine with certainty if people are emigrants before they die, for in many of their occupations it is standard to

---

others. The phenomenon is dealt with briefly in chapter 10 but merits separate study.

22. Sometimes funerals are held elsewhere and interment in Pas follows, but there are frequent funerals for emigrants in Pas as well. Children of emigrants are not normally buried in La Vega, however. The Valdemoran case is again different: only members of resident families are buried there.

be of both worlds—this is true of all peddling, of the vaquerías, of much of domestic service, of smuggling, of wet-nursing. Of the eighteen clearest cases recorded, in which people resided elsewhere for years before their return, one was self-employed and one professional; three were employed laborers and three herders from the Montaña; four were peddlers and the largest number, six, were vaquería owners. This is not a high percentage of returnees and should remind us of the fact that even people who reside in Pas are not enthusiastic about living there. The emigrant who returns to such a setting is one of the few who does not persevere in the desire to quit the place. The maintenance of property is a good measure of the insecurity, economic and otherwise, which people feel outside of Pas, but it is not a measure of their desire to establish a permanent foothold elsewhere.

Pasiegos aid one another in emerging from Pas; mutual assistance may well be more common among them outside than inside Pas. In this way is built a community whose members depend socially and in some respects economically upon one another and on their home zone as well. The Montaña herders, for example, are important to Pas herders as contacts and middle-men in cattle trade. Their roles as intermediaries in helping new emigrants become established—in discovering rental possibilities and the like—is incalculable. Vaquería owners today serve the same kind of function in assisting their compatriots into the cities, but their function here is no different from that of urban Pasiegos in other professions as well. In the past, the vaquerías had a more specific brokerage function: they were the loci in which wet-nurses made their contracts. The matrons of families wanting wet-nurses visited the vaquerías of their acquaintance, accompanied perhaps by their doctors, to interview candidate Pasiegas, who lodged in the vaquerías until they took positions.[23]

In a more diffuse way, much of the cattle transport business today is fostered by the needs of the large emigrant communities of herders, both rural and urban, just as the trade in cattle— mature cows and their female calves—links them all to Pas.

Continued intermarriage of Pasiegos results from and rein-

23. Madrid was the chief marketplace for wet-nurses. A few modern sources mention a market for wet-nurses in Madrid's Plaza de Santa Cruz. My informants were surprised by this. However, sources from the mid-nineteenth century, prior to the massive establishment of vaquerías, mention the market there (see Bretón de los Herreros 1851). Evidently, the vaquerías, once established, made obsolete this more public market.

forces the social contact and economic interests which cement the community of Pasiegos. Among E–D1 emigrants, 15.59 percent of marriages (77 of 494) are with Pasiegos from Pas and 2.02 percent more (ten of 494) are with people descended from Pas. Ties weaken in the E–D2 group. Only 5.68 percent of marriages (five of eighty-eight) are with spouses from Pas and 1.13 percent (one marriage) with descendants of Pasiegos. Of the nine E–D3 marriages, one is with a native of Pas and one with a person of Pasiego descent.

The two separate great communities—in the Montaña and in the vaquerías[24]—are not closely linked to one another, though each is to Pas. There is only a small amount of intermarriage between them, though there are, of course, ties of kinship and a history of neighborship. The economic needs of each of these two communities of milk producers are similar—access to seed bulls of the desired quality, outlets for sale of male calves, and a place to raise (or have raised by others) female calves.[25] The Montes de Pas serves these needs; the Montaña and vaquería communities do not complement and serve one another as the Montes zone complements and serves each of them. This is clearly reflected in the marriage patterns of emigrants' descendants: Montaña people and vaquería people both take spouses from Pas but not significantly from one another. This is demonstrated in table 25, where the sample of E–D1 marriages is large for both Montaña and vaquería people. Montaña people take spouses from Pas about 19 percent of the time but take spouses from the Montaña itself three times as often. Other marriages, which would include the few with vaquería people, are in a small minority. Vaquería people take spouses from Pas in nearly 16 percent of the cases, from the Montaña in less than 2 percent, and from other areas in a vast majority of cases. In this "other" category, spouses from urban areas and from the vaquería community itself figure heavily. Each of the two emigrant communities, then, perpetuates important ties with Pas and is internally cemented as well, by marriage, by some community of

24. The "community" of vaquería people is obviously more dispersed than the Montaña community and its internal ties (from city to city) weaker.

25. Sources from the period of heaviest emigration of herders into vaquerías and the Montaña describe the economy of the home zone as one heavily involved in the *recría*, or raising-up, of dairy cattle born outside Pas, an emphasis which today is negligible in comparison with the *cría*, or home-breeding, of stock. The change is due especially to the modern tendency to sell cows after they have calved, and to the fact that Montaña herders now raise much of their own stock from calf.

economic interest, and by shared status, past and present, as Pasiego herders. These ties alone might support placing the case far on the "encapsulation" end of a continuum, were similar data drawn up for other groups of Spaniards outside their home zones.

TABLE 25
MARRIAGES OF MONTAÑA AND VAQUERÍA PASIEGOS WITH SPOUSES
FROM PAS AND THE MONTAÑA[a]

A. Spouses of Montaña Pasiegos

	n	Montaña	% n	Pas	% n	Other	% n	Un-coded	% n
E-D1	174	106	60.92	33	18.97	18	10.34	17	9.77
E-D2	22	9	40.91	—	—	4	18.18	9	40.91
E-D3	—	—	—	—	—	—	—	—	—

B. Spouses of Vaquería Pasiegos

	n	Montaña	% n	Pas	% n	Other	% n	Un-coded	% n
E-D1	107	2	1.87	17	15.89	81	75.70	17	15.89
E-D2	15	—	—	4	26.66	6	0.40	5	33.33
E-D3	4	—	—	1	25.00	3	75.00	—	—

[a]Individuals of uncertain marital status are excluded from the totals. The data are not absolutely symmetrical, because there was no consistent information available on the occupations of spouses' parents. Thus, there is no figure for marriages of Montaña people with spouses whose parents had vaquerías, for example, for "vaquería" is an occupational datum and "Montaña" is a residential one. However, the "Montaña" category is almost purely composed of herders and can be used as an occupational one. Thus, the marriages between the two communities are identified in the "Montaña" columns of the table's lower section.

Finally, we must ask how the occupational spectrum changes and diversifies for successive generations born outside of Pas. The bulk of these data were presented in table 24, but I have been particularly concerned with occupational mobility not only as a function of time out of Pas but also as a function of family occupational history. Thus, I made a special study, presented in table 26, of the occupations of all descendants of emigrants whose parents, regardless of the degree of remove from Pas, were either rural herders (mostly but not exclusively in the Montaña) or vaquería owners. While there is a high rate of continuation of the parents' occupation in both groups, there are also striking differences between them which help to fill out the portraits of the communities of emigrants. Children of vaquería families continue in vaquerías in nearly one-quarter of cases, but children of herders are twice as likely to remain herders:

nearly half of them do. The statistics indicate clearly that the urban situation of the vaquerías has made it far easier for Pasiegos to educate their children for trades far above their own in social esteem. The largest single set of occupations after vaquerías themselves is the professions, and this is followed by independent commerce and clerical work. The children of herders who do not themselves become herders, on the other hand, most often become salaried laborers (largely in the Montaña), while relatively few receive training in skilled trades. The numbers of clerical employees and trained professionals are strikingly low.

TABLE 26
OCCUPATIONS OF SELECTED DESCENDANTS OF EMIGRANTS, CLASSED BY THEIR
PARENTS' OCCUPATIONS (E-D1, E-D2, E-D3 COMBINED)

Offspring Occupation:	Offspring of Herders: $n = 204$ % n	Offspring of Vaquería Owners: $n = 181$ % n
Vaquería	2.5	23.2
Herding-related	0.5	1.1
Skilled Trades	6.9	5.5
Salaried Labor	19.6	5.5
Transport	1.0	5.5
Clerical	2.5	7.2
Farming	—	1.1
Professions	1.5	14.4
Own Commerce (Except Vaquería and Milk Products)	4.9	8.3
Milk Products (Own Commerce)	—	2.2
Entrepreneurial-scale Commerce	—	1.7
Domestic Service	0.5	—
Ambulatory Trade and Seafaring	0.5	0.6
Ice-cream and Wafers	—	—
Herding	47.1	6.1
Income from Rents	1.0	1.7
Other	—	—
Unknown	11.8	16.0

The social isolation of a vaquería family in a Spanish city—except from other Pasiegos—is pronounced beyond doubt, as is the stigma on all herding peoples in Spain. Yet it is clearly possible for the child of such a family to leave his home daily, attend school, and make a good career for himself. (Such children's relations with their age-mates in school and neighborhood would make an important and interesting study.) One note on the statistics of improved status is that many of the cases occur in the same families, while other families have not apparently encouraged their youth to better themselves, so we have some vaquería families whose children are all doctors, lawyers, or teachers in the first generation born out of Pas and others whose children, grandchildren, and great-grandchildren are still to be found in vaquerías, or selling milk, or driving taxis. Part of the "encapsulation" phenomenon is, clearly, a question of motivations rather than of the simple presence or absence of opportunity. The vaquería community can make a fuller range of positive choices than can the Pasiegos in the Montaña, and there must be a considerable selective factor involved in who emigrates to the Montaña in the first place. But in both settings, new immigrants continue to find their world bounded by barriers built by the more schooled and urbane society of people better able than Pasiegos to actualize their notions of esteemed achievement. These people are anxious, just as Casco people are anxious within Pas, to disassociate themselves from others who would compromise the appearances on which their own self-esteem rests.

TEN

The Margins of Spanish Society

A people is constituted when it separates from others and affirms itself with respect to them.

Castro 1971

The transhumant Pasiego, going from cabaña to cabaña in search of pasture for his animals, reminds me of the nomadic Arab shepherd, nor are the Pasiego's commercial habits very different; he does not remain behind the counter but, like the son of Hagar, carries his wares to the towns where they are consumed, and fatigue and danger do not turn him back.

Escagedo Salmón 1921

A few other peoples like the Pasiegos have similar histories in their relations with Spanish culture and society. Like the Pasiegos, they consider themselves Spaniards, and what ethnic identity they have is the result of a set of suppositions imposed from outside. There is no active sense of not being Spanish, no positive sense of difference, but only a resigned acceptance of the fact that other people have decided that one's group must be ethnically distinct.[1]

Many groups of Spaniards have created mythologies about the origins of their neighbors. The evolution of these fabrications in some cases is buried deeper in history than are the century-old beliefs about the Pasiegos. In some cases, Spaniards have reached into their own past—to the Jews and Moors of their own history—to search out the prototypes by which to define differentness. The third foreign presence within Spain's boundaries—the Gypsies—has served less as a prototype. I do not

1. Davydd Greenwood (1977) aptly points out that "an ethnic identity is as much a definition of who you are not as of who you are."

know why this is. The Gypsy presence in Spain is not a thing of
the past, and it has been a powerless one. Perhaps a people must
be extinct or exiled, perhaps it must have acquired wealth or
power, or waged war, to be the stuff of which myths are made.

Why are some of Spain's peoples denied Spanishness by their
neighbors? What does this denial tell us about Spanishness itself? What does the choice of prototypes tell us, further, about
Spanishness? These questions differ crucially from the ones we
might ask regarding the integration into the Spanish state of
peoples with self-conscious, positive identities as something
other than Spaniards—among whom we include the Gypsies.[2]
Our questions deal, rather, with the Spanish nation and the
positions within it of certain peoples who have not struggled or
conceived themselves to be anything but members of it. Comparison of a few well-known cases can suggest directions for
broader inquiry in the future.[3]

The peoples who have been the subject of numerous treatises
and have entered Spanish consciousness labeled as *pueblos
malditos*—damned or despised peoples—are the Maragatos of
León; the Vaqueiros de Alzada of Asturias; the Agotes of the
Valley of Baztán, in Navarra; the Chuetas, or Xuetas, of Mallorca; and the Pasiegos. The Agotes, Chuetas, and Vaqueiros received wide attention earliest.[4] Of these groups, the Chuetas—a
highly localized group in the city of Palma de Mallorca—has
well-documented origins as Jewish *conversos* (converts to Ca-
tholicism) and has continued to be regarded apart by surrounding people.[5] With known non-Iberian origins, they do not belong
to the present review. Similarly, the Agotes appear somewhat
anomalous, as will be clearer presently.

---

2. The Jews and Moors who resided in the past on Spanish soil also
had their own identities, but it is hard to speak of these strictly in opposition to a Spanishness which was at that period only beginning to assume
the form it takes today, and to which they themselves contributed. Here
Hispanicists will recognize Américo Castro's thesis that these non-Iberian
presences helped to inform what we now know as Spanishness.

3. The widest spectrum of marginality within Spain is not dealt with
here. This even includes some neighborhoods whose inhabitants are despised within their towns, and many such cases have not even been published. It is important to note, however, that the margination of groups
by their neighbors occurs regularly in the countryside but often to lesser
degrees than in the cases reviewed here.

4. Lardizábal y Uribe (1786), apparently the earliest general source,
makes reference only to Agotes, Chuetas, and Vaqueiros.

5. See Lardizábal y Uribe 1786, Braunstein 1936, Moore 1976.

Maragatos are popularly said to descend from Moors or Jews.[6] Their villages lie in a hilly, upland zone in the province of León, adjacent to the mountains of both Asturias and the Galician province of Lugo. The zone is marginal for grain agriculture, though some is practiced, and more favorable for the maintenance of sheep and goats, of which the local flocks are—or were —large. Using (evidently) native wool, there developed considerable local specialization in weaving. The zone's second major specialty was in muleteering. Maragatos not only trafficked in cloth, probably including their own, but also became the chief purveyors of fish from Atlantic Spain (especially Galicia but also farther east) to inland areas, to Madrid in particular, and to the Court itself. This activity was already flourishing in the eighteenth century.

In the latter part of the nineteenth century, much of the muleteering and carting was undercut by the building of the railroads, and this apparently produced a great increase in the incidence of emigration from the home villages. As in the other cases under study, the predominant occupations of Maragatos who settled away from home were in the places along the muletrain routes, from Galicia to Astorga to Madrid, but primarily in Madrid. And the callings into which Maragatos settled were already familiar to them: they opened retail textile businesses and fish markets. The Madrid businesses in these categories which were founded by Maragatos are apparently numerous.

The Vaqueiros de Alzada, of Asturias, are transhumant cattle herders, not very unlike the Pasiegos, but they range over longer distances and through more of their province;[7] their transhumance is much more attenuated and their cattle economy less

6. Major sources consulted are Rodriguez Diez (1902), García Escudero (1954-55), and Martín Galindo (1956), in addition to the references by Caro Baroja (1943, 1946).

7. Lardizábal y Uribe (1786) dealt marginally with the Vaqueiros in his treatise on the Agotes. The major work of the following century was that of Acevedo Huelves (1893), which saw an expanded second edition in 1915. Acevedo also reproduced the lengthy letter of Jovellanos (1744–1811) to Don Antonio Ponz concerning the Vaqueiros. Since then, considerable attention has been paid the Vaqueiros, especially by Uría Ríu (1968) and Juan Antonio Cabezas, who made them the subject of a novel (1960). Caro Baroja (1943, 1946) makes brief references to them, as to the other groups. I have also had reference to Canella y Secades (1895–1900). The Vaqueiros are now the object of a cultural anthropological study by María Cátedra Tomás (1972a,b; 1976a,b). As well as from her published work, I have benefited from her personal communications on a number of subjects, including emigration styles, which contribute materially to these pages.

specialized. They are on their own ground in summer mountain pastures (*brañas*) but in winter have to coexist with settled valley villagers (dial. *xaldos*, Sp. *aldeanos*) who consider themselves ethnically distinct from the Vaqueiros and are in many ways hostile toward them.[8] The Vaqueiros share with other of the "despised peoples" the popular attribution of Moorish or Jewish origins, and these have been the subject of considerable literary speculation. There is as little substance in these, or in the speculations on the Maragatos, as in the question of Pasiego origins.

Unlike the Pasiegos and, as far as I know, the Maragatos, the Vaqueiros must share their living space periodically with people who consider themselves different and superior. This has much accentuated the kind of discrimination I have described for barrio Pasiegos in the Plaza, for in Asturias it has an ethnic dimension. Pasiego herders, according to my informants, "knew their place in church," and this was apart from the places of Plaza families. Vaqueiros, on the other hand, were told their place in church, which was often, at least in the past, set off by rails, far from the altar. One source notes that in some parishes Vaqueiros were forced to receive the sacraments at the door of the church rather than at the altar. Vaqueiros reportedly also were buried in separate space.

The Vaqueiros, like the Pasiegos and Maragatos, have emerged from their homeland as ambulatory traders, dealing particularly in wool, and as carters or muleteers, often hauling freight between Asturias and Madrid. They, too, have settled in Madrid in large numbers. Many Vaqueiros in Madrid have in the past been employed in the coal businesses. It is probably not difficult, as an Asturian, to find one's way into the coal business. The second popular occupation has been allied with the butcher's trade: Cátedra (pers. comm.) points out that urban Vaqueiros are not as often in butchering proper as in the small-scale retailing of offal meats (*despojos*). Such vendors are known as *casqueros*. I do not know of an obvious connection between Asturias and the calling of casquero. There does, however, appear to be a cultural and historical connection between outcast status in Spain and butchering and a number of allied trades. I shall re-

8. The Sarakatsani, herdsmen of Greece, described by Campbell (1964), are perhaps most comparable to the Vaqueiros, in that the ethnic designation in both cases is applied to numerous separate communities of herders, ranging over a wide territory within which systematic relationships, of generally similar type, are entered into with sedentary villagers who consider themselves superior.

turn to this presently. Here, let us simply note that the casquero is dependent upon the butchering industry but need not share the butcher's skills.

The Vaqueiros, Maragatos, and Pasiegos all occupy territories which are considered marginal for agriculture and are, indeed, exploited in alternative ways—largely for animals—which are considered in Spanish tradition to be marginal forms of livelihood. In areas like the Montes de Pas, the maintenance of animals was traditionally accompanied by maize cultivation, and maize, too, is considered marginal food by most Spaniards. People like the Pasiegos were thus set apart in both livelihood and traditional diet while in their homeland. The same has generally been the case in other upland areas where people make do with what are nationally conceived as inferior grains—rye or barley, for example—and inferior ingredients for the stew pot, such as chestnuts. Most Spaniards, in the era of the potato, consider the chestnut to be a survivor of an archaic period. People who feel themselves superior have not minced words in deprecating zones of marginal agriculture. Of the province of Santander has been said: *Mayorazgo en la Montaña: dos cucos y una castaña.* (An estate in the Montaña: two worms and a chestnut) (García-Lomas 1966:255).[9] This is the more devastating, as a mayorazgo is an entailed (that is, undivided) estate or major portion of a holding! Witness also a refrain, said to come from Santander, in the form of a conversation between maize and wheat:

El maíz le decía al trigo: 'Caña vana, caña vana, mucho creces, poco granas.' Y el trigo le respondió: 'Calla, ruincudo, que, cuando tú acabas, yo acudo' (Sbarbi 1922, 2:12).

Maize said to wheat: 'Empty stalk, empty stalk, you grow a lot and yield little. And wheat answered: 'Be quiet, you no-account: when you're all finished, I produce.'

Sbarbi interprets the entire exchange in spatial rather than temporal terms as indicating the different favorable growing regions for the two grains; even in adversity, the proud superiority of wheat cannot be ignored.

The concepts of marginality which apply to the homelands of the peoples I have described also encompass the homelands of a variety of peoples who have not, for one or another reason,

---

9. I am indebted to Honorio Velasco Maillo for this reference and in general for directing my attention to particular sections of the corpus of Spanish refrains. My analysis of it (still incomplete) helps to inform my emphasis on dominant values and views of marginality.

become despised in the same sense.[10] Among these are the various communities of transhumant herders of merino sheep who inhabit upland villages in the kingdoms of Old Castile and León. From certain montane areas in these two kingdoms, herders walked their flocks annually to winter pastures in Andalusia and Extremadura and back again. They formed the backbone of the Honrado Consejo de la Mesta, formally chartered in 1273, and, ultimately, the backbone of Spain's monopoly in wool and textiles and in merino stock itself. The academic attention paid these people (see Klein 1920) exceeds that paid to any of the others and speaks for the crucial role they played as herders outside of as well as within their native villages. Of equal interest here are the roles they have played as non-herders—that is, when they migrated at least temporarily out of their villages of origin and into non-herding occupations. Tudela (1950) has collected the best data on this movement with reference to the merino herders of the province of Soria and to migrants from other pastoral zones of that province.[11] There are both parallels and contrasts with the cases of Maragatos, Vaqueiros, and Pasiegos.

Men from Sorian zones traditionally associated with merino transhumance used to go seasonally (from November to January) to work as foremen in the olive presses of Córdoba (and probably elsewhere in Andalusia, too). They served in roles of considerable responsibility in the seasons of olive milling. Men from the same zone also traditionally ran mule trains through

10. I have not brought into this discussion of marginality the "ancient commonplaces"—to use Caro Baroja's phrase—regarding the different qualities of country and city and the virtues and vices of the life of each. The classic meditations and lore on the subject, partly summarized by Caro in a 1963 essay, clearly relate to points emerging in this chapter. However, those points—indeed, the whole study of the Pasiegos—should contribute to a general refinement of the gross category "country" and produce some notion of different types of rurality, based on the diversity of products and activities of the countryside. While most Spaniards subscribe in a general way to the "ancient commonplaces," and these make some contribution to the definitions of marginality examined here, Spaniards have also produced the more refined evaluations of place-type and activity which are more central to this study. The emphasis on activity, or occupation, furthermore, causes the evaluative system to cross the bounds of the simple countryside/city dichotomy and brings us to focus on the internal complexities of these categories.

11. The description of Sorian migrations and attitudes is based on personal communications from Julio González y González in 1963, summarized in Freeman 1970a, as well as on Tudela 1950 and on my own observation in that province (especially Freeman 1970a: 178–84).

rural areas within a fairly short radius of their homes, engaging in both trade and transport.

From a wide, montane area of Soria (as from some other parts of Castile and León), from areas favoring cattle breeding, men also engaged in long-range hauling of freight by oxcart. In their home zones, young animals were gelded and maintained as oxen precisely for the carting trade. Carters transported coal, salt, mercury, earthenware, grain, wines, and other goods from one region to another. They remained at home in summer and in the cooler months ranged as far as Lisbon and Seville. For a time, their transport of mercury was crucial to the silver industry in the New World: they carried it from the mines of Almadén to port in Seville and Cádiz.

There are reports of a variety of peddling activities, in addition to cartage, originating in these pastoral zones and involving goods produced from local resources.

So far, the list is only of itinerant professions. Herders tended also to settle along the routes of their migrations. Shepherds' familiarity with the South served as a basis for their entry into the South both in olive presses and as carters. Permanent settlement followed, and some Sorian communities in the South retained their provincial identity for centuries. They were most often in commercial callings, and frequently in the textile trade. Such communities persist in Andalusia and in parts of the New World, where the textile trade is still frequently represented.

Soria has long had one of the highest literacy rates in Spain, and its people are noted for their work ethic and their high regard for learning. Most of the Sorian pastoral groups I have mentioned seem to have managed to educate their children. All other things being equal, the social landscape of their native towns and the absence of major population displacements (such as transhumance) within them permits school attendance to be more consistent than it is in Pas. Merino herders of Soria took care to place their sons in commercial apprenticeship in establishments in towns along the transhumance routes, visited them twice yearly, and secured their entry into settled life with a rapidity which few Pasiego herders could hope for.

Sorian herders, as they follow the old sheepwalks of the Mesta or use the freight lines for the annual trip to the South, are looked upon with deprecation, suspicion, and even fear by the settled people whose towns they pass. Sorian tradition, folk and academic, dwells on their rustic appearance, wandering ways, and crude manners, as well as on some of the picturesque customs of their hometowns. However, they have never been considered a race apart (although Sorians in general are sometimes popularly likened to Jews for their commercial acuity). Perhaps they were saved this by their large numbers, high visibility, and royal support in the centuries of the Mesta's great power, or by their successful and rapid adaptation to life outside their villages. Perhaps, too, an essential ingredient was wanting in the intellectual climate of the society which—in other times and places—might have denied these people Spanishness and invented for them other origins. They did, after all, emerge in the Mesta as early as the thirteenth century and informally even earlier.

Each of the groups described above—Maragatos, Vaqueiros, Sorians, and Pasiegos—has dealt commercially outside its home zone in both the use of animals (as in carting) and animal products (wool, meat, dairy products, or livestock itself). Because in all of their homelands large numbers of animals are bred, and this in part defines the marginality of those areas, it is possible that trades like carting, muleteering, wool trading (and weaving?), butchering, and dairy production are, or were once, associated in the popular mind with such geographic marginality. The parallels between our cases are suggestive of such an association. If in fact such an association existed, it extended a stigma on geographic origins to occupational pursuits as well and may provide some basis for the different ranking of trades which are all classed together as petty commerce. I shall return to attitudes toward the trades, and some elements of their classification, presently.

Let us now turn to a case with a different aspect. A zone which has long been the object of curiosity but whose people— like Sorians—seem never truly to have entered the category of the ethnically suspect is Las Hurdes (sometimes spelled Jurdes), in Cáceres. Along with the contiguous region of Las Batuecas (Salamanca), Las Hurdes has been the subject of early description and dramatization.[12] Lope de Vega (1562–1635) wrote a play entitled *Las Batuecas del Duque de Alba.* (Las Batuecas is part of the holdings of Alba de Tormes; Lope served the Duke of Alba for a time.) Several descriptive sources appeared in the nineteenth century. After a visit of Alfonso XIII to Las Hurdes in 1922 brought publicity to conditions in the region, more writ-

12. Las Hurdes and Las Batuecas have long been in the literature, and the history of the attention paid them could be the subject of detailed analysis. I have had access only to Legendre 1927, Barrantes y Moreno 1893, and the brief comments of Caro Baroja 1946 and Muñoz de San Pedro 1961.

ings appeared, including the lengthy monograph of Legendre (1927). The villages of Las Hurdes are in a barren, montane zone, with poor communications, economically and culturally impoverished and out of touch. Even the so-called costume appears to consist largely of cast-off clothing collected from more prosperous zones nearby. There is some mention in the literature of alleged origins of Hurdanos as Goths. Generally, however, Las Hurdes is viewed by other Spaniards not as an ethnic enclave but, rather, as a cultural backwash, a corner of Spain unblessed by nature, its people a study in cultural isolation and nutritional misery.

There are other such abandoned corners of Spain, some of them unnoticed in the literature. The publicity accorded Las Hurdes brought that region to serve as a prototype for certain others, perhaps most notably La Cabrera of León. Carnicer (1964) says that even the natives of La Cabrera refer to their countryside as "Las Hurdes of León." The literature on these two zones does not stress notable systematic emigration of their peoples, though Carnicer speaks of local vending of chestnuts and walnuts in La Cabrera, and a major mode of survival in Las Hurdes in the past was begging within the region. The home zones do not have striking economic characteristics either, to catch the attention, but are remarkable only for the poverty of their natural resources. Thus, other Spaniards are apparently not tempted to see the natives of these zones as too different to be Spaniards; rather, they are severely disadvantaged rural Spaniards. Writers have raised the question of national responsibility for people in such circumstances, with little suggestion that larger, ethnic factors might be involved. A fair amount of the literature on Las Hurdes, for example, following the king's visit, appeared in medical journals. Years before that—cited already in 1893 by Barrantes y Moreno—there were a number of reports on religious and secular instruction and health care in the region, official concerns which were not much displayed for the other peoples I have described. On the contrary, in the instances where ethnic differences are assumed, as for Pasiegos, Maragatos, Vaqueiros, and Chuetas, questions of social responsibility have seldom been raised.

Viewing Maragatos, Vaqueiros, Pasiegos, and Sorian herders on the one hand and Las Hurdes and La Cabrera on the other, there is an obvious contrast between zones whose geography encourages livelihoods which are deemed marginal and zones which are marginal to the pursuit of any traditional livelihood— that is, zones which are more notable for barrenness and the destitution of their people than for "peculiarities" of their economic pursuits. Those peoples who, like the Pasiegos, come from a landscape which is productively exploited in particular ways, however peculiar these may seem, are the peoples who are most consistently viewed by their neighbors as bearers of other cultures rather than as Spaniards in misery.

The Agotes, who inhabit the barrio of Bozate in the locality of Arizcún, Valley of Baztán, in Navarra, present a different contrast. Unlike any of the peoples already described, but like the Chuetas of Palma de Mallorca, the Agotes are relatively few in number (380 in 1847, according to Michel) and occupy a very small and compact territory—their barrio. Like the Vaqueiros, they are in systematic contact with non-Agotes and subject to notable discrimination. They are truly among the despised peoples—unlike the Sorians or Hurdanos—but they differ in important ways from the Maragatos, Vaqueiros, and Pasiegos. Theirs is also the case which has received most sustained attention, beginning at least with Lardizábal y Uribe (1786), and followed in 1847 by the important work of Francisque Michel, who, in turn, was followed by de Rochas (1876) and numerous others.[13]

Almost all writers on the Agotes ally them with numerous other enclaves both in Navarra and in extensive neighboring regions of southwestern France and also in Brittany. The most general name applied to all is the French Cagots, but among the others commonly cited are Capots, Gafos, Gahets, Caqueux, Caquins. The Agotes of Navarra—principally in Bozate but also farther east in the Valley of Roncal—are generally presumed to be Cagots. Enclaves of Cagots resided in or near towns in the wide area described, where their numbers could be substantial, as in Bozate, or, in many localities, reduced to one or two families.

Cagots have been viewed variously as descended from lepers, or from adherents to leper colonies, from Goths or Romans, or from Albigensian or other heretical communities. Very occasionally speculations regarding possible Moorish or Jewish origins enter the literature, but this is not a dominant theme.

Cagots reside in restricted neighborhoods and are separated from the rest of their neighbors in the church, in the cemetery,

13. Of the other sources, I have consulted Hack Tuke 1880, Altadill 1935?, Idoate 1948, Hors 1951, and summary notes by Caro Baroja 1943, 1946, and Pitt-Rivers 1971a. Altadill's article presents a Basque nationalist approach to the Agotes which is representative of only a small portion of the rest of the literature.

at the baptismal font, and in receiving communion. They usually occupy an inferior status with respect to the juridical, military, and civil systems of their localities, in many cases not enjoying rights to share in the use of communal properties, to bear arms, or to serve as witnesses in courts of law as do ordinary citizens. Sometimes it is said that seven Cagots, or Agotes, are required to serve as witnesses in the place of any single non-Cagot. At times, Cagots have been required to wear identifying signs on their clothing. They were often prohibited entry into such places as taverns and membership in guilds, and they could not participate in certain festal observances. They have also been believed to possess physical characteristics which have vilified them more than most of the other despised peoples. Their breath is said to be pestilent; they are said to have tails, anomalous formation of the ears, a continuous flow of (menstrual?) blood and of semen, a form of plumage in place of hair; they have been said to be cretinous and to have no need of dreaming when they sleep. Given these considerations, it is almost superfluous to remark that rates of marriage of Cagots with non-Cagots—particularly in the larger and more coherent communities such as the Spanish one at Bozate—were extremely low. Individuals seeking writs of purity of blood had to demonstrate absence of descent from Agotes: this in the same era during which Pasiegos themselves were receiving writs of purity and had noble status.

Cagots were frequently but not always prohibited from holding land. In places like Bozate, they have farmed in their own barrio, however, in addition to pursuing a number of occupations which have consistently been open to them. The trades which Cagots have practiced in their own localities are varied and nearly all skilled trades and artisanry of commercial nature. Perhaps primary among these is carpentry. There are also wheelwrights, coopers, rope-makers, butchers. In Bozate specifically, most of the admissable callings traditionally plied by the Agotes have been in carpentry and wood-working trades (cabinet-making, wood-turning), but have also embraced milling, fishing, herding, locksmithy, and professional drumming. It was as drummers that Agotes entered the public social life which was otherwise closed to them. I know nothing of the forms which emigration from Bozate has traditionally taken nor what the statistics on emigration might be: the population has apparently decreased by more than half since Michel wrote. Michel mentions that some French localities rescinded restrictions against Cagot land ownership in order to reduce beggary. Agotes owned land in Bozate, but there must have been severe limits on its expansion. We have the sense, then, of a community with some gardening or subsistence farming whose people acquire most of their livelihood from a variety of commercial occupations.

The fact of their dispersion makes the Cagots—and therefore the Agotes—more comparable to the Gypsies than to the other peoples I have described. Like the Gypsies, they live in segregated districts in communities in which they have only minimal rights. Like the Gypsies, they ply specific trades. Unlike Gypsies, however, they do not have their own language or positive ethnic identity. The literature on Cagots makes little of Cagot customs, clothing, festivals, or other folklore: their traditions do not seem to distinguish them ethnographically for observers as do Pasiego, Maragato, and Vaqueiro traditions (or those of Gypsies). Indeed, the Agotes have not really been denied Spanishness. To be attributed Roman or Gothic origins is to be attributed the stuff of which Romance and Christian Spain was forged: one Spanish writer on the Agotes asked, "What greater honor? . . ." For Spanish authors in general, Agotes did not need to be denied Spanishness in any case, for they were assumed to be French! For most French writers, Cagot origins as lepers or heretics have seemed most plausible. We are dealing truly with social outcasts of a very particular type whose cultural origins have not been significantly at issue and who live entirely within the native territories of the people who despise them. These features alone suggest that their "differences" must be rooted in phenomena other than geographic marginality.

One of the insights we acquire from the Cagot case is in the question of the peoples' occupations, especially because Francisque Michel had an academic interest in the histories of the trades and this influenced his approach to the Cagots. Most sources describe the range of Cagot occupations as "those that are open to them." Farming, I have noted, is not always among them. This helps us to appreciate a hierarchy of different pursuits governed by the esteem attaching to each—a hierarchy in which most kinds of commerce or manufacture for commercial exchange, lifeways involving itinerancy, and also herding are ranked below farming.

Spaniards in the past have been much concerned with the concept of honor attaching to noble status. Caro Baroja's 1966 essay on honor and shame traces the evolution of this concern. Through much of history, the maintenance of high honor, and noble status, entailed an avoidance of commercial activity and the manual trades. The *Siete Partidas* of Alfonso X, el Sabio, (The Wise) (1221–84), is a massive codification of law and custom and one of the major sources for the study of the foundations of Spanish society and the attitudes underlying them (see Alfonso X, 1221–84). In such early codes, there is relatively little explicit consideration of the merits or demerits of specific callings within the lower social order—although a few are singled out[14]—but mercantile activity *per se* receives attention in the context which concerns us here. For example, the Second Partida, whose Title XXI is dedicated to the discussion of knights (*caballeros*) and knighthood, specifies (in Law XII) that ". . . *non debe seer caballero home que por su persona andodiese faciendo mercadorías . . .*" ("a man who himself wanders doing commerce must not be a knight"). None of the other prohibitions for entry into the knighthood specifies calling *per se*; it is far more common throughout the *Partidas* that qualifications be phrased in terms of lineage, or descent, and that a candidate be "of good lineage," sometimes within specified degrees of relationship. The study of later centuries, however, teaches us that good lineage came virtually to imply particular callings and to exclude others, but this was not necessarily fully true in the thirteenth century of Alfonso X or in his immediate past. For example, in his discussion of how knights should be chosen (Partida

14. The Seventh Partida (Title VI, Law IV), for example, defining the nature of infamy, focuses on bawds, mountebanks, jesters, wandering minstrels and entertainers, as well as on those who fight with wild beasts or other men for payment, and also on usurers. Unlike the followers of most of the other vilified callings, these people were not the productive artisans and traders in standard goods of the everyday world (though moneylenders may have been fairly common in some localities). The infamous callings enumerated in the Seventh Partida fall heavily within the sphere of entertainment and frequently involve itinerants. It is likely that we are dealing here with a category of true outcasts, of considerably lower esteem than simple traders and manual laborers. These people's callings are not only classed as vile but as beneath contempt, making them virtually untouchable. The low esteem of the theatrical and minstrel professions has, of course, survived into our times. Even more fascinating than its survival is its extension. The "pariah" castes of South Asia include ritual drummers (as we might call those found also among the Agotes). Entertainers and other itinerants are generally of low castes as well, as were the Gypsies in India, who remain at the very bottom of the social scale in their European host countries today. We are led to some compelling questions of comparison of the systems of differential distribution of honor and impurity on these two related continents, but the European system has received little enough attention that these intriguing questions are mostly premature.

II, Title XXI, Law II), he points out that in former times knights had been selected from among huntsmen, carpenters, smiths, and stoneworkers because they were strong of hand and practiced in sustaining wounds, and from among butchers, who were used to killing living things. It would be false to assume, therefore, that the butcher's trade, in particular, has always been regarded as being as utterly vile as it later came to be judged and that the butcher's place in society was always one of unmitigated lowliness. The shedding of blood, as we see in views of the bullfight and the bearing of arms, has in it something of valor as well as of defilement. But the bullfight, as well as some of the professions of strength which once made good knights, and even farming, were prohibited to clerics as unfitting, while at least some artisan pursuits were adjudged pure enough (Partida I, Title VI).

By Alfonso's time, the ancient mode of selection of knights was in question. The Second Partida relates that huntsmen, stoneworkers, butchers, and so on, had not conducted themselves with honor as knights, and had turned upon one another rather than upon the enemy. Softer men, who could display the virtue of *bondat* (moral goodness), made preferable knights. Thus, the *Siete Partidas* instructed that "above all else [knights] be men of good lineage" (Partida II, Title XXI, Law II). So already in the thirteenth century we find the clear implication that "good lineage" and the pursuit of certain callings are by definition different. Other sources of the period confirm this.[15]

In the centuries after the *Siete Partidas* were written, purity of descent, or "cleanliness of blood" (*limpieza de sangre*), became increasingly important as a requisite for access to the upper levels of the social order. Sicroff (1960:32) points out that the greatest obsession with clean blood developed only after— and probably because—Jewish converts to Christianity had rapidly acquired high status in Spanish society. The achievements of this group are a clear indication that ethnic heritage and former adherence to the callings to which Jews were restricted had not of themselves been obstacles to social success. However, with the growth of the population and of the zeal of the Reconquest, the upper echelons began to close their ranks. The first statute of limpieza de sangre was effected in Toledo in 1449. While the arguments offered for and against the statutes requiring proof of cleanliness of blood were heavily theological and philosophical (see Sicroff 1960), the motives of the whole move-

15. See, for example, the summary in Callahan 1972.

ment were as heavily social and economic, and so were its effects.

Ultimately, the issue of pure descent and the notion of impure callings were fully and explicitly joined, though as I have said, they were linked much earlier. Sicroff reports a petition from about 1600 asking why a sword-maker should be (as they apparently were) considered *ipso facto* "clean" while a doctor is always counted as a Jew (Sicroff 1960:211). By the end of the eighteenth century, Domínguez Ortiz notes, the phrase *"limpieza de oficios"* (cleanliness of callings) had become fairly general and cleanliness of blood had become effectively synonymous with "the fact of not having practiced a vile calling" (Domínguez Ortiz 1957:130). The latter half of the eighteenth century saw a great extension of the statutes of limpieza de sangre, and even fairly minor officials had to pass their tests. But Domínguez Ortiz points out that "in contrast to what happened in earlier times, nobody was harmed by these measures" in an era when "a judaizer was a rare curiosity" (1957:129). The desire to keep the ranks closed had outlived the populations against whom the statutes had been devised to protect the social order. The chief contaminant now came from within the Christian society, and the requirements of limpieza de oficio sought to keep the nobility free of the taint of commerce.

Cantabria, with the rest of the far North, saw a great number of its untitled, lower nobility engaged in trade and manual occupations, and their noble status remained intact. Callahan (1972) gives an excellent characterization of the status of the northern nobility. Nobles—exemplified by such humble country people as the Pasiegos—often outnumbered non-nobles in the population, had a small, often tiny, land base, and frequently lived in true poverty. Both their circumstances and their favorable location for trade encouraged their entry into callings shunned by the grander, better-landed nobility farther south. While northern nobles still maintained traditional attitudes about certain kinds of work, they were also particularly obsessed with their own genealogies and the roles of their families and hometowns in Spain's history, aspects of personal status which stood above whatever work they engaged in. This helped to set individuals off not only from commoners but also from the horde of other nobles: nobles' family histories were often the proudest parts of their estates.

It is significant that the entry into commerce of the nobility of the North occurred in precisely the region where uncontaminated descent was most easily—and most frequently—assumed. Indeed, the same petitioners cited above from Sicroff's work asked why the inhabitant of León or the Asturias should be treated automatically as an Old Christian while anyone from Almagro (in southern New Castile) must be a *confeso* (converted Jew). If northerners' nobility was often less grand and their economic state encouraged a descent into commerce, it was also more certain that their purity was sufficient to withstand the taint of such activity.

In the eighteenth century and in an epoch of new needs, the State and a variety of intellectuals argued for a decontamination of commerce for the entire nobility (see Callahan 1972). Callahan notes that formal moves to legitimize commercial activity of nobles and to permit ennoblement of commoner entrepreneurs did not in fact effect a major revolution within the eighteenth century: "The task of transforming attitudes and prejudices built up institutionally over several centuries was a formidable one" (1972:72). Callahan himself, and most of the authors he cites, are concerned with the institutionalization of attitudes largely from the viewpoint of the upper classes. From this perspective, all rural occupations and small trades are essentially of a single category, viewed *en masse* as manual and retail callings; with the possible partial exception of farming itself, these were uniformly denigrated. Yet the upper classes were not the only ones to hold prejudices, institutionalized or not, regarding different callings, nor were rural and commercial occupations themselves undifferentiated in the relative esteem in which commoners held them. The hierarchy of rural and commercial callings has been less formally studied for Spain, and perhaps all of Europe, than for India or the Far East. Yet a variety of sources makes possible an approach to attitudes and preferences not only of modern countrymen but of their ancestors, too.[16]

The major part of the Spanish countryside has traditionally been agrarian, with some pastoralism. The balance tips toward pastoralism in the montane and windswept upland zones, more favorable for stock than for farming. (Historians point out that the frontier lands of the Reconquest often saw more herding than farming because wealth could thus be moved, on the hoof, from embattled zones, while croplands would have to be left

---

16. Two works cited by Callahan but which I have not seen might shed light on the internal organization, hierarchy, and characteristics of the world of small trade and artisanry. They are Gaspar Gutierrez de los Ríos, *Noticia general para la estimación de las artes* (Madrid, 1600) and Pedro de Guzmán, *Los bienes de el honesto trabajo* (Madrid, 1614) (Callahan 1972:1).

behind, but definitive conquest brought farming to the countryside.) The histories of change in the last centuries, documentable locally through cadasters, show striking similarity over vast areas, even though their people have remained traditional, subsistence-oriented villagers. Wherever possible, herding has given way to farming: stock censuses are reduced and lands made more productive of grain. There are preferred grains, too: increasingly, bread is made solely of wheat rather than barley or rye. Even the Pasiegos, as herders, have consistently shown preferences for some kinds of herding (cattle) over others (sheep and goats), for sedentary rather than transhumant living, for clustered rather than isolated settlements, and ultimately for occupations other than herding. All of these preferences are widely shared, and rural history documents their realization in the Spanish countryside—at different rates and from different starting points—over the centuries. When a farmer, or group of farmers, hires a laborer, help is most commonly sought to relieve the farmer of herding rather than farming chores. It is common that whole towns employ outsiders as herders, if possible, rather than send their own people to wander with the animals beyond the margins of settlement. To live among animals and be governed by their needs, to wander in social isolation, to eat inferior sorts of bread, are things today associated with zones which have—in terms of these kinds of progress—stayed behind in history.

There is, too, in most parts of Iberia, a deeply rooted feeling against commercial trading. Traditional community life offers forms of insurance, labor exchange, and redistribution of goods and services which preclude haggling between community members and reduce the need for transactions outside the community. Market transactions are, indeed, limited to relations with outsiders. Many of the skilled services which people sell today were not traditionally for sale. In many instances, the roles of such "specialists" as tavern-keeper, butcher, miller, or baker were rotated among members of communities. Most farmer-herders possessed these skills, and enough more to serve each other's needs for masons, builders, wine-makers, and so on. In instances where true specialties and specialized equipment were required—as often happened in the cases of blacksmiths, stock-gelders, pharmacists, or teachers—communities contracted with qualified individuals, either natives or outsiders, to perform services at stipulated prices. Thus, individual villagers still did not enter independently into transactions with most specialists or bargain with them.

How to bring in the harvest was a problem for the individual farmer. He alone could decide each season whether to hire extra hands for the harvest. These were normally outsiders—itinerant men (and occasionally women) who sold their services from zone to zone as the harvests ripened. There were labor fairs in each region at which individual farmers made their contracts for the harvest season. The prices were uniform over vast areas, however, and while they might change from time to time, they were usually predictable enough that a farmer could knowledgeably calculate his needs within the rest of his budget. His mission at the labor fair was to secure the needed number of workers, not to dicker about their wages. The same must have been true in securing the services of weavers, which again was an individual matter.

Pasturing animals, even though they usually were privately owned, was often conceived as a burden which the entire community shared, particularly in the busy harvest season. Communities, rather than individuals, often hired their herdsmen—sometimes natives but often outsiders. Herders were the largest category of community employees who were not specialists.

When communities relinquish to specialists some of the functions which they formerly performed for themselves, convenience is tempered with resentment. Someone is making a living from skills which are not exclusively his; people who share those skills find themselves paying for services they formerly performed for one another. Their choice is not without ambivalence, and the entry into village life of pecuniary considerations is a difficult one. Many of the refrains in continual use in the countryside express antagonism toward local traders: *De molinero mudarás, pero de ladrón no* (You can change millers but not get rid of the robber); *Al molino y por carne, vaya de la casa el más grande* (Let the biggest person in the house go to the mill and to buy meat [so he may put up a fight]); and *Cuando el tabernero vende la bota, o sabe a pez o está rota* (When the tavern-keeper sells the wineskin, it must either taste of pitch or be torn).

In a place like Bozate, where Agotes engage primarily in artisanry and commercial pursuits, there is cause enough that such a population be considered apart from the rest on the basis of their occupations alone. However, because there is no evidence that occupation is here the only factor, and because the Cagot phenomenon is so widespread geographically, there is no way of telling that they are not despised for some other reason and confined, as a result, to lowly callings. By contrast, the Pasiegos, Maragatos, and Vaqueiros seem to be outcasts by virtue of their occupations only. They became nationally visible primarily outside their home zones in itinerant occupations; scrutiny proved that at home, too, their modes of livelihood diverged from the ideal, and the speculations on their origins began. To those who had always lived adjacent to them—the subsistence farmers of settled communities nearby—they had for all memory been placed in, and accepted, niches marginal to farm life. These were the same kinds of niches, as herdspeople or traders, which they came to fill in the nation at large. We will never know if such people as the Pasiegos ever wished to become settled farmers, but the weight of the facts shows that they chose instead to leave the countryside and its class structure to struggle upward in the social structure of town life, which they entered through the marketplace.

Even in the marketplace, which is normally in Spain supralocal by definition, and which is almost the only proper locus of exchange in the Spanish countryside, full competition was traditionally inhibited by a variety of factors. Sales in marketplaces by vendors defined as outsiders were sometimes taxed, or more heavily taxed than usual. Sometimes mere entry was taxed or even prohibited to vendors from beyond a specified zone. Regions protected their own producers and inter-regional trade was thus discouraged, though the inter-regional movement of certain products and services was protected, or at least not prohibited.[17]

There are two kinds of outsiders in Spanish rural life. The importance of the local community in the lives of its members accentuates the status of any outsider. The "respectable" individual lives within the bosom of his own community, producing his own subsistence there and living within the social and economic collectivity. One kind of outsider, then, is simply the member of another, similar community. Such outsiders one meets at festivals, at funerals, and shopping at market or fair. Such outsiders marry one's daughter or sister without meeting significant obstacles. A different sort of outsider is the one who wanders far from his own community and from the controls which its

17. Producers' associations in traditional Spanish economic life also functioned to control competition among their members. Groups of towns around Bilbao shared the tourist market for their wine, rather than compete in it, for example, by requiring that weekly rights to wine selling be held by only one town at a time in a prescribed order of rotation (see Unamuno 1902). A close study of guilds' regulations on their members would probably reveal a number of similar measures to stem open competition.

people might exercise upon him; he lives in social isolation and subsists on the proceeds of trade rather than produce his own food. He sleeps where he may; his animals (if he has them) are his most constant companions; his human interactions are based on exchange rather than reciprocity. One meets him not shopping in the marketplace but selling there; the next day he moves on. This outsider is a stranger.

The Pasiegos and people like them have played crucial roles in Spain's economic development because they have lent themselves to travel and trade. They have crossed geographic and social boundaries which other Spaniards would not cross. They have come out of their no-man's-lands to carve trails across the countryside to link countryside with city, region with region. They have helped to weave the economic fabric of nationhood and discovered themselves strangers within Spain.

Spain has housed many strangers. Official views on usury must be viewed as symptomatic of wider attitudes toward commercial activity, and it is no accident that much of commerce was left to Spain's Jews. Though their commercial achievements were scarcely confined to petty commerce, their pursuits were still not esteemed ideal. The ambivalence with which the ordinary man viewed commercial success was epitomized in attitudes toward Jews and the successes which brought them into the upper reaches of the power structure. Christian Spain offered opportunities in lesser commerce as well. Before their own expulsion, which began in 1609, Moriscos (converts from Islam) in central Spain (the two Castiles, La Mancha, Extremadura) became important in commercial callings and as artisans. They settled primarily in towns. Lapeyre (1959:131–32) lists their primary occupations: market-gardeners, water-carriers, tavernkeepers, bakers, butchers, retail dealers in agricultural commodities, weavers, tailors, shoemakers, mattress makers, rope makers, blacksmiths, carpenters, masons, pot smiths, and, in favorable areas, muleteers. Moriscos' crucial functions in these callings may be belied by their small numbers. The heaviest Morisco settlement in central Spain came with their forcible settlement there following uprisings in the late sixteenth century. Prior to that time, people with low jural status in the rural social system—although many lived on land grants—plied similar trades as shepherds, cowherds, mareherds, pigherds, fishermen, road workers, woodcutters, millers, smiths, bakers (or oven-tenders), coopers, dealers in and dressers of hides, carpenters, tailors, weavers (Valdeavellano 1968:357).

Such long lists of trades associated with low social status suggest that indeed most commercial callings have been undesirable at best and open to those who wished to follow them. For many, this would have been a step down. For others, like the Pasiegos, it was one of the most obvious steps to take and led them ultimately into the urban world and toward eventual acceptance as normal Spaniards. They have replaced such earlier groups as rural serfs or Moriscos in some of the callings they followed. In similar fashion, when the Moriscos were expelled from the city of Seville, the street vending of sweets and roasted chestnuts, which Moriscos had apparently dominated, passed directly to the Gypsies (Pike 1972:160–61, 170).

Chestnut vending is not the only pursuit which Pasiegos held in common with the Sevillian Moriscos: Pike mentions a variety of peddling activities and petty trade, noting that "None of these occupations was very remunerative, but the fact that the Moriscos managed to make a living from them at all aroused popular indignation and resentment" (Pike 1972:161). The similarity in the common occupations of the lowest classes in widely different times and places and in the common attitudes of others toward them attest to the historical depth and consistency of ideal notions of Spanishness. It is difficult to know in some cases whether a group of people is "different" for any reason other than that they are at the bottom of the social ladder and therefore perform work of low esteem. Herding is an activity which in itself marks people as different; so does most itinerancy. These attitudes are both old and modern. Others have been less persistent but indicate a true ranking within the trades of low esteem. For example, there is clear historical evidence that butchering and certain allied trades involving work with hides have made outcasts of the people who practiced them even if they were distinct in nothing else. Palacio Atard (1959:114–15) cites references to hide-curing as the lowest of professions—one whose practitioners could expect to see their descendants vilified and themselves excluded from public and religious employment and unable to marry off their daughters. In Portugal, butchers were eighteenth in a list of eighteen categories of traders, ranked by the esteem of their callings, in the organization of the processions of Evora of the late fifteenth century (Oliveira Marques 1971:189ff). Cobblers and tanners were higher in the list. Butchers thus marched first, for the front of the procession was a lowly place. (Agotes also marched first in their Spanish home communities.) The butchers of Valencia were the

subject of a 1788 tract by the Count of Aranda, cited by Domínguez Ortiz (1957:130), prompted apparently by the group's attempt to have its members enter the militia, which raised the
question of the cleanliness of their calling. Although Santander
informants have told me they believed butchers were once pa-
riahs, this is no longer the case. Nonetheless, it is well to remember the associations of Vaqueiros, Moriscos, and Agotes
with the butcher's trade in recent years. In this light, it is also
significant that of the emigrants from Vega de Pas in skilled
trades, one-quarter (twelve of forty-seven) were in butchering
and allied trades—more than in any other single category of
skilled trade. Of the emigrants' descendants in skilled trades,
nearly 16 percent were again butchers. Scrutiny of such cases,
together with what we can learn of the history of individual
trades, might shed greater light on the internal structure of
Spain's lower social order.

Modern Spain's marginal people have moved into areas of economic life which place them socially with the strangers on Spanish soil of past times. The associations evoked in the history-
conscious Spanish mind are, thus, in some sense natural. The
Jewish and Moorish peoples, however crucial in what they built
on Spain's soil, have played only the negative role in Spain's
sense of itself. They have been the presence and living memory
of what Spaniards are not, reminders of Spain's commitments
to Christianity and to its own estimation of different lifeways.
But there has been a marked tendency in Spain to fuse notions
of ethnic purity with those of social class. Spain had long had
peoples from beyond her boundaries to perform disdained tasks.
Suddenly, she had them no longer, for she had expelled them,
and Spaniards from the lower rural classes dominated the least
attractive occupations. The upper classes had tightened their
boundaries by requiring that anyone who would join their numbers demonstrate purity of blood. Because the notions of purity
of blood and calling were so closely allied, and because the
manual trades failed the tests of limpieza, a few unfortunate
Spaniards who were farthest from the ideals of occupational
purity came popularly to be considered of impure blood as well.
The images of Moors and Jews have been invoked in this cause.
Spain must need her Moors and Jews to the same degree that
she still uses them in this way, to make foreigners as well as
strangers out of Spaniards.

All nations integrate strangers and foreigners into their affairs. The patterns of this integration as we see them in Spain

are not uniquely Spanish; they are widely European. Good reflections of this are the fairly similar positions and regard in which both Jews and Gypsies have been held throughout Europe and in pan-European lore. Also this widespread are the general notions of the status of farming in relation to other rural activities and the general apprehension of the merchant, whose universal prototype is the Jew; the extension to the peddler, the tinker, and other travelers of the lowly prototype of the wandering Gypsy and the apprehension with which he is viewed; and the images of the shepherd, goatherd, swineherd, or goosegirl, who inhabit special preserves within an agrarian landscape. There are, of course, differences of texture and of color, of history and of historical imagery, but the more general forms, imagery, and evaluative attitudes are shared. The cultural supports of the social order are similar and give peoples like the Pasiegos similar lodgings. Not only are these shared patterns European; if we began to study them in detail, we would come to define more deeply what European culture is.

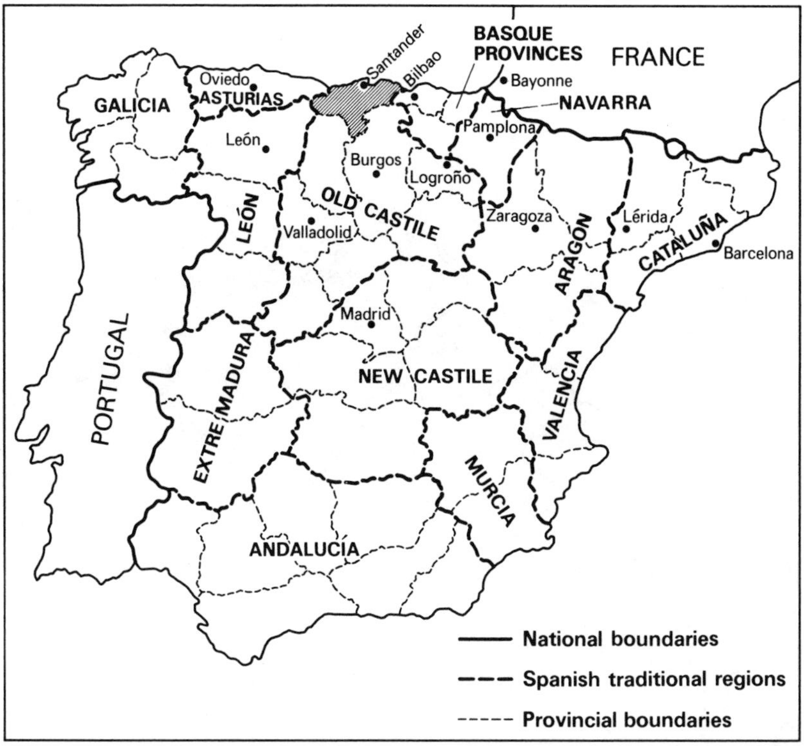

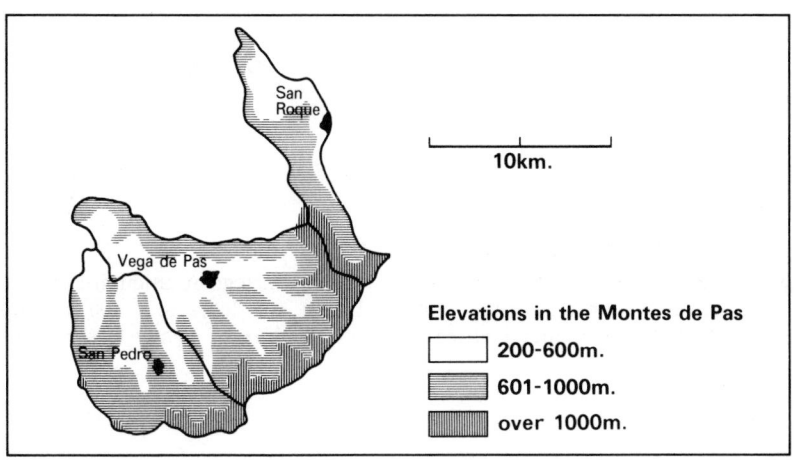

Map 1. Iberian Peninsula, with province of Santander shaded and some of the principal points of Pasiego emigration marked. (After Aguilar 1961: 142)

Map 3. Elevations in the Montes de Pas. The source places San Pedro town center above 600 m., though it is slightly lower (569 m.) according to most other sources. (After provincial map, Caja de Ahorros de Santander)

Elevations in the Montes de Pas

200-600m.

601-1000m.

over 1000m.

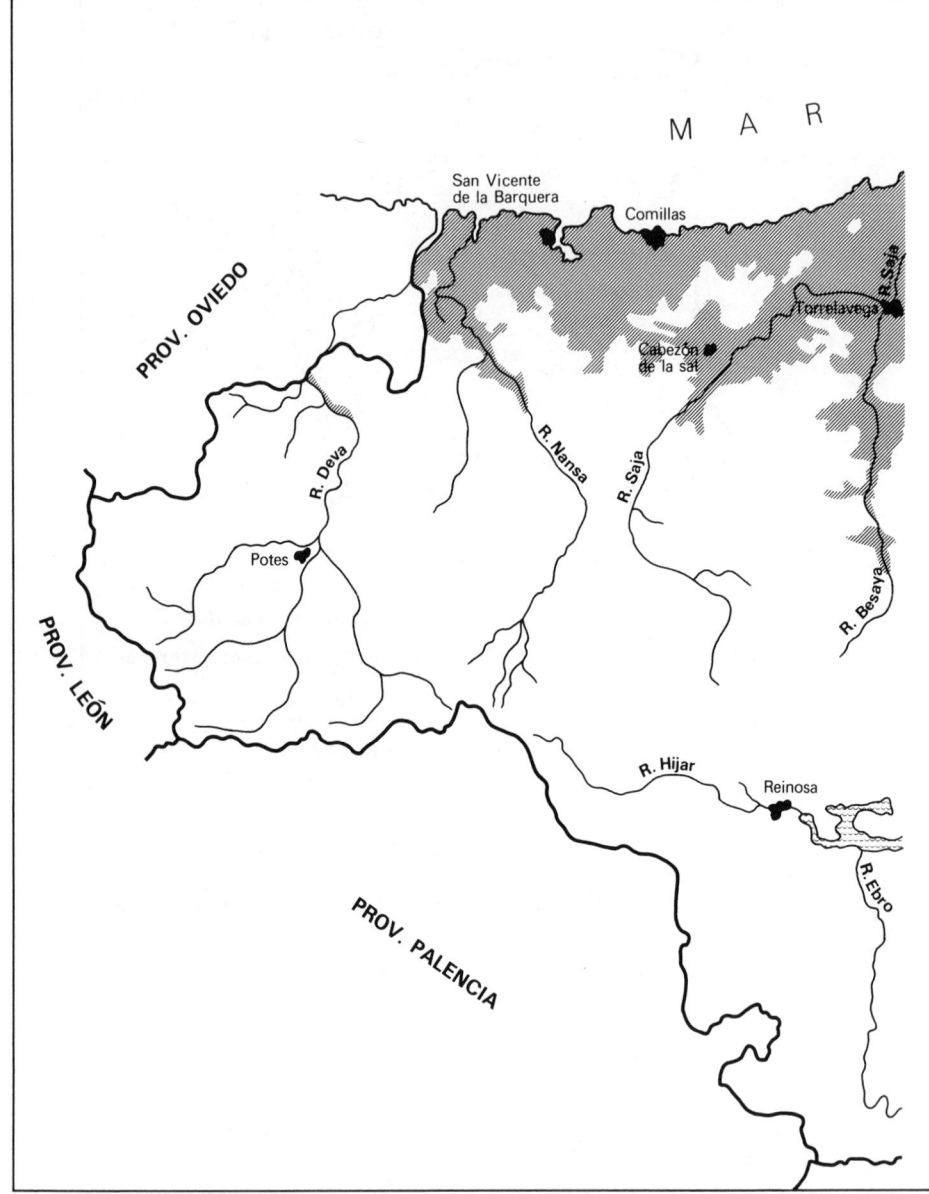

MAP 2. Province of Santander with the three Pasiego municipalities and their centers marked. Areas lying between sea level and 200 m. are stippled. Major provincial cities and some points of heavy Pasiego im-

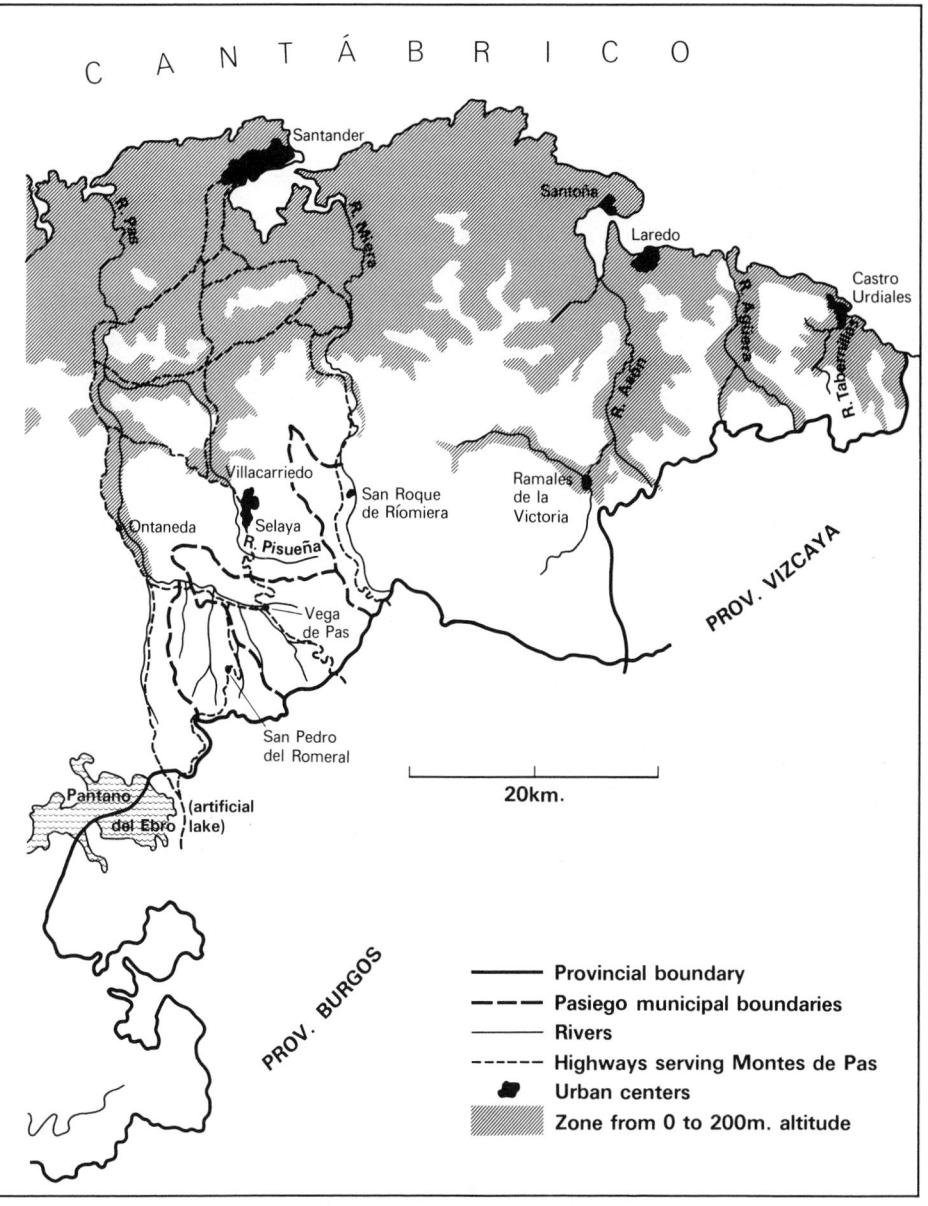

Map labels:

C A N T Á B R I C O

Santander

Santoña

Laredo

Castro
Urdiales

R. Pas

R. Miera

R. Asón

R. Agüera

R. Tabern...

Villacarriedo

San Roque
de Ríomiera

Ramales
de la
Victoria

Ontaneda

Selaya

R. Pisueña

Vega
de Pas

PROV. VIZCAYA

San Pedro
del Romeral

20km.

Pantano
del Ebro

(artificial
lake)

PROV. BURGOS

—————— Provincial boundary
– – – – – Pasiego municipal boundaries
———— Rivers
- - - - - Highways serving Montes de Pas
◆ Urban centers
▧ Zone from 0 to 200m. altitude

migration in the province are marked. Roads serving the Montes de Pas
are shown. (After provincial map, Caja de Ahorros de Santander)

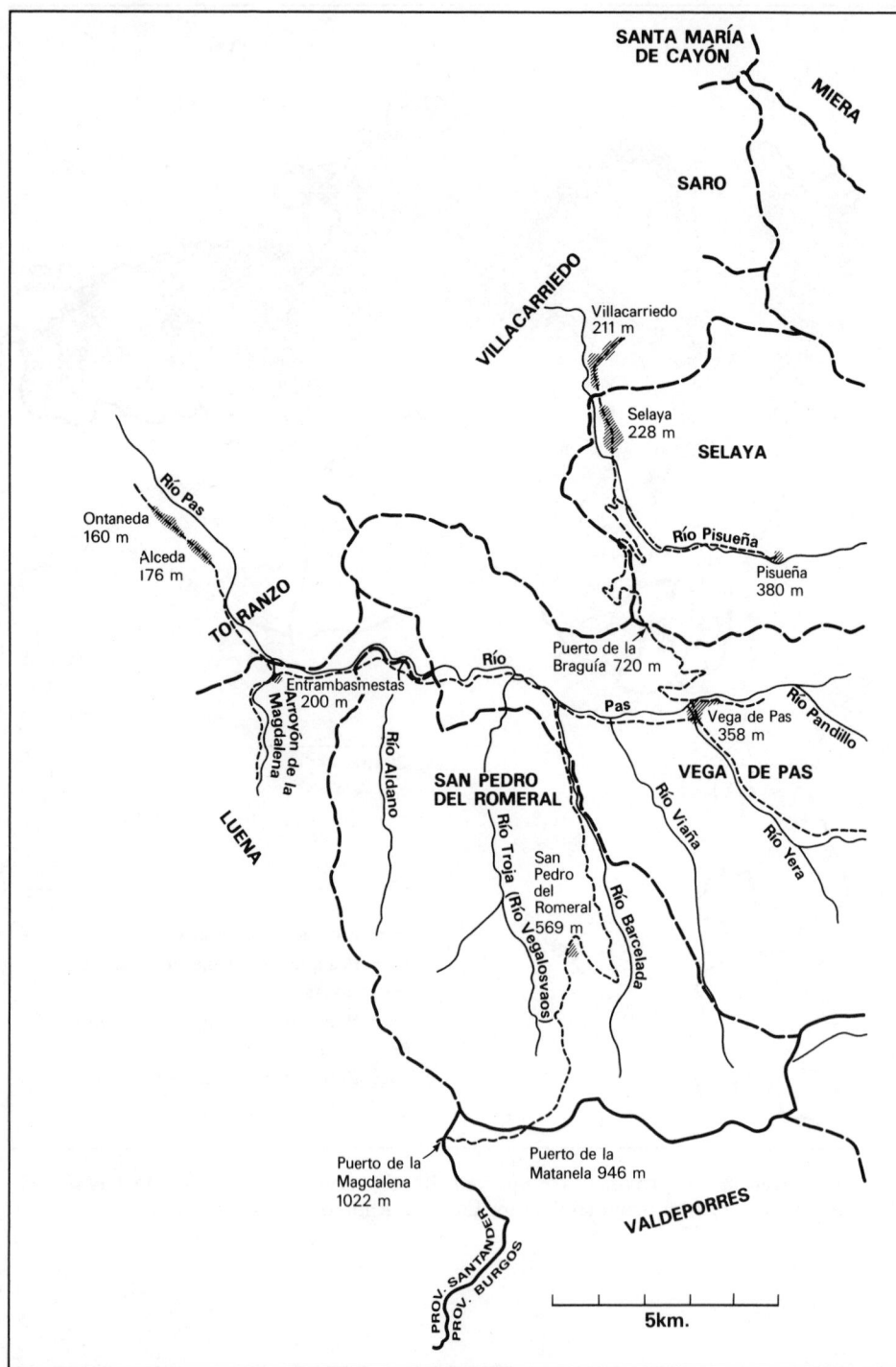

MAP 4. The three Pasiego municipalities and their immediate neighbors.

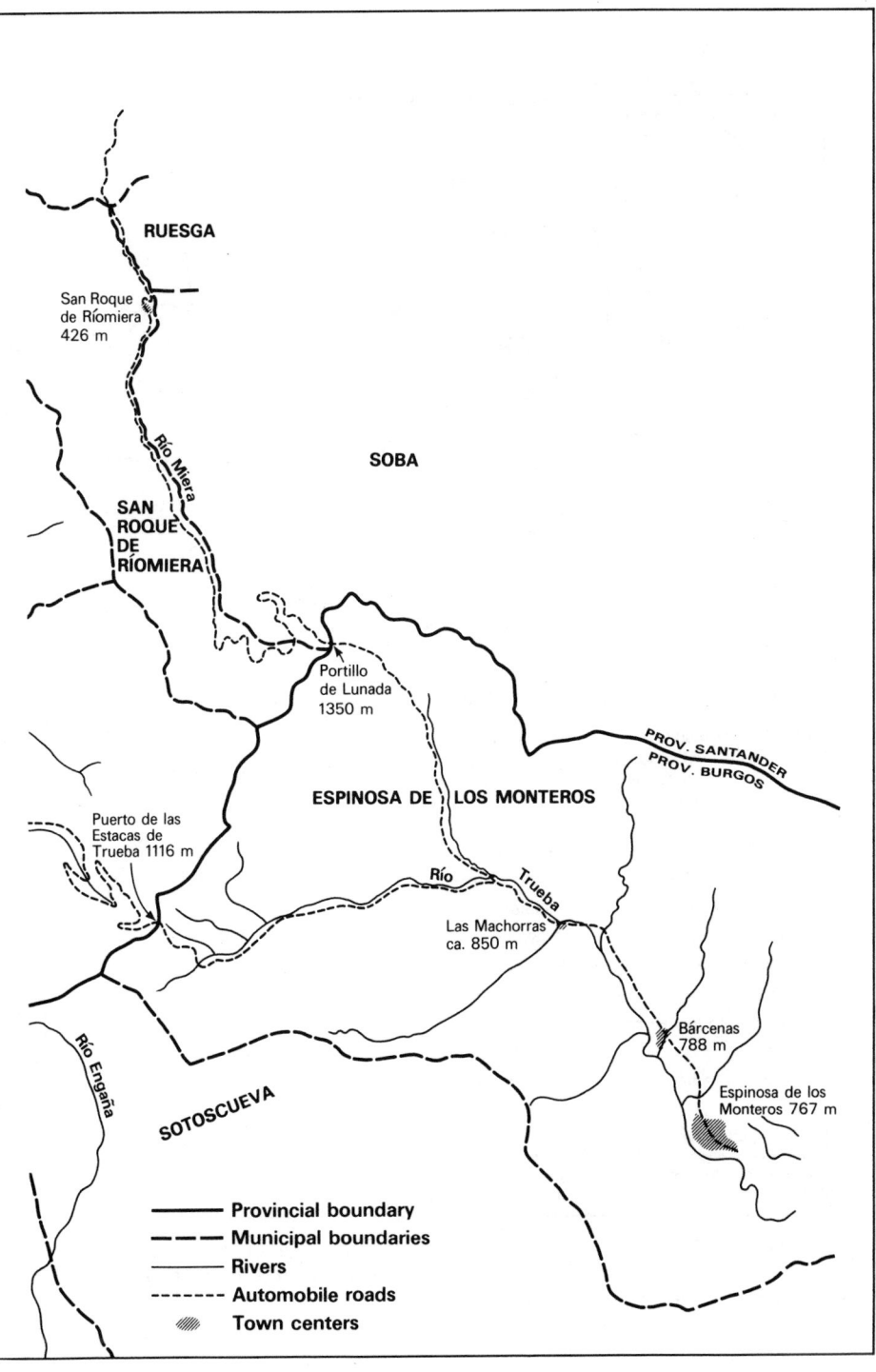

(After provincial map, Caja de Ahorros de Santander, and Instituto Geográfico y Catastral, series 1: 50.000 [Burgos])

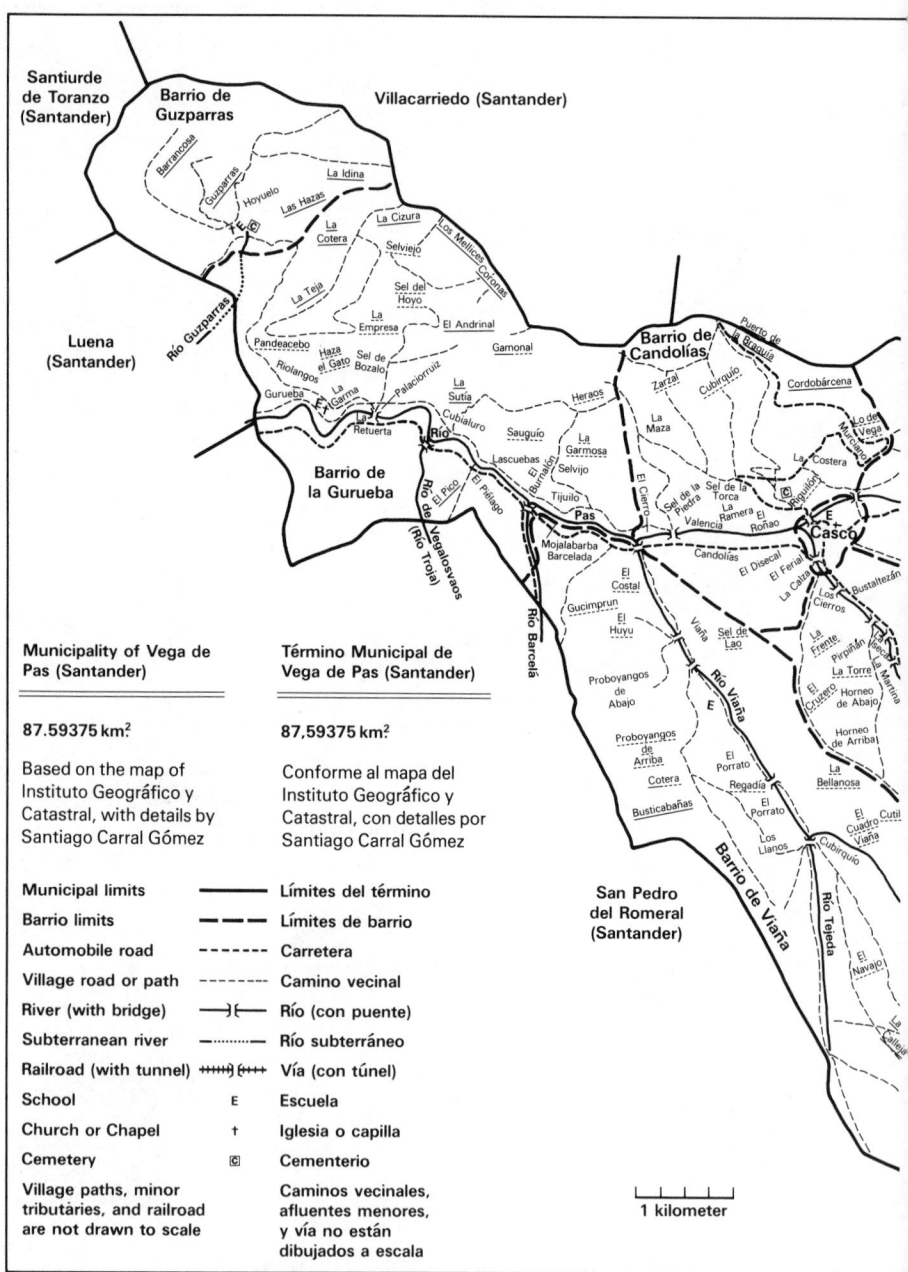

MAP 5. Municipality of Vega de Pas, with *praderas* named and their altitude zones marked. Underlined pradera = braniza zone; broken line = ladera zone; no line = ribero zone.

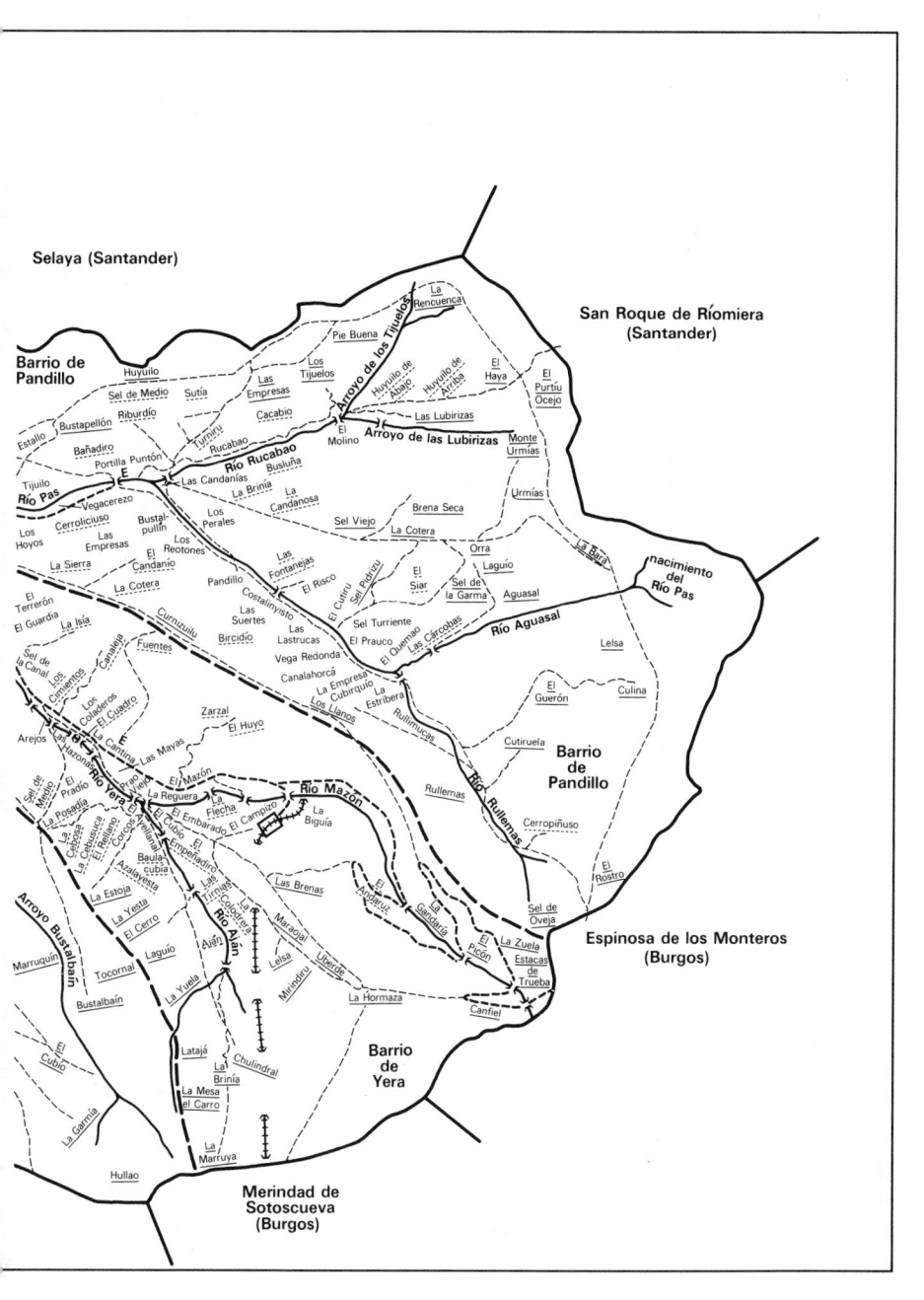

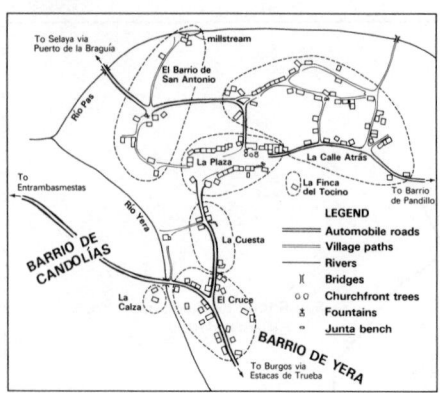

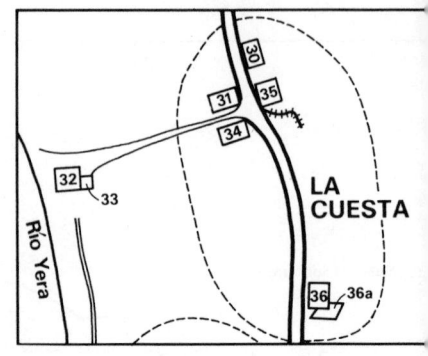

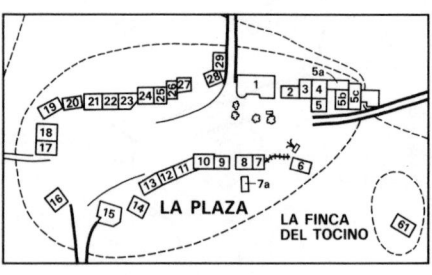

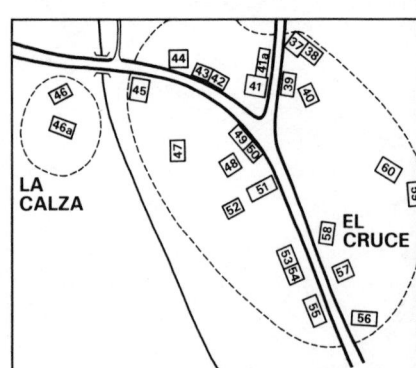

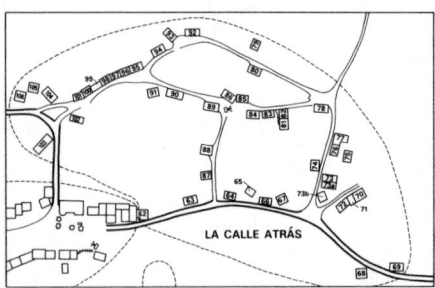

MAP 6. The Casco, or town center, of Vega de Pas.

6A. La Plaza
6B. La Calle Atras

6C. La Cuesta
6D. El Cruce
6E. El Barrio de
San Antonio

APPENDIX A

*Donation by Don Sancho, Count of Castile, to the Monastery of San Salvador, in Oña, of a large part of the territory of the Province of Santander**

Ego igitur Sanctius Comes, cum coniuge mea Comitissa Urraca, ad hanc salubrem redemptoris vocem pervenimus, et cum intentis cordis, et libero arbitrio meditando, damus et concedimus Monasterio S. Salvatoris, quod est situm in locum cognominatum Onia: in Espinosa illa nostra portione integra, cum terris, et dibisiones, quae divisit Munio Belasquiz, qui fuit nostro vicario atque Merino, cum domna Munia duenna. Quòmodo cadit ribo de Voziello in Trioba, et pergit per ad illa ponteciella, et exit ad sommas Casteruelas et ad somma la era. Et ex aliâ parte quomodo cadit ribo de Petra in Trueba, et exit ad illa cobiella, et aplicat ad Busco de Corteças, et pergit pro inde ad illa parte de rigo de Soba, et quomodo tagat ribo de Soba, et cadit in Trioba. Et alia parte usque in illos latreros, et venit proinde et ad cobas de Runino. Hic etiam supradictis terminis sic facimus decretum, ut illi homines, qui sub domine Abate, vel domine Abatissa Sancti Salvatoris Oniae populaberint, et habitatores sub eius dominio fuerint, et servierint ad Sanctum Salvatorem, potestatem habeant cum suo ganatu et omnibus suis peccoribus herbis pascuis, tam isti quam illi allii, qui in decaniis fuerint Sancti Salvatoris, et vadant omnes securi cum suos ganatos, vaccas, equas, capras, porcos, ubicumque voluerint pascere per omnes istos terminos praedictos, et per istos quod nominamus: de Espinosa usque in Salduero, et ex alia parte, usque in Samano, et venit inde ad portum S. Mariae, et aplicat ad Cabarga, et pergit inde ad ribo de Pas, et a la Mata de Nela, et ad Summo Lobato, et venit pro inde ad Mantare et ad Trioba et in Zernegega, nullos alios ganatos, nec vacas, nec peccora intrent pascere nisi illos de Sancti Salvatoris. Et si

---

*The Latin and Spanish texts are reproduced here as they were published by R. Amador de los Ríos (1891: 884–86). Asterisks in text represent handmade signs on original document.

*inventi fuerint, Abas de Onia accipiat montaticum de omnes vacas. Infra vero omnes alios terminos praedictos, omnes qui de Domino Oniae fuerint, potestatem habeant in sylvis, in vallibus, in montibus, in aquis, in herbis pascere, insulis requiescere. Et nullus sit ausus, nec potens, nec impotens hominibus de Abate de Onia, nec de suos ganatos, nec de suos porcos montaticum accipere, nec ullam inquieta-tionem Abati de Onia facere, nec in suis vacis, nec in suas cabanias aliquid per força inde accipere; qui autem inde modicum, vel multum acceperit, pariet duplatum, vel melioratum ad hanc regulam. Et ad partem Regis terrae mille quingentas auri libras pariet. Et iram Omnipotentis Dei et de omnibus Sanctis tan ipse quam omnes qui consenserint, plenarie incurrant. Ego Comes Sanctius et uxor mea Urraca Comitissa qui hoc scriptum fieri iussimus, legentem audi-vimus, manibus nostris hos signos fecimus * * et ut firmum semper permaneat confirmamus. Facta carta donationis et confirmationis in era M.XLVIIII.*

> *Ego Gutierri testis*
> *Ego Fredinando Didaz*
> *testis*
> *Ego Munio Gustios testis*
> *Ego Rodrico Telliz testis*
> *Ego Gundisalvo Telliz tes-*
> *tis*
> *Ego Rodrico Rodriz testis*

> *Ego Gonçalbo Garçiez testis*
> *Ego Petrus Episcopus confirmo*
> *Ego Belasco Episcopus confirmo*
> *Ego Gomez Didaz testis*
> *Ego Fanni Bermudez tt.*
> *Ego Rodrico Gonçalbez tt.*
> *Ego Munnio testis*
> *Ego Salite testis*

*Et nos, omnes nobiles, et infançones supra nominati, qui praetax-atos terminos divisimus, et asignavimus ex mandato Comitis Sanctii cum Munio Belasquiz, qui erat Vicario Comitis Sanctii, et de Comi-tissa Urraca, et erat Merino similiter, laudavimus, et confirmamus hoc donum, et testificamus. Et ex praecepto illius propriis manibus cum suo Merino, Aba de Onia, et suos homines in praedictos ter-minos et in nominatos montes intromissimus * * * * * **

Yo pues, Sancho, Conde, juntamente con mi mujer la Condesa Urraca, dando oído á estas saludables palabras del Redentor, y con generoso corazón y libre arbitrio, damos y concedemos al Monasterio de S. Salvador, situado en el lugar denominado Oña: en Espinosa, aquella nuestra porción íntegra, con las tierras y divisiones que hizo Munio Belasquiz, que fué nuestro vicario y Merino con doña Munia, dueña. Conforme cae el arroyo Voziello en Trueba, y sigue por aquel pontecillo, y sale á las alturas Casteruelas y á la altura la era. Y de la otra parte, conforme cae el río de Piedra en Trueba, y sale á aquella cueva, y arrima al Busco de Cortezas, y sigue por él á aquella parte del riego de Soba, y según toca al río de Soba, y cae en Trueba. Y por la otra parte hasta en aquellos lastreros, por donde sigue á las cuevas de Runino. Así pues, respecto de los mencionados términos, disponemos: que los hombres que allí poblaren y habitaren bajo el dominio del señor Abad ó de la señora Abadesa de San Salvador de

Oña, y sirvieren á San Salvador, tengan potestad con su ganado y todos sus rebaños á las hierbas y á los pastos, así estos como los que fueren en las Decanías de San Salvador, y vayan todos seguros con sus ganados, vacas, yeguas, cabras y puercos, donde quisieren pacer por todos estos términos señalados, y por estos que designamos: de Espinosa hasta Salduero, y por otra parte hasta Sámano y viene seguido al Puerto de Santa María (Santoña), y se acerca á Cabarga, y sigue al río de Pas y á la Mata de Nela, y al Somo Lobao, y continúa por él á Mantare, y á Trueba y en Zernejega, ningunos otros ganados, ni vacas, ni rebaños entren a pastar, sino aquellos de San Salvador. Y si fueren hallados, cobre el Abad de Oña el montazgo de todas las vacas. Además de todos los otros términos nombrados, todos cuantos fueren del señorío de Oña, tengan poder en las selvas, en los valles, en los montes, en las aguas, para pastar en las hierbas y sestear en las islas. Nadie sea osado, así poderoso como débil para exigir montazgo á los hombres del Abad de Oña, ni por sus ganados ni por sus puercos, ni inquietar en manera alguna al Abad de Oña; ni en sus vacas, ni en sus cabañas alguien por fuerza exigirlo; quien por tanto poco ó mucho cobrare, pague el duplo ó mejorado por esta regla, y á la parte del Rey de la tierra, mil quinientas libras de oro, y en la ira del Señor Omnipotente y en la de todos los Santos tanto él como quienes lo consintieren incurran plenamente. Yo Conde Sancho, y mi mujer Urraca, Condesa, que mandamos hacer esta escritura, y la oímos leer, hizimos estos signos con nuestras manos * * y para que sea siempre firme la confirmamos. Hecha carta de donacion y confirmacion en la era M.XLVIIII.

Yo Gutierri, testigo.
Yo Fernando Diaz, testigo.
Yo Munio Gustios, testigo.
Yo Rodrigo Tellez, testigo.
Yo Gonzalo Tellez, testigo.
Yo Rodrigo Rodriguez, testigo.
Yo Gonzalo Garciez, testigo.

Yo Pedro Obispo, confirmo.
Yo Velasco, Obispo, confirmo.
Yo Gomez Diaz, testigo.
Yo Fanni Bermudez, tt.
Yo Rodrigo Gonzalez, tt.
Yo Munio, testigo.
Yo Salite, testigo.

Y nosotros, todos los nobles é infanzones arriba nombrados, que los designados términos dividimos y asignamos por mandato del Conde Sancho con Munio Belasquiz, que era Vicario del Conde Sancho y de la Condesa Urraca, y era asimismo Merino, aprobamos y confirmamos esta donacion y de ello testificamos. Y por mandato de aquel, con nuestras propias manos y con su Merino, al Abad de Oña y sus hombres, en los dichos términos y en los montes mencionados los pusimos en posesion * * * * * *

APPENDIX B
Documents Studied

MUNICIPAL ARCHIVE OF VEGA DE PAS (VPA)

1689   Real privilegio ganado por las villas de Pas contra el Valle de Carriedo.

1699   Engecutoria [sic] ganada por la Vega de Pas con el lugar de San Martín y valle de Sotoscueva sobre el aprovechamiento de las granas de los Montes de Pas.

1789   Real carta executoria obtenida por el concejo ayuntamiento y vecinos de Nra. Sra. de la Vega, Montes de Pas, del pleito que en esta Real Chancillería han litigado con los [Regidores Generales?] y particulares de los pueblos de que se compone el valle de Sotoscueva, y consortes sobre aprovechamiento de pastos y otros en el término de Río la Engaña.

1790   Real carta ejecutoria ganada a pedimento de la Justicia, Regimiento, concejo y vecinos de las villas de Nuestra Sra. de la Vega (San Roque de Ríomera y San Pedro del Romeral), en el pleito litigado en esta Real Chancillería con la Justicia, Regimiento y vecinos de la villa de Espinosa de los Monteros y otros consortes sobre validación o nulidad de varias prendadas.

PARISH ARCHIVE OF VEGA DE PAS

Baptismal registers, 1675–present (except 1712–20 and 1925–31).

Marriage registers, 1680–1891, 1937–66.

Confirmation registers, 1731–1850, miscellaneous years between 1850 and 1901, and 1911–29.

Death registers, 1661–77, 1681–91, 1720–1966.

Accounts:

  parish, 1647–1966

  special funds, alms, and so on, 1708–50, 1752–1861

  cult of San Antonio, 1676–1755

Miscellaneous:
  membership of the Cofradía del Rosario, 1768–1881
  inventory of ornaments and vestments, 1792–1907

ARCHIVE OF EL CENTRO DE ESTUDIOS MONTAÑESES,
SANTANDER (CEMA)
1767 Ejecutoria de las tres villas de Pas

ARCHIVO HISTÓRICO PROVINCIAL
Notarial archives for Vega de Pas (of the notary Ramón Ruíz Oria,
of Villacarriedo), 1838–66 (*legajos* 4754–4762).
Catastro del Marqués de la Ensenada:
  San Pedro del Romeral, 3 volumes, E–798–800
  San Roque de Ríomiera, 4 volumes, E–803–806

APPENDIX C
Notes on Census and Genealogical Data

Field genealogies and the official census of Vega de Pas provided two large bodies of information, at points overlapping, on the contemporary inhabitants of Vega de Pas and (from genealogies only) on samples of the population of past periods. My fieldwork itself was in part guided by the attempt to make these sources as complete as possible, and the data on Pasiego sociology presented in the text derive largely from the detailed analysis of these bodies of data. The precise nature of the two sources and some aspects of their analysis are described here so that the reader may understand the basis for some of the statements contained in the text.

THE ROLLS AND THE CENSUS

The Census of Spain is published every decade. The enrollment of individuals (or households) in the localities of their permanent residence is, however, summarized every five years. These rolls are maintained in the office of local administration (in Vega de Pas itself, in this instance) and are continually updated, since Spanish law requires that changes of permanent residence for any individual be accompanied by a formal change of enrollment—that is, an amendment of the rolls in both old and new localities of residence at the time of the move. An individual is officially stricken from the rolls at death. The rolls themselves are the *padrón*; alternate rolls—those from the first year of each decade—constitute the official local census. The rolls are obviously more faithful to the reality of a given moment than is the official census, to which I refer less often. The rolls themselves, however, require some amendment also. In the dispersed social landscape of Pas, some families simply fail to enroll themselves (though enrollment is not prejudicial to them, financially or otherwise). Therefore, even the continually amended rolls do not document the total number of resident households and individuals. An accurate field census must of needs, then, be unofficial.

The rolls for both 1960 and 1965 were at my disposal in 1968 when I began fieldwork. My own copy of the 1965 rolls came to include, in addition to official amendments, deaths of adults and changes of residence which occurred during my stay; data on families who had enrolled in 1960, had failed to do so in 1965, but turned out to be resident in town; data on families whose residence in town became evident from genealogies but who had failed to enroll and also did not appear in the 1960 rolls. In the last two instances, I verified the families' status as residents before including them in my census. I did not systematically amend the rolls for births or for deaths of minors, and I did not presume to create new enrollments for new households established by marriages while I was in the field, though most marriages (as well as births and deaths) are entered in my fieldnotes. (Rearrangements at marriage, as described in chapter 6, are not necessarily completed in a short time.) Thus, even my own census does not yield a fully accurate count of individuals or of households. These failures were partially intentional, as my time was better spent otherwise than in producing a perfect census. I was only interested in having enough knowledge of the full contingent of Vega de Pas households (or of households of origin of newlyweds) to keep track of how many of these I knew firsthand or had some genealogical information on as my work progressed. Ultimately, 448 listings (not all from different households) from my adjusted rolls were also present in the sample from genealogies.

My primary object was to achieve an overview of the relationships between households which would reflect aspects of Pasiego social life not comprehensible from the rolls themselves. The rolls do not always reflect the true nature of household composition, which often fluctuates in Pas, nor do they provide good information on total family size, because marriage and emigration often reduce the figures. Personal preference sometimes leads adult siblings to enroll as independent entities, although they may share in the same domestic economy and eat at the same hearth. The rolls, of course, do not document the kinds of ties which link such separate entities. In short, my concern with a census of households was that it serve to guide me in the collection of data in a form which was both richer and more deeply reflective of Pasiego behavior—that is, genealogies. My amended rolls did, however, serve as partial basis for the study of transhumance patterns and sedentarization, and the livestock census utilized them almost exclusively.

GENEALOGIES

I conducted extensive genealogical interviews with as many adults as possible, using the rolls to guide me to households or individuals not already documented. My goal was to be able to catalog not only the kinship and affinal ties linking households in Pas, but also systematic data on emigration from Pas and the occupations of all adults in the genealogical charts. After the first several interviews, I was able strategically to select households for further interviews which were related to kin groups I had little or no information about. By checking off, in my adjusted rolls, those households on whose adult members I now had data, and noting whether those data were for one or both parental lines of that individual, I kept a running record of how much of the town I had well covered. By the end of my fieldwork, after recording seventy genealogies, I had complete genealogical information on 318 of La Vega's 392 households (as in table 3)—that is, there was good documentation of both parental lines of the head and, if relevant, of the head's spouse and/or other adults in the household. There were incomplete data for six households, and none at all for fifty-nine. These results have a spatial aspect: working from the Casco, it was systematically most difficult to complete data on the farthest barrios—La Gurueba and Guzparras; these were the areas in which I spent least time and whose networks of kinship and marriage ties extend least into the Casco and its neighbor barrios and most—as far as I can tell—into the valleys of Luena and Toranzo on the mainstream of the Pas. In other words, the spatial distribution of my complete data reflects the fact that localities six or seven kilometers apart have significantly different foci in their social relations.

In the early stages, before I began to eliminate large-scale duplication in the act, genealogies recorded networks of kin and affines to the limits of informants' memories and typically contained information on 200 or more individuals. Ideally, the following data were collected for everyone on the chart:

Sex

Living or deceased; if deceased, age at death and cause of death

Name (given name and two surnames)

Age, or year of birth

Place(s) of birth or of rearing (including barrios and praderas within Pas)

Marital status (with parallel information on spouse(s) and, in cases of lasting liaisons, of lovers)

Place(s) of residence as adult

Occupation(s)

Children, including children born out of wedlock and stillbirths, and including all of the above information on each child and his/her number in the birth-order of the sibling group

Systematic data on household composition were collected only for those families currently resident in La Vega.

Needless to say, the most complete information was available for people closest to the informant in genealogical space, and both time depth and increasing degrees of collaterality correlated with weaker recall. In general, genealogies are not deep: most informants could offer good information about their four grandparents at best and often none on their great-grandparents, though there were some notable exceptions. The numbers of people within any given degree of collaterality in ego's own generation can be formidable, as families are large, but recall in ego's own generation, in descending generations, and often even in the parental generation tended to be excellent, even exhaustive. People did not hesitate to offer information on unions between unmarried people or on illegitimate births, for these are not sources of embarrassment in Pas. Temporary affairs which produced children were not elaborated upon, however, though the children themselves were documented, and adulterous unions in particular—of which there are very few—were not discussed with me except by close friends. The single respect in which informants often had to be prodded was in the inclusion of stillbirths, deceased children, and in a few cases deceased unmarried adults without issue: because these people left no direct descendants, some informants tended to leave them out of the family record.

I transferred information on all individuals from the charts onto cards and eliminated duplicate references before submitting the entire file to analysis. A scanning of the several hundred cases of duplication indicated quite clearly that, while there were differences in the data given by different informants on a single individual, these were honest differences, usually governed by variation in genealogical and/or social and geographic distance between the referent and the different informants. Only in a few instances were differing descriptions of occupation due, I felt, to social pretensions on the part of one of the informants.

I divided the genealogical file into "generations" based largely on the absolute age of the individuals ("egos") giving the data but with some adjustments for informants who were the youngest of large sibling groups and whose networks therefore tended to include a large number of people older than themselves. Once adjusted in this way, generation assignments created little actual conflict in the assignment of individuals who appeared on more than one chart. Informants were divided into these four groups:

Generation	1	39 or younger
Gen.	2	40–59
Gen.	3	60–79
Gen.	4	80 or older

All individuals appearing on any chart were then categorized automatically with respect to the informant, depending upon the line in which he appeared in the chart: if the informant were of gen. 4, his parents would be in gen. 5, his grandparents in gen. 6, his children and siblings' children in gen. 3, and so on. This breakdown gave a time perspective to the entire genealogical analysis.

Much of the analysis concentrated on individuals reared in Vega de Pas and thus excluded the children of permanent emigrants: the study of emigrants' descendants was done separately and is described below. It is the main sample (excluding emigrants' off-spring) which I describe now. There were data on 2,949 adult Pas-iegos (1,379 males and 1,570 females) and on 1,625 marriages. There were 215 single adult females (13.69 percent of the females) and 142 (10.3 percent) single adult males. Single adults were defined as those who remained single beyond the age of thirty. Most unmarried indi-viduals below thirty were not considered fixed either in marital or occupational decisions and were excluded from the formal analysis.

Genealogies provided the basis for the study of residence patterns. A total of 917 cases are reported in chapter 9, although all 1,625 mar-riages and the residence of single adults, male and female, were submitted to analysis. Residence is coded only with reference to major territorial entities—the various barrios and different towns and villages—and some parts of the sample are not consistently codeable in this way. Marriages within barrios, for example, are not codeable for shifts to husband's or wife's localities within a barrio, or simultaneous use of meadows from both families, but only for moves out of the barrio, which account for 235 (36.72 percent) of the 640 cases of within-barrio marriage. Breakdowns of residence figures for specific parts of the sample, and their meaning, are reported in chapter 9.

Occupational data were similarly the subject of analysis and are most important, of course, for the populations of emigrants, whose choices are made within a wider spectrum than those of people who stay at home. Genealogies provided the basis for the study of emigra-tion and of occupations pursued by all individuals for whom infor-mation could be supplied. The total number of emigrant households in the genealogical sample of Pas-born adults is 1,056. All but 115 of these are married couples, as shown in table 23. The breakdown into generations again gives time perspective to the data, which are pre-sented in chapter 9.

The use of households as entities in regard to occupation requires some comment. Wives in the sample are either housewives, work together with their husbands, or do work of the same general cate-gory as the husband's in terms of prestige. There are no clear cases in which one spouse's work outranks that of the other. Thus, in all cases, couples are given a single occupational code.

The marriages of Pasiega emigrant women to non-Pasiego out-siders were included in the occupational study (table 24), although an argument could be made for their exclusion. My inspection of these cases indicated that the marriages of these women to men in particular occupational categories demonstrated approximately the same mobility—or lack of it—as did the occupational choices of Pasiego male emigrants.

The one remaining sample to be described is that of emigrants' children and succeeding generations of descendants of emigrants. This body of data, too, was drawn from genealogies—specifically from the information given on the marriage, residence, occupation, of descendants of the 1,056 emigrant families in the main sample. There was documentation (of varied completeness) on 730 descendants of emigrants. These were labeled E–D1, E–D2, and E–D3. E–D1 signifies the first descending generation from the original Pas-born emigrant, E–D2 individuals being the children of E–D1 individuals, and so on. There were 602 individuals and 494 marriages in the E–D1 group, 119 people and 88 marriages in the E–D2 group, and only nine people, all married, in E–D3. Data from this sample gave some important indications on matters of social mobility and retention of ties with Pas among individuals who were not born there. As in the study of Pas-born emigrants, the occupational study included the spouses of women descended from Pas.

GLOSSARY

Spanish or dialect terms which recur in the text are listed here with their local meanings, which may or may not correspond with one of the meanings given for the term (if it is recognized) in the *Diccionario de la lengua española* (Real Academia Española 1970). Words set in SMALL CAPS are defined elsewhere in the glossary.

ALCALDE: Mayor or chief officer of a locality's AYUNTAMIENTO

AGOSTERO: Literally "Auguster"; hired laborer for harvest tasks

ALMADREÑAS: Wooden clogs. An *almadreñero* is a maker of almadreñas

AMA DE LECHE: Wet-nurse; also NODRIZA

APARCERÍA: Literally sharecropping; in Pas the term refers to the maintenance of livestock by someone other than their owner and profit-sharing by owner and keeper; sometimes called *calda*

AYUNTAMIENTO: Municipal government; also refers to the building in which the government is housed

BACHILLERATO: Academic degree awarded upon the completion of secondary (pre-university) education

BARRIO: In Spanish usage, a strictly bounded neighborhood; in the Montes de Pas, the major barrios of towns are large rural zones, although the term also applies to neighborhoods within the population nuclei

BEHETRÍA: Territory or individual with rights to choose its own overlord

BELORTA: Hazel switch with which cut grass is gathered for transport (on the head and shoulders); also refers to the load itself

BOINA: Beret

BORONA: Maize; also formerly used in reference to millet

BRANIZA: High mountain meadow, used in summer; the highest altitude zone

BRENA: Second grass crop of the annual cycle

BRUJA: Witch

CABAÑA: The combined house and stable in which Pasiego herders live. A *cabaña vividora*, or *vividora*, is a "dwelling cabaña"—one more elaborately furnished than others, situated in the lower altitude zones, and generally the locus of longer periods of residence than characterize cabañas in other areas. A *cabaña limpia* is one in which no grass is stored

CASCO (for CASCO URBANO): Urban nucleus of settlement in the Montes de Pas; the term in native use to designate this nucleus and to differentiate it from the BARRIOS, or rural neighborhoods

CASQUERO: Vendor of offal meats (*despojos*)

CONCEJAL: Councilman in the municipal government or other elected body

CON CRÍA: In reference to cows, signifies "in calf" or "with calf"

CUÉVANO: Pasiego carrying basket. The *cuevano niñero* is the carrying basket adapted for carrying infants. A *covanero* is a maker of cuévanos

DONACIÓN, ALARGACIÓN, or CESIÓN DE BIENES: Contractual pre-mortem "donation" of property by parents to their heirs

FELIGRESÍA: Rural parish

FERIA: Stock fair

FONDA: Lodging place; village inn

GANANCIALES: Earned or acquired, as opposed to inherited, wealth or property

GARAVÍA: Falsetto or other vocal guise

GUCEO: Calling or whooping used on mountainsides

HIJODALGO (also HIDALGO; HIJO DE ALGO NOTORIO; HOMBRE BUENO, and so on): Member of the lower (untitled) nobility, or the "nobility of blood" (*nobleza de sangre*)

JUICIO: Lawsuit; see pp. 102–3 for different types

JUNTA (DEL CONCEJO): Town meeting for advisory purposes

LADERA: Hill-flank meadows; the middle altitude zone; also called *falda*

LEGÍTIMA: Inherited property; the portion of an estate which must be transmitted according to fixed rules

LIMPIEZA: Cleanliness or purity. *Limpieza de sangre* is cleanliness or purity of blood and *de oficio* of calling or occupation

MEJORA: Betterment; bequest to a favored heir

MIJO: Millet

MONTAÑA: In Pasiego usage, the coastal plain of Santander province. In national usage, all of the province of Santander is regarded as La Montaña and its natives as *montañeses*

MONTE: Hillside pasture and/or woodland. *Monte bajo* is brushland; *monte alto* is timberland

MONTERO (DE CÁMARA or DE ESPINOSA): Guard of the King's private chambers

MOZO (MOZA): Bachelor (maiden); unmarried person in a particular age range, normally between seventeen and about thirty (or younger, if marriage occurs earlier)

NODRIZA: Wet-nurse; also AMA DE LECHE

OBRERO: Surface measure in local use, equivalent to 2.772 hectares. A *plaza* is one-ninth of an obrero

PADRÓN: Census roll

PASIEGUERÍA: Pasiego lore

PESETA: Modern Spanish currency; in 1968 the U.S. dollar was equivalent to seventy pesetas.

PITU (Sp. PITO) Y TAMBOR: Pipe and drum; the instruments which traditionally provided music for events at major celebrations; their players were normally hired outsiders

PRADERA: Named meadow-cluster

PRESTACIÓN: Cooperative labor on municipal properties

PUEBLO: A population center and/or its inhabitants; a people

PUEBLOS MALDITOS: Damned or despised peoples

QUESADA: Pudding of fresh milk curd

RECELO: Suspicious reserve

RETOÑO: First grass crop of the annual cycle, which begins in May

RIBERO: Pertaining to the valley bottom, or riverside, usually in reference to meadows; the lowest altitude zone

ROLDA: The complex of courtship traditions which centers on visits by young men in young women's homes

SAM: Acronym for Sindicatos Agrícolas Montañeses, the large dairy cooperative which buys milk in the Montes de Pas

SOBAO: Cake rich in butter and eggs; from *sobado* (inf. *sobar*), kneaded

TRATANTE: Dealer in livestock

VACA PASIEGA: The Pasiego cow; the Pasiego breed of cattle, now extinct

VAQUERÍA: Urban establishment which houses cows and retails milk

VECINO: Official resident of a locality; sometimes applies chiefly to heads of household. *Vecindad* is the status of vecino

VILLA: Population center with special privileges which distinguish it from other towns and hamlets

VIVIDORA: See CABANA

ZORRO: Foxy, clever, astute

REFERENCES

Acevedo Huelves, Bernardo
1893   Los Vaqueiros de Alzada en Asturias. Oviedo.
Aguilar (publishers)
1961   Nuevo atlas de España. Madrid: Aguilar.
Ahumada, José M., Eladio Diego, and Benito Madariaga
1966   La explotación lechera en la Vega de Pas. IV Semana Veterinaria Nacional, September 1966.
Alfonso X (El Rey Don Alfonso el Sabio)
1221–   Las Siete Partidas. (1807 ed.: Las Siete Partidas del Rey Don
84   Alfonso el Sabio, cotejadas con varios códices antiguos por la Real Academia de la Historia. Madrid: Imprenta Real.)
Altadill, Julio
1935?   Bozate y los Agotes: enigma histórico. *In* El libro de oro de la patria (by various authors). 2d ed. San Sebastián: Editorial Gurea.
Amador de los Ríos, José
1960   Historia social, política y religiosa de los Judíos de España y Portugal. Madrid: Aguilar. (1st ed. 1875–76.)
Amador de los Ríos, Rodrigo
1891   Santander. *In series* España: sus monumentos y artes, su naturaleza e historia. Barcelona: Establecimiento Tipográfico "Arte y Letras".
Anderson, Robert T., and Gallatin Anderson
1962   Ukrainian night courting. Anthropological Quarterly 35: 29–32.
Aranzadi, Telésforo de
1910   De la "covada" en España. Anthropos 5: 775–78.
Arensberg, Conrad M.
1961   The community as object and as sample. American Anthropologist 63: 241–63.
Arensberg, Conrad M., and Solon T. Kimball
1968   Family and community in Ireland. 2d ed. Cambridge, Mass.: Harvard University Press. (1st ed. 1940.)

Ariès, Philippe
1962   Centuries of childhood: a social history of family life. New York: Vintage Books.
Arroyo del Prado, Ramón-Antonio
1957   Piedras armeras en Pas, I. Altamira 1957:125–37.
1958   Piedras armeras en Pas, II. Altamira 1958:387–449.
Ateneo Científico, Literario y Artístico de Madrid
1901   Información promovida por la sección de ciencias morales y políticas en el curso de 1901 a 1902, circular y cuestionario. (Village responses currently filed in the Museo Etnológico, Madrid.)
Banco de Santander
1957   Aportación al estudio de la historia económica de la Montaña. Santander: Centro de Estudios Montañeses.
Barrantes y Moreno, Vicente
1893   Las Jurdes y sus leyendas: conferencia leída en la Sociedad Geográfica de Madrid. Madrid: Establecimiento Tipográfico de Fortanet.
Barreda y Ferrer de la Vega, Fernando
1950   Apuntes para un estudio de la antigua vida económica de la Montaña. *In* Homenaje a don Luís de Hoyos Sáinz, vol. 2. Madrid.
1957   Prosperidad de Santander y desarrollo industrial desde el siglo XVIII. *In* Banco de Santander 1957.
Bateson, Gregory
1935   Culture contact and schismogenesis. Man 35: art. 199.
1936   Naven: a survey of the problems suggested by a composite picture of the culture of a New Guinea tribe drawn from three points of view. Cambridge: Cambridge University Press.
Bernard, R.-J.
1969   L'alimentation paysanne en Gévaudan au XVIIIe siècle. Annales: Économies, Sociétés, Civilisations, no. 6 (Nov.-Dec.), pp. 1449–67.
Blanchard, L. (publishers)
1892   Nueva guía de Santander y la Montaña, con arreglo al último censo oficial y con notas sobre la reciente división judicial de la provincia. Santander: L. Blanchard.
Boissevain, Jeremy
1965   Saints and fireworks: religion and politics in rural Malta. London: Athlone Press.
Brandes, Stanley H.
1973a   Social structure and interpersonal relations in Navanogal (Spain). American Anthropologist 75:750–65.
1973b   Wedding ritual and social structure in a Castilian peasant village. Anthropological Quarterly 46:65–74.
1975   Migration, kinship, and community: tradition and transition in a Spanish village. New York: Academic Press.

Braunstein, Baruch
1936   The Chuetas of Majorca: conversos and the Inquisition of Majorca. Columbia University Oriental Studies 29. New York: Columbia University.
Brenan, Gerald
1963   South from Granada. Harmondsworth, Middlesex: Penguin Books. (First published 1954.)
Bretón de los Herreros, Manuel
1851   La nodriza. *In* Los españoles pintados por si mismos. Madrid: Gaspar y Roig.
Buechler, Hans C., and Judith-Maria Buechler
1975   Los Suizos: Galician migration to Switzerland. *In* Helen I. Safa and Brian M. Du Toit, eds., Migration and development: implications for ethnic identity and political conflict. The Hague and Paris: Mouton.
Burns, Robert K., Jr.
1961   The ecological basis of French Alpine peasant communities in the Dauphiné. Anthropological Quarterly 34:19–35.
1963   The circum-Alpine culture area: a preliminary view. Anthropological Quarterly 36:130–55.
Cabezas, Juan Antonio
1960   La montaña rebelde. Madrid: Espasa-Calpe.
Callahan, William J.
1972   Honor, commerce, and industry in eighteenth-century Spain. Boston: Baker Library, Harvard Graduate School of Business Administration.
Campbell, John K.
1964   Honour, family, and patronage: a study of institutions and moral values in a Greek mountain community. Oxford: Clarendon Press.
Canella y Secades, Fermín
1895–   Los Vaqueiros o Vaqueros de Alzada. *In* Octavio Belmunt,
1900   ed., Asturias. Gijón.
Carnicer, Ramón
1964   Donde las Hurdes se llaman Cabrera. Barcelona: Editorial Seix Barral.
Caro Baroja, Julio
1943   Los pueblos del norte de la península ibérica. Madrid: Consejo Superior de Investigaciones Científicas.
1946   Los pueblos de España. Barcelona: Editorial Barna.
1963   The city and the country: reflexions on some ancient commonplaces. *In* Julian Pitt-Rivers, ed., Mediterranean countrymen: essays in the social anthropology of the Mediterranean. Paris and The Hague: Mouton.
1966   Honour and shame: a historical account of several conflicts. *In* J. G. Peristiany, ed., Honour and shame: the values of Mediterranean society. Chicago: University of Chicago Press.

Cascón, Miguel
1952   La historia del Colegio de la Compañía de Jesús, de Santander. Altamira 1952: 3–26.
Castro, Américo
1971   The Spaniards: an introduction to their history. Berkeley, Los Angeles, and London: University of California Press.
Cátedra Tomás, María
1972a   Estudio antropológico social de "Los Vaqueiros de Alzada" del occidente de Asturias (España). Ph.D dissertation, Facultad de Filosofía y Letras, Universidad Complutense de Madrid.
1972b   Notas sobre un pueblo marginado: los Vaqueiros de Alzada (ecología de braña y aldea). Revista de Estudios Sociales 6 (Sept.-Dec.): 139–64.
1976a   Notas sobre la 'envidia': los "ojos malos" entre los "Vaqueiros de Alzada". *In* Carmelo Lisón Tolosana, ed., Temas de antropología española. Madrid: Akal.
1976b   Qué es ser Vaqueiro de Alzada. *In* Carmelo Lisón Tolosana, ed., Expresiones actuales de la cultura del pueblo. Madrid: Centro de Estudios Sociales del Valle de los Caídos.
Christian, William A., Jr.
1972   Person and God in a Spanish valley. New York: Seminar Press.
n.d.   Popular devotion in sixteenth century New Castile, based on the village reports to Philip II, 1575–1580. Manuscript.
Cole, John W.
1972   Cultural adaptation in the eastern Alps. Anthropological Quarterly 45: 158–76.
Cole, John W., and Eric R. Wolf
1974   The hidden frontier: ecology and ethnicity in an Alpine valley. New York: Academic Press.
Cortés Echánove, Luis
1958   Nacimiento y crianza de personas reales en la corte de España, 1566–1886. Madrid: Consejo Superior de Investigaciones Científicas.
Costa, Joaquín
1898   Colectivismo agrario en España. Madrid: Imprenta de San Francisco de Sales.
1902   Derecho consuetudinario y economía popular de España I (Alto Aragón). Barcelona: Manuel Soler.
Costa, Joaquín et al.
1902   Derecho consuetudinario y economía popular de España II. Barcelona: Manuel Soler.
Davis, Natalie Zemon
1971   The reasons of misrule: youth groups and charivaris in sixteenth-century France. Past and Present 50: 41–75.

Dias, A. Jorge
1948 Vilarinho da Furna, uma aldeia comunitária. Porto: Instituto de Alta Cultura.
1953 Rio de Onor, comunitarismo agro-pastoril. Porto: Instituto de Alta Cultura.

Diez Manrique, Juan Francisco
1975 Estudio psicológico sobre la población pasiega. Publicaciones del Instituto de Etnografía y Folklore "Hoyos Sáinz" 7:35–101.

Domínguez Ortiz, Antonio
1957 Los conversos de orígen judio despues de la expulsión. Madrid: Consejo Superior de Investigaciones Científicas.

Douglass, William A.
1969 Death in Murélaga: funerary ritual in a Spanish Basque village. Seattle: University of Washington Press.
1971 Rural exodus in two Spanish Basque villages: a cultural explanation. American Anthropologist 73:1100–1114.
1975 Echalar and Murélaga: opportunity and rural exodus in two Spanish Basque villages. New York: St. Martin's Press.
1976 Serving girls and sheepherders: emigration and continuity in a Spanish Basque village. *In* Joseph B. Aceves and William A. Douglass, eds., The changing faces of rural Spain. Cambridge, Mass.: Schenkman.

Du Bois, Cora
1944 The people of Alor: a social-psychological study of an East Indian island. Minneapolis: University of Minnesota Press.

Escagedo Salmón, Mateo
1921 Costumbres pastoriles cántabro-montañesas. Santander: Imprenta Provincial.

Escalera, Pedro de la
1735 Orígen de los Monteros de Espinosa, su calidad, exercicio, preheminencias, y exempciones. Madrid: Imprenta de Lorenço Francisco Mojados. (1st ed. 1632.)

Esperón, Antolín
1851 El Pasiego. Semanario Pintoresco Español 1851:390–92.

Fél, Edit, and Tamás Hofer
1969 Proper peasants: traditional life in a Hungarian village. Viking Fund Publications in Anthropology, no. 46. Chicago: Aldine.
1973 Tanyakert-s, patron-client relations, and political factions in Átány. American Anthropologist 75:787–801.

Ferrari Núñez, Ángel
1958 Castilla dividida en dominios según el Libro de las Behetrías. Discurso leido ante la Real Academia de la Historia. Madrid: Imprenta Ograma.

Foster, George M.
1960 Culture and conquest: America's Spanish heritage. Viking Fund Publications in Anthropology, no. 27. New York: Wenner-Gren Foundation for Anthropological Research.

Freeman, Susan Tax
1968a Corporate village organisation in the Sierra Ministra: an Iberian structural type. Man (ns)3:477–84.
1968b Religious aspects of the social organization of a Castilian village. American Anthropologist 70:34–49.
1970a Neighbors: the social contract in a Castilian hamlet. Chicago: University of Chicago Press.
1970b Notas sobre la trashumancia pasiega. Publicaciones del Instituto de Etnografía y Folklore "Hoyos Sáinz" 2:163–70.
1973 Pasiego transhumance and internal relations in the Montes de Pas. *In* Knut Weibust, ed., Kulturvariation i Sydeuropa. Copenhagen: NEFA's Forlag.
1975 Pasiegos y pasieguería: estudio de historia e historiografía provincial. Publicaciones del Instituto de Etnografía y Folklore "Hoyos Sáinz" 7:9–33.
1976a Dos caminos a Madrid: Españoles dentro y fuera de dos ámbitos rurales. *In* Carmelo Lisón Tolosana, ed., Expresiones actuales de la cultura del pueblo. Madrid: Centro de Estudios Sociales del Valle de los Caídos.
1976b Maneras de ser pasiego. *In* Carmelo Lisón Tolosana, ed., Temas de antropología española. Madrid: Akal.
n.d. The *"municipios"* of northern Spain: a view from the fountain. *In* Robert Hinshaw, ed., Currents in anthropology. The Hague and Paris: Mouton (in press).
Friedl, John
1972 Changing economic emphasis in an alpine village. Anthropological Quarterly 45:145–57.
1974 Kippel: a changing village in the Alps. New York: Holt, Rinehart and Winston.
García-Badell y Abadia, Gabriel
1963 Introducción a la historia de la agricultura española. Madrid: Consejo Superior de Investigaciones Científicas.
García Escudero, Ricardo
1954– Por tierras maragatas: estudio e historia de maragatería.
55 2d ed. Astorga: Ind. Tip. Cornejo.
García-Lomas, G. Adriano
1960 Los Pasiegos: estudio crítico, etnográfico y pintoresco (años 1011 a 1960). Santander.
1966 El lenguaje popular de la Cantabria montañesa: fonética, recopilación de voces, juegos, industrias populares, refranes y modismos. Santander.
Gil, Enrique
1839 Los Pasiegos. Semanario Pintoresco Español 1839:201–3.
González Camino y Aguirre, Fernando
1930 Las Asturias de Santillana en 1404 según el apeo formado por orden del infante don Fernando de Antequera. Santander: Librería Moderna.
González Echegaray, Joaquín
1966a Los Cántabros. Madrid: Ediciones Guadarrama.

1966b   Casa de Velarde: Museo Ethnográfico de Cantabria. San-
         tander: Excma. Diputación Provincial de Santander.
1969   Orígenes del cristianismo en Cantabria. Santander: Institu-
         ción Cultural de Cantabria.
1977   Cantabria a través de su historia. Santander: Institución
         Cultural de Cantabria.
González Echegaray, María del Cármen
1969   Escudos de Cantabria: Merindad de Trasmiera. Santander:
         Joaquín Bedia Cano.
1970   Los antecesores de don Pedro de Velarde. Santander: Insti-
         tución Cultural de Cantabria.
1972   Don Andrés Díaz de Venero y Leyva, en el centenario de la
         fundación de la Villa de Leyva en el Reino de Nueva Granada
         (Colombia). Santander: Institución Cultural de Cantabria.
1974   Toranzo: datos para la historia y etnografía de un valle mon-
         tañés. Santander: Institución Cultural de Cantabria.
González y González, Julio
1951   Reconquista y repoblación de Castilla, León, Extremadura y
         Andalucía (siglos XI a XIII). In J. M. Lacarra et al., La Re-
         conquista española y la repoblación del país. Zaragoza: Con-
         sejo Superior de Investigaciones Científicas.
1960   El Reino de Castilla en la época de Alfonso VIII. Madrid:
         Consejo Superior de Investigaciones Científicas.
Greenwood, Davydd J.
1977   Continuity in change: Spanish Basque ethnicity as a histori-
         cal process. In Milton J. Esman, ed., Ethnic conflict in the
         western world. Ithaca, N.Y.: Cornell University Press.
Gregory, David D.
1976a   The Andalucian dispersion: migration and sociodemographic
         change. In Joseph B. Aceves and William A. Douglass, eds.,
         The changing faces of rural Spain. Cambridge, Mass.: Schenk-
         man.
1976b   Rural exodus and the perpetuation of Andalucía. In Joseph
         B. Aceves, Edward C. Hansen, and Gloria Levitas, eds., Eco-
         nomic transformation and steady-state values. Queens Col-
         lege Publications in Anthropology, no. 2. Flushing, N.Y.:
         Queens College Press.
Gutierrez Solana, José
1920   La España negra. Madrid: G. Hernández y Galo.
Haaland, Gunnar
1969   Economic determinants in ethnic processes. In Fredrik
         Barth, ed., Ethnic groups and boundaries. Boston: Little,
         Brown.
Hack Tuke, D.
1880   The Cagots. Journal of the Royal Anthropological Institute
         of Great Britain and Ireland 9:376–85.

Homans, George Caspar
1941   English villagers of the thirteenth century. Cambridge, Mass.: Harvard University Press.
Honigmann, John J.
1964   Survival of a cultural focus. *In* Ward H. Goodenough, ed., Explorations in cultural anthropology: essays in honor of George Peter Murdock. New York: McGraw-Hill.
Hors, Pilar
1951   Seroantropología e historia de los Agotes. Príncipe de Viana 12:307–43.
Hoyos Sancho, Nieves de
1969   El traje regional de la provincia de Santander. Publicaciones del Instituto de Etnografía y Folklore "Hoyos Sáinz" 1:11–45.
Idoate, Florencio
1948   Agotes en los valles de Roncal y Baztán. Príncipe de Viana 9:489–513.
Instituto Nacional de Estadística
1960,   Censo de la población y de las viviendas de España *and*
1970   Nomenclator *for each province*. Madrid: Instituto Nacional de Estadística.
1972   Anuario estadístico de España, año XLVII—1972. Madrid: Instituto Nacional de Estadística.
Kenny, Michael
1962a   A Spanish tapestry: town and country in Castile. Bloomington: Indiana University Press.
1962b   Twentieth century Spanish expatriates in Mexico: an urban subculture. Anthropological Quarterly 35:169–80.
1973   The return of the Spanish emigrant. *In* Knut Weibust, ed., Kulturvariation i Sydeuropa. Copenhagen: NEFA's Forlag.
1976   Twentieth century Spanish expatriate ties with the homeland: remigration and its consequences. *In* Joseph B. Aceves and William A. Douglass, eds., The changing faces of rural Spain. Cambridge, Mass.: Schenkman.
Khera, Sigrid
1973   Social stratification and land inheritance among Austrian peasants. American Anthropologist 75:814–23.
Klein, Julius
1920   The Mesta: a study in Spanish economic history, 1273–1836. Cambridge, Mass.: Harvard University Press.
Lapeyre, Henri
1959   Géographie de l'Espagne morisque. Paris: S.E.V.P.E.N.
Lardizábal y Uribe, Miguel de
1786   Apología por los Agotes de Navarra y los Chuetas de Mallorca, con una breve digresión a los Vaqueros de Asturias. Madrid: Viuda de Ibarra.
Lasaga Larreta, Gregorio
1865   Compilación histórica, biográfica y marítima de la provincia

de Santander. Cádiz: Imprenta y Litografía de la Revista Médica.

1889   Dos memorias: cuadros históricos y de costumbres antiguas de la provincia de Santander. Torrelavega: El Dobra.

1934   Un entierro montañés—las caridades luces—ofrendas—otros sufragios. Altamira 1934:179–92. (Publication of a 1902 manuscript.)

Lautensach, Hermann
1967   Geografía de España y Portugal. Barcelona: Editorial Vicens-Vives.

Leal, Arnaldo
1972   Notas sobre el lenguaje en la Vega de Pas. Publicaciones del Instituto de Etnografía y Folklore "Hoyos Sáinz" 4:163–77.

1974   Hacia un estudio etnolingüístico de la comunidad rural pasiega. Publicaciones del Instituto de Etnografía y Folklore "Hoyos Sáinz" 6:177–87.

Legendre, Maurice
1927   Las Jurdes: étude de géographie humaine. Bordeaux: Feret.

Ley de Régimen Local
1968   Ley de régimen local. Madrid: Instituto Editorial Reus.

Lisón Tolosana, Carmelo
1966   Belmonte de los Caballeros: a sociological study of a Spanish town. Oxford: Clarendon Press.

1971   Antropología cultural de Galicia. Madrid: Siglo Veintiuno de España.

1973a   La casa en Galicia. *In* Ensayos de antropología social. Madrid: Ayuso.

1973b   Some aspects of moral structure in Galician hamlets. American Anthropologist 75:823–34.

1974   Perfiles simbólico-morales de la cultura gallega. Madrid: Akal.

Löfgren, Orvar
1974   Family and household among Scandinavian peasants: an exploratory essay. Ethnologia Scandinavica 1974:17–52.

Madariaga, Benito
1970   La ganadería en la provincia de Santander. Publicaciones del Instituto de Etnografía y Folklore "Hoyos Sáinz" 2:173–211.

Madoz, Pascual
1849   Diccionario geográfico-estadístico-histórico de España y sus posesiones de ultramar. Madrid.

Martín Galindo, José Luis
1956   Arrieros maragatos en el S. XVIII. Universidad de Valladolid, Estudios y Documentos 9. Valladolid: Consejo Superior de Investigaciones Científicas.

Maza Solano, Tomás
1953, 1956, 1957a, 1961   Nobleza, hidalguía, profesiones y oficios en la Montaña, según los padrones del Catastro del Marqués de la Ensenada, 4 vols. Santander: Centro de Estudios Montañeses.

1957b Manifestaciones de la economía montañesa desde el siglo IV al XVIII. *In* Banco de Santander 1957.

Menéndez y Pidal, Ramón
1954a A propósito de la *ll* y *l* latinas. Colonización suditálica en España. Boletín de la Real Academia Española 34:165–216.
1954b Pasiegos y Vaqueiros. Dos cuestiones de geografía lingüística. Archivum (Universidad de Oviedo) 4:7–44.

Menéndez y Pidal, Ramón, ed.
1963 Historia de España III: España visigoda (414–711 de J. C.). Madrid: Espasa-Calpe.
1964 Historia de España VI: España cristiana, comienzo de la Reconquista (711–1038). Madrid: Espasa-Calpe.

Michel, Francisque
1847 Histoire des races maudites de la France et de l'Espagne. Paris: A. Franck.

Ministerio de Agricultura
1949 Mapa agronómico nacional: valles del Besaya y del Pas. Memoria. Madrid: Talleres del Instituto Geográfico y Catastral.

Ministerio de Justicia
1968 Código civil. Madrid: Boletín Oficial del Estado.

Moore, Kenneth
1976 Those of The Street: the Catholic-Jews of Mallorca. Notre Dame, Ind.: University of Notre Dame Press.

Muñoz de San Pedro, Miguel (Conde de Canilleros)
1961 Extremadura (la tierra en la que nacían los dioses). Madrid: Espasa-Calpe.

Netting, Robert McC.
1972 Of men and meadows: strategies of Alpine land use. Anthropological Quarterly 45:132–44.
1976 What Alpine peasants have in common: observations on communal tenure in a Swiss village. Human Ecology 4:135–46.

Oliveira Marques, A. H. de
1971 Daily life in Portugal in the late Middle Ages. Madison: University of Wisconsin Press.

Ortega Valcárcel, José
1974 La transformación de un espacio rural: las Montañas de Burgos. Valladolid: Departamento de Geografía, Universidad de Valladolid.
1975 Organización del espacio y evolución técnica en los Montes de Pas. *In* Homenaje a D. Manuel de Terán, vol. 2. Estudios Geográficos 140–41:863–99.

Palacio Atard, Vicente
1959 El comercio de Castilla y el puerto de Santander en el siglo XVIII: notas para su estudio. Madrid: Consejo Superior de Investigaciones Científicas.

Pehrson, Robert N.
1954 Bilateral kin groupings as a structural type: a preliminary statement. University of Manila Journal of East Asiatic Studies 3:199–202.

Penny, Ralph J.
1969   El habla pasiega: ensayo de dialectología montañesa. London: Tamesis Books.
Pereda de la Reguera, Manuel
1968   Indianos de Cantabria. Santander: Institución Cultural de Cantabria.
Pérez Díaz, Víctor
1971   Emigración y cambio social. 2d ed. Barcelona: Ariel.
1972   Estructura social del campo y éxodo rural: estudio de un pueblo de Castilla. 2d ed. Madrid: Editorial Tecnos.
Pérez de Urbel, Justo
1951   Reconquista y repoblación de Castilla y León durante los siglos IX y X. *In* J. M. Lacarra et al., La Reconquista española y la repoblación del país. Zaragoza: Escuela de Estudios Medievales, Consejo Superior de Investigaciones Científicas.
1969–   El Condado de Castilla: los 300 años en que se hizo Castilla.
70   Guadalajara y Madrid: Editorial Siglo Ilustrado.
Pike, Ruth
1972   Aristocrats and traders: Sevillian society in the sixteenth century. Ithaca, N.Y., and London: Cornell University Press.
Pitt-Rivers, Julian A.
1958   The closed community and its friends. Kroeber Anthropological Society Papers 16:5–15.
1968   The stranger, the guest and the hostile host: introduction to the study of the laws of hospitality. *In* J. G. Peristiany, ed., Contributions to Mediterranean sociology. The Hague and Paris: Mouton.
1971a   Cagot. Encyclopaedia Britannica 4:580.
1971b   The people of the Sierra. Chicago: University of Chicago Press. (1st edition 1954.)
Price, Richard, and Sally Price
1966a   Noviazgo in an Andalusian pueblo. Southwestern Journal of Anthropology 22:302–22.
1966b   Stratification and courtship in an Andalusian village. Man (ns)1:526–33.
Real Academia Española
1970   Diccionario de la lengua española. 19th ed. Madrid: Real Academia Española.
Ríos y Ríos, Ángel de los
1878   Memoria sobre las antiguas y modernas comunidades de pastos entre los valles de Campóo de Suso, Cabuérniga y otros de la provincia de Santander. Santander: J. M. Martínez.
Rochas, Victor de
1876   Les parias de France et d'Espagne, Cagots et Bohémiens. Paris: Hachette.
Rodriguez Diez, Matías
1902   Historia de la muy noble, leal y benemérita Ciudad de Astorga. 2d ed. Astorga: Porfirio López.

Sáiz Antomil, Miguel A.
1954   Notas sobre la cocina popular en el valle de Soba. Altamira 1954:122–29.

Sarmela, Matti
1969   Reciprocity systems of the rural society in the Finnish-Karelian culture area with special reference to social intercourse of the youth. Folklore Fellows Communications, no. 207. Helsinki: Academia Scientiarum Fennica.

Sbarbi, José María
1922   Diccionario de refranes, adagios, proverbios, modismos, locuciones y frases proverbiales de la lengua española. Madrid: Librería de los Sucesores de Hernando.

Sicroff, Albert A.
1960   Les controverses des statuts de "pureté de sang" en Espagne du XVᵉ au XVIIᵉ siècle. Paris: Didier.

Solana, Marcial
1957   Don Domingo Herrera de la Concha y Miera, señor de la Villa de Villasana. *In* Banco de Santander 1957.

Stancliffe, Merton W.
1966   Cultural and ecological aspects of marriage, succession, and migration in a peasant community in the Catalan Pyrenees. Ph.D. dissertation, Department of Anthropology, Columbia University.

Stiles, Henry Reed
1934   Bundling: its origin, progress and decline in America. New York: Book Collectors Association.

Terán, Manuel de
1947   Vaqueros y cabañas en los Montes de Pas. Estudios Geográficos 8:7–57.

Terán, Manuel de, Luis Solé Sabarís et al.
1968   Geografía regional de España. Barcelona: Ariel.

Tudela, José
1950   Notas de geografía social: las migraciones profesionales sorianas. *In* Homenaje a don Luis de Hoyos Sáinz, vol. 2. Madrid.

Unamuno, Miguel de
1902   Vizcaya. *In* Joaquín Costa et al. 1902.

Uría Ríu, Juan
1968   Los Vaqueiros de Alzada. Oviedo: Caja de Ahorros de Asturias.
1976   La caza de la montería durante la Edad Media en Asturias, León y Castilla. *In* Los Vaqueiros de Alzada y otros estudios (de caza y etnografía). Oviedo: Biblioteca Popular Asturiana.

Valbuena, Celia
1970   Juegos infantiles montañeses: "las vacas." Publicaciones del Instituto de Etnografía y Folklore "Hoyos Sáinz" 2:95–148.

Valdeavellano, Luis G. de
1968   Curso de historia de las instituciones españolas de los orí-

genes al final de la Edad Media. Madrid: Revista de Occidente.

Veblen, Thorstein
1899   The theory of the leisure class. New York: Macmillan.
Wikman, K. Rob. V.
1937   Die Einleitung der Ehe. Eine vergleichend ethno-soziologische Untersuchung über die Vorstufe der Ehe in den Sitten des schwedischen Volkstums. Sonderabdruck der Acta Academiae Åbgensis, Humaniora XI:1. Åbo: Åbo Akademi.
Wylie, Laurence, ed.
1966   Chanzeaux: a village in Anjou. Cambridge, Mass.: Harvard University Press.

INDEX

Acevedo Huelves, B., 225 n7
Adjunct household members, 91–93
Administration, local, 40–41
Adoption, 92. *See also* Fosterage
Adultery, 255
Adult men, license of, 100
Affinal marriage, 191
Age-grading in dress, 124
Agosteros, 57; newlyweds as, 131. *See also* Harvest hands; Hired labor
Agotes, 24, 224, 232–34, 240, 244. *See also* Cagots
Alcaldes de barrio, 43–44
Alfonso X, *Las Siete Partidas*, 235–36
Alguacil, 41
All Saints' Day, 160
All Souls' Day, 160
Almadreñas, 38, 59, 125, 139, 169–70, 174 n8
Alorese, 99
Altadill, J., 232 n
Altitudes of barrios, 29
Altitude zones, evaluations of as living space, 45
Amas de leche. See Wet-nurses
Ambulatory trade. *See* Peddling
Andalusia, emigration to, 50 n
Andalusian in Pandillo, 196 n3
Andrés. *See* Family histories, sample
Animals. *See* Livestock; *and names of individual animals*
Annual cycle. *See* Transhumance cycle
Aparcería, 54–56, 88

Aranzadi, T. de, 127 n8
Architecture. See *Cabañas*; House types; Styles, architectural
Archives: notarial, 55 n; Pasiego town, 9 n10
Areas of migration, lasting ties in, 209, 212. *See also* Emigration, geographic patterns of
Arensberg, C., 98
Arroyo del Prado, R.-A., 15 n19, 17 n23
Artificial insemination, 72
Ascension of the Virgin, 106, 160
Asturias, xix, 18; cattle and dairy economy of, 206 n10
Awareness of outside world, 163
Axes, 60
Ayuntamiento: methods of public announcement, 43–44; property, 42–43, 63, 65 n16; secretary, 32. *See also* Government, local

Bachillerato, 208
Bakers, 34
Bank, 33
Banns, marriage, 130
Baptism, 110, 126
Baptismal font, 12 n
Basques, xix
Basque country: chocolate factories in, 154 n; Pasiego textile traders in, 200
Bateson, G., 178–79
Bárcenas, burial of Pasiegos in, 12
Bargaining, attitudes toward, 216 n20, 239. *See also* Commerce, attitudes toward